Shadows
and Wind

Shadows
and Wind

A View of Modern Vietnam

ROBERT TEMPLER

LITTLE, BROWN AND COMPANY

A *Little, Brown* Book

First published in Great Britain by
Little, Brown and Company 1998

A CIP catalogue record for this book is
available from the British Library.

ISBN 0 316 64666 0

Typeset in Palatino by M Rules
Printed and bound in Great Britain by
Clays Ltd, St Ives plc

Little, Brown and Company (UK)
Brettenham House
Lancaster Place
London WC2E 7EN

To my parents,
Michael and Jane Templer

Contents

	Map	viii
	Acknowledgements	ix
1	Without Heroes	1
2	Imagining Vietnam	8
3	Remembering Vietnam	26
4	Famine	47
5	Feast	63
6	Empty Box	80
7	Excommunicated	101
8	Industrial Chickens	129
9	Pendulum	153
10	Cymbals and Litanies	177
11	A Mirror of Things Past	204
12	Social Evils	237
13	Faith	257
14	China Lite	283
15	Melancholy Tribe	309
16	Young and Restless	326
17	Conclusion	352
	Chapter Notes	356
	Bibliography	360
	Index	365

Acknowledgements

In writing this book, I owe the greatest debts to the hundreds of people in Vietnam, from farmers to government officials, who gave me their time and shared their knowledge. Many of these people would prefer not to be named in this book to avoid any possible repercussions, but I thank you all so much for being my teachers and my inspiration. I particularly want to express my boundless admiration and respect for Vietnamese from all walks of life who stand up without fear and speak the truth with humour and wisdom; their bravery and moral fortitude is extraordinary.

I am also indebted to all those who approached this subject before I did. I have learned a great deal from the historians, critics and others who have devoted their lives to studying Vietnam. *Vietnam Forum*, a publication edited by Huynh Sanh Thong and later by Dan Duffy, was a great source of material. I owe much to the work of Huynh Sanh Thong, whose translations have opened up the history and literature of Vietnam to the English speaking world.

I would also like to thank those who went through drafts of this book, particularly Peter Zinoman and Peter Mares. Richard Beswick and Antonia Hodgson from Little, Brown and David Miller and Deborah Rogers from Rogers, Coleridge and White provided considerable help and guidance. I am profoundly grateful to Philippe and Isabelle Agret, Frederik Balfour, Kate Bourne, Kathy Charlton, Reginald and Agnes Chua, Frank Gibney Jnr, Frances House, Kristin Huckshorn, Birgit Hussfeld, Supapohn Kanwerayotin, Tim Karr, Tim Larimer, Philip McClellan, Lois Raimondo, Abby Robinson, Alex Sauvegrain, Hans Schodder and Julie Shiels.

There are many other people who also provided support, inspiration or hospitality while I was writing this book. I would like to thank: Narawat Acosta-Wright and Victor Wright; Ilisa Barbash; Sergei and Galina Blagov; Ambassador Sue Boyd; John Chalmers; Deborah Counsell; Stephen Denney at the Indochina Archive at the University of California, Berkeley; Cynda and Ross Dunkley; John Gillespie; Jeremy Grant; Chris Greene and all the staff of the BBC Vietnamese Service; Ed Han; Bertrand de Hartingh; Giles Hewitt; Kyle Horst; Chris Hougie; Sarah Jackson-Han; Chris and Janiki Kremmer; Sarah and Paul Jean-Ortiz; Bjorn Larsson; Didier Lauras; Marc Lavine; Catherine Lugrin; Ambassador Borje Lungrren; Professor David Marr; John and Valerie McKenzie; Jamie Paterson; Geffrye Parsons; Elizabeth Pisani; Dinah PoKempner; Sheri Prasso; Teresa Raffo; Duncan Ritchie; Orville Schell; Dick Schumacher; Adam Schwarz; Milbert Shin; Judy Stowe; Lucien Taylor; Nora Taylor; Professor Carlyle Thayer; Dr. Carolyn Wakeman; Nicola Watts; Sarah Williams; and my family – Catherine, Henry, George and Mary Spender and William, Caroline, Edward and Jack Templer.

Berkeley, March 1998.

1

Without Heroes

Two great wars have passed and the medals now shine only during ceremonies. The great feats of the past have now been catalogued away in libraries where we can view them from a distance and in perspective. As doubt and boredom set in, our appetite for achieving heroic deeds has diminished and in this vacuum we now turn to half-baked entertainment instead. Money now holds the key to success and around me everyone dances around the money axis.

PHAM THI HOAI
The Crystal Messenger

I am too young to have seen the Vietnam War on television or to have read about it at the time. Before I first went to Vietnam in the early 1990s, my views of the country had been formed by American movies and books about the war. I expected a place ravaged by conflict but instead found that the war was no longer a central feature of life. A lack of memories of that time was something I shared with most Vietnamese.

More than half the population of Vietnam was born after 1975 when a demographic bubble swelled up after the uncertainties of previous years. Everyone there has lived with the aftermath of one of the longest and bloodiest conflicts of this century. It ran in many forms from the Revolution of 1945 and nine-year war to free themselves from the French through what Vietnamese call the American War, to the conflict with China in 1979. Vietnamese troops were fighting in Cambodia until 1989. These conflicts have had an enormous impact on Vietnam but for most people they are now history. The concerns of Vietnamese lie in the present and the future.

I arrived in Vietnam in February 1994 to work as a journalist for the French news agency Agence France-Presse. It was a time of optimism and recovery. A week before I arrived the United States lifted its economic embargo that had been in place since the 1950s. Hanoi was bustling with investors who thronged the lobbies of smart new hotels. There was much talk of opportunities on this new business frontier. The government was mending its relations with former adversaries and recovering from the collapse of the Soviet Union. People were getting their first taste of an emerging consumer society and were enjoying new freedoms that had been unthinkable just a few years earlier. There was an overwhelming sense that the future was just going to continue getting better.

The little ironies of life under Vietnam's new economic system – Market-Leninism, Socialism with Vietnamese characteristics, there are many possible names for this peculiar hybrid of Leninism and rapacious capitalism – were of little interest to most Vietnamese. They were mostly too driven by new entrepreneurial imperatives to pay much attention to the dusty world of politics. There was more interest in finding niches that exploited the mix of Mammon and Marxist symbolism.

Luu Quang Quyen practised what was likely to be a dying trade and yet he was making a killing doing it. The artist, who sported the straggly beard, beret and drooping cigarette that are *de rigueur* in Hanoi's mildly Bohemian circles, owned a workshop that made hammer and sickle signs and other communist emblems. The gold plastic hammer and sickles, pieced together by eight women working at the back of his small shop, sold for about $10 each. That added up to an income for Quyen of around $2,000 a month, a fortune in Vietnam, where for example teachers earn just $30 a month. The graduate of Hanoi's top art college saw his business take off in the early 1990s on the back of a bulk order for army insignia. He soon worked out that there was a market among tourists looking for communist kitsch. 'They're beautiful and political. What could be better in Vietnam?' said Quyen, holding up a large shining star. 'I don't know why, but tourists really like them,' he said, adopting a look of mock seriousness and puzzlement. 'Except our Russian friends, funnily enough.'

Quyen's shop was on a busy stretch of Nguyen Thai Hoc Street, not far from the Temple of Literature, a cluster of old wood-and-tile buildings dedicated to the worship of Confucius that was founded in the eleventh century. Adjacent to the temple is an abandoned lot where the Quoc Tu Giam, a national academy of Confucian training, stood before it was demolished and moved to the new imperial capital of Hue in the nineteenth century. Now the area is surrounded by advertising businesses that use it to paint signs. It is not unusual to see this derelict ground, once the centre of learning and culture in Vietnam, filled with the shrieking scarlet of Coca-Cola billboards propped up to dry against the crumbling brick walls.

Amid the pace and noise of urban life, the dissonance of a once impoverished artist growing rich off Communist emblems or a symbol of capitalist America intruding into the heart of Vietnamese culture seemed to hit foreigners much more vividly than Vietnamese. Few local people had the time or urge to ponder these incongruous images. Most Vietnamese simply felt that their lives were much better since the government had shed the heaviest baggage of Marxist-Leninism and abandoned central planning. Reforms had broken down many social and economic barriers and given more people the right to do what were once privileges for a political élite. People, or at least the growing number with some money, could now travel – at home and abroad, they could open businesses, educate their children at private schools and universities, visit their choice of doctor and buy more of what they want.

The envelope of personal space in which they could read, write, worship, perform or create had expanded by degrees. No longer completely at the service of the state and obliged to produce a relentless optimistic view of their country, artists and writers could produce more genuinely affecting, even melancholy work. 'One of the biggest changes,' said a Vietnamese painter, 'is that now we are actually allowed to be sad.'

Economic reforms, known in Vietnam as *Doi Moi* or 'renovation,' had opened up some doors of opportunity and shortened the reach of some state powers. Officially *Doi Moi* began in 1986 at the Sixth Communist Party Congress. Its origins go back earlier, even to the late 1960s when officials began to question the efficacy of central planning and offer market alternatives. But the changes introduced after 1986 had not been reversed like earlier experiments with the economic market and their impact had created an aura of hope in a country once crippled with disillusionment.

Everything was open to 'renovation' and the revolutionary changes it brought. *Doi Moi* made its mark on literature and movies, sex and food. 'People even talk about the "*Doi Moi*" of personal relationships, of marriages,' grumbled the writer Pham Thi Hoai, who is often described as a young star of '*Doi Moi* literature'. But there really was a 'renovation' of the personal sphere. The wheels of life began to spin faster and they meshed less often with the controlling gears of the state. A vast bureaucracy that once aspired to monitor the lives of millions of people no longer cared as much what they did as long as they stayed out of politics.

But under the glinting surface of the new Vietnam was the old darker country, a place of poverty and repression. Reforms had changed the lives of those in the cities but had not always improved the situation in the countryside where 80 per cent of people lived. Hanoi went in just a few years from being a dusty and slow city, dimly lit at night, to a bustling, glitzy place, draped in neon and throbbing with commerce. However, just a few miles outside the city centre were villages that had seen few benefits of reform.

The optimism of the early 1990s proved short-lived and indeed it had evaporated when I left Vietnam after three years. Reforms had become bogged down in the incessant debate over how much Vietnam should open up. Expectations, raised by a decade of economic growth, had soared beyond what the government was willing to allow. Investors had soured on the country, put off by corruption, bureaucracy and the myopic view of officials. Many aspects of cultural and political openness that appeared after 1986 had been reversed, creating a climate of disappointment and impatience.

I packed up to leave the day before *Tet*, the Vietnamese new year, in February 1997. Everyone was busy with the final preparations for the holiday. Outside my house in the centre of Hanoi, a crowd of flower sellers had formed an impromptu market. Hanoi is drained of colour at that time of the year when the constant drizzle forms a scrim that creates a diffuse world of greys and browns. But this was a cheerful scene, splashed with colour, noisy and fragrant. Unfortunately a harder reality intruded and provided what will be for me an enduring image of Vietnam, a thin slice of life that reflects a wider problem.

A young man, dressed in the green trousers and shirt and pith helmet worn by farmers, cycled up with two panniers filled with watermelons and stood waiting for customers. Minutes later he was followed by two policemen on a sky-blue motorbike with a sidecar. After bellowing orders for the crowd to disperse, they singled out the man with the watermelons and ordered him to load one of his panniers into the sidecar. He protested, so one of the policemen struck him hard on the face in a sudden blow that sent a ripple of shock through the crowd. The officers looked around at the others with expressions that challenged anyone else to dispute their power and then roared off with one of the baskets of watermelons. The man was left struggling with his unbalanced bicycle, which soon overturned in the road, spilling the remaining melons into the gutter as the ceaseless, hooting traffic swerved to avoid them. The young man bit his lip and pulled his helmet down over his face to hide emerging tears of frustration as he scrabbled around collecting his fruit. He had lost his pannier and half of the money that he was saving for *Tet*. He had pedalled his heavy load for three hours to sell the fruit in the city. There was no avenue for redress. This was just one of thousands of petty injustices inflicted every day by the police and other servants of the state.

When these incidents pile up, they leave a dull aching sense of the problems in Vietnam that cannot be ignored. It was no longer possible to brush over the failure to deal with many of the enduring economic, political and cultural constraints in a country where the relationship between the state and the individual was still so unbalanced. Unlike the nations of Eastern Europe, Vietnam has not tried to put in place the atmosphere of openness that was needed to tackle these issues. Instead it remains an often intolerant one-party state, one of just five Communist nations left.

This is not a book that aims to explain Vietnamese people; they are too diverse and complex to be compressed in that way. It is an attempt to examine some of the strains of life in contemporary Vietnam – the important issues facing a government that clings tenaciously to power and a people who aspire for more than their rulers can offer. I was much influenced by conversations with Vietnamese friends who steered me towards areas often outside the conventional interests and demands of my work as a foreign correspondent. The problems examined here – corruption and the difficulties of urban life, a stagnant political culture, freedom of speech and religion, the rising threat of AIDS, an emerging youth culture and the overseas Vietnamese – are all among the most pressing issues, throwing up debates at all levels of society.

The Vietnamese government devotes some effort to restricting the activities of foreign correspondents. Offices are monitored, Vietnamese staff harassed and intimidated. Foreign reporters must get permission to travel and are supposed to give five days notice if they wish to cover a news event, an impossible demand. Requests to travel to an outlying province were frequently dismissed with a curt word that all officials there were too busy to see anyone. It was an explanation that never meshed well with the somnolent lives of most bureaucrats. When interviewing officials, particularly senior members of the government, journalists were obliged to send in their questions in advance. Any found distasteful were simply ignored; the others were often answered in writing, phrased in such wooden language that they were indecipherable. There were also many officials who did their utmost to help and were open about the problems they faced; unfortunately they sometimes suffered for this.

Working in this environment means it was often impossible to identify individual sources of information. It was also very difficult to pin down particular officials associated with a policy; all decisions were presented as if they were the unanimous word of all parts of the government. In reality there were many wide fissures but it can be tough to isolate where exactly they lay so it is difficult to avoid referring to the government and the Communist Party as if they were completely monolithic institutions.

To go outside those areas hemmed in by the official line and expand a view of the country beyond that put out by people who are authorised to talk to foreigners, I have used a wide range of documentary sources ranging from reports in the official press and leaked documents to banned novels and poetry. Fiction in countries like Vietnam often proves a richer source of information and more closely reflects much public opinion than the government-controlled media that all too often has been the sole source for so many foreign books on Vietnam.

In the summer of 1997, the shaky foundations of Asia's economic growth began to give way, starting with revelations of the perilous state of Thailand's banks. A growing feeling of insecurity sent currencies and stock markets plummeting. It soon spread across the region, hitting Malaysia, Indonesia and South Korea. Even the safe havens of Singapore and Hong Kong suffered sickening lurches in their markets. Vietnam was slow to feel the pain as it did not have a traded currency or a stock market, but it too began to experience a marked decline in foreign investment. Soon the whole basis of the so-called Asian miracle – the decades of extraordinary economic growth – was under question. Authoritarian governments had once been justified because they had brought prosperity. The problems of corruption and the tangled webs of 'business contacts' had been brushed aside because they oiled the wheels of commerce. Now the conventional wisdom turned against these ideas. The new prescription for a prosperous region was open government and full accountability.

This was not the remedy sought by the Vietnamese Communist Party. The country's reforms had already been drifting as the leadership bickered, but at the end of 1997, the Party elected a conservative general, Le Kha Phieu, to the top post of General Secretary. He was a dedicated Party man who had climbed the ranks as a political commissar in the army. With his suspicion of the outside world, he represented a part of the ruling élite who feared their power would be eroded if they opened their country further. His position was supposedly balanced by a prime minister and a president who were optimistically tagged as reformers, but Phieu's appointment had a deadening impact. It signalled another step backwards, another diversion from the road most Vietnamese wished to travel.

2

Imagining Vietnam

*What I had been creating and enduring for the last four years
was a Vietnam inside my head, under my skin, in the pit of my
stomach. But the Vietnam I had been thinking about for years
was scarcely filled out at all.*

SUSAN SONTAG
Trip to Hanoi

Larry Hillblom was in love. The American tycoon, who had made
his fortune as the 'H' in the air cargo firm DHL, was known for his
taste in underage Filipinas. This affair, however, was different from
the matches arranged by well-paid Manila mama-sans. It was a
much more expensive romance that began in 1990 with a visit to the
Vietnamese town of Dalat. Hillblom fell in love with this pine-
scented colonial resort of Swiss chalets and 1930s nautical moderne
villas with curved balconies and porthole windows. The reclusive
millionaire wanted a piece of Dalat.

Skirting the US economic embargo, Hillblom pumped $40 million
into renovating the Dalat Palace Hotel, built in 1922 to attract visitors to this hill station in the cool low mountains north of Saigon.
When the town was founded by the French it was thought the climate and clear mountain air might heal those wracked with
tuberculosis or fatigued by the constant heat. Dalat won the
Emperor Bao Dai's imprimatur as the fashionable location to
summer and Air France advertised the hotel as the place to stay for
tiger hunting in the highlands. The airline commissioned colourful
posters of fierce Montagnards armed with spears. The minorities
that populated the mountain areas were for the French an ideal of
noble savagery that provided a perfect contrast to their image of the
Vietnamese as sly and inscrutable.

The Dalat Palace Hotel might have been one of the most impressive establishments in Indochina, but by the time Hillblom visited in the 1990s it was decrepit and uncomfortable, a gloomy, rat-infested pile ignored for nearly half a century. Hillblom decided to renovate not just the hotel but a number of other buildings and sixteen of the villas that lined the mountain roads. But he never lived to enjoy what he had created. A week after the hotel reopened in 1995, Hillblom was killed in a plane crash near the Pacific island of Saipan. His body was never found.

His hotel is insulated from the outside world with acres of perfect lawn and is run by a huge staff of Vietnamese and expatriates, many of them dressed in something approaching period costume of the 1930s. A water filtration plant big enough to supply the entire town was installed along with generators to guard against power cuts. The plumbing, once known for its creaking reluctance to furnish anything other than a trickle of brackish slime, was replaced with brass fixtures from which gushed very modern torrents of hot water. Striving for authenticity, Hillblom initially refused to allow televisions in the rooms, although the French management company, Accor Pacific, eventually persuaded him to change his mind. Nearby, the oldest golf course in Vietnam, originally built for the amusement of Bao Dai, was expanded and planted with the delicate European grass craved by Asian golfers. The hotel's restaurant, decorated with antique cabinets, crystal chandeliers and marble, served a rich *haute cuisine* of imported ingredients. At the bottom of the sprawling front steps, a chauffeur in a peaked cap spent his days polishing a 1930s Citroën to a depthless shine.

With Hillblom's seemingly endless spout of cash, scores of architects, engineers and Swiss-trained hoteliers manufactured the perfect fabrication of colonialism as a period of sumptuous comfort and effortless superiority. The hotel strove to be more than a rootless box for tourists. It was remade to evoke a time of brilliantined hair, Vuitton trunks and tennis whites all set in the luminous and mythical landscape of 'Indochine', a place as distant from the realities of French colonialism as it was from contemporary Vietnam.

The original hotel had never taken off, indeed the grand building overlooking the town's lake was a mirror of the economic dreams and failures of French colonialism in Indochina. Dalat had been

promoted initially as a sanatorium and then as a potential administrative capital. A plan for the town was drawn up by the architect
Ernest Hebrard, one of the foremost urban planners of his time.
Dalat was supposed to be a strictly controlled and segregated area
for the French only; the Vietnamese needed permission to live there
and were confined to a few areas on the edges of the town.
Hebrard's plan was not popular among the colonial residents, who
ignored his well-organised if antiseptic scheme and built a rambling town of nostalgic cottages modelled after those in the Alps
and Alsace.

Tiger hunting and cool summers did not attract many guests to
the Palace Hotel; it began its slow decay just after it opened. To
keep it afloat, the owners petitioned the colonial government, which
had already subsidised its construction, for permission to open a
casino. The civil servants sweating away in Hanoi had little sympathy and refused to allow the owners to save the hotel with
gambling. Photographs from the 1930s show it as slightly austere
and pinched, certainly not enormously comfortable. The menus
were not lists of gastronomic indulgence but offered the starchy
foods favoured by stout colonials. The hotel's slight grasp of metropolitan French sophistication and grandeur must have been a sad
echo of the lives of its patrons.

Hillblom had little interest in the real history of his hotel; he
wished only to create a fantasy of colonial times. In purely business
terms, the investment was a disaster. He poured $40 million into a
hotel in an almost unknown town six hours drive from the nearest
international airport. The eighteen expatriates and 170 Vietnamese
employed to service the forty-three rooms had little to do. The bell-
boys, dressed in pillbox hats and braided uniforms, lurked in the
marble lobby while maids in black-and-white dresses polished
untouched silver and changed the unused sheets.

After Hillblom's death, his Hong Kong-based company Danao,
through which he had channelled his illegal investment in Vietnam,
was struggling to finance the renovations of another hotel in Dalat.
Hillblom's $500 million estate was caught up in a tangle of legal bat-
tles that pitted his chosen beneficiary, the University of California,
against a string of illegitimate children he was said to have fathered
with bar girls in the Philippines. Without regular infusions of cash

to sustain it, the hotel struggled. By 1996 it was laying off staff and cutting rates. Most of the rooms remained empty.

In the 1990s Vietnam was attracting a new generation of fantasists and dreamers. The new arrivals were looking to wallow in nostalgia for places and times that had never been. They were drawn by their visions of 'Indochine' and 'Nam', the mythical landscapes of the West's past interactions with Vietnam. These pioneers arrived, like the first colonisers hundreds of years before them, with a rich array of preconceptions. They were nervous about their reception in this once hostile land but they were carrying trinkets that the natives craved and they had an unshakeable faith in the civilising power of market economics.

They were coming to a country they thought they knew well. Its images had been intensified in hundreds of movies and hours of news footage; these pictures of Vietnam lingered like retinal burns. There were dense jungles and sleepy rivers. The cities were lush and colonial with ochre and cream-coloured buildings, shaded streets, cafés and colonnaded hotels. The countryside was a picturesque mix of thatch and bamboo houses surrounded by glittering rice paddies. This rural idyll provided the perfect contrast to chains of bombs exploding above the jungle, the face of a man as he is shot in the temple by a policeman or a burned girl running naked from the clouds of napalm that boil up behind her.

It was 'Nam', man, and they were back. They'd gleaned the language and attitude from the cinema and a frayed copy of Michael Herr's *Dispatches*. They were 'in country', on their 'second tour', they lived a 'few clicks' out of town. Vietnamese were cool this time around, they were looking for a deal, they loved Americans. This was the new frontier, the lucrative wreckage of Communism's latest collision with capitalism. It was the land of opportunity, millions could be made by a lucky few who got in early and figured it out.

For some, Vietnam was emblematic of something in their own lives – a lost youth or a political consciousness honed in opposition to the war – and this lent it an importance that marks it out from other Southeast Asian countries. The importance attached to Vietnam by its recent history has if anything hindered a richer understanding of the country and its people. In most of this history the Vietnamese are invisible to the West, they are little more than ciphers. Both French and Americans from across the political spectrum projected their views on to them, forcing them mostly into two camps; they were either innocent victims or the faceless components of a vicious Marxist war machine.

These layered fantasies were bound to come unstuck when Westerners once again confronted Vietnam. French film director Jean-Jacques Annaud experienced a typical reaction when scouting locations for his film *The Lover*. He was searching for the 'real Indochina', for the romantic landscapes of Marguerite Duras's novel. But instead of the lush country he imagined, he found 'poverty and overpopulation' that left him stunned. 'The fancy white villas have been replaced by grey prefab council housing. The broken streets are swamped by the compact swarm of backfiring scooters,' he wrote in a journal about the making of the movie. The cities weren't to his liking but he had hopes for the countryside which he imagined as 'untouched, still Asian'.

But even the peasants were not picturesque enough for Annaud. 'No, [the countryside] too is socialist. Looking for green, we find grey . . . The Mekong, laden with motorboats with corrugated iron roofs, looks more like a freeway outside Mexico City than the legendary river flowing all the way down from China.'

Reality may be a disappointment but Annaud found that 'our memories sifted away the dirt, the pollution, the everyday troubles'. In this 'tired museum, weary and unique', he was able to create a $30 million vision of colonialism, albeit a modern confection of pale linen dresses, opium-smoking men and sinewy coolies. French colonialism in the pearl of the orient was never as stylish as it was in movies such as *Indochine, The Lover, Dien Bien Phu* and *The Scent of Green Papaya*, a number of French productions that would rehabilitate Vietnam as a land of colonial and erotic adventure.

Decades without contact heightened the allure of rediscovery in the rash of Indochina movies that were mostly critical and box office hits. They were officially applauded by the authorities in Hanoi. *The Scent of Green Papaya*, a movie by the French-Vietnamese director Tran Anh Hung, was even nominated for an Oscar as Best Foreign Film from Vietnam, even though it had been filmed entirely in studios in Paris where it was cheaper and easier to recreate 'Indochine'.

The most lavish movie, and certainly the most influential in sparking the rush of tourism to Vietnam, was *Indochine*. Starring Catherine Deneuve as a plantation owner, it was a huge hit, winning an Oscar, a Golden Globe and five Cesar awards in France. Its panoramic sweep across late colonial history was overlaid with a luxurious portrayal of life in the 1930s. The number of visitors soared, from just around 30,000 in the late 1980s to more than 1 million in 1994. They came in search of the authentic Vietnam, by which they mostly meant the Vietnam seen through the eyes of film-makers who had infused it with a French sense of loss and regret for the end of colonialism. Without irony, travel agents advertised the most heavily bombed country in history as unspoiled; the discerning traveller, they advised, should get in early before it was ruined.

With its return to the world fold nearly complete, the government proudly declared that at last Vietnam was 'not just a war, but a country'. Indeed it was no longer just a war but a country where Deneuve might spend her days dressed in tight jodhpurs disciplining the plantation workers before slipping into a silk *ao dai* to drink pastis on the terrace of the Continental Hotel.

'Indochine' is not a large imaginary space in comparison with 'Nam', which stretches across a wider and more varied topography. 'Nam' can be a place for suffering or redemption, a site of brutal US imperialism or a Communist gulag holding 'our boys' in bamboo tiger-cages. Over the scorched earth and dense jungles of its terrain wander figures as diverse as Susan Sontag and Danielle Steele, Oliver Stone and Oliver North. Nam has its own journals and university courses, political lobbies, heroes and enemies. A quick survey of a university library in the United States will turn up thousands of volumes, almost all of them about the war. A far from exhaustive survey of American movies produced a list of around 400 that feature Vietnam or veterans of the war in some significant way. A search on the Internet calls up an unmanageable number of entries; indeed the World Wide Web has given new energy to 'Nam'. There is now a virtual 'Nam', supplying everything from a complete list of American dead from the war to advice on which bars offer the most authentic 'Nam' experiences in Ho Chi Minh City.

'Nam' is a steamy condensation of life in the Saigon of the 1960s, with sex, drugs and a rock and roll soundtrack. It is bound up with images of war, of the smell of napalm in the morning and a chirruping hooker patois – 'love-you-long-time-you-be-my-big-honey'. Many of those in search of this world are looking to recreate Vietnam as an erotic playground populated by women whose national dress, the clinging *ao dai*, was designed to give an alluring glimpse of what might be on offer. More than a few mid-life crises reached their apogees in the bars off Saigon's notorious Tu Do Street (now Dong Khoi street), the epicentre of male fantasy in Vietnam since Graham Greene wrote *The Quiet American* in the 1950s. This was where the authenticity of 'Nam' was both created and challenged in bars with names like Apocalypse Now and B4 75, where to the pulse of 1960s music, young Vietnamese women again run their hands over the wide backs of shorn-haired Americans.

Vietnam in the 1990s is not just exotic, it is stylish. This is particularly the case in Saigon – nobody calls it Ho Chi Minh City – an emerging centre of media-created urban chic. It is the place to be if you are young and adventurous and have a trust fund. The *New York Times* featured it in its Sunday magazine in January 1997 under the apt title 'Saigon: The Sequel', throwing a few barbs at the collection of thrusting hustlers that had congregated there, but mostly draping the place in some comfortably worn nostalgia.

The Loud Americans were back – big, bad and posturing, according to this widely read piece. The author, Michael Paterniti, quickly throws in obligatory references to Greene to suggest that the predicaments of American expatriates in Saigon have not changed since the 1950s and 1960s. He even includes a story about a young American's naïve love for a woman who may or may not be a hooker. Vietnamese are all unsurprisingly portrayed as venal – slyly observing and manipulating the outsiders but remaining mysterious and unknowable.

The writer dutifully includes a quote from a US veteran on how Americans 'met Vietnamese in whorehouses or in battle, but we never treated them as humans'. Following decades of journalistic tradition in Vietnam, the author avoids meeting them at all, preferring just to recycle old images of Vietnamese. For Paterniti, Saigon is corrupt and criminal, it doesn't fit the supposed Confucian mould of Vietnamese society, it reeks of shit and greed. Northern Vietnamese, who are in the opinion of the writer clearly more cultured, view the city as a 'psychedelic Sodom'. Any woman with an apartment or a Honda Dream – a small motorbike that emerged as the fetish object of the new consumer age – clearly earned it on her back. In a highly suspect anecdote, a woman working in an antique shop propositions the writer. Reading from a collection of English phrases written in a notebook, she asks him if he 'will be the one to buy me a Honda Dream'.

Towards the end of this article, which stretched across ten pages of one of the most prominent publications in the United States, the writer finds some redemption for Vietnamese, who are so noticeably absent from his writing up until then. An American veteran living in Saigon tells him he sees 'people who want a little money, parents who want a better life for their children. I see innocence and energy. When I look deeply enough here, I see the beginnings of America'.

Most of the pioneers of Vietnam's latest opening to the world soon find that it is neither an optimistic proto-America nor a silken fantasy of opium smoking and sex. It doesn't take long to work out that Saigon is not the rouged and pouting temptress of lore. There is a pulsating energy, an echo of the imagined edginess of the past, but the bars tinkle with syrupy muzak rather than throb to The Doors. Most Saigonese are not the slick operators and hookers that Paterniti surmised but a range of families all dealing with the complexities of rapid change in their society. Saigon is no longer the charming mix of colonial grace and 1960s kitsch but a late twentieth-century urban disaster-in-waiting with many of the failings of other cities in the region. It has become a vast sprawl of concrete crossed with canals and rivers so polluted they bubble under crusts of garbage. By the mid 1990s Saigon had the fastest-growing economy of any major city in Asia but with this had come a tense web of problems that were hard to avoid. You might be back in Nam but it didn't always feel that way.

The layers of cultural sediment that make up 'Nam' sit so heavily on Western visions of the country that it can hardly be considered in any other light. Writers, film-makers and photographers consciously or otherwise reproduce the same images over and over. Not only does this compressed view exclude most Vietnamese, but it has stifled any reading of the Vietnamese that deviates from the widely accepted myths. They have been restricted to permanent walk-on parts in history and fiction, as sex workers, apparatchiks, guerrillas, corrupt generals and untrustworthy servants.

Ideas about Vietnam are powerfully ingrained. This is most obvious in the many American movies about Vietnam where the people appear only as small armed men in black pyjamas. But the distortion persists beyond those works of fact or fiction that dehumanise Vietnamese as the enemy. Even those works that set out to be sympathetic such as Frances FitzGerald's *Fire in the Lake* have contributed to the reduction of Vietnamese culture and society to a series of enduring stereotypes. This book, winner of a Pulitzer Prize and a National Book Award in America, had an enormous influence on the way Vietnamese are seen because it was one of the first to try to establish their place in a conflict that was dominated by stories by and about Americans. Its ambitious attempt at a cultural analysis of Vietnamese people and the war has seeped into much of the subsequent writing on the war. Unusually for a non-fiction work, it remains in print and widely available twenty-five years after its first publication.

FitzGerald sets out to establish Americans and Vietnamese as 'reversed mirror images' – essentially opposites whose differences explain their misunderstandings and conflicts. FitzGerald's Americans are endowed with creativity, optimism and a competitive spirit based on a myth of the frontier and of eternal conquest. Her Vietnamese live in a world of physical and mental constraints, hemmed in by mountains and enemies. 'For traditional Vietnamese the sense of limitation and enclosure was as much a part of individual life as of the life of the nation.'

Vietnamese 'live by constant repetition' with a grasp only of place, not time. She writes:

In this passage of time that had no history, the death of a man marked no final end. Buried in the rice fields that sustained his family, the father would live on in the bodies of his children and grandchildren. As time wrapped around itself,

the generations to come would come to regard him as the
source of their present lives and the arbiter of their fate. In the
continuum of the family 'private property' did not really
exist, for the father was less of an owner than a trustee of the
land to be passed on to his children. To the Vietnamese the
land itself was the sacred, constant element: the people
flowed over the land like water, maintaining, fructifying it for
generations to come.

By presenting Vietnamese as mysterious Asian opposites of
Americans, FitzGerald no longer has any responsibility to find out
anything more about them. Americans are caricatures of heavy-
handed bellicosity; Vietnamese therefore must be contemplative
and peace-loving. Americans are driven by a sense of historical mission; the Vietnamese are reduced to passivity by their lack of history.

Her ideas, presented in a ringing, authoritative tone but with only
the sparsest evidence, say little about the Vietnamese. By presenting
herself as a sympathetic liberal counterweight to those who wanted
to bomb the country back into the stone age, she stakes a claim to
explaining the 'true nature' of the people, a highly dubious intention in itself. FitzGerald's Vietnamese are devoid of all diversity or
individuality; they remain trapped in fixed intellectual and physical
landscapes, completely beholden to the ageless and unbending
forces of Confucianism, colonialism and village life.

FitzGerald assumes that all Vietnamese accept a single cyclical
version of history and that they scour this for precedents that justify
their current actions. She ignores, or is unaware of, earlier civil conflicts and of how contentious different readings of history have been
in Vietnam. She portrays Vietnamese as passionately hostile to outside invaders but says little about their capacity for assimilation or
how they react to their own rulers. Her assumption is that they are
all good, obedient Confucian Mandarins or subservient peasant
farmers.

What FitzGerald constructs is essentially the same as the French
colonial picture of Vietnam as the dullard offspring of a richer
Chinese culture. Vietnam's own complex history of conquest, integration, passivity and resistance does not figure here. The rich
mix of religions and political beliefs, the evolving and changing

social structures, the influences of colonialism and Vietnam's neighbours other than China are all left out; FitzGerald and many others prefer not to muddy their clear Confucian vision with any distractions.

Far from being stuck in their villages, tending their ancestors behind walls of bamboo, Vietnamese have for centuries been travelling, trading, migrating, conquering, fleeing, expanding and exploring. Village life has evolved over time and customs vary in different parts of the country; the appearance of unchanging closed worlds is deceptive.

Ninh Hiep just outside Hanoi illustrates some of the changes. At first glance this Red River village appears the archetype of the insular communities that FitzGerald describes. Densely packed together, the houses have high walls and enclosed courtyards. The town's gates could once be closed off against the world. Ninh Hiep has seen periods when it was best to huddle together to protect the village from hostile forces. It has, however, also had a long history of complex contacts with the outside world. It has a 900-year history of providing court doctors and was a training centre for itinerant healers. For centuries it has been a centre for selling silk and for trading medicines as far away as north-eastern China.

FitzGerald's work cements in place a view of Vietnamese as child-like and accepting, lacking an indigenous intellectual tradition and of being swayed by the most simplistic needs and ideas. Any Vietnamese who steps outside her framework is described as aberrant and somehow not truly Vietnamese; she doesn't consider that her framework may be misplaced. It is telling that she does not quote many Vietnamese by name; they are simply emblems such as 'an old man', 'a soldier' or 'a National Liberation Front cadre'. She may have been protecting sources with anonymity, but she doesn't make this clear. Instead, their lack of identity forms a tense contrast with the Westerners she quotes who are given names along with a sense of history and individuality.

FitzGerald's ideas could be dismissed if they were not so enduring; her eloquent and well-written Orientalist fiction has proved a tenacious barrier to a broader understanding of modern Vietnam. It is journalists and writers, not Vietnamese, who unfortunately live in a world without history where the same ideas are endlessly re-circulated. A quarter of a century after the publication of *Fire in the Lake*, FitzGerald is more often cited than challenged; this is not because of the worth of her book but because of a failure to approach Vietnam afresh. FitzGerald's ideas about the country's history of resistance to foreigners, the influence of Confucianism and the way Vietnamese see history are simply taken as fact and repeated.

Writing on Vietnam has been dominated by a small group whose exposure to the country occurred during a time of intense conflict. The Vietnam they wrote about then, and in many cases still write about now, was a country vivisected by the Geneva Agreements of 1954 into rival nations, both of which were struggling to find new political and social identities in the wake of nearly a century of colonialism. That troubled time is taken as base point of Vietnamese life, a standard by which everything is judged. There is a tendency to see the reforms of the past decades as having taken the country back to the days before 1975; Saigon in particular is seen as returning to that time. This ignores the changes that have occurred in the post-war years. The realities of modern Vietnam have not much interested any of these writers. For them, the country will forever be 'Nam' and their only vision of it can be seen through the prism of the war and its myths.

William Prochnau's book *Once Upon a Distant War*, the *Iliad* of heroic journalism in 'Nam', was a critical triumph when it was published in 1995, twenty years after the fall of Saigon. The book chronicles the Vietnam experiences of a number of well-known journalists such as Peter Arnett, Neil Sheehan and David Halberstam. Prochnau, a reporter who covered the war, is not out to challenge any of the most cherished and powerful journalistic fantasies; the book opens with the ubiquitous image of the innocent reporter striding off the plane at Saigon airport into 'this little Asian trouble spot'. From that moment on it is inevitable that he be seduced and corrupted by a city that Prochnau describes as 'not simply exotic. It was erotic. And narcotic'.

Prochnau lays down a blistering fire of clichés in just the first few pages of his drive-by reporting. The women are 'tiny, porcelain, ephemeral images of perfect grace' with 'raven hair and flowing white *ao dai*s . . . that so remarkably enhanced their femininity'.

There is a supporting cast of saffron-robed monks, 'Hindu money-changers' and Chinese 'with three-strand beards and opaque eyes who introduced visitors to the ancient pleasures of the poppy'. The countryside is 'a poet's panorama unchanged in centuries' populated by tribesmen and the followers of exuberant religious sects.

Reporting on the Vietnam War has become such a mark of distinction for journalists, particularly those in the United States who are now television anchors and senior editors, that it is almost sacrilegious to challenge it. Prochnau doesn't even try; his book, like so many about the war, exists only to celebrate a world of journalistic myth in which his young heroes challenge powerful governments with their Pulitzer Prize-winning articles. Many of these journalists did transform American journalism with their writing at that time; they were often brave and critical. Their post-war writing has, however, taken on a very different attitude as they struggle against the evidence to put the most positive possible spin on the country and its government.

FitzGerald's work sometimes seems like a template for writing on Vietnam. In Prochnau's book, the people are grounded completely in their landscapes, hidden behind their bamboo hedges that represent their closed minds or lurking in jungles which terrify the unprepared American GIs but are a natural habitat for these born warriors.

But for Vietnamese soldiers, the jungle was no easier a habitat than it was for the Americans. Vietnamese are more used to cities and paddy fields than the mountains of the Central Highlands. Thousands died of malaria and almost all suffered other illnesses and permanent hunger. Bao Ninh, a former North Vietnamese soldier who wrote the acclaimed novel *The Sorrow of War*, described the forests of central Vietnam as alien and morbid, a world of phantoms and damp nocturnal terror. 'Here when it is dark, trees and plants moan in awful harmony. When the ghostly music begins it unhinges the soul and the entire wood looks the same no matter where you are standing. Not a place for the timid. Living here one could go mad or be frightened to death.'

Bao Ninh and other writers have punctured many of the inflated ideas we have about Vietnamese soldiers; these myths were a comforting fiction for the Americans – that they were up against an almost inhuman and unbeatable enemy. The image of Vietnamese soldiers as ant-like automatons programmed to fight is undermined by these stories of desertions, drug use, draft evasion and over-whelming fear. In the world of opposites that FitzGerald and others have established, the US military in Vietnam was a drug-infested, anarchic mob with no understanding of the reasons for which they were fighting. The Vietnamese were a rigorous fighting force, tightly disciplined and motivated. Bao Ninh revealed a world in which Vietnamese were not all heroic; many did not understand really why they were fighting. War, it seems, was grim, terrifying and chaotic for all sides.

The creation of 'Indochine' and 'Nam' would not be possible with-out some complicity on the part of powerful Vietnamese officials. Rewriting the past to make it less confrontational and softening the edges of conflicts with France and the United States suited the gov-ernment after 1986 when it was desperate to resume contacts with the West. All the French movie productions were done with the approval and encouragement of the Ministry of Culture and Information in Hanoi. These cultural commissars, normally so sen-sitive to any perceived colonial slight, decided that these movies might be useful in promoting the country's new open face to the world.

They were not always so lenient. Most producers who sought permission to film in Vietnam were rebuffed by the ministry, which kept a close eye on the ideological content of scripts and rejected many, including the James Bond film *Tomorrow Never Dies*. Britain's OO7 had spent too much time fighting communism to be seen ordering a martini in Hanoi. Tran Hung Anh's film *Cyclo* was filmed almost covertly with officials unaware of its brutal presentation of Ho Chi Minh City. Far from being adopted like his early nostalgic vision of Vietnam in *The Scent of Green Papaya*, *Cyclo* was banned and attacked in the official media for 'blackening' the country's good name.

Creating a playground of colonial and war memories was a way for the government to mend broken ties and to sell the country to tourists. It had the beneficial side effect of isolating foreigners from the widening ideological, economic and social strains that afflicted the country. Visiting journalists and film-makers were allowed to indulge in nostalgia as long as it kept them away from revealing any present-day tensions. Barbarian handlers – the cadres who controlled the activities of foreign film-makers, writers and journalists – were more co-operative with projects that had an historical theme, hence a profusion of articles about the Ho Chi Minh Trail and Khe Sanh, site of a major battle between American and North Vietnamese forces. Journalists who had covered the war and were perceived as 'friends of Vietnam' in the official parlance, were given good access; they could be relied on not to stray from the path of hazy Namstalgia.

A number of American reporters of considerable journalistic heft – Sheehan, Morley Safer and Dan Rather among others – produced books on their returns to Vietnam in the 1990s that all covered similar ground and rarely wandered into areas that the Vietnamese government saw as off-limits. Dan Rather's recollections of his return along with General Norman Schwarzkopf were somewhat sour; the others were less mean in spirit but they all remained aloof from the concerns of modern Vietnam.

Guilt and sadness – the original meaning of the word nostalgia – inflected their writing, which tended to offer only the most gentle criticisms of the government. Journalists who were known for deftly challenging the assumptions and statements of their own leaders lost their edge when faced with Vietnamese officials. Instead of addressing contemporary issues and tensions, many of these journalists produced naïve accounts of the policies and personnel of Vietnamese government. Stanley Karnow, author of a best-selling history of the war, wrote a profile of General Vo Nguyen Giap for the *New York Times Magazine* that unquestioningly swallowed the general's tendentious version of history. Far from being just the adored hero of Dien Bien Phu and celebrated victor over the United States, Giap is a contentious figure in Vietnamese politics, admired by many but also vilified for what is seen as his cowardice in the face of Communist Party hardliners.

The many facets of the former defence minister's story completely passed Karnow by; the two grand old men were too busy buffing each other's egos to pose or answer the difficult questions. Karnow's portrayal added nothing to our understanding of a complex man. To find an interview with Giap in which he was pressed with difficult questions about his explosive personality, his tactical failures, his vanity and his indifference to battle losses, one has to go back to the renowned Italian journalist Oriana Fallaci, who wrote about him for the newspaper *L'Europeo* in February 1969. They did not hit it off; she described him talking 'for forty-five minutes, without letting up, in the pedantic tone of a professor lecturing some rather unintelligent pupils. To interrupt to ask a question was a hopeless undertaking'.

Fallaci's portrayal of Giap is startling when compared with the recent depiction of him as a warm and avuncular figure. He comes across as ferociously driven and indifferent to the suffering of his people. When Fallaci asked him 'So then, general, how long will the war go on? How long will this poor people be asked to sacrifice itself, to suffer and to die?', Giap responded 'As long as it's necessary. Ten, fifteen, twenty, fifty years. Until we achieve total victory, as our president, Ho Chi Minh, said. Yes! Even twenty, fifty years! We're not in a hurry, we're not afraid.'

Giap's staff, aware of the chilling tone of his words, later tried to bully Fallaci into publishing only the official text of their interview which left out the problematic parts; they were particularly angered by her challenge to him over the effectiveness of the Tet Offensive in 1968 during which troops attacked South Vietnamese cities but were almost obliterated in a counter-attack. When Fallaci, who had been intensely critical of the American military involvement, refused to restrict herself to the heavily censored and wooden answers prepared by Giap's staff, she was denounced in Hanoi as a tool of the Central Intelligence Agency.

Fallaci's critical portrayal was a rarity. Giap was a powerful seducer of the foreign media. He loved to reminisce; in his quiet, sibilant French he would dazzle journalists with his stories of founding the Vietnamese People's Army in the northern highlands in 1944, and his victory at the battle of Dien Bien Phu. He always put on a masterly show with a grace and polish that made it difficult to challenge the sprightly old general; he was history incarnate. Journalists would be invited to his large villa in the city centre where Giap would introduce his family. Stepping into the garden, he would pose for photographers under a flowering tree. If it was in blossom, he would break off a small branch and present it to the journalist. Few journalists realised that they all witnessed identical performances and heard the same speeches.

Giap is often portrayed as single-handedly responsible for the victories over the French and the United States. It is an idea he does little to discourage as it conveniently sets aside the intense debates, both ideological and strategic, that raged among the dozens of other senior military figures involved in the war. Giap often lost the internal struggles in Hanoi; his power faded from 1954 onwards and by the late 1960s he was under constant challenge from rivals.

In 1980, he was stripped of almost all powers; his job for the next few years was to head a national family planning campaign. A sardonic rhyme that circulated in Hanoi in the 1980s included a line about a victorious general whose job was now to insert IUDs. Giap's eightieth birthday in 1991 passed almost unnoticed as there were none of the special ceremonies or honours that this hero might have expected. Even his supporters started to desert him; many were bitter that he had not stood up to the ideologues who dominated Vietnam from the 1960s to the mid 1980s. Giap was among the few who could have challenged them but he chose a comfortable retirement instead. Few of these stories made it into the portraits by journalists who went back to 'Nam'.

So much written by journalists who parachuted into Vietnam was wide of the mark and often a product of desperate wishful thinking. A profile in the *Los Angeles Times* of the lawyer Ngo Ba Thanh, once a leading non-communist opponent of US intervention in South Vietnam, described her as 'one of the precious cultural bridges' between the Western world and Vietnam. Three years before this article appeared in 1992, Thanh had led a movement in the National Assembly to kill a law that might have allowed private ownership of the media and offered the press a greater degree of freedom. As a leader of the official lawyers' association, she campaigned hard to restrict the operations of foreign lawyers operating in Vietnam, a move that hindered investment from abroad. Thanh was known in Hanoi not for her liberalism but for her hostility towards the West and foreign businesses.

These reports are reminiscent of the books produced by American anti-war activists and writers such as Susan Sontag and Mary

McCarthy after their brief and closely-regimented visits to Hanoi during the war in which they described a socialist paradise. McCarthy was even struck by the rareness of acne among Vietnamese youth, which she took as a sign of a higher moral existence. These writers at least had an excuse for their weak grasp of the country; almost nothing was known in the West about North Vietnam at the time. Nowadays there is no justification for the superficial coverage, the unquestioning approach to the government and the thinly researched history. Part of the problem is the emphasis on reporting by the returning heroes of 'Nam' who rarely do more than reminisce about their youths. Creating the image of Vietnamese as mysterious and unknowable lets these writers off the hook; nothing else need be said. Even the hard-bitten Neil Sheehan, writing in the *New Yorker* in 1995, went so far as to describe the Vietnamese leadership as 'the idealistic revolutionaries of the rainforest', a phrase that seems strenuously naïve in the face of the harsh realities of their rule.

Vietnamese officials trusted to meet with foreign reporters spun the same lines and seemed to relish their stereotypical roles as Marxist Mandarins, heroic military strategists or idealistic revolutionaries. A central part of Vietnam's political culture is about presenting a façade to the outside world. In the past it covered its chaotic political divisions with the image of rigorous Confucianism or strict Marxism. It has softened its appearance now but it has not dropped its guard; officials are dedicated to preserving the images. They portray themselves to the outside world as mysterious and inscrutable, fluent in elliptical oriental wisdoms and masters of a society that outsiders could not possibly fathom. Thus they ensured that journalists and writers spent more time examining a past over which the government could exercise some control rather than a present that is slipping away from them.

3

Remembering Vietnam

Forgetting, and I might even say historical errors, are essential factors in the creation of a nation.

ERNEST RENAN
What is a Nation?, 1892

The colonial architecture that survived the wars, the damp and decades of neglect, could evoke the landscapes of 'Indochine', but recreating the country's more recent history for tourists has been a problem. There was little to offer visitors seeking the 'Nam' experience. Most of the physical damage from the war had been repaired, the bomb craters filled in and the cities rebuilt. There was much real suffering that persisted after the war – the handicapped veterans, the psychological scarring that left many with a palpable sense of anguish and the lack of reconciliation within the country and with the Vietnamese Diaspora. None of this was open to scrutiny; it was simply too troubling for a state that likes its history simple and heroic.

To shelter foreigners from the realities of war and hinder a wider exploration of the past by Vietnamese, the government offered up history in such places as the Cu Chi tunnels. From these tunnels, located in a farming district about thirty-five kilometres outside Ho Chi Minh City, the Viet Cong planned their campaigns on the South Vietnamese and American bases that ringed the city. From here, guerrillas infiltrated the city to carry out attacks or spy on the nearby bases. The tunnels were one of the few front lines in that war. This was the nearest base to the enemy's capital and was so treacherous that the only way to survive was deep underground.

Cu Chi became one of the most heavily bombed, gassed and

defoliated sites in Vietnam as US forces attempted to clear the tunnels. Now the landscape is far removed from the imaginary lushness of Vietnam. The trees are thin and etiolated, now only dry eucalypts struggle in the poisoned and scorched soil. Some areas are still pitted with vast craters left unfilled after more than twenty years.

Underneath this dry earth, Vietnamese villagers and army sappers created a vast network of tunnels. Between 1945 and 1975 they carved some 200 kilometres of narrow veins and chambers out of Cu Chi's crumbling soil. Eventually this warren became a shelter for thousands who endured relentless US bombing to clear them from what had been declared a 'free fire zone'. High explosives dropped by B-52s set off seismic shocks that rippled through the earth, collapsing the tunnels and burying hundreds of people alive.

Nguyen Thu, the head of Vietnam's state film company, was in charge of producing propaganda films during the war and saw the potential the tunnels held as a symbol of Vietnamese endurance. They were an image that could be used to boost morale across the country. Here were men and women living just outside the enemy's capital fighting a vastly superior enemy and yet they were winning because of their ingenuity and perseverance. But the risks of making such films were enormous.

'When they started fighting in the Cu Chi tunnels, we sent a crew of seven down there to film. They were all killed so we sent seven more and then more after that,' he said. 'After 1975 when the northern troops took control of Cu Chi, we found out that not one of the men we had sent there had survived.'

Cu Chi is one of a number of places where tunnels were built to shelter from bombs or hide from patrols. But this 'revolutionary bastion of bronze and steel', as a wartime song called it, has become the most important site for the commemoration of the Vietnam War. Once it was used to rouse Vietnamese to fight off foreigners, now it mostly serves to summarise the war for tourists. Cu Chi compresses the war's problematic layering of civil, international, ideological and personal conflict into a neat David and Goliath struggle.

The area, now controlled by the sports and recreation department of the army, was ripe for development into a tourist site. Part of the forest has been turned into a complete wartime environment –

a fantasy land that cries out for a name like 'Cong World'. A Vietnamese soldier with a slight cowboy swagger and a Texan twang picked up from monitoring US military radio, leads visitors around a path, pointing out the hidden entrances to the tunnels and the craters left from the constant pounding Cu Chi received. At various points along the trail, strict instructions, perhaps even orders, are given to take photographs.

At Cu Chi, it is a simple ingenuity that defeats the powerful Americans. The guerrillas left shavings from American bars of soap around the entrances to tunnels to disguise their scent from the sniffer dogs that were used to hunt them down. Smoke from cooking fires was dispersed through numerous chambers so that spotter planes could not locate it. At the end of the tour visitors are served a VC meal of stringy manioc dipped in crushed peanuts and tea brewed from forest leaves. As visitors leave they can loose off a few rounds from an AK-47 at a firing range, or shop for trinkets made from the brass shells of rifle bullets or model jet fighters crafted from Coke cans. Aware of the need to keep the attraction fresh, new additions are constantly being made to the show, which now includes trip-wires that set off firecrackers to simulate mine explosions. VC uniforms of black pyjamas and checked scarves are offered to those who wish to dress up for the occasion. The latest construction has been a culture village to give tourists a taste of life among Vietnamese minorities. There were limits, however, to make-believe; Minako Honda, a Japanese actress starring in the musical *Miss Saigon* in Tokyo, was fined and expelled from the country after being photographed in the tunnels draped only in a Vietnamese flag.

The tunnels contain a number of paradoxes as a tourist site. Their importance during the war was their invisibility and inaccessibility. Most of its occupants were members of a guerrilla army that was supposed to be highly mobile and unencumbered. Yet these qualities are a hindrance to a successful tourist attraction. So the tunnels have had to be made semi-visible, while a big show is made of their invisibility, such as when the guide uncovers a hidden entrance cunningly disguised with leaves glued together with raw latex from rubber trees. The tunnels have also been expanded so that they are now large enough for big Westerners to squeeze through;

previously they were kept narrow to keep Americans out. In its attempts to become more authentic in the eyes of tourists, 'Cong World' has had to add new layers of falsehood.

The darker side of Cu Chi, indeed of the war, remains mostly unexamined but reveals itself occasionally in the flashes of horror at the waste of lives. Nobody is sure exactly how many people died in the Cu Chi tunnels – the official Vietnamese count is 14,000 civilians and 10,400 soldiers. Maintaining this bastion just near the capital of South Vietnam was a huge symbolic victory for the Viet Cong but it came at a horrendous cost.

The ghosts of those ground up in this carnage do not appear at 'Cong World'. There is a memorial, a large ornate temple on the banks of a nearby river, but the tour groups don't stop there. Tens of thousands fought at Cu Chi but their personal stories are absent. In a film shown to tourists, they are all simple peasants battling an evil foreign enemy that shows its contempt for Vietnamese by shooting at images of the Buddha and killing their chickens for fun. 'With a rifle in one hand and a plough in the other', these hardy warriors fight only foreigners, not other Vietnamese, and are rewarded for their bravery with the title of 'American killer hero'.

The constant repetition of this honour, which the film tells us was awarded to a young woman who, despite being weak and peaceful by nature, 'continuously shot down the enemy', is one of the few notes that might jar tourists in a history that attempts to remain as inoffensive as possible. History is reduced to a tradition of fighting off foreigners. This mantra of heroic resistance is now presented as the single, unifying theme of Vietnamese history.

A few kilometres from the Cu Chi tunnels Nguyen Thi Lanh lives with her only surviving son and his wife and young children in a small concrete house decorated with blue tiles. The house was a reward for the 85-year-old for her many years of revolutionary struggle. In the 1950s, Lanh had taken the red and gold flag of North Vietnam and buried it in a bronze pot under a tree on her small plot of land. On 29 April 1975, Cu Chi fell to the communist forces and Lanh dug up the flag so that it could fly from the liberated town hall. She described it as a moment of extraordinary happiness.

As Lanh recounted her story in language that fitted the approved mix of sentimentality and revolutionary rhetoric, the head of the local chapter of the Women's Union, which had set up the interview, listened attentively and smiled in a mildly patronising way. But the cadre's lips soon pursed into a tight bud of disapproval when Lanh's tale shifted away from flag-waving heroics and turned to the realities of war.

'I lost three of my sons and my husband and I lived a life that was indescribably horrible,' she said, her eyes flickering up towards an altar where she had placed framed pictures of the dead: four men, all polished and neatly dressed in white shirts, all frozen in handsome youth, the father looking no older than his sons. Two of her sons died in Cu Chi and another at a Viet Cong base in Cambodia. Her husband had died in the French colonial prison on Con Dao Island. She could not bring herself to talk about how it felt to have your children die in war and instead spoke of the constant hunger, deprivation and isolation of a life tarred by conflict and the bleak years that followed it. A quiet cough from the Women's Union cadre reminded her to get back to the glories of the revolution and ended this brief glimpse into her private world of loss. Outside the house her sole surviving child, a tired-looking, middle-aged man with a thin, bruised face, smoked a cigarette, looking as though he too had carried far too much of the burden of grief in silence.

In 1994, Lanh was one of 20,000 women awarded the title of 'Heroic Mother' given to those whose children had died in the conflicts that blighted Vietnam from 1945 to 1989. It was an honour 'that you don't go looking to win', Lanh said, summing up the strangeness of being rewarded for enduring the loss of your children. Several hundred women, dressed in formal black velvet *ao dais*, attended a ceremony at the Presidential Palace in Hanoi where they were serenaded by a rock band and greeted by past luminaries such as General Giap and Pham Van Dong.

The writer Bao Ninh watched the ceremony on television and was left stunned and tearful at the sight of these old women whose suffering was finally being acknowledged by the state so long after Vietnam had honoured its men. 'It has taken us nearly twenty years to recognise their grief,' he said, shaking his head with incredulity.

Honouring these women was an attempt to heighten patriotism

at a time when the country was experiencing rapid, unsettling change. For many Vietnamese, however, the ceremonies reinforced resentment that so little had been done for the people who had suffered the most during the war. A samizdat leaflet that circulated in Ho Chi Minh City after one of the ceremonies in 1995 pointed out 'the heartbreaking contrast' between 'these pale walking skeletons pinned with medals' and the 'fat, perfumed officials' who attended. It was the first recognition that women had got for their roles in the war, as heroism was centred very much around men. For years, the army had been bathed in a warm glow of heroism and it did not brook any dissenting views. Casualty figures were never released, injured men were given little help and the maimed or shell-shocked were brushed aside. Those, who like Bao Ninh tried to strip away the images of square-jawed heroism and restore some humanity and individuality to soldiers, were accused of lacking patriotism.

The Communist Party still feels a political imperative to pare the complexities of the war down to a simple narrative, turning soldiers into cardboard heroes. As a low hubbub of dissonant voices began rising, the government tried to restore some order to its history. Part of this was a matter of isolating those people whose versions of the war did not follow the official line, but it also involved changing that official line. There was a clear effort to tone down the memories of the war, to ease some of the inflammation of those times by turning down the volume of propaganda and by reworking museums and monuments. The American War Crimes Museum in Danang was closed and a similar repository of grim artefacts from the war in Ho Chi Minh City was renamed The War Remnants Museum. Several local authorities quietly removed the tanks and jet fighters from town squares and parks. The toning down of aggressive martial images gave more of a holiday feel for tourists who did not want to be too troubled by the dark side of the country's history. Even the War Remnants Museum, which contains shocking images of conflict and torture, now offers a water puppet show and souvenir stands.

A number of wartime locations have been opened up for tourism. Dien Bien Phu can now be reached by plane and American investors planned a huge resort at China Beach near Danang, hoping to capitalise on the market of US veterans and the popularity of the eponymous television series. The project eventually collapsed due to a lack of funds but is likely to be resurrected. A whole list of 'Nam' museums were being planned for tourists. Quang Tri province, where the Seventeenth Parallel once divided the country, has a scheme to build a museum devoted to the McNamara Line, a rinky-dink and unworkable 1960s answer to the Maginot Line in which various detector devices were installed to spot North Vietnamese troops infiltrating the South.

Officials from the province, one of the poorest in the country and littered with unexploded ordnance that still maims and kills, estimated that recreating a stretch of the line complete with bunkers, observation towers and sensors would cost $2 million. The Ministry of Defence is planning a museum devoted to the Ho Chi Minh Trail to be built at its official starting point just outside Hanoi. Museums about the war have become a way to extract money from the central government and promote tourism.

Only tourists and schoolchildren seem to visit these museums with their malfunctioning dioramas of battle scenes and scratched vitrines. Most of the objects on display have the *Boy's Own* quality of war museums – weapons, military banners and ingenious booby-traps fashioned from everyday objects. Vietnamese forces though were generally mobile and did not carry much around with them. This bequeathed a problem for museum curators searching for the heroic objects that could represent this period of history. They have masses of abandoned American equipment and tonnes of unexploded ordnance, but little with which to represent themselves. The Hue Museum has a display of a 1960s Air France PVC flight bag, an unlikely object to stir the patriotic heart. The bag sits proudly illuminated and labelled in a glass case in the Hue Museum because it was apparently used by a local cadre to carry secret documents. It is one of the few 'genuine' articles in the museum.

Most objects on display in Vietnamese museums are fake. Even if the museums have genuine pieces, they prefer to keep them around the back, safe from damage or theft. Visitors are offered poorly crafted replicas of Dong Son drums and ancient Buddhas. Authenticity is not centred in the objects; what are important are the political and historical messages they send. It is acceptable to question the origins of an object, such as an ancient drum, but it would be offensive to question what it represents; in this case the antiquity and richness of Vietnamese culture.

Few Vietnamese seemed perturbed by the fact that tank number 843, famous for being the first to smash through the gates of the Presidential Palace in Saigon, has been displayed for years concurrently in Saigon and outside the Army Museum in Hanoi. Neither was there much concern when in 1996 it was revealed that neither of these cloned tanks (it is unclear which is the original) was even the first one through the gates. The tank represents reunification, revolution and victory, which are very much sacred territories off-limits to any challenge. To make this clear, a clause in Vietnam's constitution makes it a criminal offence to 'doubt the fruits of the revolution'.

Tank 843 got all the glory because it led a re-enactment staged for the cameras. This was common after battles; immediately after the collapse of French forces at Dien Bien Phu, it was all re-staged for the film-makers. Some of the key moments in Vietnamese history that were captured on film were actually performances in which the past could be tightly controlled.

The museums and war theme parks may offer a simple version of the conflict but the country is covered with much more troubling sites that recall the war. Every few kilometres along Highway One, the pocked two-lane road that runs the length of the country, there are cemeteries for war dead. Hundreds of these have been built after 1975 to hold some of the 3 million people who are estimated to have died in conflicts since 1945. One of the largest military graveyards is the Truong Son Cemetery in Quang Tri where they buried many of those who died on the central stretches of the Ho Chi Minh Trail, the thousands of miles of roads and paths along which supplies and men infiltrated the South. High up on a bleak plateau, a landscape cross-hatched with rows of heavily scored rubber trees, the cemetery is filled with the graves of 20,000 people. The wind whips through the small concrete gravestones, each of which has a small blue china incense holder. The paths are warped and cracked and paint has peeled from the central monument. The names of all those buried there are scored into granite columns that give the

dates of when they joined the army and when they died. The gap
between these dates is often tragically short – often just a few
months – as thousands of boys from the villages of the Red River
delta were ground up along the muddy route.

The dead are honoured in cemeteries with an obelisk bearing the
cold inscription: 'Your country acknowledges your sacrifice'. Some
cemeteries are untended and nearly derelict; they rarely seem to be
a focal point for remembrance. Officially the war was glorious, not
the tragedy it was for the United States. A sense of the nation as
victim is encouraged in history and in the constant remembrances
in newspapers. Individual grief is not seen in the same way and so
sorrow in Vietnam has often turned inwards. When almost everyone has suffered terribly, it is hard for anyone to express that
suffering.

Mourning and remembrance are largely private affairs. Even the
military funerals offered to veterans are now often shunned in
favour of more traditional ceremonies that restore a personal and
religious content to the rituals. Thousands of families lived for years
without being given any details of missing relatives; the bureaucracy was unhelpful and unwilling to acknowledge publicly the
extent of the losses the war had caused. For those who can afford it,
mourning has become a matter of a quiet pilgrimage to a war cemetery in the South to recover the remains of a relative for reburial at
home. Many searched for more information about their families,
cajoling officials into giving out 'state secrets' so they could find out
when and how a son, father, uncle or brother died. These journeys
into the past are mostly unrecorded and unnoticed. Yet they consti-
tute a more powerful force of remembrance than the multitude of
official events and anniversaries that are more about the
Communist Party shoring up its sagging legitimacy than they are
about restoring harmony to troubled lives.

Official memorials and museums are intended to create a simpli-
fied history that erases troublesome memories of war and even of
the very existence of South Vietnam. But despite enormous efforts
on the part of the state, the country is charged with tensions over
how history should be written, whom should be deemed heroic
and what should be commemorated. While the state has tried to
monopolise history through its control of academia and the media,

it has not been possible to stop Vietnamese from creating their own stories, often by resurrecting and reworking what were once darkly condemned as 'feudal practices'. The decade after 1985 saw a resurgence in apparently traditional forms of worship or celebration in villages across Vietnam. People revived village festivals and saints' days, staged cockfights, cheered as buffaloes locked horns at bloody tournaments and stood in silent, absorbed crowds to watch 'human chess' played with costumed people in temple courtyards.

The resurrection of traditional village life involved not just the recovery of festivals and religious rituals but their reinvention. It required that they be anchored in the past, after all a tradition gains its legitimacy from at least appearing to be ancient, and so they borrowed from a rich cultural idiom that had been suppressed since the 1950s or lost during the war.

The desire to maintain a uniquely 'Vietnamese culture' in the face of external influences is strong; Huu Ngoc, a prominent historian and folklorist, described it as 'the country's third and most difficult war of resistance'. But this is much more a civil conflict over ideas of history and modernity than a battle against foreigners. For decades the pre-revolutionary past was dismissed as feudal or colonial and therefore in need of change.

Now redefining the past requires difficult decisions. Much of what is described as Vietnamese culture has its origins in China. This presents a challenge to national identity that has perpetually troubled the country. Likewise the Red River delta, seen as the primordial heartland of this culture has been given a leading role that is not wholeheartedly accepted elsewhere in the country. In the south and centre, areas with distinct cultural traits, the murmurs against the hegemony of northern Vietnamese culture are growing louder. For decades, the state tried to reform 'feudal' practices that discriminated against women or heightened inequalities in society; now some of these practices have returned presenting a conundrum to a government that can no longer clearly delineate this re-emergence of culture.

The government generally favoured the restoration of certain practices when they were seen as conducive to good order and national cohesion. It started pushing for families to take an interest in their lineages and to restore clan meetings. Previously family ties had been frowned on as feudal. 'Vietnamese ancestries have been scattered through thousands of years of resistance wars against foreign invaders. It is time to eliminate disagreements and unite ancestries together,' Nguyen Song Tung, a vice minister of labour, told a ceremony to honour the Hung kings, the mythical ancestors of all Vietnamese. A strong sense of clan identity was useful 'in the development of the social and moral conduct of Vietnam,' he said, overlooking centuries of internecine wars between rival families.

The media has taken on an important role in the reinvention of tradition, often attempting to arbitrate what is acceptably Vietnamese and which traditions should be preserved. A newspaper campaigned for a ban on the paper models of such objects as houses, cars and televisions that are burned so that deceased relatives can enjoy them in the afterlife. 'Currently this traditional industry does not pay any taxes,' sniffed the *Vietnam News*, urging authorities to ban it as a 'social evil'. 'Their contributions to state and local budgets are negligible or non-existent. As the government gears up to tackle a host of cultural problems, will it also go after this wasteful superstition?' it asked.

The recreation of these different traditions and their historical justifications has been muddled by an important cultural change that took place in Vietnam in the first few decades of the twentieth century. In an effort to detach the Vietnamese élite from their heavily Sinicised culture, the French introduced *quoc ngu*, the romanised writing of the Vietnamese language that had previously been written in variants of Chinese characters. Within a few decades the use of the western alphabet, supplemented by accents, had completely replaced the use of characters. Vietnamese are almost totally cut off from anything written before 1920 unless it is transcribed into *quoc ngu*. This has meant that there is very little direct access to history. Very few Vietnamese understand the inscriptions written in characters in their homes or temples. Only a tiny number of people have much sense of history beyond the selection of martial episodes constantly replayed by the state to build a sense of cohesion against foreign enemies. The fact that few people can look back to the documents of the past has created tensions over the 'correct version' of the past, but it has also freed Vietnamese to play out some of this cultural invention on a clean slate, not on the usual layered palimpsests of history. The Communist Party encouraged this process in the hope that a reassertion of traditional identity could fill the ideological gaps exposed by the withering of Marxist-Leninism. But by relinquishing its role as the sole scribe of national history, the party has had to face the loss of an important means of control.

At a temple in Vinh Phu, a province just outside Hanoi where the highlands rise from the Red River basin, a shrine was erected in 1994 to a deity believed to be a descendent of the Hung kings. This deity had led Vietnam into an era of pride and abundance. His worshippers were mostly old men with gaunt figures and wispy beards. His image, cast in white clay, was placed on an altar of red lacquer and gilt along with figures of the eighteen Hung kings. On the eighteenth day of each lunar month, worshippers offered fruit and flowers at the altar and the deity blessed his followers with celestial waves that brought prosperity and success in business.

As the number of followers grew to more than 200, its leaders decided it was time to receive official recognition of their religion and they duly applied to the authorities in Hanoi. The response of the Religious Affairs Commission came as a surprise to the applicants. The sect's unauthorised worship of Ho Chi Minh was irregular and would not be tolerated. The religion, known as Doan Phu Tho 18, was banned and its followers ordered to desist from their practices.

By establishing a temple dedicated to the father of modern Vietnam who died in 1969, the men had been following an ancient practice of turning heroes of war and resistance into gods. Across the country there were pagodas honouring men and women who had led rebellions or helped fight foreign invaders. Many of these temples had been reopened and were popular centres of a spiritual revival. They were a collective celebration of the strength, ingenuity and recovery of a nation.

But there already was a temple to Ho Chi Minh in Hanoi and a cult that worships him there. This intolerant faith would not allow any rivals, even those that offered a similar message. They may have blurred the lines between earlier heroes and the frail, ascetic man who led Vietnam to independence, but this was a closely controlled process. Only a select priesthood could interpret Ho Chi

Minh's work or approve the use of his image. There was no room for spontaneity or individual initiative in his worship.

Pictures of Ho are so common in Vietnam that they almost fade into invisibility. He is usually shown either in a Spartan environment deep in thought, or playing with young children. He is normally middle-aged or elderly and dressed in a loose shirt and trousers, not the suits he wore in Russia and France. The images are aimed at portraying his kindness, humanity and modesty. The stories that are endlessly recycled in the press are most often of his self-deprecating humour and his refusal of gifts and honours. His life is shown in a number of unlinked set pieces: he grows up the child of a poor but patriotic mandarin, he leaves for France as a young man where he learns about Marx and starts the struggle against colonialism, he returns to Vietnam in 1941 and four years later takes over in the August Revolution, proclaiming independence in Hanoi.

Even the relatively modest state religion of Ho Chi Minh, the only personality cult allowed by the Communist Party, has come under quiet but sustained attack. Ho, who devoted much of his time to buffing his image as a saintly national uncle, has come down to earth. His closest colleagues have admitted that he was less than infallible, questioning his passivity as the Party lurched towards Maoism in the 1950s; the catastrophe of land reform later in that decade; his role in the decision to reunify through war and the refusal to defend those purged because they disagreed with the Party's move towards China.

In 1990 the writer Tran Huy Quang published a story in the journal *Van Nghe* called 'A Prophecy Fulfilled' that slyly undermined Ho's cult and attacked what the author saw as the false allure of Marxism. In the story, Hinh, the son of a mandarin, hankers to lead others. He is visited by the envoy of a deity who tells him to walk down a certain road, resist various temptations and then 'bend down and walk very slowly, step by step with thine eyes fastened to the ground in order to look for this. Continue on . . . it shall take only one moment and thou shalt possess the world'. When he starts looking for 'this' he is joined by a huge crowd of people who think he is looking for hidden treasure.

And they were now as numerous as ants, these people crawling around in the flower garden, looking for anything in hope of a bit of security. Hinh suddenly noticed the noise of the crowd and, startled, looked around at them. Why, there was the world, swarming all about him. In just one moment he would possess the world. Fulfilled and serene, his eyes welled up with tears of bliss … and he went home. But the crowd continued on like a torrent of water in a stream that never runs dry. They had no idea what 'this' was that they were looking for but they still hoped.

There were many more subtle attempts to reassess or undermine Ho's image. *Farewell Saigon*, a movie released in 1990, portrayed the young Ho as torn between his love for a girl and his duty to his country. The country, of course, won out in the movie which stunned audiences for even suggesting that Ho had any relationships. Newspapers even published reports alleging that he was married. One wife might have been shocking enough for a man who portrayed himself as a celibate ascetic but there seem to have been at least two wives, one of them a French woman.

Many Hanoians affected to have known all along about the multiple wives and young mistresses that top officials kept in a compound of government villas on West Lake, but most people were wide-eyed with curiosity at these stories. National Assembly chairman Nong Duc Manh was rumoured to be Ho's son with a woman from the Tay minority who live in the northern highlands. The gossip proved useful to this rather bland political figure and Manh never bothered to deny it even when confronted directly.

Countering the hagiographies of Ho were much darker stories that circulated as gossip or appeared in the writings of dissidents who had left the country. Their allegations are almost impossible to prove – they exist in a murky historical realm of the Vietnamese élite that may never be completely illuminated – but they illustrate the degree to which Ho's heroic and kindly persona is challenged overseas and at home.

Stories about some of Uncle Ho's nocturnal wanderings were much more troubling. Vu Thu Hien, the son of Ho's personal secretary Vu Dinh Huynh, has accused a senior official of killing Ho's

mistress and her sister. In his book *Darkness at Noon,* Hien said Tran
Quoc Hoan, the head of public security and a member of the
Politburo, raped and killed Ho's lover, a woman from the Nung
minority called Nong Thi Xuan. Ho is said to have kept her at a
house in central Hanoi, sending out his bodyguards to collect her
occasionally. In late 1956, according to Hien, she gave birth to Ho's
child. A few months later in February 1957 Hoan, the country's
chief policeman, went to the house to demand that Ho's mistress
have sex with him but was rebuffed. He returned later and raped
Xuan. A few days after that she was found dead near West Lake,
apparently a victim of a car accident, a highly unlikely occurrence in
a city with so little traffic. The few cars that were allowed were all
owned by officials. The child disappeared, although after Ho's
death he was said to have been adopted by another man who
worked for the president.

Most of this information may never be verified but it is something
more than titillating gossip. Hien got his information from his
father, one of Ho's closest associates for many years. Several other
officials, including one who held the post equivalent to deputy
mayor of Hanoi, corroborated details and in the 1980s some members of Xuan's family demanded an investigation. Letters they
wrote to senior officials suggested strongly that the public security
minister was responsible for her death. There has been speculation
that Ho may have approved of the murder having tired of Xuan;
some Vietnamese find it hard to imagine Hoan being so brazen as to
rape the president's mistress without some inside knowledge that
she had fallen from grace.

That these stories circulate at all shows that the Party's control
over Ho's image is always under threat and has to be constantly
monitored. The photographs of him playing with small children,
the refusal of all honours and his supposed modesty have been
effective in retaining an emotional attachment from many
Vietnamese although his cult is something of a fading force.

At the centre of the Holy See of Ho's cult is the necropolis on Ba
Dinh Square, the place where he declared independence in 1945.
The square is dominated by his mausoleum, a large stone edifice
surrounded by columns. It presents itself as a chilly and not greatly

heroic sarcophagus; like so much Soviet-influenced design, the mausoleum lacks a powerful architectural presence.

Many Vietnamese have been inside on a school trip but few Hanoians go there; it was more popular in the days when it was the only air-conditioned public building in the city and could provide visitors with a refreshing blast of chilled air. The queue nowadays is largely made up of people from the countryside and foreign tourists eager to catch a glimpse of the dead unburied as they are marched hastily past the carved catafalque that holds the glass coffin and the pallid remains.

'I have requested that my remains be incinerated,' Ho wrote in his will. 'I hope cremation will become a common practice. Not only is it good for the living from the point of hygiene, it also saves farmland. When we have a plentiful supply of electricity, "electric cremation" will be even better.' He asked that his ashes be divided into three ceramic boxes to be buried on hills in the north, centre and south of the country. 'Let no stone stele and bronze statue be erected on the grave. Instead there should be a simply designed, spacious, solidly built and cool house where visitors could rest.' Around these houses he wanted trees planted to create wide forests.

But his death was too important to lose the opportunity for a national monument. On 29 November 1969, nearly three months after he died, the Politburo decided to preserve his body and erect a tomb that would 'reflect a modern character while preserving the national character. Solemn but simple'.

It took more than a year to come up with a design. The General Secretary of the Vietnamese Architects' Association, Hoang Nhu Tiep, wrote: 'When we enter the tomb of Uncle Ho we will have the feeling that he is still alive and we will feel extremely peaceful, quiet and respectful before the sleeping Uncle Ho'. The flow of people through the building had to symbolise 'the endless vitality of Uncle Ho in the hearts of everyone and the lasting mark he left upon the Fatherland'.

The mausoleum, Tiep wrote, should not 'create a gloomy feeling in the nature of religious worship' nor should it encourage the gathering of noisy crowds. While it had to have the solemnity of a burial place, it also needed to be filled with life. 'When completed, the tomb of President Ho will be a historical monument of special importance to our people and our friends throughout the world, a monument befitting the noble undertaking of President Ho and the age of Ho Chi Minh, the most brilliant age in the glorious history of our people.'

With this demanding list of instructions, teams from architecture and building institutes set to work. Most of the ideas harked back to traditional Vietnamese landscapes or images such as the lotus flower. An idea for a replica of a rural three-room house was dismissed as lacking in dignity, as was a scheme that involved building an artificial mountain in central Hanoi that would have been topped with an apartment building and a fake river. Another design incorporated a sweeping avenue that would have cut through some of the most beautiful areas of Hanoi.

Five competitions were held and eventually a number of ideas were blended together. The Vietnamese asked for help from the Soviet Union, experts at building tombs as well as stuffing and pickling dead leaders. According to the Vietnamese, the Russians barged in and took over the project, leaving the locals to provide only the workmen and the raw materials.

The mausoleum, placed at the symbolic heart of the capital and therefore the country, seems somewhat inappropriate to many Vietnamese. It is too grandiose and socialist for Hanoi, a city that has remained remarkably unscathed by pompous official architecture. Soon after it was built, large groves of bamboo were planted on either side of the structure to soften its hard edges and to create a sense that it was in Vietnam, not Red Square.

Ho's mausoleum stands in an area originally designed to evoke not just raw colonial power but an ethic of French culture and superiority. Next to the Presidential Palace were the Botanical Gardens, representing nature tamed. Along one side of the square was a large school; on the other the ornate Treasury building with its oriental flourishes. Just nearby was the citadel with its armouries and barracks. Since 1954 the area has gradually been reworked and added to in order to shift the emphasis to a national identity centred around the cult of Ho and undefined Vietnamese tradition. The curving roads and paths laid out by the French were straightened to make them more suitable for military parades. A permanent reviewing stand was added on either side of Ho's mausoleum in another martial touch. The mausoleum was built at the centre of one side of the square. The scale of Ba Dinh Square is still human, but it feels austere; there is less of the vibrant street-life that runs rampant across the city.

Much of the criticism of the mausoleum by architects and others has focused on the violation of Ho's wish to be cremated and the imperial pretensions of the monument. An urban myth in Hanoi, repeated often in all seriousness, is that Ho's body has decayed alarmingly and that the pale pink corpse on show in the mausoleum is a waxwork. The writer Nguyen Huy Thiep, the leading figure of the literary revival of the 1980s, used the mausoleum's link to Vietnamese feudalism in a story to criticise the current leadership, a dangerous and shocking move at the time. In the short story Vang Lua (Fired Gold), Thiep looked back to a past era of mausoleum builders – the Nguyen Dynasty in the nineteenth century – and compared the officially reviled Emperor Gia Long with today's rulers.

There is a sense that a better memorial to Ho is the wooden house in the grounds of the Presidential Palace where he is said to have lived. This small structure built on stilts next to a fish pond was carefully juxtaposed next to the ornate French building where the governors-general of Indochina lived. The house contains Ho's modest belongings; some books, sandals, an alarm clock unwound since the day of his death and now protected by a Lucite case. The polished wood and bare furnishings actually give the house more a sense of minimalist luxe than the Spartan ambience it is supposed to recreate. There is even doubt over whether Ho actually lived there; little about the man is certain, such is the myth-making that surrounds his life.

Just behind the mausoleum is a vast concrete and marble museum, distinguished only by the fact that it was the last Soviet-designed structure to be built in Vietnam before the collapse of that empire. No longer in awe of their Russian mentors, Vietnamese architects have criticised its unwieldy bulk and ugliness. Nguyen Truc Luyen, current president of the Architects' Association, complained of its 'heavy design' that left visitors alienated by the vast masses of concrete. It would have been impossible to speak out against Ho's actual mausoleum, but the museum was a fair target for scorn.

The museum was the last of the monuments in the Ho necropolis, finished only in 1991. It is an extraordinary, almost surreal, journey through Ho's life, played out in a series of brightly coloured tableaux that represent his travels overseas and events in Vietnam. It is richly appointed and detailed compared with other museums across the country; no expense was spared in setting up the elaborate permanent display.

The circular gallery is divided into three concentric rings with the outer part representing the world, the central part Ho, and the inner part Vietnam. Along the outer wall is the whirl of early-twentieth-century modernism, represented by Picasso, the machine age and the Great War. At the same time, Vietnam is under the imperial yoke, illustrated with a gilt and lacquer palanquin and other feudal accoutrements of the collaborating class. Ho Chi Minh's life is chronicled in letters and photographs in the middle ring of the museum, mediating between the outside world, which moves through war, peace, fascism and revolution, and the inner ring that represents Vietnam.

The gallery plays out Vietnamese history from independence from France in 1954 to the arrival of US ground forces and the escalation of that war in 1965. The connections between the objects on display and the historical events are sometimes obtuse. A life-size model of a Ford Edsel car bursts through a wall. The connection with Vietnam is that Robert McNamara was head of Ford, which built the disastrous Edsel, a by-word for automotive failure. As Secretary of Defence, McNamara had escalated the Vietnam War. The inner wheel of exhibits has debris from planes and a flying suit from a captured American pilot, before the display ends with the glories of reunification and peace, represented by some giant plaster fruit set on an oddly shaped table.

The museum paints a glowing picture of Ho and gives an overwhelmingly privileged position to ideas of independence and national sovereignty. Inadvertently it reveals some of the sadder legacies of Ho Chi Minh. In another gallery downstairs there is an exhibition that outlines the success of reforms. Here the museum loses its oddly playful tone and reverts to drab illustrations of what communist countries take as industrial triumphs and the rest of the world takes for granted. There are cases of cheap light bulbs, displays of plastic buckets and a stack of vacuum flasks. Everything, even the building with its cracked marble and patches of bulging damp, seems sadly drab.

Opposite Ho's mausoleum, across the shaggy grass of Ba Dinh Square, is a new monument that not only commemorates the dead of Vietnam's many wars but seems to symbolise many of the changes of recent years, the shedding of so much ideological and historical baggage and a renewed, but still uncertain, sense of national identity.

The monument was born out of a sticky problem of diplomatic protocol. Official visitors were expected to lay a wreath at a memorial, but the Vietnamese were aware that many Western leaders still found it distasteful to honour Ho Chi Minh. What was needed was a new, less charged memorial, one that was not dedicated to any specific war but to all wars that Vietnam had fought.

A competition was launched and Le Hiep, an architect at the Hanoi Housing Department, was chosen from the eight entries. Hiep had been one of the Vietnamese architects who worked with the Russians on the Ho Chi Minh Museum and had felt frustrated by the brutalism of the building. In this commission he wanted to use something Vietnamese, but found there were few models of grand architecture to plunder for inspiration.

Instead he decided that he would look to the village for ideas and came up with a design that includes the shape of traditional monuments in the recessed sides of a square arch of granite and bronze. 'I wanted to incorporate elements of national identity and design in the monument,' he said. The outer line of the arch on each side follows the shape of a traditional temple roof, while the inner line is taken from a stele or gravestone.

The arch is set on a platform of granite with a low balustrade that echoes the designs of mausoleums in Hue. At each corner there is a lamp and in the centre of the arch a large incense urn. 'What makes the war memorial persuasive is that it is simple and small – there is nothing excessively grand about it,' Hiep said. The lack of grandeur and its few immediately readable symbols were controversial choices in a country that was more used to vast socialist obelisks. There are no hammers and sickles, no golden stars and no slogans carved in the granite. The memorial does not refer to any particular event or even a specific war. 'It doesn't shout anything obvious, it doesn't speak any ideological language,' said Hiep. 'Instead it is open for everyone.'

What Hiep created was a monument not to memories of conflict but to forgetting the divisions of the past; it is a monument to the end of ideology. A certain amnesia is important now in Vietnam. The country is trying to shed the horrors of war, the recriminations of division and the pain of its forced reunification. At the same time it has had to endure the difficult and protracted process of scraping off the sticky tar of communism. All this has required that Vietnamese give up many of their grievances and hatreds and move beyond the political battles of the past. This monument does not celebrate war; instead it honours those who survived it. That is the ambition that Hiep set up for his memorial. 'Suffering doesn't last for ever but I want this memorial to last thousands of years,' Hiep said. 'It has to go beyond suffering.'

4

Famine

One day by mishap my rice portion got overturned
In my disappointment I was still figuring out what to do
When quick as a bunch of pigs
Four, five guys, white-haired, scrambled one on top of another
And just as quickly, made a clean job of the stuff
Grumbling, cussing and chewing all at the same time on that
*   mixture of rice and dirt.*

NGUYEN CHI THIEN
My Rice Portion

In the spring of 1945 they came in an interminable line from across the Red River basin. By the time they had reached Hanoi, some were naked. Others stumbled forward dressed only in cloaks of rough bamboo matting. Their dry skin, darkening with decay, formed a thin parchment over bone and their hair came out in handfuls as they took palsied steps towards the city. Those who witnessed this terrifying parade said it was impossible to tell young from old. Hunched over and silent, they stopped only to bury the dead in shallow graves where the bodies released a pervasive stench and brought forth a riot of green weeds.

Even some of those who reached Hanoi died, too weak to absorb the small amount of food available. In death there was little dignity; Hanoi's sanitation department paid its workers by counting the ears cut off corpses collected from the streets.

> And day by day, towards cities, toward Hanoi,
> more corpses, yet more corpses dragged
> themselves,

> bringing a trail of flies, a stench of smells,
> then crumpled down along some street or lane.
> At dawn you'd gingerly push your door ajar,
> to check if there was someone dead outside.

This poem by Bang Ba Lan, a writer who chronicled rural life, showed the horror of 1945, celebrated as the year of the Revolution but remembered for a famine that killed two million people. Across the northern provinces, the famine cut a swathe through the population even as rice piled up in the Mekong Delta and grain taken by the Japanese and French rotted in storage. When their meagre stocks of rice were gone, villagers ate cassava and banana roots. Eventually they stuffed their burning stomachs with straw. In some villages, up to half the population died.

> You'd hear a whiff of breath still throb with life,
> a body stir or gasp . . . And teary eyes
> watched humans bury humans not quite dead.
> Four suburbs opened rows and rows of graves,
> which corpses would soon fill without a break
> and clouds of flies would darken all the land . . .

Nothing else in the catalogue of horrors endured by the Vietnamese shares the same dark hollow of the collective memory as the famine of 1945. Elderly Hanoians still take an edgy, stunned turn when they remember that time. The suffering of wartime has been softened with tales of heroism and sacrifice in the name of a grand cause, but famine still evokes nothing but fear and shock. The deaths and suffering of so many helped strip the French of their colonial pretence to a higher morality and doomed their rule. Japan, which had put Vietnam under military occupation, cemented in place a suspicion that would last for decades, becoming another chapter in the history of resentment that still smoulders across Asia.

Since the start of colonial rule in the late nineteenth century, the Red River delta had relied on rice from the south of the country. The plains that surround Hanoi are not known for their bounty; the land is watered and revitalised with layers of silt from the river, but it also suffers from flooding and the ravages of typhoons that blow through in the summer and autumn. It has been densely populated and closely farmed for centuries. A region whose economy allowed little flexibility and was a considerable distance from any alternative source of food was always susceptible to the political and economic forces that create famines.

In 1945 it was war and colonialism that caused this extraordinary loss of life. Average incomes measured in paddy, or unmilled rice, had fallen over the thirty years of French rule while exports had soared. Land was put under textile crops such as cotton or oil-bearing plants that could provide lubricants. In the three years from 1942 the area growing these crops trebled in the north. Japan had sent its forces into Indochina in 1940 and ruled alongside the colonial government which had sided with the Vichy regime, allies of the Germans. The Japanese turned over more land to industrial crops and stockpiled rice, diverting the area's meagre resources to their efforts at colonising Asia. The French dominated sales of rice through government offices, distorting a market and making it unprofitable for southerners to ship the grain North. In 1942 the government instituted compulsory purchases of rice, often forcing peasants to hand over three quarters of their crops at obscenely low prices. The black market price rose to twenty times what the colonial authorities were paying.

By 1944 Allied bombing had cut the roads and railways, while submarine patrols blocked shipments of food from the Mekong Delta, where an abundance of rice was being turned into ethanol to fuel engines. The colonial authorities also confiscated rice shipped from the south and set a limit on transportation fees so it was not economical to ship the grain to the Red River basin. The French put 500,000 tonnes of rice into storage in the two years ahead of the famine, while more than 2.5 million tonnes were exported to Japan between 1942 and 1945.

The death and suffering of this famine, the worst in a century, sucked out what little oxygen was left in the moral order of colonial Vietnam. Officials refused to release stocks of food as thousands died in the streets. Parents sold their children for a few cups of rice. Most Vietnamese blamed the French, many still believe that the shortages were part of an effort to subjugate the country and put off independence. That sentiment was eagerly mobilised by the Viet

Minh, the coalition of Communist and nationalist forces who fought the Japanese and the French. People were urged to raid granaries and distribute the food.

The Viet Minh listed hunger as one of its primary enemies. Declarations from the Communist Party stressed that sufficient food and independence were indelibly linked. 'It is no exaggeration to say that the Communists gave the famine a predominant place in their political strategy and that the campaign against hunger placed them at the head of a large movement of the population, explaining a large part of why they were able to come to power,' wrote the historian Nguyen The Anh.

After the Allied victory in 1945 and the revolution that briefly swept Ho Chi Minh to power, the French themselves tried to turn the famine to their benefit. General Jacques Philippe Leclerc, the commander of French forces in Southeast Asia, wrote in a cable to Paris that 'considerable attention should be drawn to the catastrophic situation in Tonkin in our absence', conveniently ignoring the fact that the Vichy French had been running the country for all but a few months of the war and that the famine was in good measure a creation of colonial agricultural policies. Leclerc tried to pin the blame on the Japanese by reminding the Vietnamese that it was the Japanese and not the French who ate rice. The Japanese had also reduced the area under paddy to produce crops to help their war effort. He added that it should be put out that the French had been unable to carry out emergency measures during the famine because they had been replaced by Japanese military officers or incompetent Vietnamese.

As hunger helped bring about the revolution, it would later become a rebuke to the revolutionaries. The famine is a central theme in the Vietnamese Declaration of Independence, a brief document that Ho Chi Minh read to a crowd in Ba Dinh Square on 2 September 1945 that reminded Vietnamese of the famine and the other injustices of the French rule. Ho Chi Minh ranked food as the top priority for his government. He didn't exactly promise a chicken in every pot, but he did offer a system that would not promote famines and stand idly by while millions died.

Forty years later, the failure to meet pledges to feed the people had become a source of shame for the Communist Party. Ruinous

agricultural policies that took land from peasants to create inefficient collective farms left Vietnam reliant on aid from its socialist
allies. That meant a diet of cassava and a few handfuls of crumbling
rice. Rationing allowed those in cities a bland diet of grains and
pickled vegetables. Many survived on animal feed sent from
Eastern Europe, aid so humiliating that people still flinch when
talking about it.

The formal history of Vietnam may read as a litany of foreign
aggression and great victories against the odds, but when
Vietnamese tell their personal stories the focus is more prosaic and
human – tales of hunger and plenty, famines and feasting. The
country is still mostly agricultural, indeed 80 per cent of the people
still work the land and live in part by the rhythms of rice-planting
and harvesting. In the bustling cities it seems half the population is
engaged in providing sustenance or refreshments to the others.

The relative plenty of today is in stark contrast to the years of war
and its aftermath. Memories of that time are mostly of hunger, a
bone-wearying, grinding hunger that weakened the body and
frayed the spirit. They were times when hunger bubbled constantly
into thoughts, interrupted sentences, burned the physical and moral
fibre in a slow persistent smoulder. Vietnamese knew that while
the newspapers were reporting illusionary rises in crop outputs,
food was getting scarcer, parents were getting more tired, children
were small and undernourished. During the war between 1960 and
1975 the deprivation could be blamed on the United States and was
generally accepted by the population as one of the burdens they had
to bear. After 1975 it was more difficult to pin the blame on war as
food shortages continued to have a devastating impact on daily
life. There was a growing rancour at the failure of government policies to improve living standards.

In 1988 the film-maker Viet Linh made a movie that was a rare
open criticism of the Party and expressed a growing sentiment of
the time. In *The Wandering Circus* a group of prospectors tries to
win the trust of some villagers in an area where they are searching
for gold. The villagers are suffering from a famine and are suspicious until shown a trick in which a basket appears to produce an
endless supply of rice. Fooled by this magic, they follow the
prospectors and agree to work for them. After they fail to find gold,

the prospectors all leave. The villagers, who have not planted their crops that year, are left even hungrier than before. It took two years for Linh to get this allegory of the Party's behaviour past the censors.

People recall those times as the 'brick days' – from the bricks they would leave in queues to mark their places while they went off to do errands or join other interminable lines. Not only did the collection of food take up vast amounts of time, the rewards were meagre. Rationing gave bureaucrats almost complete control over people's lives, adding to a sense of malice and suspicion. Even to eat a decent meal in plain sight of another was shockingly ostentatious. In Hanoi one needed a good reason, such as a funeral, to buy a whole chicken. To find one would often require risky ventures into the black market. Luxuries such as fish were eaten covertly; one Hanoian remembered trying to plug the gaps around windows and doors with newspaper to stop the incriminating odours of frying carp from reaching the noses of neighbours.

The defining elements of Vietnamese food – rice, fish sauce, the rich array of herbs and spices – mostly disappeared from city markets to be replaced by alien substances such as cheap Bulgarian jam, millet and wheat. Only top cadres received the best imported goods. Lower-rung officials could buy food in a shop near the Hanoi Cathedral, using their ration cards to get about 100 grams of meat and half a litre of fish sauce a month. Others got about half that from state food stores.

In a short story called 'The Blessed Alms', the writer The Giang, now a restaurateur in Germany, gave a taste of what shopping for food was like in Hanoi in the 1980s. The story, set during the September 2nd National Day celebrations, is about a man's search for the extra ration of fish to be doled out to mark the holiday. People began queuing from five in the morning outside markets. When the fish arrived in a small truck the crowd surged forward. 'You have to admire the flies: in a flash they were swarming all over the fish. I forgot my dignity and waded into the crowd with all the strength I could manage.' After gorging himself on the fish, the protagonist finds himself sick, along with everyone else in his housing block. In the queue for the squalid shared bathroom, neighbours gripe about their boiling bowels while bickering and slapping their children. 'Outside it was hardly light when the information and culture truck began blaring out its message ". . . as if Uncle Ho himself were present on the happy Great Victory Day." The cadres of "the civilised way of life" were poking their bull horns in every house inviting people to take in their washing and put up flags instead.'

Hunger is a frequent theme in stories and novels of this time – not of course in the 'official' writing that clung to a relentless rosy-cheeked Marxist cheer – but in the stories that came out of the re-education camps and in the post-1986 literature that directly questioned the privations of socialism. In 'The Two Ducks', a story of life in a re-education camp in the 1970s, Nguyen Ngoc Ngan tells of a soldier becoming enraged when some policemen order half a chicken in a restaurant and 'eat it all as a snack, without rice!' Phuc, a young former South Vietnamese soldier incarcerated in the highlands is given two ducks by his mother. Becoming increasingly fond of the ducks, he refuses all entreaties by his friends to kill them or to bleed them to make duck blood pudding, a favourite delicacy. His aim is to breed them, figuring that he could then eat duck twice a year. Even the commandant of the camp suffers from constant hunger as food shortages cut into the military when China ended its support of Vietnam. The commandant tries to steal the ducks, setting off a wave of resentment among other officers who use the incident against him. The ducks end up getting eaten, shared out among twenty camp guards.

Rations in the camps consisted at best of one or two bowls of rice and a few vegetables. After 1978, prisoners received mostly manioc or flour and almost no protein. The Aurora Foundation, a human rights group that published a report on the Vietnamese re-education camps, included a letter from a man called Cao Ngoc Phuong:

> In my forced labour camp in the highlands, the event that dominates everything is the experience of hunger. We are hungry permanently. All we can think about day or night is eating. Many of us catch lizards to eat, knowing that they provide protein. Very soon the lizards in the whole area were exterminated . . . Such foods as mice, rats, birds, snakes and grasshoppers must be caught and eaten secretly. It is forbidden and if the camp guards find out about it, the

prisoners will be punished . . . What little food is eaten is
chewed very slowly. Still it makes no difference. We feel even
more hungry after eating.

The most graphic descriptions of hunger come from the re-education camps, but others also described how deprivation among the
general population tore at so much of what Vietnamese held dear
about their families and social life. They examine the tensions that
the dogmatic policies of the time imposed on families, on identity as
Vietnamese and on traditional roles. Food shortages and hunger
are at the centre of this moral and physical dystopia that is in sharp
and deliberate contrast to the propaganda of the times.

In Tuong Nang Tien's short story 'Communism and Guigozcanism', the grasping individualism caused by shortages
undermines all communal sense as people carefully guard their
food in old cans that once held a brand of Dutch powdered milk
called Guigoz. The lessons of Marxist theory taught in re-education
camps set up in the 1970s for former South Vietnamese soldiers and
officials are eroded daily by the panicked reaction to hunger by
those who had grown up in the generally prosperous south.

Guigoz cans were prized for cooking and storage. 'Though larger
than a Nestlé can, it was still of a handy size and light weight so it
could be easily moved around or hidden away.' The cans were filled
with a fistful of greens grabbed from a field, or rice gleaned from the
dirty floor of a storage shed.

'The prison camp turned into a limbo haunted by some of our
fellow soldiers, all ghosts of their former selves, who now lived in
mute isolation, each hugging his Guigoz can. They symbolised an
unwholesome individualism spawned in an environment of black
despair as a counter to the morbid collectivism enforced by the
Communists.'

When the narrator is released from the camp, he goes to stay with
an elder sister whose family has experienced similar privations on
the other side of the camp wall. He is shocked to see his niece scoop-
ing rice into a Guigoz can to take off to work, telling his sister that
this is 'rather individualistic and undesirable'. This sends the sister
into a rage as she explains how collective eating was organised at
factories and farms.

'A gang of bandits. Every month they deduct and withhold money for meals . . . when it comes to meals they never fail to cheat you. After you've finished your first bowl of rice there is nothing left on the plate. If you're a slow eater, as soon as you are through with your bowl of rice, that's the end of lunch. Well, every man for himself – that's best. To each his own Guigoz can. What's wrong with a little bit of individualism, heh?'

The Guigoz can also hid the new forms of class that emerged, as the protagonist sees when a man carrying in the cans used by foremen on a construction site trips up, spilling out abundant quantities of such rare delicacies as meat and fish from the humble containers. 'Tell me what you hide in your Guigoz can and I'll tell you what class you belong to in the classless society,' he says.

Food had been about cohesion, bringing families together and reaffirming the structure of society. Suddenly it was about individualism, hoarding and the straining of social structures. Food came to represent those things in life that are to be endured, the tough and bitter. Rather than sharing, people saw the selfishness and divisions of the Communist system, which completely overturned any sense of ambition or pride. 'The one endeavour left for everyone is to hustle and eke out a living less wretched than that of his or her neighbour: that is the extent of human ambition and pride now,' Tien wrote.

The contrast between the poverty of the 1980s and the revitalised Vietnam of the 1990s is a testament to improved policies. A country that could not feed itself emerged in just a few years as the world's third largest exporter of rice. A government that had once tried to limit family stalls from selling *pho* – the restaurants producing the national dish of beef noodle soup were regarded as irredeemably capitalist – encouraged the development of a vast private sector of farmers, distributors and sellers. The worship of production statistics, most of them ethereally untrue, was replaced by the primacy of the consumer.

The most important economic changes in Vietnam have been in the realm of agriculture, particularly the farming and selling of rice. Seven out of ten Vietnamese are involved in growing rice. It is the staple for all Vietnamese, providing on average 85 per cent of the calories eaten each day. It is the second largest export earner after oil. Rice is the central agricultural concern of the government, which intervenes at every step of its production from deciding which land should be used for paddy fields to organising its export.

Rice extends way beyond the economic realm into areas such as identity, humour, sexuality and death. It is the breakfast of champions for the heroes of Vietnamese mythology and the food on which armies marched. Rice gruel is the country's equivalent of a healing chicken broth, and rice is a major ingredient in the traditional pharmacopoeia. Glutinous rice, a breed more commonly grown in the mountains, is connected to festivities such as *Tet*, the lunar new year, and with weddings and death. The rice is served at funerals – the Vietnamese equivalent of the phrase 'to kick the bucket' is 'to eat sticky rice'.

The language of rice is intimately female – seedlings before they produce grains are said to be 'young girl rice' (*lua con gai*). When the stalks produce ears of rice they are said to be pregnant. Along with these associations of fertility and nourishment, there is inevitably sexual language and innuendo. Vietnamese adore telling foreign men that they should not live on rice alone but try noodles and porridge as well. This is barely-coded advice for not remaining satisfied with one partner but also having a mistress and visiting prostitutes. With clicking tongues and mostly mock disapproval, people will say a young couple are 'eating rice before the bell' if they are having sex before marriage. This is said to come from the time during the war when children evacuated to the countryside ate in communal halls where a bell, usually made from the hollow casing of a US bomb, would toll before each meal. The hungrier children would creep in before the bell to eat more than their share.

Ly Quy Don, an eighteenth-century historian, recorded that farmers distinguished between seventy different strains of rice, each producing a different grain or thriving under varied conditions. Even cooking and preparation was complex. The rice was first washed and carefully cleared of stones, stems and insect turds. Once in the pot, grains had to be conserved closely, it was considered improper to spill any or allow it to stick to the large chopsticks used to stir the pot. The cook, however, was not allowed to tap the chopsticks against each other to release any sticky grains as the sound of bamboo clacking together was said to recall the sound of the skeletons being reburied, a ritual that takes place several years after a first burial. Chopsticks had to be wiped gently against the lip of the pot which would then be sealed as tightly as possible for cooking.

Rice and the rituals that surround its cooking and serving are part of the way children learn respect for their elders, who must be served first from the communal pot. The manner of serving has as much meaning in Vietnamese meals as the food itself. Indeed there are few universal dietary constraints, but there is a fairly elaborate system of serving and ensuring suitable deference to one's elders. The manners that were once so much part of meals have changed markedly, influenced by communal eating halls, the emergence of street-side restaurants and even the modern electric rice cooker that has freed many urban women from the chore of boiling the grain over coals.

The emphasis of Vietnamese policy from the late 1940s up until 1979 was collectivisation. The derided class of landlords, in many cases peasants only marginally richer than their peers, were dispossessed and hundreds of thousands of hectares were redistributed or merged into vast collective farms. In the north, where much of the land had long been farmed collectively, there was only some resistance. In the south after 1975, farmers destroyed equipment and killed animals rather than hand them over to collective farms. In the South, pre-1975 land reforms had distributed farms to many families; later they would refuse to let go of their land and only 7 per cent of households joined co-operatives, compared with about 90 per cent in the north.

Collectivisation remade the hierarchy of rural life. The richest villagers were no longer those with the most land, but those who had family members in positions of power in the communes. A survey by Vietnamese social scientists in 1990 found that in areas where co-operatives had endured, 'democratic freedoms are not being guaranteed, a plague of "new local despotisms" has appeared in many areas, law and order are almost non-existent, social and moral dislocations have increased, unemployment is widespread, the peasants are uncomfortable in expressing themselves and feel repressed and village solidarity has decreased'. Revelations of these problems in the official media shocked the country.

As disastrous as collectivisation, was the intrusion of the state into the buying and distribution of rice. Between 1976 and 1980 rice yields fell markedly. Stockpiled rice was eaten by rats or wasted; surplus grain from the south did not make it north. Farmers slackened off as there was no difference in what you took home to eat whether you laboured hard all day or dozed in the shade; either way the government paid a pittance for rice. The gulf between the official price for the staple and what it could fetch in the black market widened. Food imports soared and the overall economy spiralled downwards. When Chinese food aid halted in the later 1970s, the government was forced to relax its restrictions on private enterprise and trading, allowing the provinces limited autonomy to set policies that worked. Co-operatives were allowed to grant short-term leases to farmers who then had to fulfil a contract to supply rice to the state. Production surged, yields rose by a quarter and overall food output went up by 27 per cent.

However the heavy hand of the state gradually off-set the gains made by farmers. The government raised taxes, fees and the costs of inputs such as fertiliser. Production and yields once again declined and famine hit parts of the country in 1988 when grain output sank to new lows. This was an economic nadir for Vietnam, which was stricken with hyperinflation of more than 775 per cent, declining aid from the Soviet Union and a disastrous attempt at currency reform.

In the northern provinces three million people were left on the edge of starvation while another 12 million were seriously short of food. Monthly wages bought only enough food for ten to fifteen days. The rapid decline sent another wave of boat people fleeing the country to Hong Kong to escape the unendurable poverty and hunger. Those with connections desperately tried to get jobs in Eastern Europe. It is a measure of how low Vietnam had sunk that its educated élite were coveting dangerous or unpleasant jobs in East Germany. Almost everyone was affected; even government workers did not receive their rations for several months. Despite the impact of the shortages, the official media went on trumpeting successes without any reference to the famine. State controls over food had failed again and all except the most privileged suffered.

The shock of this famine precipitated further reforms that have become something of a success story. In 1988 farmers were allowed to lease land for up to fifteen years and could choose what to grow and where to sell it. Giving responsibility back to farmers had an enormous impact on the whole economy and society, in many ways making socialism untenable and setting the country firmly towards a market economy. Overseas sales of agricultural goods trebled from 1988–1996, earning the country more than $500 million in foreign exchange. Nutritional levels and the diversity of diet improved and agricultural growth spurred a revival in the richness of village life and customs.

The turnaround, however, disguised some of the problems that persist in part because of the government's ambivalence towards the market. The state sector still controls the distribution and export of rice – according to the Party line, to protect farmers from the vagaries of world prices and to limit inflation. Most of the recent growth in agriculture has been unbalanced. Output is up 40 per cent since 1988 in the Mekong Delta region, but the rest of the country has seen just 8 per cent growth, less than the rise in population over that period.

Much of the blame for slower growth in the north can be pinned on the heavier impact of the state in that region. Land is more difficult to trade in the north because of bureaucratic interference and land use rights are offered for shorter periods than in the south. Village officials are also more inclined to appropriate land for redistribution to the landless or for themselves. The state, far from being the guardian of property, adds to the risk that farmers feel. This means they are less inclined to invest in better irrigation or other inputs. Farmers in the North have less access to loans that might help them upgrade their land and increase output of food.

Land is not the only area where state interference harms farmers. The state controls all exports, doling out quotas to a number of state companies who buy their rice from private middlemen. Quotas, taxes and monopolies penalise farmers while benefiting bureaucrats and the managers of state firms. A United Nations report in 1996 said that removing quotas could boost gross domestic product by $800 million, with the main beneficiaries being the farmers now struggling under ever-mounting debts.

The price controls and quotas under which farmers have to sell their crops are aimed at protecting them from variations in international rice prices, but the price is set below already low world prices for the commodity. Farmers rarely get this price anyway. State firms mostly buy from intermediaries who deliberately depress prices around harvest time. For example in the first half of 1997, the government's minimum price for rice in the Mekong Delta was around 1,500 dong per kilo of paddy. However at the height of the harvest when most farmers are forced to sell, traders rarely paid more than 1,100 dong per kilo. This meant that while farmers were barely able to cover their costs, the private traders and bureaucrats in the state rice trading firms were sharing out profits of at least 400 dong per kilo. The cost of growing a crop is about 900 dong per kilo, leaving the farmers with only the narrowest of margins out of which they also have to pay interest on loans and a multitude of taxes imposed by local officials. To add insult to these injuries, the government makes farmers pay taxes based on them receiving 1,500 dong per kilo, while trading companies are subsidised with cheap credit from state banks.

State intervention in the rice trade subsidises the price of food for rich city residents at the expense of poorer farmers, a common problem across the developing world. If the government were to remove what it portrays as a safety net for farmers, their incomes would rise markedly, in some cases nearly doubling. But the income earned by state enterprises that trade in rice would plummet. The system lays bare Vietnam's political reality. The power of the state bureaucracy to demand subsidies and protection is overwhelming and corrosive. It sucks resources away from the most productive and the most needy sectors into the sinkholes of bureaucratic self-interest.

Fickle policies have also hurt exports. In 1995 with inflation rising alarmingly in the first half of the year, the government simply stopped exports, even on those contracts that had already been signed. Vietnamese rice is already cheap because of its poor quality, but defaults on contracts, changes in export taxes and the capricious management of state firms has depressed it further. Tax policies that levy the highest rates on the best quality rice mean that Vietnam mostly exports its low-grade product that contains a high percentage of broken grains and is therefore worth less. All this translates into lower incomes for farmers and lower government revenues.

The government is unapologetic about keeping control over almost all aspects of rice farming despite the damage to the economy and to the poor. Rice is such a strong political, economic and social force that it is extremely difficult for those in power to relinquish control over the crop. The government remains wedded to responding to problems with spurious technological changes or by slapping yet more regulations on farmers and traders. The Ministry of Agriculture and Rural Development does not see fit to allow too much freedom; farmers are ordered to grow certain crops and land is kept under rice even when villagers could make more growing other crops.

Ninh Hiep, wealthy from its spice and silk trading, has just 300 hectares of land for its 13,000 people and cannot grow enough food for itself. Instead of even attempting to reach the impossible goal of self-sufficiency, the head of the local people's committee wants to turn land over to grow ornamental trees for sale in Hanoi. The government insists the village continue to grow rice even though it can easily afford to buy its food supplies from elsewhere. In some areas, mostly those close to cities where many villagers are engaged in manufacturing or trading, this insistence of making people grow rice diverts labour and capital away from more lucrative activities and does little to ensure food security.

One statistic that never appears in the official press is that there were no improvements in the diet of Vietnamese between 1960 and 1990, a thirty-year wilderness of malnutrition. Throughout this period most Vietnamese ate an average of 1,800 calories a day, well below the required 2,500. Nutrition in rural areas is still a serious problem. Around half of all children are malnourished and about a third of all adults suffer similar problems. A United Nations Children's Fund (UNICEF) report in 1997 said that there had been no improvements in the overall nutrition of children since 1991.

During the period of collectivisation, almost all farming production was focused on rice. The crop took up 85 per cent of all land, leaving the country with a monoculture that only increased the risk of terrible famines and heightened malnutrition, most importantly among small children who cannot absorb the needed calories from rice.

The problems of rice and nutrition were not limited to the poorest members of the population. Nowadays richer peasants are able to afford significant amounts of rice. With its image as clean and nutritious, rice is fed in large quantities to children who end up surprisingly malnourished compared with children from poorer families. Women are now encouraged to stick to the 'poor' diet that included greens and tiny crabs from paddy fields that is regarded as *déclassé* but has all the necessary nutrients for children. Another adverse development is the supposed improvement in milling rice that leaves it completely polished and thus depleted of protein and minerals. Previously farmers used hand mills or bought cheaply-milled rice that provided them with more nutrients than are left in highly-polished rice.

Famine still lurks in Vietnam. Shortages still occur and the government continues to ignore the lessons that each famine has brought. Communism, an ideology that came to power on the back of peasant farmers, has weighed heavily on them; reforms have made some headway but the government refuses to release its grip and aid the majority of people who would benefit from further liberalisation. Thailand and Indonesia were able to buy time by allowing farmers to expand into forest areas; the policy destroyed the environment but it gave governments breathing space in which to tackle rural poverty.

Vietnam will have no such luxury. Its forest cover is already massively depleted by migration and the ecological impact of the war. It is among the most densely populated countries in Southeast Asia with around 205 people per square kilometre, twice the regional average. The density in the two main river deltas is much higher and neither have more land to be planted. Any economic gains will have to come from gains in productivity, not from new land. The state intervention in agriculture keeps farmers poor. These people migrate to cities to earn a living and by swelling the urban population contribute to a host of social problems. No consensus has emerged in the government on how to tackle these issues so the cycle of state intervention, low investment and poverty grinds on.

5

Feast

Best is forbidden sex, next best is hog haslet.

VIETNAMESE SAYING, REFERRING TO
PATÉ MADE FROM PORK OFFAL

Phu Quoc lies at the periphery of Vietnam, off its southern coast in the Gulf of Thailand. The island's dry hills and sandy beaches, wrapped year round in a rubbery heat and humidity, give it a tranquillity that belies its history as a prison colony and the site of horrifying massacres by Cambodia's Khmer Rouge. Its main town, Duong Dong, straddles a narrow salty river crowded with the wooden fishing boats that have brought Phu Quoc fame and fortune.

Along the river, tucked between clusters of palms, are rows of prosperous two- and three-storey houses decorated with curved balustrades and colourful tiles. Behind the houses are large warehouses from whose dark interiors leaks a thick, almost eye-watering miasma, an insistent, concentrated aroma of the sea. The fumes come from large wooden barrels, taller than a man, filled with *nuoc mam*, a fish sauce that is the essence of Vietnamese food.

Nuoc mam is Vietnam's olive oil, its vinegar and its soy sauce, a condiment that defines the food and adds its own layers and complexities to any dish. Making *nuoc mam* is as simple as letting fish rot in a bucket of salt and water but as subtle as making wine. It ranges from a thin, lightly perfumed and coloured liquid to a thick oily tar that some people find powerfully emetic. For Vietnamese, who use it in most dishes, this sauce sets their food apart even though variants are produced and used across Asia.

The best *nuoc mam* is said to come from the private companies that line the river. Here the boats unload their catch of tiny, almost transparent fish, called *ca com*, which are mixed in the wooden barrels with a few shovelfuls of sea salt that looks like dirty snow. After a few days the fish decays and ferments, losing its oils into the brine which becomes a rich mix of amino acids and phosphates. Not only does the salty richness provide a wealth of taste possibilities, it compliments a rice-based diet well, providing minerals lacking in the grain.

The 'first pressing' of *nuoc mam*, as with olive oil, is the richest, and is served at the table rather than used in cooking. Further pressings, taken when the barrels are again filled up with water and allowed to stew, produce a thinner sauce that is used as a marinade. The demand for high quality sauces has soared and unscrupulous wholesalers are now selling cheaper Vietnamese or Thai *nuoc mam* labelled as if it comes from Phu Quoc. The sauce-makers on the island have reacted to the faking of their product with the indignation of champagne viticulturers when the name of their product is violated. So far, however, they have been powerless to stop counterfeiting or the over-fishing of local waters.

So far, Phu Quoc has spurned the industrialisation of its processes; factory owners say any changes would ruin the unique taste of each company's sauce. Wooden barrels have yet to be replaced by stainless steel vats; the barrels are still hammered together in sandy yards outside the warehouses, the staves of wood bound with thick rope bands. The wood lends colour to the sauce which can vary from a rich oily purple to nearly clear, and is among the factors that influence the taste.

Truong Van Hoa, one of about eighty owners on the island, proudly displays certificates from the Pasteur Institute in Ho Chi Minh City attesting to the quality of his sauce. His *appellation controlée* for his finest cru of fish sauce speaks volumes about the importance attached to *nuoc mam*, which has rescued Phu Quoc from its place as a backwater haunted by a history of incarceration and invasions. Fish sauce and the island's main agricultural crop of pepper have brought it prosperity as Vietnam underwent a revival of its culinary culture. The elevation of Phu Quoc's fish sauce above all others has come at a time when there was a resurgence of the need to assert Vietnamese identity through such things as food.

As the bleak sumptuary laws imposed by central planning and austere Marxism went out of the window, Vietnam went on an orgy of culinary rediscovery, remembrance and consumption. Food once again became a part of cultural identity and reclaimed a primary place in life. Meals are at the heart of celebrations, of nurturing, even of control and guilt; Vietnamese find the stereotypes of Jewish or Italian mothers very familiar. Food doesn't get much attention in the intellectual definitions of national identity but it does in the popular notions of what marks people out. The Vietnamese have been declaring their food as distinct since at least the eighteenth century and maybe earlier. The first writings about food are really medical texts, the most famous of which was written by the Buddhist monk Tue Tinh in the fourteenth century.

Tue Tinh is said to have written *The Miraculous Effects of the Southern Pharmacopoeia* on orders from the Tran dynasty emperor who wanted a text book of medicinal herbs that could be grown in Vietnam rather than imported from China. The work was also to include local remedies that followed customs from Vietnam, not those from 'the north' as China was known. Tue Tinh's medicinal homily was 'use southern medicine to treat southern people'. His work listed 3,873 recipes to cure 184 diseases, bringing together local folk remedies with the traditions of Chinese medicine.

In what was an extraordinary scientific achievement, Tinh documented 630 plants with medicinal uses. About half of these were also used as foods and more than eighty were Vietnamese in origin. The list includes many of the ingredients that provide the flavours of contemporary Vietnamese food – lemon grass, various types of mint and basil, garlic, ginger and coriander.

Tue Tinh's work provides much of the basis of Vietnamese home cures to this day. For blurred vision, he recommended liver of either fish, pork or chicken mixed with *xi* beans and onions. Liver would provide a good dose of vitamin A and the beans would help the uptake of the nutrient that prevents the eye disease xeropthalmia. For diarrhoea, Tinh prescribed boiled rice liquid, salty rice gruel and a tea made from motherwort or young lotus leaves, a remedy that would be endorsed by the World Health Organisation today. For the elderly, he recommended cow's milk and enough roughage to avoid constipation.

None of Tue Tinh's original writings still exist, so it is not clear whether he really set out with strong intentions to mark out Vietnamese medicine and food as distinct from Chinese. Certainly today he is seen as one of the key figures who separates a Vietnamese intellectual tradition from the overbearing weight of Chinese culture. In his life-time, his work was not appreciated for the impact it would have. After he completed his *Pharmacopoeia*, Tue Tinh was one of a number of monks packed off to Beijing in 1385 as part of Vietnam's tribute to the Ming emperor.

We know about his works today because they were copied down in the eighteenth century when clearly setting out a distinctly Vietnamese cuisine and medicine did become politically important. Hai Thuong Lan Ong, a scholar and doctor born in 1720, furthered Tue Tinh's work and carved out clearer distinctions between Chinese and Vietnamese medicine. He rejected a central text of Chinese medical practice – Chang Chung-ching's *Treatise on Ailments Caused by Cold* – as he said it was not applicable in tropical Vietnam. People from the South, he warned, reacted badly to Chang's cures that relied on 'hot' medicines such as cinnamon.

Lan Ong's recommendation for good health, included in a 28-volume encyclopaedia, could have been written by a modern nutritionist. Therapies concentrated on foods that were readily available, not exotic potions. Much of his work on diet stressed the need for hygiene and keeping water sources clean. He was an advocate of moderation long before dieticians, recommending people eat soya, vegetables and cereals more than meat. Salt, he said, made the heart cold. Too much sugar 'was not useful' as it damaged the kidneys. He even warned about smoking and the dangers of cirrhosis from alcoholism.

The twentieth-century heir to Tue Tinh and Hai Thuong Lan Ong is Tu Giay, an elderly and professorial man who is the Director Emeritus of the National Institute of Nutrition in Hanoi. Giay has the courtly manners and formal French of the emerging Vietnamese bourgeoisie of the 1930s that either gave up everything for the Revolution or fled. Giay, a doctor, stayed and worked for the

Revolution, writing newspaper columns on nutrition for farmers and the peasant soldiers fighting the French.

Giay was eventually put in charge of the Research Institute of Military Nutrition and Clothing which was set up to keep soldiers fed and alive in extremely difficult conditions. Most of the work involved finding ways to preserve foods in the heat and humidity and allow the soldier mobility so that he was not weighed down with huge quantities of provisions. Research had a definite political tinge – considerable time was devoted to finding ways to prevent the rampant diarrhoea that afflicted people forced to eat in the unpopular communal canteens that were introduced in the North in the 1960s.

Throughout the war against the French, the army had tried to live off the land, paying the peasantry for food or growing their own. They were supposed to follow Mao Zedong's dictum of living like fish in water, blending into the rural environment without disrupting it. After 1960 this proved more difficult for troops fighting in the South; the forces were more numerous and had to be mobile, making it impossible for them to meet their own needs. The war reversed the normal balance of food in Vietnam under which the South shipped its surplus to offset the meagre yields of the North. During the war, food went south, down the dozens of mountain tracks that made up the Ho Chi Minh trail.

Giay led the team that had to find out how to pack rice so that it could last up to two years and survive the tough conditions along the 2,000 kilometre supply route to the South. Unhusked rice normally lasted only six months and consuming spoiled rice left soldiers with beri-beri, a disease that the French had once called *Boufissure d'Annam* because of the swollen faces of Vietnamese children suffering from the protein deficiency.

The institute devised a way of enclosing rice in four sacks – the innermost and outermost of hemp, interleaved with sacks made from plastic and from PVC. The hermetic seal was so tight that during the long siege in the battle of Quang Tri, bags of rice were floated down rivers to provision troops.

The highly mobile forces needed to carry with them lightweight, high-calorie foods. Soldiers had used toasted rice, but it lacked nutrients and still could not be used over long periods. The army needed a nutritious food to be used by special forces on surveillance missions that would fulfil minimum dietary requirements in just 300 grams of food a day. This was achieved by providing soldiers with intensely sweet biscuits and a type of pork pickled in highly concentrated fish sauce that could be turned into a bouillon with vegetables. Even with special foods, most soldiers lost an average of five kilograms during a month-long mission – a large amount for fit young men who probably weighed less than fifty kilograms.

Vegetables presented a daily problem if soldiers were to avoid constipation, but were difficult to grow if they were on the move. There was little in the way of a surplus that could be taken from the local peasants. So nutritionists and botanists produced a guide to edible wild plants that grew in jungle areas and could be eaten. The initial guidebook identified for soldiers more than 100 plants and their nutritional value. It has become part of the 'Nam' mythology that Vietnamese were at home in the jungle while for GIs it was a perilous world. In reality, the forest and mountains were alien territory for most Vietnamese. Soldiers had to be taught how to survive in the jungle; the fact they did better than Americans is testament to their training and fortitude, not because it was an environment that was familiar to them.

Despite these efforts, most soldiers suffered unbearable hunger and malnutrition. Those living in bases were better fed than the general population but the many living along the Ho Chi Minh Trail or fighting across the South faced serious starvation. The writer Do Kim Cuong recalled being so hungry he would slip into American camps to steal food and cigarettes under cover of night despite the enormous risks. He still has a nostalgic love of Lucky Strike cigarettes and the fatty blandness of Spam.

The notions of self-reliance bred during the war have gone deep into the mentality of the country, even though between the 1960s and the late 1980s, Vietnam was a net importer of food. Food security is defined only in terms of self-sufficiency. There is, however, overwhelming evidence that access to trade routes, a market economy and an open society are more important factors in keeping famines at bay. The Indian economist Amartya Sen has shown how Communist countries – the Soviet Union, China and Vietnam in particular – have been prone to devastating famines in the past century while more open societies such as India have not.

Nationalist ideas of self-sufficiency were further promoted by what was known as the VAC system of food production, from the Vietnamese words for garden, pond and animal. Peasants were encouraged to keep animals, have a pond and grow a garden, using the by-products of each to sustain the other. The name comes from the Vietnamese words for the three areas of production. This system did increase output in many areas of the country and has reduced an over-reliance on rice monoculture. But even VAC has not had as great an impact as liberating farmers from the constraints of the centralised economy by freeing prices. Allowing farmers to sell what they had to grow at market rates saw food production soar in the late 1980s. For the first time in years, the government's swaggering grain production figures had some muscle to match their manner.

People remember the war as a time of terrible shortages, although most say it was worse after the war when Vietnam's food aid from China dried up and economic policies cut domestic production. But despite these memories, even foods that evoke the hardships of war have aroused a warm nostalgia in the new era of relative plenty. Pressed rice cakes – rice flavoured with sesame seeds and peanuts and wrapped in banana leaf – were a common sustenance for children evacuated from Hanoi during the bombings. The cakes are durable, lasting for several days even in tropical heat and were carried by soldiers during the war. Indeed there is a long martial history connected with them going back to the legendary Giong who as a three-year-old boy grew into a giant and kept the Chinese invaders at bay with strength derived from the stodgy packets.

To Huu, the poet laureate of the Revolution, even devoted a verse to them after the Battle of Dien Bien Phu when the army 'moved mountains, slept in shelters and ate compressed rice'. Along the Ho Chi Minh Trail, hundreds of kitchens prepared the cakes for soldiers travelling the dangerous roads south. Rice cakes were traditionally given by mothers to their husbands and sons for long journeys. Few people bother now with the hard labour of boiling and pressing the rice, but the cakes are still sold in railway stations, now wrapped in polythene rather than leaves. For one writer, the cakes

are still 'a celebration of the spirit of our nation'. It is perhaps a
hefty burden for a ball of rice to bear.

Just as many soldiers would as soon forget about the food they
ate back then. An overseas Vietnamese, irritated by the demands of
his local business partners during a meal with some American
guests, related that he deliberately ordered a range of simple peasant dishes rather than the luxurious fare they were expecting. The
foreigners munched through the meal appreciatively but the old
soldiers sat scowling and refused to eat, insulted when reminded of
their humble pasts and the hardships of the war. They were also
probably offended that their host had not judged them important
enough to warrant a spread of expensive delicacies.

As food supplies and incomes rose in the late 1980s, food
regained its place as a social indicator. The privileged who ate meat
and fish bought in special shops no longer had to hide away and
these luxuries were more widely available to the urban rich. A love
of food was no longer a dangerously bourgeois affectation but
something to revel in as satisfyingly Vietnamese. Newspaper articles rhapsodised over traditional foods, glorifying dishes as cultural
icons.

One newspaper carried a thousand-word elegy to *bun thang* – to
an outsider a simple bowl of chicken noodle soup, but to a
cognoscenti a vivid expression of the riches of domestic life, a
boiled-down essence of what food means to Vietnamese. The writer
went so far as to insist the noodles be served in bowls made from
white porcelain from Hai Duong, a town half-way between Hanoi
and the coast. A stock was prepared from pork and chicken bones,
boiled 'until it acquires a natural sweetness without the aid of sea-
soning'. Chicken, preferably a castrated cock that would give the
'right whiteness and softness of meat as well as the right degree of
fat', is cut up and placed on top of the noodles. Thin slices of a
sausage that resembles baloney goes in another corner, followed
by small pieces of omelette. The dish is topped off with crushed
dried shrimps, spring onions and coriander before the hot stock is
poured over. Then the final touches – a spoonful of black prawn
paste and the tiniest drop of musk produced by a male belostomatid
insect, a large and rather fearsome beetle, is added with a bamboo
toothpick.

Bun thang, the author of this article tells us, is eaten only on special occasions. It should only really be sampled at home, where the true techniques of the cook are developed to their highest degree. 'Most Vietnamese agree, however, that nowhere in the country is *bun thang* made as well as in Hanoi – a delicacy that no doubt stands up to its country's culture.'

Writing about food and exulting its domestic and cultural roots may not seem remarkable, but in the 1950s the writer Nguyen Tuan was condemned as a bourgeois reactionary for writing about the soup noodle dish *pho*. Writers were supposed to focus on the glorious onward march of the Revolution, not trivialities such as food. Many *pho* stalls in Hanoi were closed in the 1950s and owners served their hurried clients surreptitiously, hoping police would not raid these speakeasy soup joints and take away the pans.

The age-old links between medicine and food have returned to the forefront of life along with the many taboos that go along with meals. Villages that specialise in the production of a certain food have reasserted the links between their product and identity. Ninh Hiep is among the country's richest villages with an average annual per capita income of $850. A couplet inscribed in Chinese characters on an ancient gate in the village set the tone for its economic recovery: 'This is a land of unostentatious virtue, passed on by our ancestors, where goods are abundant and the markets are wide'. Much of its trade is in lotus seeds, which are grown in Cambodia and used in soups and desserts. Nguyen Tach Vien, a third generation trader in the seeds, said that in recent years the volume of seeds traded had gone from just a few dozen kilograms a year to several tonnes. Lotus seeds are just one of about 200 medicinal plants and spices that are processed in the narrow alleys and stone-flagged courtyards that are saturated with the rich scents of anise and cinnamon.

The village has recently resuscitated festivals celebrating the tenth-century doctor Ly Nhu who is said to have founded the trade in medicines and spices based here. The wealthy drug lords of Ninh Hiep, who in a matter of a decade have renewed trading links that stretch as far away as the frozen northern provinces of China, gather at their restored gilt and red lacquer temple in the village to honour their ancestors and compete in the ostentation of their gifts.

For many years these sorts of celebrations were banned. Many villages imposed strict sumptuary regulations to stop people spending money on the feasts that were required for weddings and funerals. Some districts even forbade the offering of cigarettes to guests; many banned the slaughtering of animals and instead held austere ceremonies in local government offices. Families had once gone heavily into debt for funerals and weddings which required lavish displays of food and gifts. Ceremonies often had a competitive edge to them; not just in the amount of food on offer but in the way it was cooked. Cooking rice in clay pots over coals was a competitive event in the Red River basin, with women vying to show off their skills in tournaments.

Even if they could be a grinding financial burden, the religious ceremonies and feasts were popular and much missed. When the regulations were eased, villagers went back to almost unprecedented levels of indulgence. Residents of Ninh Hiep say these festivals have restored a sense of social cohesion; an important part of life for traders who operate a complex cartel to keep prices up and competition down. Festivals created solidarity and eased the competitive edge of the market; in Ninh Hiep all traders were expected to return home for the major ceremonies held once a year. Economic reforms have also meant a slackening of state power, and in the countryside traditional ways of governance are coming back. Much of this centres around rituals and displays, feasting and celebrations.

In the cities, there has been a resurgence of interest in the diversity of Vietnamese foods, with restaurants springing up selling regional specialities or dishes that evoke a nostalgia for the countryside. Cooking lessons have also been a hit among urban women. Dieu Ho, a Canadian-Vietnamese who worked as head chef at the New World Saigon Hotel, was stunned by the response to a show he did on television in which he prepared a Christmas turkey. He cooked the dish just to show a traditional meal from another culture, but was soon inundated with people wanting to know how to prepare the meal themselves. 'The whole culture of food and a demand for new tastes is coming back now that people have more choice,' he said.

Food takes on its richest meanings on special occasions and the biggest of the year in Vietnam is *Tet*, or the lunar new year. It falls in January or February, a time when the north of Vietnam is chilly and overcast. Celebrations at *Tet* have become, at least for richer city-dwellers, increasingly sumptuous with guests offered huge arrays of nuts, sweets, Western and Vietnamese biscuits and *banh chung*, a cake produced from sticky rice, beans and fatty pork wrapped in leaves and boiled for hours into a substance of throat-clogging density. It takes days of preparation to make the square brick-like cakes and often involves collaboration between households. In the alleys and courtyards of Hanoi before *Tet*, the damp greyness of winter lifts a little as groups of women cut up the pork bellies that provide the lard at the heart of *banh chung*, wrap up the bricks in leaves and then boil them over smoky open fires.

Banh chung origins are said to go back to the Hung kings, the first rulers of Vietnam. A king with twenty-two sons held a competition to choose an heir. He ordered them to find a food that could be offered to the ancestors. One of the princes, named Lieu, despaired as he watched his brothers engaged in a furious competition to find rare or expensive delicacies. Divine intervention was at hand in the form of a goddess who advised Lieu to find a simple dish that was rich with significance. She told him to make two cakes, one square to symbolise earth, and another round to symbolise heaven. The square cake would be green and contain beans and meat to represent the flora and fauna of the earth. The round cake would be made of ground rice and would be white. When the king decided to judge the dishes, these simple cakes were up against peacock sausage, bears paws and rhinoceros liver. The king chose the cakes of which he said: 'They are not only a tasty, valuable food, they also convey important meanings; they express a son's devotion to his father and mother, his worshipping them like heaven and earth; they imply all his love for the homelands and the fields. They are very easy to make because they are made with the most precious gems among all gems under heaven and earth, yet those gems can be grown by everyone'.

Nowadays people are not so modest when it comes to seeking out the exotic and expensive. Conspicuous consumption during *Tet* – a time when expensive French cognac and Scotch whisky are given and guzzled – has begun to worry government officials who have

never quite shed their insistence that at least other people live a
puritan existence. In 1996 Prime Minister Vo Van Kiet urged people
against over-indulgence in alcohol and ordered them to curtail their
spending during *Tet*, making a point of saying that he would not
accept any gifts during the holiday.

Kiet's impotent edicts, repeated each year before *Tet*, only served
to highlight the government's weakness in the face of Vietnam's
new appetites. They were the latest in a long series of sumptuary
laws imposed by governments. Under the Nguyen Dynasty there
were rules that set how long funerals and weddings could last and
banned participation in the 'one hundred amusements' – mostly
entertainments such as cock fighting. There is still an array of
restrictions on what government officials can consume, but in any
restaurant the noisiest table with the most lavish choice of food and
the largest number of brandy bottles seems to be populated by a
group of cadres or men in uniform.

Tet gifts and splendid meals are about much more than greed.
They establish important bonds among families, business colleagues and officials. They offer a polite and sanctioned form of
competition, a way of showing off to the neighbours that can now
be indulged. After years when nearly all consumerist desires were
suppressed, they have now exploded. The day before the holiday,
markets and the new supermarkets in Hanoi were crushed with
the same joyless, hard-faced consumers scrambling with last minute
purchases that you would find in any western city on Christmas
Eve.

Food has become such a part of asserting identity that to criticise
it, or to even not enjoy it, risks causing offence. Amid all this lip-
smacking celebration, it would be almost sacrilegious today to write
about food in the way that Tam Lang did in his article 'I Pulled a
Rickshaw', published in 1932. Taken to a sidewalk stall in Hanoi just
after he becomes a rickshaw puller, the author experiences a meal
that is almost gothic in its horrors.

In front of me, one bowl of beef offal soup stood with steam
belching off it. Even though it was as hot as that, I predicted
that it wouldn't be very tasty, because the soup looked like
drain water with a few slices of offal floating around like

drowned corpses . . . Holding the rice bowl, I poured the soup into it and felt my stomach jump into my mouth. Perhaps the dish of large intestines was not carefully prepared, for after I'd finished one mouthful, I thought I had swallowed a whole field of bullshit.

Nothing else on the stall appears at all appetising. The fish sauce was 'mixed with brine to discourage consumption', and some bean curd 'fried for some days had begun to change colour from yellow to dirt brown'. He is left looking with wonder and nausea at a fellow rickshaw puller who guzzles the offal soup with relish.

Tam Lang's descriptions, which were intended to reveal the horrors of poverty in the 1930s, now seem almost at odds with the celebratory cult of Vietnamese food that allows for little criticism. In the north it often seems that palates and cooking skills were dulled in the lean years of socialism. Hanoi lost its restaurant culture after 1954 when they were mostly closed down. After 1978, the city's Chinese population was expelled. Among those leaving were many of the better cooks and keepers of a culinary tradition that enriches Vietnamese cooking. While almost no Chinese live in Hanoi, Ho Chi Minh City still has a population of more than half a million who have kept their varied and rich cuisine alive in the city.

Buon Ma Thuot is a quiet town in the central highlands of Vietnam, famous in the West as the site of one of the last battles of the war that precipitated the collapse of South Vietnam. In Vietnam it is better known for two rare and expensive products – a venison biltong that comes in chewy purple sheets, and also one of the rarest types of coffee in the world – a bean that is organically grown and processed without the touch of a human hand. *Ca phe cut chon* is processed by the earliest known type of wet processing known to man – the gut of another animal. In this case it is a small and inquisitive fox that is said to select only the ripest, reddest berries from the coffee bushes. In its gut the bean is stripped of its outer layers at exactly the right temperature to induce a gentle, flavour-enhancing fermentation. The coffee beans emerge in long strings that are collected by farmers, washed and then roasted to produce what experts say is a sensuous and rich coffee, mellow by the normal rough standards of the robusta variants grown in the area.

Both the dried venison and the coffee are very hard to find nowadays, such is the hunger for exotic products and new tastes. Farmers around Buon Ma Thuot say the fox is nearly extinct and is almost never seen near the town. Asked what happened to the animal, a farmer rubbed his stomach and leered hungrily. The deer have nearly all gone as well, lightly grilled and served with herbs and a garnish of peanuts in the beer gardens that have sprung up in cities.

Exotic foods have won a growing place in the diet of the wealthier urbanites as people search for new experiences and new ways to spend their money or show off their gastronomic sophistication. Connoisseurs now all know the best places for dog, cat, rat, snake, rare frogs or jungle meat – the term for game. There is nothing in Vietnam's Red Book – the list of endangered species – that an epicure cannot find on a menu in Hanoi.

Dogs and snakes attract perhaps the most gastronomic attention. Dog is a northern dish, its scented meat is hot, vaporous and unsuitable for women as it breeds lust and is believed to harm an unborn child. For men, it gives strength and promotes the same lust that women suffer from, although of course men don't regard this as such an obstacle to consumption. It can be served in a number of ways, grilled with a lemon grass sauce, steamed or fried until a crispy golden skin encases the flesh, which is traditionally tenderised by beating the dog to death over several hours with a short length of hose pipe. Most restaurants are far too busy to do this any more; the dogs are despatched more quickly. Dog comes undisguised. There are no euphemisms here, dog is simply *thit cho*, or dog meat, not fragrant meat or any of the more delicate phrases the Chinese prefer. In Vietnam, dogs are not man's best friend, a full stomach is.

When supporters of the Thai military government were organised into protesting against Communist forces in Vietnam during the war, they carried around signs calling Vietnamese 'dog eaters'. It is not an appellation that troubles many Vietnamese, for eating dogs is no source of anxiety, indeed before the Year of the Dog, a time when the animals might expect a little respect, many men in Hanoi went off to welcome in the new year with a meal of barbecued dog sausages at the bamboo restaurants along the Red River dike. There is a playful defiance against Westerners who are shocked by eating dog. When US Secretary of State Warren Christopher visited Hanoi in 1995, his security detail arrived first with a dog to sniff out explosives. Vietnamese customs officials were initially unsure about how to categorise the animal. Embassy staff handling the paperwork later found the black Labrador had been labelled 'an imported food product'.

Restaurants in Hanoi now compete to come up with increasingly rare dishes in a culinary pursuit like something from a medieval European royal court. The exoticism is linked in part to the romantic pastoral memories, or more likely mythologies, many Vietnamese men have of hunting, and to a medicinal tradition that prizes rare animals for their curative powers. Exotic foods are frequently chosen from a cage or displayed live at the table to prove their authenticity and to heighten the sense of importance of the meal, rather in the way sommeliers create small performances over serving an expensive bottle of wine.

The emerging culture of restaurants and public consumption marks quite a change in Vietnamese society; food was mostly consumed at home and people rarely ate out. Echoing the transformations that have taken place in the West over the past fifty years, Vietnamese are eating out and choosing restaurants and foods as a way of marking out class and status. As a certain type of restaurant becomes popularised, new establishments or forms of cuisine emerge where the cognoscenti can mark themselves out from the masses. Much of this social differentiation has centred around restaurants that serve exotic or wild foods that are rare and pricey.

Just outside Hanoi is a village crowded with snake restaurants. The snakes are displayed tangled together in cages. Skilled hands reach in and dramatically pluck out the snake chosen for a meal and kill it at the table. Often the bile is drained off and drunk with alcohol; other wines in which toxic species of serpent have been marinated are also served. One speciality is to kill cobras at the table by cutting out the heart, which is served, still beating, in a glass of rice wine.

When an animal becomes hunted out, which they frequently are, restaurateurs are inventive at coming up with a substitute. Wild cats, including tigers, are a hot food, strongly aphrodisiac and masculine. Unfortunately the many men requiring this sexual boost vastly outnumber the few furtive animals living on the fringes of Vietnam's depleted forests. Instead, restaurants in Hanoi serve 'baby tiger' – domestic cat that is cooked in dozens of ways. The basic dish is small kebabs of cat marinated in a medicinal concoction that effectively disguises any flavour the meat may have. More adventurous diners could try 'false dog meat' – cat with mushrooms in a thick sauce – cat's liver with testes or even a rare dish in which the cat's skeleton is cooked for hours before the white bone marrow is extracted and served up. These are exotic dishes by any standards; many Vietnamese would squirm at the thought of eating cat. Most prefer more mundane and less expensive meat.

Black cats are valued over other colours and according to the owner of one stall near the railway line that cuts through Hanoi, it 'can cure a thousand ailments related to imbalances in body temperature'. Black cat steadies your nerves and clears your kidneys, he reassures patrons. These claims provoked some scepticism among practitioners of traditional medicine who say that the only part of a cat that is commonly used is the gall bladder, and that is only prescribed for asthma. The efficacy of black cats as a curative would be hard to test as few cat restaurants ever have any. The menus may offer costly black cat dishes, but the animals in cages out at the back of the restaurants generally have piebald brown fur.

Cats and other exotic foods, like many Western delicacies, are intimately connected to sex. Many dishes are aphrodisiacs or at least enhance virility. There is also an overlap between commercial sex and food. A night out for a group of men will centre around an expensive meal followed by a visit to a prostitute. The meal is part of the preparations for sex. Brothels and stalls selling exotic foods have sprung up together in parts of Hanoi to cater to an increasingly sybaritic public in search of a whole range of fleshy temptations.

Amid this Epicurean frenzy, expectations are on a constant rise. After so many years of not having enough food, Vietnamese are hankering after more, looking with nostalgia at food they remembered from the countryside, childhood or even the war. Exotic foods can create distinctions of class, wealth and even gender. An appreciation of foreign food is starting to emerge; fast food has already returned to Ho Chi Minh City in the form of fried chicken restaurants and expensive ice-cream parlours. Vietnam has seen the arrival of a huge array of imported foodstuffs, most of them more appetising than the goods once shipped in from Eastern Europe. A stall set up by Kraft Foods was a huge hit at an American trade fair in Hanoi just after the lifting of the US embargo in 1994. Even Phan Luong Cam, the wife of Prime Minister Vo Van Kiet, stopped at the stall to massage a plump bag of marshmallows and to marvel at the exotic Day-Glo yellow of Cheezwiz.

This emergence of a complex consumer-oriented society, many Vietnamese believe, heralds the start of a time of enormous social and political change. Hunger is still widespread in Vietnam but the preoccupation with getting enough to eat is no longer quite so pervasive. The journalist, artist and restaurant owner Ly Qui Chung believes that time for radical social change may nearly be here after a decade of reforms. 'Now that people have full stomachs, they can start to think about something else apart from eating.'

6

Empty Box

The Party is like a big box. It looks impressive from the outside,
makes a good sound if you tap it. But if you open the lid you'll
see there is nothing inside.

PAVEMENT ANALYSIS FROM A HANOIAN DURING THE
PARTY CONGRESS IN JUNE 1996.

Tran Trong Tan could have hardly picked a more theatrical moment
to throw a spanner in the works of the Eighth Congress of the
Vietnamese Communist Party. On a steamy July day in 1996, the
final session was about to end. Four days of interminable speeches
and Marxist pageantry as anachronistic as a gathering of Druids
were winding up in a televised display of unity as the faithful voted
on new Party statutes. Then Tan, a former top ideology official, rose
to his feet. A Mexican wave of astonishment went through the
crowd; lolling heads perked up, elderly generals, their chests jan-
gling with medals, turned in their chairs and craned for a better
view.

The changes to the statutes were ideologically unsound, Tan said.
The Party had no right to take power away from the Central
Committee and the Politburo. These are the top two institutions of
power in Vietnam. The Central Committee has around 160 members and meets twice a year to set the broad brushstrokes of policy.
The Politburo is a group of about sixteen of the most powerful officials who run the country. Almost all power resides in this secretive
body that only occasionally makes its decisions public. The
Standing Board of the Politburo – five people who would hold the
purse strings, keep the keys to the armoury and have a free hand in
policy-making – had not been elected by the Central Committee. 'I

am afraid that if the Standing Board is given the right to make decisions on too many issues, this would not be beneficial,' Tan said.

Another ripple of amazement crossed Ba Dinh Hall, the building normally used for sessions of the National Assembly. It was extraordinary that anyone would actually stand up at such a gathering and voice an opinion, even one as understated as this. President Le Duc Anh, deaf and incoherent, his voice lurching in irritation at this unscripted interruption, kept on pressing Tan to spell out his objections more clearly. Tan did so, receiving a mutter of support from the audience, many of whom objected to this concentration of powers. As Tan and Le Duc Anh continued their exchange, General Secretary Do Muoi, the head of the Communist Party, brusquely intervened, snapping at the President. 'Mr Tan has expressed his views quite clearly. The Politburo Standing Board handles affairs on behalf of the Politburo and it does not make decisions. The amendment of the article should be made with this in mind.'

It turned out it was fortunate Do Muoi did step in at the last minute. The wording of the changes, one of the most radical shifts in the Communist Party's power structure in decades, had simply been an error inserted by a careless typist. Or so said Do Phuong, a Party propagandist and Central Committee member who headed the Vietnam News Agency. Writing in one of the agency's newspapers, Phuong breezily dismissed suggestions of any internal divisions. It was all just a misunderstanding. Never mind that the 'error', moving vast power into the hands of these five men, had occurred nineteen times in the statutes, drafts of which had been circulating for months. This excuse was needed to rebut reports that the incident had been a symptom of the rising discontent and division within a Party that in Do Muoi's words was trying to keep the Congress focused on 'unity, unity and unity'.

For decades historians, journalists and spies have been trying to fathom the workings of the Vietnamese Communist Party. For many years Ba Dinhology, the local variant of Kremlinology, was almost an arcane branch of palaeontology with its acolytes turning out wild hypotheses based on tiny fragments of ancient information. As Vietnam opened up, the study became more akin to ornithology. Party watchers would exchange news of rare sightings of top officials but could only wonder at their hidden habits. In recent years, a rising level of disarray in the Party and many leaks of documents has made it easier to get a better view of how the organisation works.

Tan's intervention capped a period when the musty velvet drapes of secrecy were pulled back to give a brief official glimpse into the sepulchral world of the Communist Party of Vietnam. It wasn't an edifying sight. The top three men, their bony hands gripped tensely around the reins of power, did not step aside. Ideologues played word games while the ship of state drifted. The deep fault lines and personal disputes between the handful of people who run Vietnam were papered over with ludicrous excuses and a stifling insistence that the Party put its power ahead of everything else.

Do Phuong amply illustrated the real level of political debate. In a lengthy article, in which he claimed to explain the Vietnamese political process to foreigners, he revealed that before the congress there had been some heated argument over whether Do Muoi should say that the country would 'gradually shift to industrialisation and modernisation', or whether he should favour some other variation such as 'push up to industrialisation or modernisation', or 'strongly push up to'. These were not just word games, Phuong insisted; it was spirited discussion.

These gatherings are more about ceremony than debate or decisions. The 1,200 delegates from across the country are supposed to elect a new Central Committee which in turn would elect the Politburo. Unsurprisingly everything is worked out long before the Congress, a point illustrated when the Eighth Congress elected a corpse to the Politburo. The scientist Nguyen Dinh Tu had a heart attack and died the day before his election to the Politburo. As a mark of respect he won a seat anyway.

It didn't seem to trouble the delegates that the final list of Politburo members had been drawn up at least four days before Central Committee members got a chance to vote. Most of the delegates spent the Congress dutifully applauding speeches and then rushing out to drink beer in the gardens of Ba Dinh Hall or flick through the Disney *Lion King* colouring books on sale at a book stall along with the less entertaining works of President Anh. Word circulated in Hanoi that several delegates wandered further astray and were sent home after being caught in a *bia om*, literally 'a hugging bar', where young hostesses provide services to a male clientele.

From this meeting stemmed the defining theme for the next five years – more control. It also ended the illusion that Vietnam's transition from Marxist-Leninism was going to be a smooth evolution to democracy and openness. The epigrammatic phrase of the Congress was spoken by Do Muoi in his political report: 'Leadership without control is tantamount to no leadership at all'. What this meant was more of the same divisions and policy paralysis as the Party demanded not new reforms but a tighter grip on the economy and a firmer hand in dealing with social problems. They were reaping the whirlwind of rapid social change seeded by economic reform; all they could do in response was to fall back on their coercive powers.

This sclerotic beast was the same Communist Party that had briefly seized power in a daring revolt in 1945, fought the French for independence and led the country to reunification by fighting one of the most gruelling wars of modern times. Now it was almost alone in a world that had roundly rejected Marxism. It was led by men of limited knowledge whose unchanging rhetoric framed unimaginative policies. It was corrupt and discredited to the point of being scorned by many of the people who had once been among its most fervent supporters. And yet despite all this it remained very much in power, sixty-six years after its founding meeting was held in the stands during a football game in Hong Kong.

Why, when Marxism has been rejected so forcefully, so rapidly and by so many, has it survived in Vietnam? There is no single answer. Vietnamese Communism was always closely tied to nationalism and the Party's own identity has been so closely woven together with the country's that they are hard to separate. The message is constantly reinforced that to attack the Party is to attack the country. Communism in Vietnam was home-grown rather than being imposed by the Red Army as it was in Eastern Europe. It made some effort to fit in with local customs. Even though for decades the Party rejected Confucianism as feudal and outdated, it recently decided that Communism meshes well with Vietnamese Confucian tradition as both aspire to provide a firm moral structure to society as well as a model for government.

Asked why the Party should remain in power, an elderly general who heads the veterans association in Ho Chi Minh City said bluntly: 'Because we won the war'. This conflict, always framed as a great victory over foreigners but never as a civil war, has always been milked to legitimise the government, but it is a fading force. The younger generation doesn't remember the war and is more curious than hostile to the outside world. Now the Party is trying to shift its base of legitimacy to its management of the economy. This requires that it essentially bribe people with rapid economic growth which in turn requires quick thinking and adaptable policies that are grounded in pragmatism, not dogma.

Power, as Mao Zedong said, comes out of the barrel of a gun, and in Vietnam the Party still controls the guns. The top brass in the military and security services are all in the Party, indeed they hold three of the five positions in the Politburo Standing Board. Downsizing hit hard in the late 1980s but the army has a privileged position in the economy that has allowed it to survive budget cuts by transferring its energies to joint ventures with foreign companies. The military may be massively weakened as a fighting force, but it is a growing commercial enterprise with thirty-five joint ventures and foreign investment of more than $335 million by the end of 1996. It also holds a vast stock of land which it has repeatedly refused to turn over to other government agencies.

The Interior Ministry, which is responsible for domestic security, has also joined the rush to make money, strengthening some of its capacity for political and social control with the purchase of new technology. In a country where most men in uniform, even the guards at Ho Chi Minh's Mausoleum, look fairly ragged, the Ministry's riot police are extremely well equipped. To earn money it has gone into a number of businesses, principally property. Its main import-export company has a $500 million joint venture with a Taiwanese firm to construct a hotel and office building on the site of a Ho Chi Minh City jail that once housed political prisoners. This interweaving of the state, the economy and the personal interests of officials has created formidable barriers to political change.

The Party has been able to soften opposition by abandoning its more doctrinaire positions. The idiom of communism lingers on, but it only provides a flimsy scaffolding on which the Party can hang its banners. Lenin's works are available in fifty-four thick volumes in Vietnamese, the language rendered even more impenetrable than in the original. They are found in government offices, bound in ruptured plastic with strata of dust and dead insects testament to their lack of use. But Lenin remains, nevertheless, among the most influential thinkers in Vietnam not for his economic ideas but for his political views. His works are pored over at special institutes of Marxist-Leninism and quoted approvingly by government leaders. On his birthday, the newspapers are filled with slogans honouring him.

Lenin's legacy is the model for the political structure of a Marxist state in which the Communist Party insinuated itself into every aspect of life. Adapted to local concerns, this has been a powerful means of maintaining control in Vietnam. Through its cells of members, the Party channels information, maintains political discipline, rewards the obedient and monitors the others. The structure has sagged a little, indeed it is in need of some repairs, but it remains surprisingly effective.

Huu Tho, a former editor of the Party newspaper *Nhan Dan* and head of the Party's External Relations Committee, attributed its survival to its collective leadership, its willingness to admit mistakes, a relative lack of corruption and a distaste for personality cults. If this is the case, then it is in big trouble. The degree of collective leadership, always vastly overstated by the Party, has come near to collapse. The system now works to block most new ideas rather than to moderate them and has created repeated crises of succession. It might have been easier to get some measure of consensus around fighting a war, but peace presents more options and often more tension. Unless the leadership is operating in an environment of crisis, it seems nearly impossible nowadays to reach agreement on any innovative new policies.

Huu Tho's assertion that Party members are not corrupt is simply laughable. His idea that it is willing to admit its mistakes is disingenuous in the extreme. Nobody has admitted that the influence of Maoism was a mistake, or that the Tet Offensive that destroyed Viet Cong networks in the South was ill-conceived. The Party has never confessed that it may have erred in the decade-long involvement in Cambodia after its invasion in 1978 to remove the Khmer Rouge, even though this is almost universally regarded as disastrous. Far from admitting its errors and righting wrongs, the Party has tended to meet legitimate grievances with stony silence or vengeful punishment.

It is true they have avoided cults of personality, except the one surrounding Ho Chi Minh. But this hasn't stopped massive abuses of power by senior Party members. Le Duc Tho, winner of the Nobel Peace Prize along with Henry Kissinger and the late head of the sinister Organisation Department of the Party that kept files on members, will be remembered with loathing by most Vietnamese for his reign of fear. Le Duan, the former general secretary, nurtured Ho Chi Minh's cult rather than his own, but that didn't stop him bringing the country to its knees with his dogmatic imposition of socialism.

Huu Tho's four-step programme for eternal Marxist-Leninist rule inadvertently outlines four of the main factors that are eroding support for the Party and might prompt its eventual rejection. The Party's messy internal divisions, its cancerous corruption, the dark secrets that lurk in its history and its lack of charismatic figures could eventually doom it.

In 1960, Ho Chi Minh remarked in a speech that the thirty-one members of the Central Committee had spent 222 years in jail between them. In the crowded cells of colonial prisons they had forged bonds that created the remarkable unity of the Party. This was a vital factor in their victories over the French and South Vietnam, but by the early 1990s it seemed to be fading. The former Foreign Minister Nguyen Co Thach promised an American delegation that he could get General Le Duc Anh, then serving as Defence Minister, to agree to a major change in thinking on the search for US troops listed as missing in action because the two of them, he claimed, had shared a prison cell once.

Thach's faith that the warm glow of shared cell-time would overcome ideological and policy differences was touching but mistaken. Le Duc Anh did not make the policy change and in 1991 was instrumental in ousting Thach from the Politburo and the Foreign Ministry.

Not only have the small group of men and women seen their

sense of common experience fade over the years, they have lost a sense of common purpose. There is no war to fight, no enemy to hate and no rousing slogan. Today's mantra of 'industrialisation and modernisation' hardly rallies the masses. The only issue this ageing coterie can agree on is that they must stay in power, unchallenged by any other organised political force. How they should do this remains a matter for intense debate in their secretive world.

In August 1995, nearly a year before the Eighth Congress, Prime Minister Vo Van Kiet kicked off the political season in an explosive manner. He sent a letter to the other members of the Politburo, outlining his vision for the future. He urged the Party to cut the Gordian knot of Market-Leninism – the contradiction between the legal needs of a market economy and the desire for the Party to keep its hands on power. Vietnam needed the rule of law, private enterprise needed a level playing field and the government needed officials chosen for their expertise not their party loyalties.

The letter gave a blunt assessment of the level of corruption in the Party and outlined how outdated Vietnam was in its ideology. It was time to abandon democratic centralism and the dictatorship of the proletariat, central articles of the faith since the founding of the Party. International socialist solidarity was dead, he said. This might not have been much of a surprise in a world that watched the fall of the Berlin Wall on television, but it was a jarring heresy to the ears of some members of the Politburo. He defended himself from accusations that he was 'deviating from socialism' by listing his accomplishments as premier. Socialism was what worked, he told them. Deviations from it were the corruption, authoritarianism and factionalism that plagued the Party.

Kiet believed the Party should give up even pretending to nurture the withered vine of Marxism and instead shelter under the tree of Vietnamese nationalism. His letter was unusually direct for a Party document. It marked out the successes of the past five years, clearly claiming credit for them, but warned that the Party needed to keep moving forward if the country was not to lose more time in its race for development. His analysis was couched in some of the necessarily wooden and often martial vocabulary, but its message was clear: the Party would only survive in power by keeping up the pace of reforms.

The Prime Minister had come a long way since the early 1980s when he told an interviewer of how his burning class hatred had been aroused as a child by the sight of exploited farm workers in the Mekong Delta. His career had been long and unorthodox. His friend, Nguyen Ho, a former Party official who turned against the leadership, described Kiet as a 'great revolutionary but a poor Marxist'. As the Party Chief in Ho Chi Minh City in the late 1970s, he tried to soften the blows of collectivisation by allowing a measure of free enterprise to prosper despite a furious blizzard of edicts from Hanoi. His career had mostly been in the South during the war where he fostered an independence of mind and pragmatism that is often lacking in those who built their careers in Hanoi's ideological environment. Kiet had lived much closer to the hardships of the war than his more cloistered colleagues. His first wife and children were killed in an American bombing raid in the jungle near the Cambodian border. Later his strength of character and reputation as a practical man in the midst of ideologues, brought him considerable popular and bureaucratic support in his rise to the post of Prime Minister.

Kiet has been a strong advocate for reforms but he doesn't even come close to being liberal. The Premier has taken some of the toughest lines on social and religious issues, indeed he has been more outspoken than any other senior leader in his criticisms of the Roman Catholic and Buddhist churches. In this letter, he was not repudiating the Party but trying to save it. Kiet was keenly aware that the fate of the Party now depended on its success as an economic manager.

Kiet, who had travelled widely in Asia and the West, was shocked by Vietnam's backwardness and poverty compared with its neighbours. Thailand had long been denounced as the impoverished and weak puppet of American imperialism and yet it was decades ahead of Vietnam. Even averaging the 8 per cent annual growth it had managed in the early 1990s, Vietnam would still need twenty-five years to reach the level of Thailand in 1995. Desperate measures were needed to catch up.

He listed five points that he said should define a new socialism for Vietnam. To the distress of some of the members of the Politburo, the Communist Party's continued power was fifth on this list, below measures calling for improved social welfare and environmental protection. Achieving this nebulous vision of socialism required that the Party abandon all formulas and work out a mixture of policies best suited to the prevailing economic climate, he said. This meant, for example, giving up the Party's insistence that state industries remain dominant over the private sector.

His letter whipped up quite a stir in Hanoi's political circles, where Kiet was widely respected for his competence. It also galvanised the doctrinaire Party officials who began muttering about Mikhail Gorbachev and the slippery slope to the collapse of communism. To them, Kiet's letter was a dangerous manifesto that could only weaken the Party's power. They moved into action, putting out a number of documents that attempted to counter Kiet's position. The Interior Ministry published a list of subversive organisations and ranked the threats posed by different groups. Few people had ever heard of most of the groups; there was some suspicion that they existed only in the fevered imaginations of the Interior Ministry. A Party circular warned of the rising threat from the United States, saying that the normalisation of diplomatic relations in 1995, which Kiet had touted as one of his main achievements, was part of this plot.

Kiet's letter unleashed one of the most vicious political battles of recent years. There was little support for his views in the Politburo, where economic reforms were viewed with suspicion if they weakened the Party's power. Broadly, the Party divided between those like Kiet who wanted to see it withdraw from daily government affairs and to operate within a legal system, and those who felt the leading role of the Party was only ensured by its continued intense involvement at all levels of the bureaucracy. The collapse of communism had shocked the latter group deeply. They pinned it on Gorbachev's tolerance of reformers in the highest levels of the Soviet Party and on a sinister Western plot of 'peaceful evolution' that used decadent culture, democracy and human rights to discredit communism. Nguyen Duc Binh, the rector of the Ho Chi Minh Political Academy and a member of the Politburo, concocted his theory of peaceful evolution, borrowing liberally from the Chinese, to explain why Communism had been so roundly discredited.

Most Vietnamese intellectuals and many Party members ridiculed the idea of peaceful evolution. 'Who toppled the Communist governments and parties in Eastern Europe?' asked the dissident Nguyen Ho in a widely circulated letter. 'The United States and its armed forces did not contribute to this victory. Rather, it was achieved by these countries' own citizens who suffered under the leadership of Communist parties for forty-five years. These people had no weapons except their anger against the Communist parties' outdated and ineffective policies.'

The Party was still a mass of anxieties about the demise of Communism and peaceful evolution was a more palatable explanation than the truth. In this climate, Kiet's blunt criticisms of the Party were seen as almost treasonable. To stop them gaining any currency, a senior Politburo official, Nguyen Ha Phan was sent out to denounce Kiet's ideas at Party meetings, particularly in the Prime Minister's power base in the south of the country. Hanoi's gossipy world began to talk of Politburo meetings at which the main players spent their time screaming abuse at each other. Kiet's letter was soon leaked and hastily distributed around Hanoi. President Le Duc Anh was said to have demanded Kiet's resignation and a lengthy article in the Party newspaper *Nhan Dan* written by a Politburo member warned of the growing rifts at 'even the highest levels of the Party'.

Political battles in Vietnam tend to be complicated by the overlapping circles of interests, like some fabulously complex Venn diagram. Each of the three 'pillars of state' – the Communist Party, the Government and Vietnam People's Army – has groups that reflect different political and economic viewpoints. The cohesion of past years has all but evaporated; what Vietnam has now is a form of 'fractured authoritarianism', with power divided among often hostile groups within the state structure. What has emerged from the shift away from communism is a wild menagerie of personal fiefdoms, provincial power bases, ideological blocs and competing financial interests.

The army, for example, has long been divided between those who see defence as a matter of technology and training that requires a clear pragmatic view, and those who take the Maoist line that it is a political issue that demands the mobilisation of the masses under the complete control of Party cadres. Now that Vietnam is no longer at war, the military tends to divide into those who see the establishment of a rich military-industrial complex as the key task, and those who want to maintain a tight ideological grip on the soldiers.

President Le Duc Anh and his protégé Le Kha Phieu, now General Secretary of the Party, are among the ideologues. Neither was popular among those officers who saw the military's role as one of national defence, not political control. A letter circulated by some army officers in 1995 denounced the Party's errors and called for political reforms and the rule of law. 'There should be no privileges for those who used violence to come to power,' the letter said. 'We are determined to smash all the selfish, conservative dogmatists who use the guise of the Revolution to obstruct the wheel of history.' The letter ended with the slogan: 'President Ho Chi Minh lives forever in our cause.'

Within the government and Party there are different interest groups such as the managers of state enterprises, ministerial bureaucrats and provincial cadres who all have conflicting views. What this means most of the time is paralysis, as each group can block a project or policy that might diminish its influence. These squabbles are mostly over less lofty ideals than the letter from the army officers might suggest. They tend to be about control of resources and the placement of officials in the lucrative positions as gatekeepers for foreign aid or investment, but they are often framed in the idiom of ideology or in accusations of corruption. These interest groups rarely coalesce around individuals except when threatened.

The attacks on Kiet and the replacement of several officials, particularly in the military, who were seen as close to him, provoked his supporters to fight back. One of their targets was Dao Duy Tung, a neo-Stalinist ideologue whose ideas were inimical to reforms. But Tung was sick. Cancer had metastasised throughout his body and he no longer presented much of a threat. His protégé, however, did. Nguyen Ha Phan, the head of the Party's Economics Commission and Vice Chairman of the National Assembly, was being touted as a possible successor to Kiet. He was a conservative on economic affairs and had the advantage of being a southerner. He also had a past.

How exactly someone with Nguyen Ha Phan's background made it into the Politburo is a mystery. Whenever officials move up in the hierarchy they are checked by the Party's Organisation Department that monitors their past records and activities. Phan's detailed personal file must have been checked dozens of times during his rise, but it was only in early 1996 that rumours of a murky secret began to emerge.

How Phan's history caught up with him has not been explained completely but it appears that documents surfaced proving that in 1963 Phan had betrayed some of his Viet Cong comrades to the South Vietnamese secret police. 'His fingerprints were found on the documents,' one official said. Another said handwriting analysis had proved his guilt. The evidence must have been convincing enough for the Politburo, which gathered in a special session and expelled Phan for his 'serious errors'.

The official line, according to a document circulated to all Party cells, was that: 'In the struggle to liberate the South and to unite the Fatherland, when comrade Nguyen Ha Phan was arrested and imprisoned, he did not maintain the honour of a Communist and revealed to the enemies many revolutionary underground units. Since his release in 1964, he has not reported his mistakes to the Party. Comrade Nguyen Ha Phan's mistakes are serious. The Party Central Committee decided to discipline Comrade Nguyen Ha Phan by expelling him from the Party.'

The document specifically said this information was not to be used by the media. No Vietnamese newspaper published reports of his expulsion but news about it travelled quickly around Hanoi. Although most people believed it was quite likely that Phan had some skeletons in his closet, the whole incident left intriguing questions about who had exposed him.

The most probable answer appears to have been Vo Van Kiet. Phan was being touted as his successor, even though he lacked much of a public base. Phan had also been sent to the southern provinces in an attempt to undermine Kiet and discredit his policies. Phan – economically and socially conservative – would have been an acceptable southerner to put into Kiet's job.

Kiet might have won a battle, but it was not clear if he would win the war. As the Congress approached, he seemed almost invisible as his more conservative colleagues dominated public appearances. There appeared to be an ideological drift back to state control and tighter regulation of the economy. The rhetorical volume and its xenophobic tone, always cranked up ahead of a Congress, was getting very loud. In a flashback to the pre-*Doi Moi* days of intense suspicion of the outside world, the government stopped issuing visas to foreigners, a move that crippled the tourist industry in the lead up to the major holiday season in Europe and the United States.

The Central Committee began its series of meetings to prepare for the Congress by drafting documents and selecting a new leadership as part of a regular process to bring younger blood into the elderly top ranks. The conservatives wanted Kiet to go, but he resisted. No consensus emerged on who would replace the troika of President, Prime Minister and General Secretary who were all in their late seventies. The list of successors illustrated the problem the Party faced. None had the gravitas of the current leadership or the level of political support. Few of them had any international exposure or had dealt with the prickly issues that the top rung of leaders had faced. Several were tainted by ideological extremism or corruption. Just before the Congress, the Central Committee reached a decision on the rejuvenation of the leadership. The current elderly troika would all stay in their jobs for another year.

The change did come after more than a year. In 1997, Kiet's deputy Pham Van Khai, replaced him as Prime Minister. Tran Duc Luong became President and General Le Kha Phieu finally won the battle to becomeGeneral Secretary of the Communist Party at the end of the year. It was not an inspiring selection. Khai and Luong are both tainted by the corruption of their families and Phieu is widely regarded in Hanoi as an unthinking ideologue with no exposure to the outside world and only a limited grasp of market economics. This generation of leaders are likely to have less in common with each other and less will to fashion a consensus. None of them has much in the way of revolutionary glamour; few have spent any time in prison. Phieu, the most powerful figure of the younger generation, is unpopular, even among the military, and has had little success developing a warm public persona despite shedding his uniforms for business suits.

Several political scientists have tried to show that the Congress actually brought in a new generation which they believed was a reason for optimism. In fact the turnover was much the same as at previous congresses and there was no reason to believe that younger officials are likely to prove more open. It is likely that this Soviet-educated generation forged in the war against the United States may actually be more rigid than their predecessors who made their names fighting for independence, not as bureaucrats. Certainly there is little to suggest that generational change will bring with it increasing liberalism or political reform. It is likely that it will usher in a period of even more fractious leadership.

None of the intense wrangling over the leadership went on in public. The Vietnamese ruling class has largely managed to keep its battles to itself although it has become increasingly difficult to control the spread of information. Unlike Western politicians whose egos are kept in check by sharp cartoons, satire or stiletto questioning, the leadership in Hanoi is rarely touched. Their political world may offer up the Byzantine behind closed doors, where they endure back-stabbing and intrigue, but they have no taste for even the mildest public humiliation. When Kiet visited Australia he encountered a small and peaceful demonstration by overseas Vietnamese calling for respect for human rights. More than a year later he was still brimming with rage when he met the outgoing Australian ambassador at a farewell gathering. It was simply incomprehensible to him that he should have had to endure even a little distant jeering.

While the real debates are kept hidden, the public is fed an unappetising diet of slogans and ineffectual political ritual. Political language has become so debased that it no longer communicates anything. Speeches and Party documents are like mantras or a Latin mass – they are to be repeated even by those who cannot understand them. This has been reinforced under the leadership of Do Muoi who has tried to strengthen the Party bureaucracy after it was weakened under his predecessors. Nguyen Van Linh used grand gestures and media barrages to out-fox the Party bureaucracy and push through reforms. Muoi has returned to a cautious, foot-dragging approach that has explained the lack of vitality in the reform process since the early 1990s.

Muoi, a warm and garrulous man who looks remarkably well preserved and energetic for his years, is the last of the leaders to have come out of the 1945 revolution and the only member of the Politburo with the magical scars of time in Hoa Lo jail, later nick-named the Hanoi Hilton by American pilots held there. Muoi, who came from near Haiphong in the north of the country, parlayed prison-time and his revolutionary fervour into a job as a provincial Party secretary at the age of twenty-eight, a position that marked the start of his steady climb up the ladder.

By 1960 he was on the Central Committee and rose through the government ranks to become Minister of Construction, an impor-tant job at a time when so much was being destroyed by bombing. He was an effective bureaucrat, willing to hector people into giving him what he wanted. He also appears to have blown well with the political wind, remaining in favour whoever happened to be dom-inating at any time. This is one of the things that grates with so many Vietnamese, who are not nearly as taken with Do Muoi as most foreigners. For the Marxist Mandarins of Hanoi, a surpris-ingly refined and snobbish group, Muoi has always been a little too much the horny-handed son of toil for their tastes. He appeared to have so few real beliefs or principles, a trait that while pragmatic can also come across as craven. A professional revolutionary since his teens, Muoi was self-educated and like so many autodidacts he cannot resist having an opinion on everything.

According to those who have travelled with him on his inspection jaunts, he thinks nothing of telling peasants how to raise their ducks or how to get more out of their rice fields. Part of this is an avuncu-lar concern but it also indicates a disturbing degree of self-delusion and a will to delude others. Muoi is a master at telling audiences what they want to hear, making his every utterance slippery, a useful trick for all politicians. He is equally happy urging delega-tions of American CEOs to invest in Vietnam as he is telling Cuban journalists that they must remain at the vanguard of the world rev-olution that will defeat capitalism.

At the Congress, he exhibited his usual tendency towards mixing all signals, applauding hard-line speeches and yet trying to sound tolerant and open with the foreign media. On several occasions he emerged from Ba Dinh Hall, waved off his bodyguards and plunged into the grappling cluster of journalists. He said he was hail and hearty, flirting with any woman who came within grabbing distance as if to prove it. Communism would 'last forever', he said, quickly leaning into the microphones to add that foreign investors were still very welcome.

Muoi's vapid speeches may not be unusual for a politician but nevertheless the lack of content is important. There is a widening gap between rhetoric and reality in Vietnam that saps support for the rulers. The lack of clear statements on policies breeds a perpetual uncertainty that undermines confidence in the government. The political idiom has become debased by a bureaucracy that shrouds its lack of ideas in a glorious gobbledegook. The Party has stuck to the international Esperanto of Marxism, the same ugly phrases that rang so hollow in Brezhnev's Soviet Union and throughout Eastern Europe. Visits by foreign officials are 'highly appreciated', achievements are described with heavy hyperbole and enemies are pinned down with leaden accusations of being reactionary, revisionist or hegemonic.

In the early days of the Revolution, propaganda had been inventive and effective. Ho Chi Minh's 'Letter from Abroad', written from China in 1941 and widely circulated, was a model of concise and informative writing. In two paragraphs he sets out the international situation in a way that was bound to rouse the people to action:

> France has been lost to the Germans. French strength here is dissipated, yet they still raise our taxes to loot us, still they mount white terror against the people. In foreign dealings they hold their breath fearfully, giving some land to Siam, kneeling down in surrender to Japan. Meanwhile, our people have to wear two yokes, continuing to serve as buffalo and horses for the French but now also being slaves of the Japanese.
>
> In such painful tormenting conditions shall we simply fold our arms and wait to die? No, absolutely not! More than 20 million descendants of Lac and Hong are determined not to be perpetual slaves without a country.

Ho's 'Letter from Abroad' was one of the most important

documents of the Revolution. It was just 600 words long yet it captured the spirit of the time. No Vietnamese leader nowadays would
attempt such brevity or directness. Today political rhetoric func-
tions mostly to disguise a lack of ideas, fashion a weak consensus or
to hedge a promise. A society without a coherent legal system
requires a government that can articulate values which can be
broadly accepted. For several decades, the Communist Party was
able to produce men who could do this, but times have changed. Its
political structure, its internal battles and its own limitations mean
that it is hard for such a voice to be heard.

Lenin still stands in Hanoi. There is no graveyard yet for the sole
statue of him in Vietnam. He is set in bronze five metres high and
frozen in mid-stride in a small triangular park across from the Army
Museum in an upscale district of Hanoi. One hand points towards
the bright future of Marxism, the other remains stuffed in the pocket
of his coat. Lenin went up in Hanoi in 1985, only a few years before
he came tumbling down across Eastern Europe. It is known to the
Vietnamese as 'the stop thief statue', as the slightly startled Russian
looks as though he is pointing at a fleeing pickpocket and clutching
for his wallet. The joke slyly throws back the belief that was
common among Russians working in Hanoi that the Vietnamese are
wily and light-fingered.

Another piece of doggerel about the statue ran: 'If Lenin is a
Russian/then what is he doing in a park in my country/he's frown-
ing and pointing his finger/and saying "Socialism is still a long
way off."' CCCP, the Cyrillic letters for the USSR that for decades
was Vietnam's main aid donor, was said to stand for Vietnamese
words that mean 'The more they give us, the more we destroy'.
Billing meals to an expense account is still known in Vietnam as
'spending Soviet money'.

Vietnamese have come up with hundreds of ways to mock their
leaders and their system of government. Many of them are the same
jokes that were told in Eastern Europe. Q: Why do the police patrol
in groups of three? A: One to read the regulations, one to write out
tickets and the third to monitor these two dangerous intellectuals.

Many jokes hinge on the language's enormous capacity for puns.
As words can have up to six tones, a slight shift can change the

meaning. By changing the tones of the numbers in the words Sixth, Seventh and Eighth Party Congresses, the meaning changes to 'the hoax congress', 'the obscene congress' and 'the temporary congress'. Inverting the words and changing the tones of the common slogan 'make progress' gives 'very hungry'.

There seem to be fewer political jokes nowadays. The state is less involved in people's everyday lives and there is certainly less to gripe about. Political humour was a survival tool during those days, but it is no longer quite as necessary. People are simply less engaged, something that offers a present salvation to the Party and a problem for the future.

While the Communist Party spent months pumping up the Congress as the glorious culmination of another five years of socialism, it went almost unnoticed by the public. Most attention seemed to be focused on the European Cup soccer matches, broadcast in the early hours on Vietnam Television. The intense passion for soccer is extraordinary. There were nearly riots in Hanoi when the government declared a day of mourning for North Korea's dictator Kim Il-Sung and cancelled the broadcast of a World Cup quarter-final. Grown men talked in awed tones or with adolescent fervour about different teams from the other side of the globe. Village boys unable to locate Britain on a map could give you the run-down on the latest star striker playing in England's Premier League. During the European Cup, quiet Hanoi nights were punctuated with roars that followed each goal. Slack-jawed and yawning throughout the day, very few Hanoians were in any state to follow the meandering Congress.

The indifference, particularly of the younger generations who make up the majority of the population, poses a long-term threat to the Party. The Party was always supposed to be the 'vanguard' of the country, not necessarily a mass movement. Applicants once had to jump through many hoops before winning the privileges and trust that went with membership. Entry criteria have been relaxed, but fewer people feel the need to join now.

The demographics of Vietnam have already become a challenge, according to membership figures released by the Party in 1996. Pensioners now make up the biggest group of members. People aged under thirty make up around 60 per cent of the population but they account for just 11.6 per cent of Party members. The share of younger members had declined by about a quarter since 1991 when the figure was 15.6 per cent.

Those aged over forty-one made up 52.4 per cent of the membership in 1991, when 24.5 per cent of Party members were pensioners. Five years on, 56 per cent were over forty-one and 27.4 per cent were pensioners. Along with all its other divisions, the Party gerontocracy and the people are now facing each other across a huge generation gap.

Membership has risen, but not by the impressive figures given out by the Party which neglects to mention that thousands of old Party members die each year. In the five years between congresses it was up just 19,129, or 0.9 per cent. At the time of the Eighth Congress, Party membership stood at 2,128,742 out of a total population of 75 million.

The vast majority of Party members are in the North, particularly in and around Hanoi. Ho Chi Minh City, with a population of 5 million, had just 85,294 members. Just 1.7 per cent of the city's population were Party members.

Educational levels of Party members were generally low. Fewer than one in seven members had a university degree. Nearly half had no education beyond the age of fourteen. Vo Van Kiet complained that 'many Party members no longer set an example', and that cells were 'paralysed and degenerate'. He summed up the problem by saying: 'It should be concluded that the standards and quality of cadres and Party members has not kept pace with the development of the country.' The issue of the education levels and the corruption of Party members 'pose a direct challenge to our leadership role', he warned.

Despite these problems, the Party persists in its claim to speak for the people even though this has become an absurd act of political ventriloquism. The people are expected to remain dumb while a handful of people claim to represent them. All the Party's efforts to overcome public indifference have failed. Government officials are still pushed into joining. Almost all senior officials, newspaper editors or directors of state enterprises are members of the Party, so if you aspire to those jobs, you join the Party. Admitting that you joined the Party purely to advance your career became far less embarrassing than saying you joined because you believed in it.

Even those who followed the Congress were unimpressed. Asked what he thought about all the talk of stepping up Party control, one official, himself a member, rolled his eyes and said: 'Vietnamese always love talking about things they don't have.' Others complained of a complacency and self-congratulatory tone at the meeting, which offered nothing new in the way of policies. Nobody expected this timid gathering to revive the fortunes of the Party, but the complete lack of bounce felt afterwards was depressing.

Muoi, Kiet and Anh were the last leaders to benefit from the aura gained from being present at the creation. This generation, Khai, Luong and Phieu, who climbed the political ladder under socialism were more influenced by Eastern European Communism than the struggle against colonialism. There is no guarantee that they will be more open or more liberal than their predecessors; many fear the opposite may be true. These new leaders will face the true challenges of reform.

Apathy and the diverting desire for a little more money have muted opposition to the Party and kept it afloat through the tense years when Eastern Europe and China erupted. Czech President Vaclav Havel put it bluntly in his essay 'The Power of the Powerless', a work with many insights into the relationships between rulers and ruled in communist societies. The state 'by fixing a person's whole attentions on his mere consumer interests . . . hoped to render him incapable of realising the increasing extent to which he has been spiritually, politically and morally violated'. There is widespread discontent and cynicism in Vietnam, but political dissent is dulled by boredom and the need to focus on earning a living. 'We all know that this is a terrible way to run a country,' said the writer Nguyen Huy Thiep with an air of resignation. 'But none of us knows what to do about it.'

7

Excommunicated

Whenever human beings are repressed, there appears an uprising and struggle.

HO CHI MINH

The television news went through its usual dull cycle, stirring little interest among the patrons of a café in the central highlands town of Pleiku. Government leaders visited factories and opened housing for the poor, cameras lingered too long on stiff socialist tableaux of officials in armchairs. Then the amateur hour of forced enthusiasm that passes for television journalism in Vietnam shifted suddenly in tone. On the screen were images of what looked like a Stalinist show trial shot on grainy black-and-white film.

The café fell quiet as everyone turned to watch this shadowy fragment of newsreel that seemed to come from some distant totalitarian past. On the screen rows of middle-aged men in the cheap grey suits of officialdom filled the wooden pews of a dirty courtroom. Armed guards stood to attention in front of a raised dais where the judge and prosecutors presided. At the centre of the room stood two men bundled up in ragged clothes, one of them almost impossibly old and frail, his face narrowed with cold and pain. The other man, younger by several decades, looked downcast and broken.

The camera panned across the room, briefly catching a hard-faced judge attempting to exude some moral authority as he wielded the instrument of state power. The television announcer read out a commentary, doubtless echoing the tone of the judge. Relief that it was someone else in the dock showed on the faces in the public gallery. Nervous glances at the camera and a certain shiftiness betrayed a sense of complicity in some wrongdoing. In the café, the silence stretched out after the news had ended. No one wanted to be reminded that for some people, Vietnam's present is not very different from much of its past.

On 8 November 1995 the elderly defendant, Hoang Minh Chinh, was sentenced to a year in jail. His friend Do Trung Hieu was imprisoned for fifteen months. They had been tried on nebulous charges of harming state interests. Chinh had given an interview to a Polish journalist in April of that year in which he irritated the controllers of information in the Communist Party by discussing its long history of abuses. When police came to investigate they found copies of Hieu's writings. That was enough evidence in Vietnam to accuse them both of anti-government agitation. Their trial lasted just a few hours and the prosecution had taken up most of that time. They were not allowed to call witnesses in their defence. Instead they were only permitted to make humiliating appeals for leniency. The judge deliberated briefly with two 'People's Jurors' and then read out a long statement that had clearly been prepared well in advance.

While the court had marshalled the paraphernalia, costumes and rituals of law, it had not worked any notion of justice into the proceedings. But that was almost irrelevant, as the audience watching the murky political drama through the cameras of state propagandists would have understood the performance. It had served only to create what Vaclav Havel once described as 'the pleasing illusion that justice is done, society protected and the exercise of power objectively regulated'.

The jail terms were not harsh by the standards of Vietnam, where dissidents have been executed or imprisoned for decades. This pair, however, were unusual. They were not former South Vietnamese soldiers, nor were they exiles, but had once been senior Communist Party officials. Their trial was another episode in a history of internal dissent that still haunts the Party, another one of the accumulations of regret and repression that go back as far as the origins of Communism in Vietnam.

It is no surprise that revolutions devour their children. It is, however, a surprise to revolutionaries that the taste doesn't go away. The Vietnamese Communist Party has been unable to find a cure for the indigestion and meaty repetitions that have followed its gorging over the years. Nothing in its ideological medicine cabinet has yet been able to cure what has become a chronic and painful problem. Each decade since the Revolution in 1945 has brought its own episodes – the land reforms and crushing of intellectuals in the 1950s, the Anti-Revisionist Movement of the 1960s and the gulag of re-education camps that lasted from reunification in 1975 up until the late 1980s. Even in the bright new Vietnam of the 1990s, it has been impossible to hawk out such a legacy of bitterness.

The Party has always left out these strands of history when it weaves what are not so much tissues of lies but great gilded tapestries of untruths about its past. Unity is prized above everything and the Party must maintain this pretence at all costs. But even when rigorous social control left few cracks in society where dissent could breed, there were still people who challenged the Party, its policies or its belief that it alone could determine the political and cultural identity of Vietnam. As in all societies that lack the freedom of expression, there are men and women who have refused to remain silent. Their stories are of prison, exile or the near complete isolation from society, a form of modern excommunication mastered by the Communist Party.

In the past, the past had been less of a problem. But by the 1990s the Party was losing control of its well-crafted history, as remorseful former officials admitted responsibility for staged trials, and jailed men who had been heroes of revolutionary battlefields came forward to demand justice. Personal and political grievances boiled over into outright challenges to the legitimacy of the Party.

Hoang Minh Chinh was an honoured war hero and rising Party academic when in 1967 he was secretly detained and taken to the notorious Hoa Lo prison in Hanoi. There he was accused of handing over secret documents to the Soviet Embassy in Hanoi and conspiring with it to stage a military coup to overthrow the leadership. These accusations stemmed from the fact that Chinh had studied in Moscow and was known to favour Krushchev's advocacy of peaceful co-existence with the West over Mao's ideas for a 'permanent revolution'. There were fears among the leadership that the Soviet Union was using Chinh and others to prevent a closer relationship with China, then in the midst of the Cultural Revolution. The anti-Maoist line that Chinh took would eventually become political orthodoxy as the leadership in Hanoi were terrified that unleashing a Cultural Revolution in Vietnam would undermine their positions and threaten the war effort.

But Chinh's persecutors did not later offer a shame-faced apology. Instead he remained in jail or under house arrest. Out of jail in the late 1970s, he urged the Party to begin economic and political reforms. Many Party members shared his ideas, but Chinh was still under attack from Le Duc Tho, the man who ironically had inducted him into the Party. He was sent back to jail in 1981 for six years. These incarcerations left him ill and weak but they served only to harden his views. Despite the danger and difficulties of countering the intellectual torpor and fear in Hanoi, he kept alive notions of freedom and attacked the official dogma in writings that influenced a wide group of cadres and military officers.

Like many Vietnamese dissidents he had criticised extreme infections of socialism but had not believed that Marxism was inevitably equated with the repressive totalitarian force it had become in Vietnam. He accused the Party of absorbing a 'feudal form of Maoism' that had undermined its legitimacy. By the time of his latest arrest in 1995, Chinh was far down the path of many dissidents in Eastern Europe, who started off as advocates of cautious reform within the Party only to end up radically opposed to its rule.

A peculiar bravery marks out some people who will not be cowed by lies, who turn their iron logic and morality back against a repressive system. Vietnamese who find themselves banging up against walls of bureaucracy and corruption often display a flared-nostril determination that seems to derive strength from each rebuff and humiliation. Hoang Minh Chinh's wife, Le Hong Ngoc, also in her seventies, is one such person. A week before her husband's trial in 1995 she was still trying to find a lawyer, but had been unable to find a single one in Hanoi who had the courage to take on the case. Her last hope was a lawyer from overseas, but Vietnam does not allow foreign lawyers to advise on its law let alone defend people in criminal trials. There was little Ngoc could do to cajole the terrified Vietnamese legal establishment into representing her husband.

Chinh had been arrested after meeting Do Trung Hieu, a former religious affairs cadre who had exposed religious persecution and the mistreatment of prisoners. To make out a case of criminal association, the police produced a letter from Hieu to Chinh that showed they were linked. Ngoc pointed out that they should try Hieu first to prove that he was a criminal before they could arrest her husband. But her protests were useless in dealing with a police force unused to any challenge to its vast powers. They stonewalled her right up to the trial, refusing her access to documents and blocking any opportunity to prepare a defence. They even stopped Ngoc from giving her husband a volume on Vietnamese criminal law. The book, they told her, was clearly subversive.

The Vietnamese legal system is really more 'an excuse', as Havel said about Czechoslovakia's laws. 'It wraps the base exercise of power in the noble apparel of the letter of the law.' Chinh was charged with 'abusing the rights and freedoms of democracy and free speech to harm the national interest' under Article 205A of the Criminal Code. There is a chilling contradiction that snakes through this line of the law. The state is not obliged to present any evidence of harm to the national interest nor is this concept ever defined.

After the trial, Ngoc sent a letter to all the top leadership listing the ways in which the trial had violated Vietnam's laws. 'Our family is very unhappy that the trial did not take place in public and did not respect several articles of the Criminal Code,' she wrote. 'The trial should have been held in public, but only six members of our family were allowed to attend in violation of Article 19. Chinh should have been allowed to speak without any limitations, but he was only allowed to answer "yes" or "no" to questions posed by the court.'

Ngoc complained that the court had not allowed Chinh to submit documents to prove his innocence and his request to call twenty witnesses from the ranks of retired and active officials had been refused. He attempted to defend himself in the end because he had never been allowed to meet the four lawyers he had chosen. 'My husband is a man of seventy-six years who had contributed much to the Revolution, who had been injured during the war when he was shot, and now suffers from many illnesses. The sight of Chinh during this trial has aroused strong emotions among people of conscience.'

Chinh was first arrested in 1967 during the purging of dozens of other senior officials in what was known as 'The Anti-Revisionist Movement'. The detention of these officials, supposedly for their links to the Soviet Union, still resonates today in the dusty corridors of power and in the clubs and cafés where retired cadres meet to gossip and reminisce. The injustices done to these people in the name of ideology are perhaps even more sharply felt now that those ideologies have diminished in importance. It would be hard to find anyone in Hanoi who would measure another person by standards of political thought, and impossible to find anyone who believed that opposing the excesses of Maoism was a crime.

Patriotism and a good war record still, however, hold considerable currency in these circles and Chinh is untouchable on those counts. For many his prosecution revived resentment and perhaps guilt among those who had stayed silent for so long. Chinh's name may be almost unknown abroad except among a handful of human rights activists, but his words can still galvanise the Communist Party's more truculent ideologues into bursts of fury. Partly it is his background. The fact that he was a revolutionary hero, Party intellectual and confidante of Ho Chi Minh makes him that much more difficult to ignore, particularly as his calls for justice and for a resolution of the errors of the past have considerable appeal. Many cadres found it hard to stomach the sight of a venerable revolutionary being punished again. After his arrest in July 1995, there was much debate at even the highest levels of the Party over whether to put him on trial. But in the tense political climate ahead of the Eighth Party Congress, it was almost inevitable that he would be punished to prevent others from speaking out.

Chinh has spent his life in the adamant pursuit of his beliefs since he joined the revolutionary forces aged seventeen to fight against the French. He was almost immediately jailed and on his release two years later he joined the Communist Party. He rose up the ranks, making his mark in 1947 when he was injured leading a daring attack on the French air base at Gia Lam near Hanoi. His bravery won him a medal from General Vo Nguyen Giap and the revolutionary kudos to secure a good job after the Communist victory in 1954. His reward was political training in the Soviet Union.

He arrived there in 1957 at a time when the Communist world was experiencing turmoil it would not see again until its collapse more than thirty years later. Khruschev had denounced the crimes of Stalin in a secret report that soon made its way down the Party ranks in Vietnam. The Hungarian Uprising shook Eastern Europe and in China criticisms of Mao were unleashed in the 100 Flowers Movement. Far from being an awesome monolith of Marxist-Leninist faith, the Communist world proved to be fractious and riven with intense rivalries between Moscow and Beijing. Chinh later said these events planted in his mind the seeds of doubt about the suitability of Marxism in Vietnam, but nevertheless he returned to Hanoi to take up a key ideological post as rector of the Institute of Marxist-Leninism.

In 1963 he was asked to help prepare a report for the Ninth Party Plenum, a meeting of those top Party figures gathered together in the Central Committee. Chinh was handed this poisoned chalice at a time when the Party was splintering into increasingly distinct factions aligned with either Moscow or Beijing. The two camps were also divided over policy towards South Vietnam. Le Duan and the generally pro-Soviet group favoured an emphasis on the fight for reunification, while Truong Chinh – who had adopted this *nom de guerre* meaning Long March in deference to his Chinese mentors – felt the country should concentrate first on the North and the task of 'building socialism', a euphemism for applying the radical models of social change borrowed from Maoism. Hanoi was wobbling on the high fence that divided the Communist world. After a pro-Soviet shift in the first three years of the decade, the Lao Dong Party, as it was then known, moved rapidly towards Maoism.

The draft documents Hoang Minh Chinh had prepared for the plenum in December 1963 were torn up and denounced as revisionist, a label attached to any deviation from the Party line. Truong Chinh himself delivered a report that did not hide its anti-Soviet line ('It is the Chinese Communist Party, headed by Comrade Mao Zedong, which has carried out most satisfactorily the instructions of the great Lenin.'). Truong Chinh, himself demoted for his role in the disastrous land reform programme of the early 1950s, harked back to that and was withering in his attacks on those who had won that earlier battle against the Party's excesses. His speech included this ominous sentence: 'In the past few years, while an acute ideological struggle was taking place within the international Communist movement, a small number of cadres have supported the erroneous viewpoints and lines of the revisionists.'

Those words were to mark the start of purges that swept through

Hanoi's élite, isolating all those like Hoang Minh Chinh who opposed the Maoist turn. For Truong Chinh, the purges were a delicious act of revenge against those who had forced his humiliating demotion from the post of Party General Secretary in 1956. Ho Chi Minh, by then ill and old, had little power to stop the whirlwind of retribution that eventually sucked in dozens of men with whom he had worked closely. The purges consolidated the power of Le Duan, the southerner who had become General Secretary and Le Duc Tho, head of the Party's Organisation Division that monitored Party cadres and all their activities. Tho kept an iron grip on the Party from behind the scenes. Even at the Paris peace talks that ended the war with the United States, he claimed to be only an advisor to chief negotiator Xuan Thuy. In fact Tho, who later turned down the Nobel Peace Prize which he won along with then National Security Advisor Henry Kissinger, was an increasingly powerful figure.

Although Vietnamese are now reluctant to admit it, there was a definite swing against the Soviet Union after 1960. The Russian historian Ilya Gaiduk found evidence in Soviet archives that there was a marked decline in relations in 1964, with the Vietnamese even requesting the withdrawal of Russian military advisors. Tensions were heightened when Vietnam allowed anti-Soviet exhibitions donated by China to be shown in Hanoi despite the intense objections of the Soviet Embassy. The move towards Maoism divided the ruling élite; Maoist policies introduced after 1949 had been unpopular and had contributed to the failure and violence of land reform, so few people were keen to embrace them again.

Some Vietnamese intellectuals now cast these events less in terms of ideology and more as part of the personal settling of scores and the class battles that pitched urban intellectuals against 'professional revolutionaries' from the peasantry. The Anti-Revisionist Movement tore the intellectual heart out of the Party, clearing many posts for those who felt their class backgrounds and endurance of French jails gave them the clear mandate to run the Revolution. Red was better than expert, and intellectuals could not be trusted with power. The legacies of these cultural and political campaigns of the 1950s and 1960s sadly live on today with the impoverishment of ideas and the stiff reliance on dogma that still weigh heavily on the country. Many of those who stirred up this sentiment were themselves from relatively privileged backgrounds, but that did not stop them using class warfare to serve their own ends. The list of those purged in the 1960s includes many people who had been in prison with Le Duc Tho in Son La province; this has led many of those purged to speculate that he wanted to cover up his activities before 1945.

For those purged by the Party, life meant a persistent, throat-tightening fear of the secret police and a tangible insecurity in every waking moment. Children were denied entry to schools, applications to university were repeatedly rejected. Jobs were unavailable, there were none of the slow sinecures that were the main source of income for the middle classes in Hanoi. Families were left to fend for themselves in the darker fringes of the economy, exposing them to further persecution if discovered. Friends and family would only rarely support these outcasts and more often acted as informants. Once-privileged people joined the former Hanoi grandees and the despised bourgeoisie as prisoners of poverty, crowded into houses with unsympathetic or even hostile neighbours, suffocated by the absolute control that strangers wrought over their lives.

Nguyen Manh Tuong, a French-educated lawyer who was purged in the 1950s for his criticisms of land reform and the campaign against intellectuals, described the slow progression into poverty and isolation that his family suffered. Breakfast was the first meal to go; meat and vegetables became an infrequent part of their diet. As lunch and supper declined to a bowl of watery rice gruel, the family desperately tried to find ways to earn money. But Tuong's French classes were broken up by the police, the family didn't have the cash to buy cigarettes for resale on the street, and he was too old to pedal a *cyclo*. Even repairing tyres on the street proved impossible for Tuong whose doctorates in law and literature left him ill-equipped for fixing punctures, 'just like a eunuch in front of a beautiful woman', as he wrote in a biography published after he went to live in France.

By 1995, Hoang Minh Chinh's persecution had aroused the consciences of some of the very men who had orchestrated the Anti-Revisionist Campaign, including Nguyen Trung Thanh and Le Hong Ha, officials who once occupied top posts in the Party's

feared security apparatus. Thanh had been head of the Security and
Protection Department of the Central Committee between 1951 and
1988, acting as the hard man who ensured complete obedience to
the diktats of the Party. More than any other person he was responsible for maintaining the clenched, pathological secrecy and fear of
even those cadres who lived at the Olympian levels of Vietnamese
communism. It was his men who stood outside houses and offices
of senior officials, reporting back their every meeting and conversation. His men kept a tight grip on everything that went on in the
villas and offices around Ba Dinh Square.

Many of the Revisionists and their families who had lived
through decades of isolation and poverty began speaking out about
the injustices they had endured in silence. As the Party came under
pressure from these swelling voices, Thanh was called out of retirement to review the files of the Revisionists. Looking back into those
dusty archives and reading the accumulations of lies and distortions
used to convict the innocent led Thanh to make an extraordinary
admission. He wrote to the Politburo saying the accusations had
been based on forced confessions and distorted reports. 'Some of
these comrades might have violated Party regulations,' he wrote in
documents that circulated in Hanoi, 'but they never committed any
crimes nor did they violate any laws. Based on real evidence that
has been double-checked, I can conclude that these victims should
not have been accused, tried and condemned for anti-Party, anti-
government and espionage activities.'

Among those purged were four members of the Central
Committee, the foreign minister, a deputy minister, four department heads, a general and four colonels. Vu Dinh Huynh, Personal
Secretary to Ho Chi Minh and a member of the Party since the 1930s
was also a victim along with his son. 'I believe the most urgent
problem is immediately to clear these comrades who were wrongly
accused and held for many years,' Thanh wrote. 'This will benefit
the unity of the Party and society as well as ensure the political stability of the current situation. Our priority must be to admit and
correct these errors.'

The Politburo didn't see it that way and simply ignored Thanh's
letter. Furious at the lack of a response, Thanh released his letter into
the close circle of officials in Hanoi where it had the effect of

crystallising years of disaffection. Thanh received dozens of letters from his victims, reminding him in no uncertain terms of his own role in the Party's repression but welcoming his repentance. 'After reading your letter, I was very touched by your sincerity. During the thirty-seven years you spent in your job, it is obvious that you contributed to those errors and crimes, the fake trials and distorted reports. Consequently a number of innocent victims, as well as their relatives and friends, suffered the insufferable. You now repent for your past actions against the people of Vietnam. People will forgive you,' wrote the journalist Phan Que Duong.

Phung Van My, a former professor of philosophy at the Institute of Marxism-Leninism jailed from 1967 to 1976 also wrote that he had been deeply moved by Thanh's letter. But he rebuked Thanh for saying the Party should 'clear' the victims of the purges, saying he was glad to have been expelled from that world. 'The word "clear" doesn't mean anything today,' he wrote. 'We live normal lives, not those of the condemned. Spiritually our lives are peaceful and independent. We are no longer slaves or members of any department or system. Why do we need anyone to clear us? Will we be cleared and returned to the old system? I can't tell you how much that idea scares us.

'With the outcome of these trials, did we win or lose? Yes we lost a lot, a great part of lives, our youths. Dozens of us died as a result of hunger, poor health, mental problems. An uncounted number of the victims' families had to suffer an immense burden. But ironically we gained more than we lost. The most important gain was our liberation from the system to live in a state of peace with no fear.' My rejected any idea of compensation or redemption from those who had jailed him. 'We do not need compensation from the Party because many years ago the people around us had already compensated us with their trust and understanding and considered us heroes. We all know who were perpetrators of these crimes. Our lesson is that only the freedom we gain ourselves is real. The freedom given by others is not.'

Thanh's switch from enforcer to campaigner provided the perspective that could reveal the mendacity of the Party, turning a powerful light back on a system that rested on fear. Having the past so brightly illuminated did not please the Politburo and Thanh was finally summoned to a meeting with Do Muoi and the head of ideology Dao Duy Tung in the office of the Central Committee on Ba Dinh Square. The meeting did not begin well. According to notes of the conversation that Thanh kept, Do Muoi began with a patronising remark that at the age of seventy-two, Thanh should 'relax, write poems, take care of flowers rather than write letters like this one'. Thanh replied that Do Muoi, no spring chicken himself then at seventy-eight, was still working for the Party and he was only doing the same.

Throughout the conversation the main concern of both Do Muoi and Dao Duy Tung was that Thanh had openly discussed the Party's past. 'You made this letter public rather than meeting with me quietly,' Muoi said. 'What if the United Nations obtained this letter and used it to accuse us of violating human rights. It would cause a lot of damage.'

Muoi complained that the cases of the Revisionists had been reviewed twice by the Central Committee, which still accepted that they had been correctly handled and that they were guilty of political crimes. When challenged by Thanh's confession that he was part of the whole fabrication of evidence that had led to this injustice and that he was now fighting for redress 'on behalf of my conscience as the responsibility of a Party member before the Party and the people', Muoi could only come up with this response: 'You're saying that I have less of a conscience and less responsibility than you. I was also imprisoned like these other comrades; I quite understand them. However the main point is that the Politburo is so busy, especially with the Eighth Congress coming up and many other priorities and we have no time to review this issue.'

If Thanh's memory of this conversation is correct, it shows that Muoi recognised both that Vietnam has a case to answer on human rights issues and that the jailing of those purged is comparable to his own five years incarcerated in the Hoa Lo prison in Hanoi under the French. For Vietnamese leaders, time in French jails has always been a mark of bravery, even a necessary credential to win a powerful position. Certainly no Vietnamese leader would ever publicly acknowledge that dissidents in their jails have suffered as much as they did under the French.

Muoi's attempt to project a tolerant and reasonable attitude was belied by his actions. Dao Duy Tung admitted in his conversation with Thanh that it was Do Muoi who had ordered the confiscation of the letter. Later Thanh was expelled from the Party and held under close surveillance. Le Hong Ha, a former colleague in the Party security apparatus who had joined in his campaign to clear the names of those purged, was jailed in August 1996 for two years on trumped-up charges of circulating classified documents.

By speaking out and accepting responsibility for the past, Thanh and Ha had broken two key rules of political life in Vietnam. Under the principle of democratic centralism, debate or dissension is only allowed, in theory, before a decision is made. Once the hierarchy has reached agreement, the decision is final and must be obeyed. Leadership in Vietnam is supposed to be collective, as is responsibility, which serves as an excellent way for everyone to avoid blame for mistakes. While the Party will occasionally loosely acknowledge some 'errors', it favours the use of a grammatical construction that should be known as the 'passive exonerative' tense. 'Mistakes were made,' Do Muoi told a parade to mark the twentieth anniversary of the fall of Saigon, without acknowledging the Party's role, yet alone his own personal responsibility, in the subjugation of the South after 1975. The crowd, unsurprisingly, did not roar its approval at this less than forthright appraisal of policies that had led to the incarceration of hundreds of thousands of people and sent more than one million fleeing abroad.

The Party has often found disingenuous ways of pinning the blame for its failed policies on someone else. Land reform and the cultural purges of the 1950s were caused by the cold winds of Maoism blowing down from the north. Over-reliance on Soviet advice led to the economic collapse and repression that followed reunification, according to many Vietnamese officials, who offer this up in a conspiratorial whisper as if it were a radical revelation. Blaming outsiders serves to put Vietnam and the Party in the position of victims whose only mistakes have been to put their faith in perfidious foreigners.

Whenever the Vietnamese wanted to ignore their patrons in Moscow or Beijing, they did just that, always aware that their brand of triangular diplomacy after the Sino-Soviet split in 1960 meant that neither side could express too much irritation. While Hanoi occasionally portrayed itself as a weak client in these relationships, its patrons often had to suppress their rage at this upstart who refused to swallow all the guidance offered by Beijing or Moscow. Russian diplomats today scoff at the suggestion that they ever had much ideological control in Vietnam. The Chinese made their position clear by invading Vietnam in 1979 to 'teach it a lesson', a phrase that hardly suggests a history of passive compliance from Hanoi.

The Party cannot afford to have its legitimacy sag under the weight of demands that it deal with its history, demands that are increasingly coming from people who were among its core supporters. For years it relied on its victory in war to sustain the idea that only it could rule. Now it offers up the argument that only it can provide the stability and policies needed for rapid economic growth, a highly questionable assertion given its past performance. This shift of the basis of legitimacy has left the Party uncertain about how to deal with criticisms. Party members can raise issues in the correct fora, but the organisation will not tolerate any public appeal or challenge. Most of the prominent critics of the Party started off inside the system, but found it unresponsive to their demands. Eventually they stepped outside the secretive world and expressed themselves openly. Most were immediately stripped of Party membership and many have been jailed. Statements that might have been tolerated within the close confines of the super-family of the Party became criminal acts when spoken outside.

By the late 1980s, the General Secretary Nguyen Van Linh was encouraging a measure of open discussion among Party members. Linh, who during the war had used his vast political skills to forge pacts with hostile religious groups, knew the value of co-opting enemies. The country was in a state of economic crisis, the Party's legitimacy had been eroded by corruption and a series of disastrous policy decisions. Linh appeared sympathetic to Party members who wanted to see a shedding of ideological baggage and concerted steps to alleviate the country's crisis. One way to force change through a moribund bureaucracy was to open up debate and tolerate greater criticisms of the Party, channelling the bitterness of the previous decade to clear away many of the most corrupt and incompetent officials.

Among the first to take advantage of this were a group of veterans of the Viet Cong, many of them in senior positions in the hierarchy in Ho Chi Minh City, who banded together in the Club of Former Resistance Fighters in 1987. Their unofficial leader was Nguyen Ho, one of the longest-serving revolutionaries in the Party who had held important posts in Ho Chi Minh City and the labour movement. Ho started out running what was supposed to be a charitable group, but which emerged as a form of loyal opposition and a focus of dissent.

The Club declared it would encourage 'a broadening of the patriotic tradition in Vietnam' and the 'building of socialism'. Despite this apparently unthreatening agenda, the government refused the group permission to form an official association and allowed it only to become a club – a status that would give it fewer rights in the important hierarchy of Vietnamese organisations.

Many members were motivated by anger at the degradation of the Party that followed victory in 1975. They had fought for decades against the French and later to reunify a country, but they had not expected to end up mired in poverty and led by corrupt ideologues, or to see their country slip backwards as the rest of the region moved forward to prosperity and international respect. Those in the South were also less committed to the centralised socialism that was handed down from Hanoi and deeply resented the lack of trust shown by the leadership.

There were perpetual political tensions as local leaders in the South tried to resist the implementation of socialist policies by allowing markets and some measure of free enterprise. The sight of the North Vietnamese behaving like a conquering army still arouses anger. After their victory they stripped South Vietnamese bases of their American equipment and shipped it north, took over the luxurious villas of those who had fled Saigon and issued edicts with no sensitivity to the different attitudes of the South. Many former Viet Cong and Party members in the South, among them the 'Winter Cadres' who had narrowly escaped eradication under South Vietnamese President Ngo Dinh Diem, felt that they had borne much of the brunt of the war and now faced all the burdens of peace.

The Club soon justified the Party's suspicion that it would not stick simply to good works. A petition signed by more than a hundred of the great and good from Ho Chi Minh City was sent to Hanoi demanding changes in the political system. The Club then published a clandestine journal called *The Resistance Tradition*. The first copies were seized by the police, but two further editions were printed by compliant local governments in provinces outside Ho Chi Minh City. The journal offered up a few pieces of unwelcome advice for the Party by urging elderly and incompetent cadres to resign. Positions should be allocated on the basis of ability, not time served in the Party. A choice of candidates should be given for the post of Chairman of the Council of Ministers, the equivalent then of Premier, and voting should be by secret ballot. The Club managed only three editions of the journal before the administration moved in and closed it down.

An axiom of Vietnamese Communism has always been to incorporate or destroy any organisation that might speed up the development of a civil society outside Party control. Panic was rising as Communist parties collapsed in Eastern Europe and when it became clear that the Club would only become increasingly outspoken, the Party closed it down. Many of its members were denounced as spies and counter-revolutionaries. An official Veterans' Association was set up to deal with the concerns of eight million former soldiers and to stop the coagulation of any more groups like the Club.

Nguyen Ho went almost immediately from being a Party elder statesmen to becoming an outcast. An outspoken man with a powerful charisma even in his eighties, Ho had begun a career of insurrection as a labour organiser at a French navy shipyard and was jailed in 1940 on Poulo Condore, the beautiful tropical island 250 kilometres from the coast, also known as Con Dao, that housed a notorious penal colony. Ho spent five years on the island, graduating from what the Communists came to regard as a 'university' for many Southern revolutionaries including Le Duan and Nguyen Van Linh.

After his release from Poulo Condore, he returned to Saigon and the stealthy campaign of violence and political insurrection against first the French and then the government of South Vietnamese President Ngo Dinh Diem. Ho's entire life had been marked by these conflicts. His brother had been killed in an American bombing raid and his wife beaten to death by South Vietnamese police during the Tet Offensive in 1968. Ho stepped down from his posts in the Ho Chi Minh City hierarchy in 1987 although he was reluctant to go quietly into retirement.

In disgust at the closure of the Club in 1989, Ho left the Party and began a self-imposed internal exile, living in a farmer's shack about sixty kilometres outside Ho Chi Minh City in what was a typical gesture by this emotional figure. He was soon visited by the then Deputy Premier, Vo Van Kiet, who rose up through the ranks of the Ho Chi Minh City Party ultimately to become Prime Minister in 1991.

Kiet arrived with a dish of salted turtle meat, apparently the premier's favourite food. He talked with Ho about how Vietnam could match the economic successes of its Asian neighbours, even admitting that he believed that more democratic institutions were needed for Vietnam to advance. Kiet promised Ho that he would be protected if he returned to the city and did not cause any problems. But Ho fully expected to be arrested and remained outside the city. The pair talked all morning while walking around the small house where Ho was living. Not long after the meeting Ho was arrested.

Ho was out collecting edible greens from the shallow water of a nearby river when a police launch pulled alongside his small boat. He was taken back to Ho Chi Minh City while a nervous young policeman held him at gunpoint. From then on, the Party excommunicated Ho, subjecting him to arrest and harassment. He was repeatedly questioned and asked to write self-criticisms, a vindictive practice aimed at trapping people into confessions of guilt. 'Usually self-criticisms are only carried out within the Party. However my case was different. They had pointed guns at me, put me in jail and later placed me under house arrest. They went beyond the line and no longer considered me an insider. Rather, I was considered an enemy of the Party,' he wrote.

Ho was masterfully aware of how to use the Party's vocabulary of past persecution against it. Many of his writings focus on his imprisonment and periods under house arrest, echoing the long tradition in Vietnam of glorifying suffering in prisons as a badge of revolutionary honour. Prison literature, particularly Ho Chi Minh's own *Prison Diary*, are central to the Party's image of itself and a vital part of staking a claim on leadership. The American historian David Marr compared the experience of French colonial prisons to China's Long March, as the central act of Communist heroism and endurance that established their legitimacy. In 1993, after spending three years under house arrest, Ho followed this tradition by releasing an autobiography that detailed his own incarceration in much the same tone the old revolutionaries had used for their prison memoirs.

While under arrest Ho latched on to the legal system for hope, but in Vietnam it offers none. 'At the time of my arrest, no warrants were issued from the People's Court of Investigation or any other court. Moreover, after two years of house arrest, my case has not yet entered the courtroom. This clearly shows the constitution and laws are not respected in Vietnam,' he wrote. 'The Resistance Club was suppressed, and I, like many other comrades have been arrested for involvement in the Club. We experienced the iron manacles of the Vietnam Communist Party, which are no different from the iron manacles of imperialism. We were imprisoned and isolated and became completely captive and separated from the world.'

Ho was to languish under house arrest for years and was denied access to proper medical care for a serious heart condition. Friends and family slipped his writings out and he talked to Vietnamese-language radio stations in France and the United States, where the recanting communist was treated like a elder statesman. In one interview, his voice throbbing with emotion, he pledged 'to involve myself in a struggle until my last breath for democracy, freedom and pluralism'. Ho placed the security services in a quandary by threatening suicide if they tried to arrest him. 'The Southern regime killed my wife under the eyes of my children and grandchildren who will also witness the Vietnamese Communist Party kill their father and grandfather in the house of a veteran hero and a retired and ageing cadre.'

Ho remained under house arrest but was easy enough for the authorities to control. His grandiloquent style and his old age put off many potential supporters. Ho's constituency in the south was also not that large and lay mostly among elderly officials or disaffected former Viet Cong who had been sidelined by northerners.

Greater efforts to ease the problems faced by veterans, including the hundreds of thousands then being demobbed after serving in Cambodia, and a closer watch on old soldiers through the new official association blocked the emergence of more groups like the Club of Former Resistance Fighters.

All Vietnamese dissidents have found themselves victims of campaigns to discredit them, both in Vietnam and among the overseas community. At home they are normally dismissed as tools of foreigners, traitors who have sold out to the Central Intelligence Agency or been co-opted by dark forces aiming to overthrow Communism. Writers have been denounced for the mere fact of being published overseas, a process that can turn a book showered with awards at home into 'a poisonous cultural product'. No diatribe is too mean-spirited or petty for the official press. When Human Rights Watch honoured Nguyen Ho with a Hammett-Hellman Award granted to jailed writers, there was a spate of snide articles expressing astonishment that he could be considered a writer on the basis of some samizdat publications. Those who are tried are accused of being common criminals and are denied special treatment in jail, a privilege that even the French gave its political prisoners in Vietnam.

Few people who have spoken out against the regime have faced such a barrage of abuse as Colonel Bui Tin. A senior military officer, a high-ranking Party member, trusted propagandist as deputy editor of the Party daily *Nhan Dan* and 'barbarian handler', Tin came from a milieu where he was both able to form pertinent criticisms of the Party and knew how to express them. Tin was well known as the officer who had accepted the surrender of the South Vietnamese government in 1975. He had been the public, reasonable face of Vietnam for outsiders and his journalism was widely read at home. But to reach the widest audience for his message of reform he was obliged to leave Vietnam, a painful personal decision and one that has left him vulnerable to the age-old Vietnamese suspicion of those who cavort with foreigners.

Bui Tin's ebullient manner and cheerful patter cannot disguise the hardships of exile. He lives alone in a tiny two-room apartment in La Courneuve, a Communist-run area of municipal decay in the northern suburbs of Paris that is cut through with rail lines and motorways. 'They say in Hanoi that I live in a chateau paid for by the CIA,' he said. The reality is a cramped, sparsely furnished room where he heats his meals in a small microwave oven. He supports himself by writing and speaking at conferences. The physical discomforts of his life clearly don't bother him, but his bright face occasionally shows the sadness of being parted from his wife, daughter and grandchildren who remain in Hanoi. When he left in 1990, he thought he would be gone for a few months, long enough to attend a conference organised by the French Communist newspaper *L'Humanité* and to have a heart operation in Paris. Before his departure he had already resolved to issue a petition and knew that he would face problems. Six years later he was still optimistic about being able to return 'in two years as it is probably too dangerous now'. The tone of attacks emanating from Hanoi suggests that he will have to endure a much longer separation from his family.

In December 1990, tens of thousands of people across the country sat around radios and listened to Bui Tin on the British Broadcasting Corporation's Vietnamese language service laying out his criticisms of a system that he had spent his life supporting. Communism's demise in Eastern Europe charged his words with additional importance. Normally only televised football internationals clear the streets in Vietnamese cities, but Tin's interviews, broadcast in short segments over two months, caused most activity to cease as his words came over crackling short-wave radios. What Tin had to say was hardly news to anyone who lived under Vietnamese Communism, but to hear the words spoken by a top official, and one with close and well known family connections to Ho Chi Minh, was exhilarating. After carefully establishing his credentials as a senior Party figure, Tin then laid into the security apparatus, the press and the Party, particularly its cruel and arbitrary Organisation Department. His complaints were direct and focused compared with the nebulous ideas and drifting rhetoric that are the norm in Hanoi.

The Party was corrupt and directionless, guided by mindless bureaucrats, he said. It had co-opted the ideas of Ho Chi Minh in a rigid, dogmatic manner. Instead of seeing Ho Chi Minh's 'flexibility, dedication and integrity', they had tried to turn his ideas into 'sacred pronouncements' with no reference to the real situation in the country. The interviews picked apart the shibboleths of Vietnamese politics and called for a 'calm, scientific and convincing discussion' of democracy. The people wanted the Party to renew itself but real democracy would only be possible if there was a legal opposition, he said. Vietnam needed to avoid the chaos and anarchy that had been seen in Eastern Europe, but he attacked the Party's oft-repeated theme that its policies could be justified in the name of stability. This idea, he said, had been the cause of some of the worst abuses of the past. 'Stability does not mean the preservation of the status quo, the maintenance of prolonged inactivity, stagnation and sluggishness, as this is even more dangerous.' The fear in the leadership and its undue obsession with stability had led to a massive exaggeration of the dangers of subversion from outside and within the country. 'For this reason there are still unnecessary arrests, deportations and confinements of some people, even religious leaders. This has created a tense situation and an unfavourable and unattractive image of Vietnam abroad.'

Bui Tin's ideas, like those of Nguyen Ho and Hoang Minh Chinh, were tempered by a deep knowledge of the reluctance of Vietnamese to see rapid, unsettling change. Far from calling for the overthrow of the Party, he urged it to reform, to select a brighter, younger generation of leaders. The Party should thin its ranks, abandon its control of supposedly elected bodies such as the National Assembly and introduce real debate. The top leadership should not be swept aside completely, but should bring in people with a flexible mindset. He openly appealed to General Vo Nguyen Giap to take over. The hero of Dien Bien Phu, still in the political wilderness at the time, was 'a man who enjoys prestige at home and abroad, has the virtue of integrity and also commands a relatively vast knowledge . . . I hope that, with his new thinking, the general may steer the ship of state safely through the storm'.

Reaction in Hanoi was one of incredulity that such a senior figure had committed such a profound violation of the rules and had used a radio station that the authorities loathed. Vuong Tinh, director of the external relations department at the Ministry of Culture and Information, gave the first response to a foreign journalist. 'It is our wish that Tin returns to Vietnam and expresses his views here, since putting forth his views abroad may cause misunderstandings.' After attempts to lure him back failed, the denunciations flew, particularly from journalists who had worked alongside Tin. He was denounced as a reactionary and traitor who had blackened the history of the Party. Senior officials disparaged his high Mandarin family background and his upbringing by 'imperialist elements', showing that the Party had done little to update its invective since its spasms of Maoist class war. He was sacked from his job at *Nhan Dan* and stripped of Party membership, but only after considerable debate and resistance from some quarters. Tin was unfazed and gleefully pointed out in his memoir that attacks against him merely drew more attention to his ideas and broadcasts.

They were able to hurt him, however, through his family. The police repeatedly summoned his wife to report any contact with her husband and kept her under constant surveillance. She refused to co-operate and told her husband that many people had offered their moral and financial support. Tin's daughter, a surgeon at the eye clinic in Hanoi, was demoted and made to work in a hospital shop selling spectacles. After Tin complained in letters to the Minister of Interior, she was reinstated. Her husband was refused permission to take up a scholarship to study in the United States. His son had earlier fled the country on a boat and was granted asylum in Canada. Years later the family were still under suspicion, unable to leave Vietnam to visit Tin in Paris. Tin's wife, a retired teacher, remained defiant, berating security agents who harassed her for behaving 'like the French before independence'.

The reaction of the overseas Vietnamese to Tin's statements disappointed him. Although he had supporters who have provided him with help in exile, he has been viewed with deep suspicion as someone who spent too much time in the system to be able to repent. His comments that Viet Kieu, those Vietnamese living overseas, still harboured extremist views that hurt chances for reconciliation did not endear him to this tough audience of people he had once fought against. In Orange County, California – the largest community of Vietnamese outside the country – those who met him refused to be named in newspaper articles for fear of retribution from others offended by the appearance of the man who had orchestrated the final moments of South Vietnam's history in

1975. 'He is guilty of many heavy crimes against the homeland and he still dares to show his face in the Vietnamese community here,' said Hung Le, head of a local association, in the *Los Angeles Times*. 'If we had a court of citizens we should try him.'

The Vietnamese communities in the United States, France and Australia are divided into a stunning array of political factions that defy any attempt to unite them. Most have formed around personalities or religious groups rather than politics, but the most vocal are the hardline anti-Communists. For these groups, Tin's attacks on Hanoi did not go nearly far enough. Some believed Tin had been authorised to leave the country and make his criticisms as a way of relieving tensions at home and to sow divisions among the Viet Kieu. The idea was that he would provide some catharsis for the past without the Party having to admit its errors. It has startled Tin that he is regarded in this manner, particularly given the attacks on him at home and the high price his family has paid. It is inconceivable that the Party would authorise someone to make such deep criticisms, to publicise its most grotesque actions and ideas in the way that Tin has.

Like so many exiles, Bui Tin has faded somewhat from real political relevance. Many in Hanoi see him as an opportunist, someone who mistakenly felt the political winds were shifting in Vietnam and tried to switch sides. He was criticised for leaving and not working within the system for change. At this he protests that he had been working for years to push reforms forward. He had submitted manifestos, written critical articles and argued with many top figures in private. In 1986 in the midst of economic chaos and just ahead of the Sixth Party Congress that launched reforms, Tin and other army officers pleaded with Giap to take over, to use his credibility and popularity to push through reforms. Giap refused, saying that he could not act alone and was fearful of the possible repercussions if his attempt to win power failed.

Tin is now openly bitter about his former mentor, whom he once saw as the heir to Ho Chi Minh and the only man who could have saved Vietnam during the long years of Le Duan's rule. Rather than making him out in his normal guise as a dashing hero, Tin now sees Giap as politically timid, afraid to rescue fellow officers who were persecuted, and unwilling to use his position to help Vietnam. Tin believed that a 'cruel system had destroyed the integrity of a military genius' and became increasingly bitter in his attacks on Giap. In a letter written to Giap in 1995 asking him to intercede in the trial of Hoang Minh Chinh, Tin bluntly reminded him of an old Vietnamese saying that the 'honour of a general is built on the corpses of ten thousand soldiers'.

In his book, *Following Ho Chi Minh*, originally published in Vietnamese in two volumes, Tin showed that many of his positions had hardened since his initial manifesto and the BBC broadcasts. The book presents an unvarnished view of Vietnamese history and even of Ho Chi Minh. None of the revelations put Ho in anything like the same bestial league as Mao, but Tin does accuse him of emulating Stalin by building up his own personality cult. The gentle consensus politics that the Vietnamese present as their system of government Tin reveals as occasionally gladiatorial in its brutality. Like many memoirs, the book is enormously self-serving and is a heavily romanticised account of Tin's life, but it does offer up an unusually forthright view of Vietnamese politics. Tin, however, gives no prescription for political change, beyond saying that discussion and honesty would be a good place to start.

Tin still has some respect in Vietnam. Officials on visits to Paris often slip off to see him and take letters back and forth to his family. The Vietnamese ambassador in Paris would take his calls, although they avoided discussing politics. His book is banned and copies sent in by mail are confiscated, but photocopies and tapes of his BBC interviews are eagerly consumed by many officials, even apparently Vo Van Kiet. A picture of Tin's father, Bui Bang Doan – a former minister in the Imperial Government who also served under Ho Chi Minh – was published in the minutes of a session of the National Assembly in 1996. It was taken as an oblique signal of the support Tin still had in certain circles.

Tin's political impact has, however, been diminished by his exile and the fact that the dynamics of Vietnamese society work against groups forming around dissidents. Political change mostly appeals to a small group of intellectuals frustrated by the restrictions targeted on them and alienated by the repression of critics of the Party who try to change the system from within. The population is far from inert, in fact Vietnam seethes with an uncontrollable subversion as people wilfully ignore the authorities. But that energy is translated into corruption, crime and foot-dragging, or by evading any contact with the authorities. Pervasive mistrust of the government and officials is channelled into simple deceptions that might enrich the individual but do not pose an immediate threat to the political system.

The Party professes to be unhappy at this political torpor, but indifference and the moral uncertainty of people who have been forced to accept the system saves it from more intense criticism. The middle class is too small to form a political bloc to demand more say in the way the country is run. Political dissent is proving fairly easy to control as the number of people involved is tiny and their ideas have been easy to isolate from a mostly indifferent or fearful population.

Separation has been the main punishment applied by the Vietnamese – in its most extreme form in the re-education and prison camps that cover the country, or through the forced relocation of hundreds of thousands of people to new economic zones after the war. Since the dramatic purges of the 1950s and the 1960s, most people who cause trouble have been moved aside in a quiet, careful manner to avoid stirring up too much resentment. Political figures were retired or shuffled off to stagnate in bureaucratic backwaters. Others, like Nguyen Ho, were placed under house arrest, cut off from most contacts with the outside world. Excommunication meant removal from arenas in which they could put up a fight or challenge the Party. The Party tolerates criticism at its secretive meetings and in the circulation of highly confidential documents, but those who step outside those boundaries in the hope of appealing to a larger audience are dealt with swiftly.

Part of the maintenance of unity is the strict application of Party discipline on middle-rung officials. If they step out of line, they must be punished. The cultural roots of this attitude go deeper than Marxism. In Vietnamese families, problems must be solved within the group and without any outside help. To discuss problems outside the confines of the group is a serious breach of traditional ethics that give the Party considerable moral weight when it attacks dissidents for this transgression. Form is more important than substance in discussion, a legacy now not just of Marxism with its limited vocabulary and reduction of the complexities of life to historical simplifications, but also of Neo-Confucianism, an ideology that tolerates little behaviour outside the boundaries of established rituals.

A general rejection of personality cults – except the closely controlled cult around Ho Chi Minh – makes it difficult for a charismatic figure to emerge in opposition to the Party. Anyone presenting themselves as a potential leader would have to challenge or co-opt the primacy of Ho Chi Minh as a political totem. A rival would also have to skim off the potent political elixir of nationalism from the homogenised soup of Party rule, cultural identity and victory at war, that the current leadership use to gain legitimacy. There have been no dynastic politics either because that would violate the image of collective leadership, which itself lends an aura of reasonableness and competence to the Party. To suggest that the Party was less than infallible in the past opens the door to public questions about the omniscience of the current leadership. The fear of those questions makes it almost impossible for them to deal with the errors of the past.

Much of the dissent that arose in the late 1980s and early 1990s had an impact initially because it was phrased in the vocabulary of Marxism. Few have ever dared to challenge socialism as a whole, but instead have challenged its form. They have never declared that Communism must inevitably lead to the monolithic authoritarian structures, but have merely regretted the direction of socialism in Vietnam, often harking back to a more idealistic time that almost certainly never existed. But their opinions were feared precisely because they were comprehensible and appealing, particularly to a younger generation of Party members. They did not talk of an immediate leap to some 'foreign' form of democracy and could not easily be dismissed when they reflected views that were widespread within the system.

The people who emerged as the public critics were the most vocal of a large group inside the Party who felt the need for change. As in Eastern Europe, many have resisted the notion of being dissidents, it marks them out too easily. Many of those labelled dissidents around the world have disliked the term because it suggested they were something of a protected species, a group of special people who were allowed to speak out, perhaps to release some pressures or to offer proof of the regime's generosity. The label also tends to suggest that only a small group of intellectuals are unhappy, and that the politically passive population were all content. By pushing critics into the margins of society, governments are able to deny them their status as normal people with everyday concerns who have said publicly what most others only dare to say in their homes.

Critics of the Vietnamese government have received little attention from the outside world. While human rights organisations have followed their cases, they have not been able to win the international support extended to Burma's Aung Sang Suu Kyi or the Chinese dissident Wei Jingsheng. Some of the overseas Vietnamese community have tried to bring them into their causes, even though most dissidents are wary of too close an association of groups that are easily discredited by Hanoi. Even though many overseas Vietnamese have been active in supporting political change, the government has been able to use them as a way to counter any dissent. Their absence from Vietnam has helped the Party immeasurably by ensuring that two million of its potential critics were overseas and mostly too busy arguing amongst themselves to present much threat at home. At the same time, a very small number of extremists provide the Party with a handy justification for maintaining a massive security apparatus and rousing people with the threat of instability.

Just as the more prominent figures have been unable to rouse grassroots support at home because of their isolation, they have been unable to maintain much interest overseas. The residual sympathy for Vietnam and its long history of suffering at the hands of the West, has made it difficult to criticise Hanoi. It is usual for diplomats to seek some contact with those in opposition to a government, but in Hanoi they remain aloof from any critics of the Party. The United States, Australia and the Scandinavian countries have tried to keep human rights on the agenda but without much success. Informed of another arrest or trial, diplomats from other countries would scowl and hurry off, wishing they had not been told. The rationale for their timid response, disguised by the phrase 'quiet diplomacy', was neatly expressed by a European ambassador: 'We don't talk about human rights because we don't want to upset the foreign minister.'

The emergence of dissent paralleled other changes in society. Those who had been purged in the 1960s were old and fearless, they no longer cared what might happen to them. Their children were grown and some had left the country. Market reforms had given people considerable independence from the state. People were no longer trapped by their reliance on the bureaucracy for ration books, medical care or housing. For the first time in forty years in Hanoi it was possible to live life with only minimal contact with a system that had once been able to use its management of every aspect of a daily routine as a very strong deterrent to speaking out.

Chinh, Nguyen Ho and Tin have been neutralised. But the Party only compounds its problems by punishing those who raised embarrassments from the past or challenged its direction in the future. By doing this it ensured that ideological battles and personal grudges that would otherwise be long forgotten have re-emerged as the focus for dissent.

8

Industrial Chickens

Rob by night and you're a bandit, rob by day and you're a mandarin.

VIETNAMESE SAYING

When Pham Huy Phuoc took the stand in the People's Court in Ho Chi Minh City, a nervous tapping of fingers echoed through the dingy offices where Vietnam's rulers wield their power. 'How far would he go?' they asked as the muddy waters of scandal crept higher, lapping closer to their doors. Swinging between bouts of venom and weepy self-pity, Phuoc unburdened himself in an incriminating stream. In Hanoi and Ho Chi Minh City they sat and waited. These cadres, who had wallowed in his largesse, who had shared the brandy and the women, who had found layers of hundred-dollar bills tucked between their sheets in five-star hotel rooms, braced themselves as Phuoc sang and wept and pleaded for his life.

Le Van Thi, a former deputy mayor of Ho Chi Minh City, was called to court where she indignantly denied allegations that she had received $11,000 in 'travel expenses' during a trip to Tokyo. She was also said to have received a car from Phuoc. Thi was a low-roller in Phuoc's world, a middle-rung bureaucrat who could be bought off cheaply with some pin money and a Japanese sedan. This was, after all, a man who gambled away hundreds of thousands of dollars in a single evening in Macau. Even his girlfriend did better than Thi. Vu Thi Hien got a car and a $200,000 villa. Phuoc's billfold was legendary in the karaoke bars and those restaurants in Saigon where the cognac comes in crystal bottles inside satin and leather cases. The drinks tab was nothing against his

losses at the Vy-Club, a gambling den where Phuoc's pals took him
for fleets of cars and thousands of dollars. He was reputed to carry
$50,000 in cash on his business trips to Hanoi. With a wiseguy flour-
ish, he would peel off 10 years' wages for some low-level pen
pusher who got in his way.

Despite the flamboyance, Phuoc's world was one of obsessive
secrecy in which nobody broke the inviolable code of silence. Deals
were done between people who had forged their bonds in prison
cells decades earlier. These were people who could trust each other.
You knew these people. You kept your friends and family by your
side. They ran the front companies, cooked the books, hid the
money from your bosses, hid the money from yourself. When
Phuoc's day of reckoning came, he didn't even know where the
money had gone.

They caught up with him eventually. Or did he catch up with
them? Phuoc's trial would blow open their business dealings,
undermine their feared image, threaten their leaders. It would
undercut them just as they were feeling the heat. But they had to
take him down, even if it meant sacrificing one of their own. Phuoc
had done good work for them but now he was expendable. The
Communist Party of Vietnam no longer needed him.

Many Vietnamese were incredulous when Phuoc's trial began in
January 1997. Very few corruption cases were ever brought to court,
particularly those cases involving senior officials of the Communist
Party. One newspaper produced a cynical lexicon of legal phrases
for corruption that reflected the widespread scepticism that the government was ready to deal with the problem. The report listed a
number of different offences: if you were a peasant and stole 5,000
dong (about fifty cents), you would be charged with 'gross violations of socialist property' and sentenced to a long spell in jail. If
you were a middle rung official and stole 500,000 dong you would
be charged with corruption and fined. If you were a senior official
and Party member who stole 5 billion dong, you would be charged
with minor violations of administrative procedures and would only
face an internal disciplinary enquiry.

The sense of public disbelief heightened when the prosecution
team appeared to be genuinely interested in uncovering the true
extent of the tangled financial web that Phuoc had left behind.

Tamexco, the Party-owned company he managed, collapsed in 1994 with debts of $40 million. The trial of Phuoc and another nineteen defendants had revealed 'just the tip of the iceberg', according to a prosecutor, who puffed himself up with lawyerly indignation and warned that those involved in Tamexco could run, but they could never hide.

Phuoc was charged with 'violating socialist property' and 'contravening regulations on state economic management', dry words to describe his lurid spree from 1989 when Ho Chi Minh City's Communist Party cell set up Tamexco to benefit from the lucrative trade in fertiliser and cars. Phuoc positioned himself close to the centres of power so that the company could win valuable licenses to import goods. Phuoc had ambitions beyond the import-export business. He bought land earmarked for agricultural use but had it illegally reclassified for housing or for use by foreign investors, sending its nominal value skywards. The land was used to raise loans from compliant bankers, who were paid off if they thought to question the real value of the collateral. While a Vietnam State Bank deputy governor was in the bathroom of his hotel suite in Jakarta, Phuoc hurriedly lined his bed with $8,000 in crisp green paper.

As the damaging revelations poured out at his trial, Phuoc realised he was sunk and started to beg. He had three daughters and an elderly mother who was sick. He urged the court to spare him for their sake. He said it had all been his responsibility, he should take all the blame and the others should be spared. His pleas did not make any difference. The prosecutors had asked that he be sentenced to death and the judge followed their recommendation. Three others were sentenced to death. Prison terms for the others, including Phuoc's brother, sister and girlfriend, ranged from life to three years suspended. A crowd of 2,000 gathered outside the court house in Ho Chi Minh City to hear the verdicts, savouring the death sentences that added to the festive mood of the approaching *Tet* holidays.

A few years earlier Phuoc might have got off with a light sentence or might even have gone free. After all, he had not done anything that hundreds of other managers of state companies hadn't done. Bribing officials, shuffling assets, defaulting on state bank loans, giving contracts to companies run by family members – all these were standard practices in the state sector.

Phuoc and two others were executed by firing squad on 7 January 1998. A fourth man had his sentence commuted to life in prison as his family had contributed to the Communist victory. They were woken that day and read the final decision that they would be executed. After being offered a final meal of chicken and steamed buns. At 7.00 a.m. they were taken, blindfolded and gagged, to a field outside the city where a crowd had gathered hours earlier. A woman called out Phuoc's name and he gave a garbled response through the gag. After the firing squad had done its work, the commanding officer fired bullets from a revolver into their heads to make sure the job was done.

Phuoc's mistake was that he was a little too crooked. Like some virulent disease, he burned through his host too quickly, killing it off far too fast where a more successful parasite might have kept the animal alive longer. He also fell victim to bad timing. The mood was changing. Members of the National Assembly were asking when the government was going to stop talking and start acting against corruption, a problem that had become 'a national disaster' in the words of Prime Minister Vo Van Kiet. Pham The Duyet, former head of the Hanoi Party committee, berated cadres at a meeting, saying that one in five of the city's party officials had been disciplined for corruption. Statements like these raised the question of whether anyone in the government was clean.

An incident in 1996 probably provided something of an answer. Fire fighters were called to put out a blaze at a villa in Ho Chi Minh City. They quickly dealt with the fire and then helped themselves to some bottles of whiskey and wine from a liquor cabinet. Searching through the blackened wreckage of the house, a fireman found a safe. Inside were 47 taels of gold worth about $24,000. The firemen decided to help themselves. It didn't take long for the police to track down the larcenous firemen who had taken their haul off to a nearby building to share it out. The gold was quickly returned to its somewhat embarrassed owner – Nguyen Ky Cam, the head of the Anti-Corruption and Smuggling Committee, who held ministerial rank in the government.

Press reports on the incident never asked the question of how

Cam came to have such a large amount of gold in his house while subsisting on a modest government salary of around $100 a month. Instead the figure of $24,000 was allowed to hang in the air. Cam spent a few months twisting in the wind before being sacked in a cabinet reshuffle.

Nothing much comes as a surprise. The anti-corruption chief was sacked for corruption, the deputy head of the national drug squad was caught smuggling heroin. The head of the People's Inspectorate, a body that is supposed to monitor government performance, was sacked for being involved in what a senior official discretely called 'a business wrongdoing'. Health ministry officials stole donated contraceptives and sold them in Russia. Top officials in the foreign ministry enriched themselves by using the diplomatic bag to smuggle with impunity. The list of corrupt officials seems depressingly endless.

There is little that remains untouched by the blight. If you are sick, you have to pay extra for even the most basic medical treatment whether or not you are covered by government insurance. If you want your children to pass their exams you have to pay teachers for 'private tuition'. If you want to move house, change jobs or leave the country, you'll have to pay someone.

No business, from billion-dollar foreign joint ventures down to pavement soup stalls, can evade the grasping hands of bureaucrats or the police. Vietnam's economic boom of the early 1990s meant the opportunities and stakes were growing every day. Unfortunately so was the epidemic of corruption. The Political and Economic Risk Consultancy, a firm in Hong Kong that issues annual rankings for corruption among Asian nations, put Vietnam in at number one on the list in the first year it was considered, honouring it with the Imelda Marcos Golden Shoes Award for grand larceny.

The optimism of the early 1990s was such that investors were prepared to ignore much of what was going on. Vietnam was virgin territory but located at the heart of Asia; its cheap labour force, raw materials and large market were enticing. If it lacked a legal system, that was not a problem. Investors had gone into Thailand, Taiwan and Indonesia before they had got their commercial codes sorted out. Foreign investment surged to more than $20 billion in pledges in less than a decade; Vietnam had done better than Thailand

during a similar phase of development. But signing a deal and actually carrying it out were two very different things in Vietnam. The
glittering promise of Vietnam soon proved evanescent. Corruption
and red tape appeared at the top of the list of complaints among
investors. Even the Keidanren, the association of top Japanese companies whose members were no strangers to the idea of corrupt
politicians, found the level of graft in Vietnam unacceptable. By
1997, the Swiss-based World Economic Forum ranked Vietnam near
the bottom of its list of competitive economies because of problems
with corruption and the legal system.

Economic crime, from bribery and abuse of power to extortion and
smuggling, costs the government hundreds of millions of dollars in
lost revenues each year. In 1997, countries across Asia suffered an
economic meltdown that was in no small measure caused by the
corruption and lack of transparency of their governments and businesses. Connections between banks, governments and businesses
undermined any attempts at clear regulation. Banks lent without a
clear idea of risk, eventually precipitating a near economic meltdown. Beyond the economic costs, the political and social impact is
enormous. Corruption strips away the already denuded faith in
government and legal institutions. It creates an atmosphere of risk
that crushes initiative and undermines the environment in which
businesses and individuals prosper. On an individual level it leads
to terrible cases of injustice. A teacher who left the profession briefly
could not return to his maths class because he could not afford to
pay a $400 bribe to a local official to get his job back. Instead a man
who could be a cog in the vital machine of education was left ped-
dling trinkets on the beach at Nha Trang.

Some graft is accepted by the population; officials who rigidly
apply regulations are seen as unbending and cruel. People expect to
lubricate their progress through the tortuous bureaucracy with
bribes and are shocked when they cannot. Corruption is one of the
many moral confusions thrown up by reforms. Business activities
that were illegal under central planning are now officially allowed.
What might have been corrupt under the previous system is now
good business practice and vice versa. Officials who built up elaborate networks of connections to operate in a system where they

alone allocated all resources, have now had to learn to adapt to a new way of doing business. The gaping moral and legal holes in the fabric of society benefit officials who use them for personal profit. With more money sloshing around and enormous opportunities for corruption it is hard to imagine how else a bureaucracy would behave. Given the advantages the system has to the limited group of nomenclatura, there is little incentive to change it.

Some economists see corruption as a sign of robust economic activity and therefore not really a problem. Businesses are able to factor it in as a cost and as long as it is predictable, there is not too much to worry about. But part of the difficulty in Vietnam is that corruption has not yet become a routine form of taxation on businesses and individuals. The country's bureaucratic structure allows for many gatekeepers, all of whom must be paid off as each can block a decision or license. Officials can be bought, but they don't always stay bought. They often demand ever larger sums of money without sticking to their side of the deal. By the mid-1990s many foreign investors were muttering about how much easier it was to do business in Burma where the sleazy and vicious military junta was deeply corrupt but kept to a code of honour among thieves; bribes were paid and obstacles were lifted. In Vietnam the cash was handed over only to have new difficulties arise.

Corruption has already sparked demonstrations in Hanoi, which has seen very few street protests in the past few decades. The leadership is haunted by the student protests against corruption in Beijing in 1989 that escalated into demands for full-scale political change before they were crushed by gunfire and tanks. Nothing that dramatic has happened in Hanoi but there have been a growing number of protests by victims of official abuses. In May 1997, riots erupted in Thai Binh, south of Hanoi, over the predatory activities of local officials; members of the Politburo were sent in to cool down irate farmers. A media blackout was imposed for five months before the government acknowledged that it had a serious problem on its hands. It sacked a few of the worst offenders among the local officials but it also rounded up those involved in the protests, detaining them under a law that allowed people to be held for up to two years without trial.

Commentators in the media and government often trot out the

idea that corruption has only emerged since Vietnam began its reforms. Pinning the scourge on the introduction of market principles reflects the deep ambivalence many feel about reforms and the subsequent erosion of some government powers. Blaming the rough and tumble of the market also seems to have some resonance among a public that is sometimes nostalgic for a simpler, more egalitarian and apparently less corrupt past. But markets themselves do not create corruption. Hong Kong, Singapore and New Zealand, regularly ranked among the world's most open economies, have reputations for very clean government.

It is also hard to pin corruption on the corrosive effects of free enterprise, given that Vietnam does not yet have anything close to a market economy. The government still retains enormous powers over economic activity, requiring a license for almost all transactions, and the emerging legal structure is mostly cementing these powers in place. A little bit of reform can be a dangerous thing. It gives officials wide discretionary powers but does not create the channels or means to contest those powers. As officials see reforms taking some of the means of control away from them, they reach out for others. This means a frantic grasping for money before the opportunities disappear.

Talk of developing the rule of law has become something of a mantra among Vietnamese officials. What they mean by this, however, is different from its accepted meaning elsewhere. There is little evidence that the Communist Party is willing to tolerate an independent judiciary or a situation where laws can be used to challenge and curtail the powers of the state. There is no sign of an end to the fusion of state and Party interests or to the idea that laws are a means to codify and implement the Party's ideas.

What officials tend to mean by the rule of law is that regulations will be written down and made available to the public. Previously decisions were made secretly with no reference to any legal authority and were rarely announced. Ending these practices has the benefit of curtailing some of the discretionary powers of bureaucrats but it does not provide a situation where the individual and the government official are truly equal under the law.

The emphasis of legal reform is on creating order, not establishing due process or protecting individual rights. Rights tend to accrue to the government and not to individuals. For example, Vietnamese have a constitutional right to freedom of speech and assembly. But they are not allowed to 'abuse' this right by harming the interests of the state. What is in the interests of the state is not determined by an independent judiciary but by the government. The result is, of course, that Vietnamese actually have no right to speak their minds or to organise themselves free of government interference.

The lack of individual rights extends far beyond political activities. Businesses must obtain official permission to do almost anything. A study by an Australian lawyer found that setting up a small guesthouse in Ho Chi Minh City required the submission of forty different documents that were stamped with eighty-three official chops and signed by 107 bureaucrats from twenty-six different offices. At almost every step, officials would demand a 'fee'. Officials have almost unlimited discretion to block licenses, so either people pay bribes to get the paperwork in order, or ignore the rules and pay off inspectors. Either way, you pay.

The response to this has not been to strip officials of their powers, but often to give them more. There is a widely propagated idea that there is nothing wrong with the system that cannot be cured by weeding out a few corrupt people and punishing them as an example to others. The notion of this inculcating a higher morality in those who run the country has met with withering public scepticism, but nevertheless the government clings to this notion of a perfect mechanism undermined by a few officials who lack the necessary rectitude.

The government has constantly pushed the image of the government as a rational model of Confucian and Leninist principles even though this is undermined by everyday experience. Few Vietnamese have much sense of the operations of a legal system or of their rights and responsibilities, but they all know the value of family links and old connections from the village, school or the army. Vietnam has much more in common with other Southeast Asian countries to the degree that patron-client relationships and other ties dominate more rational Confucian systems of bureaucracy.

There have been demands from aid donors and investors that the government deal with corruption by relaxing their grip on the economy. So far, however, the government's main strategy has been to demand yet more control over the population. Control became the leitmotif of discussion at the Party Congress in 1996 as the leadership vowed to exercise its already enormous powers with more vigour and to acquire a few more means with which to force people to toe the line. Do Muoi had no doubts about how the best results might be achieved. Speaking outside the Congress he said that corrupt officials 'should be severely punished, even shot dead'.

Vo Van Kiet followed up with a more populist appeal. What Vietnam needed was more men like Judge Pao, the Prime Minister said in a newspaper interview. Judge Pao, a fearsome ninth-century crime-buster dressed in silk brocade and an elaborate hat, appeared on a popular programme on Vietnamese television in the mid-1990s. His favoured judicial response to corruption or other abuses of power was execution by beheading but in a manner that duly noted the hierarchies of the Confucian world. High-ranking officials were killed with a dragon-handled sword, lower rungs of society suffered decapitation with a blade carved with a dog's head.

Millions tuned into the Taiwan-made costume drama to watch the dread-locked judge gruffly dole out the muscular justice they craved. Nobody seemed to notice the sad irony that Vietnam could only locate a symbol of incorruptibility in a fictional television character based on a mythical Chinese hero.

Learning from the wisdom of Judge Pao, the government introduced mandatory death sentences for those caught stealing more than $27,000 from the state, and by mid-1997 at least ten people had been tried and sent to death row for economic crimes. Courts were ordered to impose tougher penalties across the board and to deal with a vast backlog of corruption cases. Very little was proposed to tackle the real structural problems that led to such widespread graft.

The response of neo-liberal economists to corruption has been to urge deregulation and the removal of powers that put officials in a position where they can extract bribes. Instituting the rule of law and reducing the intrusive power of the state can indeed cut back on the problem. In Vietnam, an end to price subsidies reduced many opportunities for corruption in the trade of consumer goods. Those areas of the economy where controls are still strong are notorious for their corrupt practices. The rice market is still heavily regulated by the state and is still distorted by corruption and smuggling.

Market economies require a legal system to enforce rules and mediate disputes. Vietnam is supposedly moving in the direction of the rule of law but as yet the legal system is completely inadequate; the country is caught in a terrible limbo between the law and central planning. Judges are notoriously poorly trained, indeed most are not actually lawyers. They do not have real powers to interpret the laws; instead they mostly avoid coming to decisions in civil cases by pressing the two sides to reach a settlement. Judges do not act in the way they do in the West; they are more like facilitators in an often tortuous negotiating process that can involve bribery, cajoling and consensus building. Judges have been known to throw in the threat of criminal prosecution to concentrate the minds of those unwilling to settle a civil suit.

Vietnamese lawyers who deal with court cases try very hard to avoid going in front of a judge. Close political connections or a briefcase full of cash are needed to win a case. What little deregulation there has been has transferred the problem from a corrupt bureaucracy to a corrupt court system. All this means is that lawyers, rather than officials, get rich. Rapid deregulation is not likely to solve many problems; it just privatises sleaze.

In 1997, the Party did tentatively announce changes that might have cracked open its hard shell of secrecy by forcing all officials to disclose their assets. The measures were half-hearted as it was unclear if they applied to family members of Party officials. It is most often the spouses and children of cadres who run businesses profiting from their family connections. Party members themselves are supposed to maintain the fiction that they cannot dirty themselves in the exploitative world of capitalism. Plans for officials to declare what they own were quietly dropped as unworkable; nobody was willing to stir up such a hornet's nest of problems.

Nguyen Thi Xuan My, who in 1996 became the first woman to enter the Politburo, had a particularly revealing suggestion on how to combat corruption. Xuan My, who headed the Control Commission, a body that disciplines Party members, gave an interview to a women's magazine in which she urged wives to turn in their corrupt husbands. Beyond this sinister attempt to return to the days when the state was placed ahead of families, Xuan My had little else to offer in the way of policy ideas, instead mouthing familiar platitudes. 'We need more than just slogans against corruption,' she intoned, coining what was for a time the latest slogan against corruption.

The bureaucratic state has proved heavily resistant to the economic, political and legal changes that Vietnam will need to carry out if it is to sustain its economic growth and lift its people out of poverty. The bureaucracy serves a very narrow base of interests. These officials are the 'industrial chickens' of Vietnamese slang; plump and atrophied battery hens doing little but feeding at the public trough.

Asia's most economically successful countries have done well by separating politics from policy-making to some degree. From Thailand to Japan, much of the complex work of running a fast-growing economy was left to a corps of highly educated technocrats who are kept insulated from the more ideological and rhetorical side of political life. This achieved some spectacular results, but politics and corruption in these countries were still powerful enough forces to contribute to the economic slump of 1997. Increasingly economists and political scientists are seeing Asia's success less in terms of a peculiar culture that fosters growth and more in terms of good policy-making by élites who have been allowed to take long-term views without being too buffeted by politics. When the policies that had created their economic success were not carried out with sufficient vigour, their economies started to go bad.

In Vietnam a technocratic class is still embryonic. There are some excellent civil servants with imaginative ideas for policies and the skills to carry them out. But being seen as politically sound still counts for much more than being expert in the higher rungs of government.

The definition of being sound has changed with the political winds, but there are some powerful symbolic forces that political leaders still harness to haul themselves up or to buttress their claims to power. Most of those at the top of the ladder are there because of their war records, time spent in colonial or South Vietnamese prisons, family connections or good works for the Party. Very few hold their jobs because of their educational qualifications; indeed very few actually have educational qualifications although the number of top officials with degrees has been rising.

In the first few years of reform, a time of open and imaginative activity, a number of non-Party members, even former South Vietnamese government officials, were brought in to advise the leadership. Two examples were Nguyen Xuan Oanh, a former central bank governor under the Saigon government, and Hoang Ngoc Nguyen, a British-educated economist; both were close to Vo Van Kiet who was then leading the push for economic change. There was even talk of appointing ministers who were not members of the Party as a way of bringing in new talent and broadening the government's base of support.

The collapse of the Soviet Union changed all that. The leadership became nervous that allowing outsiders to stroll the corridors of power might weaken discipline and undermine the Party. Maintaining control over the bureaucracy was central to staying in power. Those who were not Party members were gradually nudged aside and plans to allow them into senior government positions were dropped in favour of rewarding those with the right Communist credentials.

The right to hold high office was often won decades ago during the war. Many small acts of heroism or simple good luck started off as a ripple but turned into powerful waves that carried cadres into power. Vo Thi Thang is one of the most startling examples. A brief smile turned her into a political icon, a major step on her way to becoming a member of the powerful Party Central Committee and Director General of the Vietnam National Administration for Tourism.

Thang had been a member of an opposition student movement in Saigon and was jailed in 1969 on charges of subversion against the Saigon government. As she left the court, the 24-year-old smiled for the cameras and in an instant became the international political pin-up for the Viet Cong. Her radiant smile and her beatific demeanour were in perfect contrast to the Saigon police goons snarling under their dark glasses. Thang's beauty, her defiance and her calm in the face of a twenty-year spell in an appalling South Vietnamese prison, earned her a place as an icon of the war at home and abroad.

Thang is not unusual in parlaying her wartime suffering into a political career. American prisoners of war came back from Vietnam to be lauded as heroes. Many of them were able to convert their experience and the myths and fame that surrounded it into successful careers. Senator John McCain of Arizona and former Representative Douglas 'Pete' Petersen, the first US ambassador in Hanoi, were residents of the infamous Hanoi Hilton. The conversion of Thang's role as a saintly, youthful martyr into a political authority hasn't come without some resistance. A Vietnamese newspaper noted after her appointment to head the tourism authority that tour operators believed 'it would take some time for Madame Thang to settle into the job as she has limited business or economic management experience'.

Having informed its readers that Thang had no place in such an important job, the newspaper quickly returned to how Thang had been tortured while in jail, reaffirming her political credentials. Many people openly scoffed when she was appointed. Those in the tourism business described her as purely a Party hack who had worked her way up through the youth and women's unions. Some were openly disappointed, saying Vietnam's struggling tourism industry needed an infusion of sharp management, not more politics. 'She's famous only for her smile,' said the owner of a Ho Chi Minh City restaurant that relied on foreign tourists. 'It's a whole career based on a smile. Maybe they can use it in a marketing campaign.'

Corruption is often blamed on the low salaries paid to government workers and indeed this is part of the story for the lowest paid, such as traffic policemen. But the reality is that state enterprise employees and government officials are among the highest earners in the country. Wages in state businesses average about $100 a month, putting annual incomes at around five times the average. In addition to fair pay, state jobs often come with housing and lucrative opportunities for making money on the side. It is no wonder that these people tend to protect their positions.

In Hanoi, the richest 20 per cent of the population have an average income seven times that of the poorest 40 per cent, according to government figures. The city has the widest gap in the country, significantly higher than in Ho Chi Minh City which has suffered less from bureaucratic intervention in the economy. According to Tuong Lai, head of the Institute of Sociology and an advisor to former Prime Minister Kiet, most of the top income earners are employed by the state, in ministry jobs, trading companies, the economic police, customs and transportation businesses. The richest households tend to include both an official and an entrepreneur who could take advantage of government contacts while operating in the private sector. Lai was understated in his description of the rampaging greed and larceny among the families of officials. 'It is very difficult to define among the *nouveau riches* whether their wealth is a result of their real capabilities or their social position,' he said.

Vietnamese officials are generally more interested in their own enrichment and self-aggrandisement than they are in any broader national interest. Indeed the country has not so much gone from plan to market, but from plan to clan; this idea is neatly reflected in an old adage that 'once a man becomes a Mandarin, his whole lineage can depend on him'. The country manager for Daewoo Corporation, the South Korean conglomerate that was the largest investor in Vietnam, summed up the problem in an interview with the *Asian Wall Street Journal*: 'Government officers – they don't have patriotism. They are thinking of themselves first.' The system that creates a warm and nourishing environment for corruption, also nurtures a hubris and arrogance that threatens Vietnam's future by blocking any solid commitment to reforms.

Once in lucrative rent-seeking positions, officials latch on with vice-like grips and resist all changes that might undermine them. In the early 1990s, the Central Research Institute of Economic Management, a Hanoi think-tank run by the economist Le Dang Doanh, floated the idea that the 6,000 state companies on the government's books should be reduced to fewer than 500 by closing the weaker firms and merging others. This smaller group of companies would be run by a special government department and not by ministries. With 'fewer children to look after the government could feed its businesses better so they could play the key role in the economy that they are supposed to play', the think-tank report said. A company law would be drafted to control their workings and management. Reporting procedures would be standardised in preparation for their eventual sale to the public. This followed the line being pressed on Vietnam by its aid donors and the major financial institutions who wanted to see more privatisations of the generally inefficient state sector.

Three years on, the issue had disappeared from the official agenda. Fumbling around for a new definition of socialism, the Communist Party had decided that maintaining a major role for the state sector was key to their grip on power. Reforms that might have revitalised moribund businesses were dropped in favour of increased subsidies and continued preference in lending from banks. Ari Kokko, a Swedish economist, estimates that the state sector expanded from 33 per cent of GDP in 1991 to 44 per cent in 1995. *Doi Moi* has actually increased the role of the state in the economy. Much of this growth came from foreign investment drawn in by state firms. The great irony of the economy is that multinational investors have been propping up the state sector in Vietnam which the government takes as a central aspect of its definition of Communism. International capitalists, once a force for evil in their top hats and striped trousers, have now become the great benefactors of socialism.

At the same time as the state sector was expanding its share of the economy, the power of state managers, always great because they combined political and economic leverage, was enhanced as yet more were brought into the Party Central Committee. These managers wanted to see more protection for their industries, not a situation where they would have to compete with foreign companies on an equal footing. Most wanted tighter import regulations, notably on manufactured goods, and higher tariffs on raw materials. Domestic competition from the private sector could be controlled through the system of export licenses and allocations of quotas. State sector companies enjoyed much better access to capital, land and technology than the private sector and their managers were determined to preserve these privileges.

Very few managers saw anything to be gained in closing or merging companies to create economies of scale. Provincial and city governments that controlled state firms were not keen to see any reorganisation that would reveal the extent of so-called 'triangular' debts between state firms. Many local authorities quietly removed some state firms from their books to avoid having to take responsibility for their debts. As companies disappeared, their debts, which have been estimated by economists such as Kokko to be as high as $24 billion – more than the annual GDP – became irrecoverable and were left on the books of the nearly bankrupt state banks. State sector debt has become a financial time bomb that is ticking away ominously.

Corruption was endemic in the state sector long before the introduction of limited market mechanisms. Factory managers routinely paid bribes to planning officials to get consignments of parts or to off-load surplus stocks. Trading companies bought and sold their licenses to import or export goods. Reforms have opened up this system but enough of the bureaucratic bottlenecks have been kept to ensure that these practices continue. Preserving these powers in the hands of bureaucrats benefits the tiny stratum of officials and Party members at enormous cost to the rest of society. In the past decade, only the private sector has been able to create jobs for the one million new workers that join the labour market each year. State employment has declined and yet the sector still swallows most of the capital available for investment.

One of the country's best known state factories has gone from representing socialist industrial achievement to being a symbol of the failure of central planning. The Nam Dinh Textile Company is one of the largest producers of cloth and yarn in Vietnam. Its vast complex of mills south of Hanoi were built by the French seventy years ago and production has continued ever since, even through the American bombing of the town. By the 1990s the weaving equipment was completely obsolete, the plant in debt, and the market for its low-quality cloth eroded by better, cheaper products from China.

To counter the company's decline, managers drew up an investment plan and between 1992 and 1995, the mill spent more than $50 million of government money on new machinery. But more money was put into spinning than dyeing or weaving equipment. Growing stockpiles of yarn that couldn't be used were sold at a loss or thrown out. Despite wages for skilled workers of about $30 a month and a huge demand for cloth, the mill still failed to turn a profit.

One of the reasons was the company's management, which mixed corruption and incompetence in equal measures. A director had his family provide the factory with machinery and raw materials at inflated prices. At least half a million dollars went for entertainment and bribes. By 1995 the mill had debts of more than $50 million and was losing about $18 million a year. Whilst racking up these losses, the business had been reporting profits of millions of dollars each year, which were dutifully signed off by government officials who were well aware that there was trouble at the mill.

While Vietnamese officials are inclined to look with disapproval on the private sector which they regard as a hotbed of tax evasion, shady accountancy practices and other misdemeanours, they seem less outraged by the behaviour of state enterprise managers such as those at the Nam Dinh textile mill. Vietnam is not burdened by a vast state industrial complex like the former Eastern Bloc or China. It never got that far. But what little industry it does have tends to be crumbling and inefficient, a drain on resources that could be used better elsewhere. The steel and cement markets are dominated by two giant state conglomerates that control everything from manufacturing to trade. They are models of Stalinist inefficiency and both have been ensnared in scandal, but they are kept running for reasons of self-interest, national pride and a wilful refusal to look clearly at their books.

Most Vietnamese government officials are middle-aged Party members. The better educated officials studied mostly in the former Eastern Bloc before spending their entire careers in government. The majority of these studied technical or scientific subjects and only a few are educated in economics, management or the social sciences. This educational background has meant a preference towards engineers who see the world in terms of physical accomplishments of construction rather than looking at a project's costs and benefits, both economic and social.

These men, and they are almost entirely men, tend to prefer big masculine schemes. Concrete is the favoured building material, steel electricity pylons are powerful objects of beauty – they are a regular motif of socialist poster art – and size really does count.

They have an institutional preference for dams, tunnels, freeways and vast power lines over rural road-building schemes, education or health care. And thus are loosed the herds of white elephants that rampage through the jungles of Vietnam, the only species of pachyderm that has remained off the list of endangered species. Nearly every day the Vietnamese press announces a new government programme to build a vast impractical project that would seem to offer little economic benefit while swallowing a great mouthful of the gross domestic product.

One of the latest projects was a scheme announced by Vo Van Kiet to build a new highway the length of the country. The road, estimated to cost around $6 billion, or about one quarter of the country's annual output, was to be built through conscripted labour. When the government announced that it would require all Vietnamese to work on the road there was a shudder among officers of the multinational lending organisations – the project raised the spectre of forced labour and horrible environmental damage. Many Vietnamese dismissed the idea as yet more governmental blather; they were confident that the government had neither the funds nor the ability to mobilise so many people.

In 1994 the government decided to build an oil refinery and industrial complex at Dung Quat, a barren stretch of central Vietnam with a pristine beach and little else. The site was chosen to help development in the poor central provinces and to avoid what had come to be known as the 'dumbbell effect' of rapid development in northern and southern Vietnam but nothing in the middle. This enclave development in which small regions of prosperity are surrounded by hopeless poverty is starting to become a serious problem.

The government announced that the cost of the project would be about $1.3 billion. The French oil firm Total wanted to invest in petrochemicals in Vietnam, but had been making its calculations on the basis that the refinery would be in the South, near both the offshore oil reserves and the major markets in Ho Chi Minh City.

After studying the cost of building at Dung Quat, which would need new roads and an artificial port to protect tankers from the frequent typhoons, Total concluded the project was not feasible and pulled out. LG Group, a South Korean conglomerate with ambitious plans in Vietnam and a desire to curry favour with the government, declared itself willing to take over and the feasibility studies began again. By this stage, the government had adopted a defensive tone about the project, which was described as 'a fact' and 'inevitable'. Dung Quat was no longer just a bad political decision by Prime Minister Vo Van Kiet, it was now a force of nature.

A new group of investors lined up to join the project but after crunching the numbers they too came to the same conclusion; it just did not make economic sense. There was over-capacity in refin-ing across Asia, profit margins were tight, and there was doubt that Vietnam needed a refinery for any reason other than to satisfy national pride. Hanoi would have to offer huge incentives, better market access for the investors, or pay for the additional infrastruc-ture themselves if the refinery was to be built. It was to be a hugely expensive means of kick-starting development in central Vietnam. While the project pleased those who hunger for vast industrial pro-jects, it was clear from the start it would provide little in the way of profits for investors or economic benefits for local people.

By 1997, even the new group of investors was having second thoughts. The project, initially due for completion in 1999, was now years behind schedule. The only economic impact had been to draw hundreds of families into the area where they set up shanty towns in the hope that eventually they would be evicted and compen-sated. Even they were disappointed by how far the project had progressed. By the end of the year there were mutterings about call-ing the project off although the official line was that Vietnam would go it alone if necessary; it would have its belching smoke stacks at any cost. Ground was finally broken at Dung Quat in January 1998, but it remained unclear whether the project would ever be com-pleted.

The Vietnamese bureaucracy is well-schooled in slogans; officials are remarkable for the discipline they show in remaining 'on mes-sage' by parroting the latest political line. They rarely, however, show much connection to economic and social realities. A foreign health specialist who dealt regularly with high-level bureaucrats said that in the many years she had worked in Vietnam, she had never heard a Ministry of Health official ask whether an aid project was actually helping to improve people's health. Their concerns were always about their bureaucratic turf wars, their own prestige and how much they could extract from aid donors. 'They are never interested in the real issues, only in how well they can do out of whatever project you are discussing,' she said.

Indeed, the greed, graft and nepotism seemed most sharply delineated at the ministries of education, health and at Molisa, the ministry of labour, invalids and social affairs. One of Molisa's responsibilities was to implement a scheme funded by the European Commission to assist in the reintegration of boat people who had fled Vietnam only to languish in camps across Southeast Asia and in Hong Kong before being sent home. The programme was to assist particularly vulnerable returnees – those who were coming back without any family or suffered debilitating illnesses. Many also had serious mental health problems after spending years in appalling conditions in camps. The Returnee Assistance Programme, or RAP, was also to equip vocational training centres that would serve the wider community.

Problems began when Molisa refused to hire more than 200 Vietnamese who had worked on an earlier programme for returnees funded by the European Commission. They were 'not of good character', an official from Molisa said. Instead of these well-trained motivated people, Molisa officials tried to hire what an EU official described as 'their cousins and drinking buddies', who most often were completely under-qualified for the jobs. Molisa also refused to relinquish control over a programme to aid small businesses which was to have been administered by the more efficient and less corrupt Finance Ministry. At every step Molisa officials displayed an attitude of contempt for returning boat people, heightening the anxieties they felt about their reintegration and the threat of persecution for having fled the country. The attitude of these officials was one of haughty Mandarin contempt for the needs of the people they were there to serve, and was at complete odds with the righteous humanitarian rhetoric they trotted out for foreign donors.

Sleazy officials benefited from the nature of foreign aid and the bureaucracies of organisations such as the European Commission, themselves not untouched by corruption. EC officials were mostly concerned at pushing projects through, not ensuring the Vietnamese people benefited from European money. In one of the most brazen misuses of funds, a training school for returning boat people, built in the beach town of Do Son near Haiphong at a cost of $40,000, was converted into a seaside brothel. The blue and gold-starred flag of the European Union was still proudly displayed outside.

Corruption and bureaucracy are not unique to Vietnam, but the situation is worsened by the structure of the Leninist system that gives officials too much power and deprives people of a legitimate voice in government. Bureaucrats constantly throw obstacles in the way of projects that could only benefit the country. The Fred Hollows Foundation, an Australian NGO that establishes self-financing factories to produce ocular lenses, was blocked from opening a facility in Hanoi for two years because of bureaucracy that could not even be removed by the personal intervention of General Secretary Do Muoi. NGO workers were jailed, harassed, threatened, occasionally even arrested by local government cadres who felt slighted in some way or had not been able to extract benefits for themselves. NGOs and aid schemes played into this game; instead of refusing to pay bribes or countenance the skimming of money, the international aid industry often prefers a smooth path over the morally correct choice.

Corruption could be the force that cracks open the Communist Party and becomes its undoing. Most of the demonstrations that have taken place have been because anger over corruption boiled over. It has also had a corrosive effect at the highest levels, battering the sense of consensus that once existed among top officials. Corruption has replaced ideology as a way of fighting political battles. Throughout his tenure in office, Vo Van Kiet was dogged by accusations that his wife, a university professor who teaches metallurgy, was corrupt. Phan Luong Cam was a frequent target of innuendo in Hanoi where everyone from officials to street vendors had a tale of her alleged avarice. It was said that the Politburo had banned her from travelling abroad without approval because her spending sprees were being noticed. But despite the incessant drum beat of gossip about Cam, no solid evidence of her corruption has emerged. She may well be a new Imelda, and certainly there is something about the high, lacquered hair and the make-up that suggests the former Filipina first lady, but her activities were much more discreet than those of the families of other Asian leaders. There is good reason to believe that some of the stories about Cam were invented by her husband's enemies to attack him or to deflect attention from embarrassing lapses by their own families. High-level corruption is still played out discreetly; the top families may be draped in the designer clothes and jewels of an emerging plutocracy, but they keep it all hidden under a shroud of Communist burlap.

The near absence of institutions that limit or check government power has created this monster and most efforts to tame it have had only a limited impact. As the economic situation improved in the mid-1990s, the government saw little need to keep up the pace of reform. What they wanted to see was a consolidation of their power, not a weakening of it through deregulation. But by giving powers to bureaucrats they have not necessarily strengthened state control. The high level of corruption, the general lawlessness, the difficulties in imposing policies on provinces, all illustrate that the Vietnamese state suffers from some major weaknesses. The problem is paradoxically too much power – over speech, symbols and the political channels through which people could address grievances – and too little control over such areas as the legal system, the behaviour of cadres and the use of money.

This is the great contradiction of Market-Leninism. On the one hand it ensures the power of officials and subsidises the bureaucracy who receive their wages through a form of taxation, on the other hand it weakens the rule of law and undermines the legitimacy of the Party, which once put considerable emphasis – at least in the realms of symbolism and rhetoric – on people and their needs. While the Party needs to be seen to act against corruption, it has little to gain from exposing the true extent of graft in its ranks or from giving up the secretive, closed system of decision-making that nurtures the criminal above the honest. They have learned the lessons of Gorbachev's Soviet Union. When Leonid Brezhnev was in power, everyone was aware of the corruption and indolence that afflicted the system but nobody said anything; people were able to maintain some pretence that everything was working. Gorbachev, on the other hand, opened the door to criticism and saw

Communism collapse. Once laid bare, the system was untenable.

Immediately after the Tamexco trial, newspaper editors were told to tone down the coverage and a few months later when Phuoc and his fellow defendants appealed their sentences, the reports were sketchy and uncritical. By then the government had decided that it had little to gain in exposing the real extent of corruption, particularly in areas such as the banking system which was becoming increasingly shaky. In March 1997, the government introduced new press restrictions on reporting about the financial sector that included a ban on unapproved stories that revealed official malfeasance. Even the sacking of dishonest officials could no longer be reported in case it undermined confidence in the financial system. A senior journalist was jailed for exposing corruption in the purchase of ships from the Ukraine, thus deterring others from looking too closely at state enterprises. Having set the press to help clean out the Augean stables of government, the Party has now backtracked, fearing that the exposure would assist the erosion of its legitimacy. Instead of dealing with the problems, the Party has reverted to shooting the messenger.

9

Pendulum

Do not look unless it is in accordance with the rites;
do not listen unless it is in accordance with the rites;
do not speak unless it is in accordance with the rites;
do not move unless it is in accordance with the rites.

CONFUCIUS
The Analects XII.1

The end of Vietnam's decades of conflict and isolation have not been easy for the newspaper *Quan Doi Nhan Dan* (the *People's Army*). The ghosts of the Cold War still rattle around the grand villa in the Old Quarter of Hanoi that houses the publication's offices, searching for a new threat, never settling down to enjoy the peace. Diplomacy constrains them from pointing the finger at the looming presence of China, probably the only security issue that really worries the government. Instead the enemies have become democracy and human rights promoted by the forces of 'peaceful evolution'. In the minds of the paper's editors – all military men – the United States lurks patiently in the shadows, determined to undermine Communist rule by stealth. The martial vocabulary, still brimming with indignation, sounds sadly outdated now that the enemy jets in to unload tourist dollars and foreign investment rather than bombs.

Vietnam may have transformed many of its institutions since the mid-1980s but until recently not much had changed at *Nhan Dan* (the *People*) and *Quan Doi Nhan Dan*, the official organs of the nation's two most powerful institutions, the Party and the military. Both still carry a heavy freight of Marxism. Their one-sheet format hints at paper shortages, the grubby ink tells of manual typesetting and ancient presses. Something in the amateurish design suggests their origins as inflammatory pamphlets, but nowadays the papers are singularly the mouthpieces of the conservative establishment. Their motionless pages are dominated by speeches by Politburo members, the words rambling on to one or more of the inside sheets. Information is rare, entertainment almost unknown. Marxist-Leninism provides the vocabulary, although the ideas are grounded more in the rich vein of nationalism that is still mined by the Communist Party.

Quan Doi Nhan Dan has become a master at inventing new enemies to excite its military readership. In 1996 it located a hidden menace 'sleeping under trees around Hoan Kiem Lake' in Hanoi. This undercover force spoke the language and ate Vietnamese food. They were up to no good riding around in *cyclos*, dressed in shorts and singlets. Vietnam could no longer ignore the threat they posed. It was 'too easy in this age of information flow to mistake enemies for friends', the newspaper told its readers. The country, the army daily warned, was under siege from young foreign backpackers.

Doubtless Vietnamese breathed a little easier knowing who was the enemy in their midst. But the *Lonely Planet* Legions were not the only security threat. Executives from overseas, the newspaper said accusingly, were attending business seminars because of their interest in 'information that helps them work out their investments, calculate prices and put pressure on their Vietnamese partners'. Foreigners were even using these meetings to get their hands on 'secret technological information'.

These newspapers continue to devote many of their pages to anxious jibes at foreigners as they struggle to keep intact the fractured image of Vietnamese as square-jawed heroes, peasants, workers and intellectuals toiling together under the guidance of an omniscient leadership. It is here that the Party and the army remind themselves of their glory days, their victories at war and their once formidable capacity to unite the country.

Even these papers, however, have not been able to cling completely to the past. *Nhan Dan* has expanded to eight pages and has attempted to spruce up its design and increase its foreign news. Feature pages that were once grey trails of type exalting Marxist doctrines, now have stories on lighter subjects such as the winter marriage season in Hanoi. The windy polemics of *Quan Doi Nhan Dan* are now occasionally leavened by feature stories. The revolution that rippled through the Vietnamese press has finally reached the last holdouts.

The market reforms that have transformed Vietnam have also freed an urgent entrepreneurial spirit in a once moribund media and have opened up areas of reporting and debate that were unthinkable only a few years ago. Supermodels have edged aside reports on Stakhanovite feats, colour has infused pages that were once only filled with leaden propaganda and newspapers now print stories of real interest to real people. Around 350 publications now fight for circulation and advertising, their ranks swelled by ninety newcomers in the five years after 1990. Editors talk about sports weeklies, economic dailies, special supplements and co-operation projects with foreign publishing giants. Suddenly the language is more multimedia than Marx. 'Five years ago it was all propaganda, now there is real news and the relationship with the government is a two-way street,' said Ly Qui Chung, former editor of two major newspapers in Hanoi and Ho Chi Minh City.

But this circulation of information has proved one of the most difficult problems for Market-Leninism. A country that was once only connected to the outside world through a cluster of telex circuits and a radio line to Moscow now has to contend not just with a more vibrant domestic media but an invasion of foreigners, fax machines and the Internet. It has also been buffeted from within by a market economy's pressing need for information, balanced by the fear that knowledge could undermine a government that has always preferred to shroud itself in secrecy.

In the late 1980s, the government bowed briefly to a powerful force – its own people. Throughout the decade the declining economy and the war in Cambodia led to a festering sense of resentment among Party members and intellectuals. The conflict with China led them to question the Maoist dogma that had worked its way throughout the party. Slowly a body of critical literary and artistic work emerged, most notably from veterans and Party members. As the country sank to its nadir in the middle of the decade, the voices demanding change grew louder.

General Secretary Nguyen Van Linh latched on to this resentment and openly encouraged writers 'not to bend the nibs of their pens' with propaganda but to write the truth about a country weighed down with economic and political problems. Like long-caged birds, writers emerged cautiously, mindful of the purges and jailing of critical writers in the 1950s. But as their confidence grew, sharper articles appeared in the press, writers railed at a government veined through with corruption, and journalists began to tackle the policies that had plunged Vietnam into its dismal decade after 1975.

The first reaction of the more liberal members of the Party was to go along with the growing openness, trying to harness it to their own ends. Linh was a master of manipulating the media, using it to push against the inertia of the sullen ranks of apparatchiks and to raise issues without going through convoluted consultations. He wrote numerous columns signed 'NVL' that challenged the political orthodoxy of the time.

But like many bad columnists he soon descended into the trap of writing a weekly litany of querulous complaints. His supposedly anonymous musings made him a laughing stock among officials, particularly when other members of the government started pointing out that his views were often absurdly impractical. In one 'NVL' article he questioned why diplomats serving at Vietnamese embassies in Asia drove Nissan or Toyota cars rather than flying the socialist banner in the Volgas and other sinister black-curtained Soviet models that belched and slunk their way around Hanoi. The rather more practical Foreign Minister Nguyen Co Thach had to tell Linh that the cost of buying and maintaining Russian cars in cities such as Jakarta was prohibitive compared with running Japanese vehicles. 'NVL', Linh said, stood for '*noi va lam*' or 'speak and act', but it was soon spread around that the initials were more aptly interpreted as '*noi va lua*' or 'speak and deceive'.

His columns continued long after he had been kicked upstairs into an advisory position. Having launched the reforms, he seemed to lose his taste for them; it was said he feared being known as the Gorbachev of Vietnam, the one who consigned Communism to the rubbish heap of history. In 1994, he let loose with a long diatribe against the foreign investment policies he had initiated, saying that 'joint ventures will only make capitalists richer while Vietnamese remain sellers of their labour', a point that while not exactly untrue, hardly meshed with the government's attempts to promote an investment-friendly image. Linh also left out the telling fact that foreign investment was keeping the state sector afloat; without this influx of cash from overseas few state enterprises would even be functioning. Far from being the challenge to the system that he liked to think, his articles were generally a mish-mash of half-truths and demagoguery.

In the mid 1980s, there was an important revival of a type of journalism that had once had a profound impact on the way Vietnamese saw the world. Known as *phong su*, which literally translates as 'to enlarge', this colourful, socially charged writing originated under French colonialism. In the 1930s there was a flurry of documentary writing on poverty and exploitation that did much to crystallise resentment against the French. Journalists exploited the emotional power of fiction and intensive research to create a way of looking at the world. Their articles exposed the poverty of city life and the difficulties faced by farmers. Instead of just publishing edifying tracts, newspapers took it on themselves to expose a seamier, realistic world of a floating urban population detached from the links of family and village. These articles were some of the most powerful writing in Vietnam this century; they played a vital role in establishing a modern national identity and rousing the emerging middle class against colonialism.

Phong su returned in a number of publications led by *Van Nghe*, the weekly journal of the Writers' Association. Among the most powerful was 'The Night of That Day, What a Night!' by Phung Gia Loc, that told of life in a northern village called Phu Yen. The story chronicles a life of unremitting poverty and anxiety. Not only do the people endure hunger and deprivation but they are also raided by predatory officials demanding taxes they cannot afford to pay after floods destroy their crops.

His hands were holding an iron crowbar as thick as a thumb. My wife invited the men to sit down. The old grandmother, who was lying on the bed tried to get up. She greeted them, trembling.

'According to the team's list, you still owe more than 100 kilograms of paddy. We request it to be submitted right away.'

My old mother answered on behalf of her daughter-in-law: 'Dear uncles and brothers! There is nothing left to be submitted. Uncles and brothers, don't you see that her children are pale with hunger? Uncles don't you see that I am sick with oedema, wrinkled as a yellow leaf?'

'We're not asking you, old hag, get it?'

The officials search the house looking for valuables they can take in lieu of rice; they end up with a pathetic array of bicycles, earthen jars, pigs and poultry to hold until the peasants pay their taxes. Eventually they find the stash of rice that the protagonist's mother had been saving 'so the villagers can have a small bowl to eat when they come over to help my family with the funeral'.

Loc's article prompted a torrent of letters to *Van Nghe* about conditions in the countryside and whether he had reported it truthfully. A furious former cadre accused him of gross exaggerations in portraying modern Vietnamese officials as no better than French colonists; others wrote in support, thanking him for exposing the abuses of debt collectors and rural administrators. The former official opened his letter by asking 'what sort of bastard is this Loc?'. He went on to question his loyalty as a Vietnamese and said if abuses did occur in the countryside 'they are very rare'. The letter's supercilious tone and oblivion to the realities of life in the countryside sparked off a wave of support for Loc with letters venting spleen at obstructive and ignorant officials.

Publishing this story had immediate repercussions for Loc. In an interview with the publication *Tien Phong*, he was asked whether there had been any 'negative reactions' to his article:

Of course. And they came pretty quickly. I hadn't even returned home when the story had caused the local authorities to keep an eye on my family. They called up my wife and five other people mentioned in the story for interrogations at the production team office . . . Only after Mr Ha Trong Hoa no longer held the position of secretary to the People's Committee of Thanh Hoa province did I feel somewhat safe.

Loc's story had an extraordinary impact on the public. Soon photocopies were being churned out by the thousand and sold at higher prices that *Van Nghe* usually cost. It galvanised a generation of writers to look back to the critical styles of the 1930s *phong su* and write about the social problems afflicting Vietnam. Exposés of corruption and official abuses were favourite subjects for the more daring newspapers which competed to find the ripest scandals. It wasn't quite a 'Hanoi Spring', but it was an intense period for journalists who emerged from their roles as glorified stenographers and Party propagandists to become drivers of change. For the first time in decades, they were able to challenge and inform; it was an exhilarating time for writers and readers.

It didn't last long. Communism collapsed in Eastern Europe and Vietnamese leaders shuddered at the execution of the Ceauşescus and the indignities heaped on their close friend Erich Honecker, the late leader of East Germany. Writers were jailed, those who called for political reforms, even distinguished former soldiers, were branded 'reactionaries' and several prominent figures in the media left the country or retired. The pendulum weighted with fear had once again swung back on its path between liberalism and repression, between a fear of being left behind by the world and the knowledge that openness could widen the cracks in the system.

Vietnam's press, which is entirely owned by Communist Party or government organisations, is still one of the most tightly restricted in the world, operating in an environment where private ownership is banned and publications can be closed overnight by government fiat. *Nguoi Hanoi* (the *Hanoian*), a weekly run by the capital's Arts and Literature Association, was shut down in January 1995 after it said people were 'worried and sad' about a government ban on firecrackers that are much enjoyed during the *Tet* lunar new year holidays. The magazine's editor and others responsible for the article were ordered to write 'self-criticisms' after being accused of violating press laws. Other newspapers had also written about the ban in critical terms, discussing the devastating impact on villages where firecrackers are made, but their coverage swiftly turned to toadying praise of the government's success in ridding Vietnam of such a wasteful and dangerous tradition. As soon as the government signalled that this campaign was serious, the press adopted it as their own, although some journalists grumbled at the coverage they were forced to write. A year after the ban came into force in January 1995, the government was still having problems keeping journalists in line.

A newspaper published by a council of co-operatives was given a strong dressing down for reporting, without any criticism, that football supporters had set off firecrackers in Nha Trang to mark a victory by the national team. *Doanh Nghiep* was cited for being 'too objective' in its reporting (which was supposed to be more subjectively supportive of the Party) and for 'not carrying information in line with the government's propaganda campaign'. The eradication of firecrackers had become a near obsession for Prime Minister Vo Van Kiet as it tested the government's ever-diminishing capacity to control people. Ahead of the *Tet* holidays, newspapers ran front-page reports on the long sentences handed down to those caught with contraband firecrackers, once again proving the government could force the press to toe the line, even if it couldn't force compliance of the law on firecrackers outside the major cities.

As the Communist Party sees an increasing decentralisation of power and an inevitable ideological deflation, it has become even more reluctant to cede control over the media for fear it would aid in the development of the civil society that could undermine its rule. Indeed it has been tightening restrictions in recent years, replacing independent-minded editors and urging greater attention to the Party's authority. At the Sixth Congress of the Association of Vietnamese Journalists in March 1995, Party General Secretary Do Muoi reminded the audience that they were there 'to serve the government and the people'.

'In Vietnam, press freedom is meant to serve the interests of the entire people, the whole country and the new political system,' Muoi said, serving up the argument of collective rights taking priority over the individual that has often been used by authoritarian Asian governments to justify their tight hand on the press. 'We will not allow the abuse of press freedom by people who seek to destabilise the socio-political situation in our country and impede us in our development and our integration into the world community.'

Since the tightening of the screws with the draconian Press Law in 1989, few Vietnamese journalists are willing to challenge this idea or even enter into serious debate about their role. Newspapers exist once again for propaganda. Tran Cong Man, a former editor of the *Quan Doi Nhan Dan* and for a while a barbarian handler wheeled out to explain Vietnamese policies to foreign journalists, summed up this view for a Western researcher: 'We have never advocated that the people get a free press. The so-called free press of the West is a disgrace. It is violent and negative and sensationalist. Our press is better. It is positive and there to help people stay united.'

After the Communist victory in the North in 1954, controls over the press were tightened, a process that was stepped up after a very brief flurry of critical publications in the late 1950s. With the advent of war in 1960, the media was prevented from revealing any criticisms and instead was marshalled into support for reunification. The government forced journalists into completely passive roles as distributors of propaganda that was drafted each day by senior Party officials.

Independent journalism was simply not on anybody's list of priorities at a time when reporters were soldiers first. In the struggle for national liberation there could be no straying from a path that united the country. Political vocabulary and journalistic ethics are still mired in this era, and as the editors who now run the newspapers are mostly former war correspondents steeped in this tradition, they are rarely a force for change.

Officially television, radio and the state news agency are under the direct control of the Prime Minister's office and their director-generals have the rank of vice minister. All other newspapers and local television stations must be licensed by the Ministry of Information and Culture. All the media is monitored through Party cells that exist in every publication from *Nhan Dan* down to provincial papers to channel directives down from the top. All editors must be Party members and must justify their actions to the Party, ultimately to the Ideology Commission of the Central Committee. Even the most senior journalists still have to send their articles through checks and controls that generally dilute them into the watery intellectual gruel served up in the media.

Bui Tin, a former deputy editor of *Nhan Dan*, gave some rare insights into the secretive workings of the press in his autobiography *Following Ho Chi Minh*. After years working as a war correspondent for *Quan Doi Nhan Dan*, Tin held a top post at the Party daily in the late 1980s, working at the highest levels of Vietnamese journalism as one of those who decide what the masses can be allowed to know. He describes a system where bureaucracy has paralysed imagination and the demands of a tiny élite outweigh all other considerations in a world dominated by the purges, factionalism and corruption that are essential themes of Vietnamese politics.

Journalists at *Nhan Dan* began a debate on whether the paper genuinely served 'the people' as its name suggested. Or was it merely an official gazette for government announcements and speeches by members of the Politburo? The newspaper briefly adopted a more critical tone, particularly in the Sunday magazine edited by Tin. He published an article about the doctoring of Ho Chi Minh's will and promoted the new and exciting literature that was emerging. However, as the countries of Eastern Europe rejected Communism, the ideological leadership in Hanoi began to fear the impact of the limited opening they had allowed. When in August 1989, the Solidarity trade union won elections in Poland, the Party daily ran a furious editorial written by the head of the ideological committee, urging Poles to close ranks and fight this 'counter-revolutionary coup by reactionary forces'. This earned a rebuke from the Polish Embassy and, according to Tin, made the newspaper 'a laughing stock', among Hanoians.

As Communist parties crumbled across Europe, *Nhan Dan* increasingly reverted to its earlier tone and a more compliant editor was chosen. Tin's articles on the arrogance of the Communist leadership after their victory over South Vietnam in 1975 and the corruption that had become central to the political system were censored or not published and he grew increasingly disillusioned that the changes that had swept the world would not reach Vietnam.

Tin described the press as 'antediluvian' and journalists as 'suppressed and annihilated' by the system of Party and government control. 'There is a whole range of bureaucratic journalists who specialise in hectoring and intimidating their readers. In the spirit of class warfare, they learnt mechanistically about the power of the press to make propaganda, although it is really distorting the truth and is altogether wrong,' he wrote. He provides several examples of the mindless fear that dominates editorial decisions. In one case journalists were rebuked for innocently placing a picture of an anti-aircraft brigade so that its gun pointed across the page at a photograph of Ho Chi Minh. After 1989, the list of taboo subjects expanded to include political pluralism, calls for open debate, even the crimes of Stalin that had been discussed in Russia for years. A number of hard-liners were appointed to key posts to reinforce control. The Party appointed eight tame journalists to the Central Committee, the largest number ever, indicating the importance that has been attached to the media and propaganda as the leadership increasingly feels itself under siege.

The top figures at the main publications and the Vietnam News Agency hold top government posts and many are also members of the National Assembly. VNA employs more than 2,000 people and yet it would rank as one of the world's least informative news agencies. Its stories are drab and poorly written, are often inaccurate and are laden with an obsession with government targets and spurious statistics The agency, far from becoming a vital means of communication as Vietnam opens up, has simply become more restrictive.

The former director-general of VNA, Do Phuong, typified the sour suspicion that many Hanoians believed characterised cadres from the central province of Nghe An, a place summed up with the powerfully bleak description that it was 'so poor that the dogs eat rocks and the chickens peck at graves'. Phuong's prime achievement as opportunities swirled through Vietnam was to open a number of doctrinaire newspapers filled with laudatory stories about Iraq and Cuba. His influence stemmed from membership in a group of senior Party members who were still squaring the circles of Marxist dogma long after most of the country had shrugged it off. Unfortunately it is this small clique, headed by the Politburo's top ideologue Nguyen Duc Binh, that still have their hands around the media's neck, squeezing occasionally just to let everyone know who is really in charge.

For most of those who work in the media, the machinery of control is almost frictionless, generally requiring little input of energy from the security system. People do not become journalists unless they know the rules and are aware that self-censorship is a key to survival. 'It isn't much different from life before 1975,' said Ly Qui Chung, who managed to go from editing newspapers in Saigon to running one in Hanoi after 1975. 'You weren't allowed to question the leadership back then and you aren't allowed to question the leadership now.'

Journalists do chafe at the restrictions and many privately show their boredom at the more ideological aspects of their work, aware that much of what they publish is ritualistic cant. The freedoms that have been allowed are still a bit of a novelty and journalists are discouraged from asking for more. Those who do push the envelope are often sidelined or cowed with official rebukes. A young reporter who asked Vice Foreign Minister Le Mai at a press conference if journalists would still have to refer all stories about the United States to the Foreign Ministry for checking after the normalisation of diplomatic ties, was answered with a savage look and some waffle. His boss later tore a strip off him for breaching the pretence of press freedoms that must always be maintained in front of foreigners.

Even the most senior journalists can be subject to punishment. Vu Kim Hanh reached the peak of her career in the early 1990s when as editor of *Tuoi Tre* she transformed the newspaper of the Communist Party Youth League into one of the country's most influential and widely read publications. But in May 1991 she overstepped the mark, publishing a story about allegations that emerged from Paris that Ho Chi Minh had been married. Later Hanh visited North Korea as part of an official delegation to a youth festival and gave a forthright description of the country as 'a land of robots' that was ruled by 'a despicable government'.

That insult against another Communist country, albeit one that had a history of animosity towards Vietnam, provided the excuse the authorities were looking for and she was dismissed from her post. She resurfaced in 1995 with *Saigon Tiep Thi* (*Saigon Marketing*), a tabloid that offered consumer advice to a growing middle class that built up a circulation of 60,000 within a year. While this was a respectable, and at least useful publication, it was a step backwards for one of the country's most capable and intelligent journalists.

Readers don't often publicly question the press but neither do they seem to regard it highly. *Nhan Dan* tends to remain crisply folded on desks throughout the day. For many people, the repetition and stock phrases seem familiar, perhaps even comforting, but they are rarely taken on board. They are part of the political culture; they are a normal form of political discourse read only by those who need to find out what are the correct rituals of the moment. 'You don't buy to find out the news, just to find out the Party line. You never know when you might need to know it,' said a retired Vietnamese official of the newspaper. The newspaper has a circulation of around 200,000 a day but most copies are delivered to government and Party offices, which are obliged to buy it.

Nguyen Ngoc Lan, a Roman Catholic priest and magazine editor before 1975, illustrated what Vietnamese think about *Nhan Dan* in a commentary on the Vietnamese service of Radio France International: 'On one hot afternoon as I was watching a soccer match, a clever newspaper vendor announced his product in a very practical manner: "Strong sun. No headache . . . buy the paper." I am reminded of the time when there was a severe shortage of paper across the country. People literally lined up daily to buy the inexpensive *Nhan Dan* for household uses.'

Vietnamese may have found *Nhan Dan* useful in the bathroom, but for information they turned to their radios and the Vietnamese language services of the British Broadcasting Corporation (BBC), Radio France International (RFI) and Voice of America (VOA). These broadcast intermittently during the day, providing mostly international news but also reporting on subjects that do not make it into the Vietnamese press. For years all radios had to be registered with the police and it was a serious offence to be caught listening to foreign broadcasts. For decades, many Hanoians kept abreast of the news that *Nhan Dan* did not see fit to print by tuning illicit radios to these stations.

The government seems strangely ambivalent to the BBC. Phan Quang, the director of Voice of Vietnam, sternly lectured the BBC Vietnamese service about its inappropriate coverage, such as broadcasting interviews with Bui Tin, and then asked if they would offer training to his journalists. Officials seem to reserve most of their contempt for RFI because of its commitment to giving a voice to Vietnamese dissidents and because it is run entirely by overseas Vietnamese, several of them apostates from the

Communist cause. The War Remnants Museum in Ho Chi Minh City singled out RFI as a 'subversive force' in an exhibit on attempts to overthrow Communist rule. The Foreign Ministry in Hanoi has repeatedly complained about its broadcasts, which have included interviews with prominent critics of the government. Prime Minister Vo Van Kiet asked the French ambassador to close the station, threatening a downturn in relations if it remained on the air. Even the French government is not that craven and RFI continues to broadcast.

In 1997, Radio Free Asia (RFA) began broadcasting in Vietnamese. The station, modelled on the broadcasts to Eastern Europe during the Cold War by Radio Free Europe, created near apoplexy in Hanoi. *Quan Doi Nhan Dan* denounced the station as an attempt to spread 'America's pornographic lifestyle' to Vietnam; the station was seen as intruding into Vietnam's internal affairs. RFA defended itself by saying it merely broadcast the news without any political commentary. In retaliation for RFA's broadcasts, the government held up an agreement for the US Information Service to open a cultural centre in Hanoi.

The almost daily attacks on RFA in the press may have stirred up interest in a station that few Vietnamese had heard of or cared about. Hanoi seemed to ignore the fact that the radio stations that had nourished listeners through decades when they were deprived of news now pose much less of a threat to the government's grip on information. The radio stations' listeners are greying and declining in numbers; they have had little success in attracting a younger audience lured away by television, videos, karaoke and numerous other distractions.

Gossip is a mainstay of life and news tends to travel quickly along the pavement telegraphs. The advent of the photocopier, a formidable foe of information controls, has formalised this into a true samizdat press that now circulates widely. Most of these pamphlets tend to be about a single issue, attacking an official for corruption or complaining about a particular policy.

One of the most interesting underground papers emerged from Saigon in the mid 1990s to provide witty and scathing attacks on the leadership. Written by 'the Saigonese', a laconic character who spent his time gossiping in cafés, it gained a readership abroad when translations were put out on the Internet by an overseas Vietnamese organisation in the Californian city of San Jose.

The Saigonese remains anonymous but given his political insights, he is certainly well connected in Ho Chi Minh City and was probably at some time a member of the Party. His sardonic and humorous articles have savaged the leadership in the city; he described them with typically Saigonese hauteur as 'peasants from small provinces'. In a response to a directive on control of the media issued by Dao Duy Tung, the Party's chief ideologist until 1996, the Saigonese made his feelings clear about the state of the Party:

> Your mouth is used to saying: 'The leadership of the Party is reinforced and escalated'. What does that mean? Your Party today is seen by the people as a little cult at a roadside temple in the countryside. How proud can you be? . . . Please just stay quiet. Stop issuing the kind of nonsense that will give the world good reason to damn your Party and cause the wrong image of the country and the people of Vietnam.

The Saigonese rubbished the view expressed by Tung that 'adversary forces are using means of communications and electronics to oppose and ruin us'. The United States, the Saigonese pointed out, now accepted the children of top leaders for medical treatment and was providing Vietnam with investment and expertise. 'Are there any imperialists left for you to hate Brother Tung?' the Saigonese asked. 'Why do you keep preaching this message of hate and animosity? The truth is that after the first two sentences of the usual rhetoric, the rest of your directive is simply a net with which to capture freedom of speech.'

Vietnam dawdled for years before allowing anything other than the most limited access to the Internet, which has been used effectively by the overseas Vietnamese community to spread information on politics and human rights. The World Wide Web has allowed rapid communication among the diaspora, but so far has had only a very limited impact in Vietnam, where few people own computers.

Senior officials have, however already warned of the dangers of these 'ultra-modern forms of media' that were being used to attack the Party. Regulations on Internet are draconian, partly to control access to information and because the state telecommunications company wants to monopolise this potentially lucrative business. There is certainly plenty of information on the Internet that the government would rather not have people read. As well as all the latest news from Vietnam that is not covered in the press there is also much noisy debate, mud-slinging and reassessment of history. The Internet crackles with the sort of democratic flow of information that terrifies the Party.

The pendulum is already swinging over the Internet; at first the government seemed to encourage its development, later it closed down several cyber-cafés and announced a series of restrictions in a doomed attempt to maintain an hermetic seal on the country. A strong financial imperative may yet undo this desire to control a medium that has defied government restrictions. Telecommunications companies are eager to get Vietnam wired up to what could be a new source of income; likewise academics and some technocratic officials are concerned about the country being left even farther behind in the information age unless they permit more freedoms. The Party wants to divorce 'useful' scientific and technical information from other material; it has not worked out that the world of inquiry and critical thought is indivisible.

Outside of the realm of politics, journalists working for the official press have been able to express their views more openly and without such heavy constraints. Issues such as corruption, poverty, prostitution, the labour movement and abuses in the workplace have come under scrutiny by newspapers that increasingly see themselves as responsible primarily to their readership. *Lao Dong* (*Labour*), the trade union newspaper, has been foremost among a new breed of campaigning publications that have taken on key social issues without pushing too far. 'Vietnamese workers are interested in the fight against problems that afflict the country,' said editor-in-chief Pham Huy Hoan. 'Our writers are very active investigating cases of corruption as these are of great interest to our readership. Another important issue for us is the conflict between employers and workers.'

Vietnamese editors and journalists often point to stories on corruption as evidence of their independence from the government. But it is clear that newspapers rarely initiate corruption investigations. Corruption has replaced ideological correctness as a means of overpowering opponents in political battles. Now that accusations of straying from the correct path of Marxism have no resonance, the best way of attacking a political opponent is to catch his hand in the till. Most newspaper stories on corruption or fraud are either about pervasive petty graft or they are officially approved. Few go much beyond general exhortations against corruption; only a handful have the impact of Loc's story on village officials. Even before investigations are complete, prosecutors will hand documents over to newspapers whose stories are loaded with the assumption of guilt. This pretence of investigative journalism satisfies both the reporters who imagine they have a social role, and benefits officials using the information against rivals.

While this newspaper and others such as *Nguoi Lao Dong* (the *Worker*), *Thanh Nien* and *Tuoi Tre* (both mean *Youth* but, like all youth organisations in Communist countries, are controlled by people edging into late-middle-age) have had some success in keeping corruption and labour issues on the agenda, a little freedom has occasionally been a dangerous thing. These newspapers have waged remorseless campaigns that owe much more to xenophobia than concern about workers' rights. In a few cases, they have become arenas for vendettas and an apparent need to vent steam building up in society over growing inequalities. A senior union official acknowledged that newspapers singled out foreigners in cases of labour abuses because the unions felt they had no other way of dealing with the problem. Vietnamese management could be subjected to self-criticism or the sanction of the law, but the easiest way to deal with managers from overseas was by vilification in the press.

In almost all cases, the reporters neglect to speak to the person or company being accused of wrongdoing. A Frenchman who ran a furniture company in Ho Chi Minh City found himself at the centre of a fierce campaign by several newspapers to have him thrown out of the country. For several weeks, the city's newspapers screamed about abuses of Vietnamese workers at Saigon Mobilier Internationale and urged authorities to deport the manager,

Georges Wache. Almost all the city's press jumped on the story with a relish reserved for cases that push all the Vietnamese buttons – sexual abuse and humiliation at the hands of foreigners. Wache was accused of forcing his employees into 'shameful acts' and prompting the resignation of three men who then went to the authorities to complain. Reports stated that national honour was at stake and that Wache should have to undergo 're-education', an ominous prospect for anyone in Vietnam.

Wache insisted all he had done was use a party trick to hand out some free cinema tickets to staff that involved some of the staff bending over and handing the tickets through their legs so they couldn't see who was getting them. This explanation and his protestations that one of his accusers was simply getting his revenge after a dressing down from a supervisor did not clear up the issue. He said he had once made a Vietnamese worker stand on his head after the man had assembled a piece of furniture the wrong way around; he insisted it was just in fun. Wache was reported to the police, and perhaps more dangerously, to the press. Later the government office that licenses foreign businesses sniffily issued a statement demanding that he desist from any 'just-for-fun tricks that are against Vietnam's customs and decent habits'. Wache left Vietnam, having never once been given a chance to defend himself.

There are no libel laws, no right to reply and no avenues for redress if one is wronged by the media. Only those with political clout would be able to get a retraction or punish a journalist, and as few foreigners fall into this category they are seen as an open target. Editors tend to brush off such complaints by pointing to their inexperienced staff and say that while they want to improve ethics and writing, their priority has been to bring in a new generation of writers and clear out some of the dead wood that in Vietnam is more heavily ligneous than anywhere else. 'To improve the newspaper we had to replace older journalists,' said *Lao Dong's* Hoan. 'That generation were too used to the old system and they bored the readership.'

There is a greater emphasis on professionalism and ethics, although these are still extremely loose, with payments commonplace for favourable coverage. Money plays an important role in Vietnamese journalism – reporters receive envelopes of cash for attending news conferences and officials often expect a small *pourboire* for giving an interview. Several journalists in Ho Chi Minh City took this half-hidden side of journalism a step further by planting an insect in a soft drink and then demanding that the foreign bottling company pay them $20,000 not to write about it. After they were arrested, the company decided to pre-empt any rumours with a news conference to deny any contamination of their product and to reassure the public. Shortly afterwards the city government fined the company $1,000 for holding a press conference without the permission of the Ministry of Culture and Information.

An end to government subsidies has meant a fight for advertising revenues even as the overall market grows at 60 per cent a year. Some publications have provided internal subsidies by renting property to foreign businesses or by hooking up with international publishing companies. These changes have produced a glossier, more entertaining and essentially more trivial press, where the bottom rung of the market is prospering because its readership is only interested in uncontroversial coverage of gruesome crimes, movie stars and soccer. Editor of *Phu Nu* (*Woman*) magazine, The Thanh, led her publication in the shift from ideological correctness to entertainment. 'When we started to write about clothes and make-up, we were condemned for being "bourgeois". Now even newspapers that belong to Party organisations have fashion sections. They see it as a natural need for people.'

It is the most conservative groups in Vietnamese society – the security services – that produce the most lurid newspapers. Public Security Bureaux in many provinces and cities publish either weekly or monthly newspapers filled with the sort of crime stories and sex scandals that are grist for tabloid mills everywhere. Rather like Fleet Street tabloids, the newspapers combine a prurient interest in sleaze with a grating moral tone; a winning mix, it appears, the world over. The bottom rung of newspapers in Vietnam have learned the tricks of the trade amazingly quickly. A headline screamed across the front page of one such magazine: 'WILL VIETNAM'S TOP MODEL MARRY A FOREIGNER', promising a tale of beauty and some hairy Caucasian beast. Inside less space was devoted to the model's answer to the question: 'No.'

Ha Phi Long is one of the few journalists in Vietnam who exudes complete confidence. As a senior official in the security forces and editor-in-chief of *Cong An Thanh Pho Ho Chi Minh City* (the *Ho Chi Minh City Police Weekly*), he is too high up on the political food chain to suffer from the caution that afflicts officials when speaking to foreigners. There is no fear of letting slip an indiscretion, no anxious demands to see the questions before an interview.

Long, a youthful 46-year-old who joined the police as a teenager, presides over two magazines and a film division from a baronial suite of offices near the former presidential palace in Saigon. The circulation of the weekly is more than 500,000, making it highly profitable even though it doesn't take advertising. The newspaper started out as an in-house publication for the city's police, but ten years ago realised it was sitting on an important journalistic resource – access to all the sleaze they could print. Now it flies off the newsstands; it is by far the best-selling paper in Vietnam. A newspaper vendor in Saigon said she sold at least 3,000 a week as people 'rushed to buy it'. She only sold about ten copies of *Nhan Dan* a day.

Like many tabloids, the police paper plays on the public's capacity for cognitive dissonance by sending out a very mixed message; it offers up a dystopia of rampant crime and deviancy and at the same time reassures the public that the police have got it all under control. Long maintains that only 15 per cent of the paper is devoted to crime stories and that its real aim is to propagate government views on law and order. It is hard, however, to imagine eyes pausing for long on a dense tract about land taxes when giant type nearby screams out 'MONSTER OF THE FOREST CAUGHT', or 'POLICE BUST MACAU SEX TOUR RING'.

The attraction of the paper is the same frisson of fear and disgust that tabloids offer up everywhere. But in a country where for decades bad news was no news, the mere fact of the publication of crime stories is a breakthrough. With their vast and attentive audience, these newspapers are important political tools for the Interior Ministry, ensuring a glowing image for the network of police but also creating the undercurrents of concern about crime that they say justifies the vast security force.

While filling his newspaper with such characters as 'a horrible, monstrous, second-to-none, woman gang-boss' and stories of young pimps terrorising prostitutes with acid attacks, Long maintains that Vietnam is happily a low-crime country thanks to the attentions of the police. The newspaper is hardly subtle in its glorification of the Interior Ministry, an institution that acts as the Party's main means of suppression. In these pages it is able to promote the idea that more social controls are needed.

It also enjoys latching on to those issues that can be relied on to raise the sap of public indignation across the world. In a country that is generally quite tolerant of homosexuality (possibly because most people believe it does not exist except among Westerners), the *Ho Chi Minh City Police Weekly* has made an unusual point of trying to have it classified as a 'social evil' even though there is no statute on the books making it illegal. The paper has taken great delight in attacking homosexuals and urging efforts to crush this decadent Western influence. Likewise it has been a leader in campaigns against a number of writers.

Any challenge to the view of the police or crime that the newspaper presents tends to come under intense fire. It hated the movie *Cyclo* by French-Vietnamese director Tran Anh Hung that explored the seamy underworld of Saigon in which the police are seen as either powerless by-standers to crime or active participants. The movie is indeed shockingly violent, but what worried the newspaper's reviewer (who admitted he had not even seen it) was that it 'blackened Vietnam' with its 'poor ideological content'. While it is permissible for the police to cultivate a climate of fear to justify its own ends, the newspaper does not look kindly on anyone else examining the realities of crime in Vietnam.

Despite the insidious aspects of the police newspapers, the Vietnamese tabloids have had an invigorating impact on the press. For the first time in decades, Vietnamese have newspapers that they want to read. Not only have some of these papers occasionally raised challenges on social issues, they have freed the press from the dreadful language used in *Nhan Dan* and other 'serious' papers. The strident tone, the white noise rhetoric ('President Le Duc Anh said he highly appreciated the absolute unanimity and traditional amity between our countries . . .'), the formulaic delivery of news has all been subverted by editors.

Kim Hanh of *Saigon Tiep Thi* has a gnomic slogan that sums up her strategy for her newspaper: 'Fewer words, more information.' Newspapers have been forced to discard some of the worthless diatribes of the past and hook into the pungent language of the streets. One publication that has particularly played off this is *Tuoi Tre Cuoi*, a satirical paper that publishes mostly cartoons. There is a long tradition of subversive caricatures and political lampooning although much of this died after 1954. It has returned with some astringent cartoons on corruption and government mismanagement although the leadership are spared any comment. The paper has pushed the boundaries of what is acceptable, frequently irritating the Party with its subversive tone. *Tuoi Tre Cuoi*, however, rarely fails to play to the lowest common denominator. It has a tendency towards the cynical and xenophobic; one cartoon showed pregnant Vietnamese women parading with placards on which were pasted photos of Western men. The caption: 'Where are they now?'

Ahead of the Eighth Communist Party Congress in 1996, all newspapers were ordered to tone down their coverage, dropping even the officially sanctioned criticisms of corruption. President Anh issued a warning to journalists that their coverage had become too negative and that now that the bright skies of economic stability had returned, newspapers had better turn their attention to the successes of the Party and the leadership. In a sly rejection of this order, several newspapers enacted a quiet revenge on the leaders by devoting many column inches to the Clean Hands campaign in Italy, as well as the trials of former South Korean presidents Chun Do-Won and Roh Tae-Woo.

Editors may be able to get away with some indirect rebukes of the leaders, but even the lightest of topics can arouse the fury of the authorities or rival editors when they appear in foreign-backed publications. A Singaporean firm, Communications Indochine Pte. Ltd., ran into problems with its Vietnamese-language women's magazine called *Femme*. Before the magazine had even hit the newsstands, an editor of a rival magazine accused it of an 'ugly and distorted' vision of the country. 'Vietnamese would be unable to recognise the depiction of their society in this magazine,' wrote

Nguyen Thi Van Anh, editor of *Phu Nu* magazine, in a front-page article in *Nhan Dan*.

What caused offence was a fashion spread depicting a foreign model in a tumble-down but picturesque village, surrounded by grubby children and toothless peasants. Fashion magazines have often featured such images, but in Hanoi they provoked a furious response from Anh, who, of course, categorically denied that she was prompted by a fear of competition. The Ministry of Culture and Information seized 30,000 copies of the magazine at the docks; it was never distributed or published again. *Femme*'s publisher was left muttering bewildered protestations about how she was Asian and thus understood Vietnam; meanwhile there was no shortage of those who enjoyed the irony of seeing a publication from Singapore, no friend of a free press, so swiftly dispatched by the Vietnamese.

The *Vietnam Investment Review*, a publication officially owned by the Ministry of Planning and Investment but run by an Australian company, has faced a similar array of problems although it had managed to navigate the shoals and craggy reefs of political sensitivity for more than five years. The English-language *Review* was more PR rag than serious publication, as its publisher admitted, but even so it frequently ran into difficulties over its articles or photographs. Pictures of a farewell party for an expelled foreign journalist that were featured in a social section sparked off an Interior Ministry investigation and the newspaper narrowly avoided closure. Any negative news about investment had to be slyly woven into stories as the main focus of the newspaper was relentlessly upbeat.

The Vietnamese media no longer serves up the monolithic view of society it did before 1986 but neither will it push debate beyond the boundaries set by the Party. But even the harshest ideologues bear in mind the role of rising consumer demand in the collapse of Communism in Eastern Europe. They now have to allow entertainment and even criticisms that would not have been tolerated in the years immediately before 1986. They are very much aware of the usefulness of the press as an escape valve in a society with few means of public expression or debate.

It will be a long time, however, until Vietnam develops a

combative media that in any way stands in opposition to the government or that seriously questions its policies or personalities. The press may be able to attack corruption, but it cannot examine the causes of graft or the moral bankruptcy of the system. It can criticise the implementation of policies but not the policies themselves; it can entertain but cannot inform too deeply. It can stand slightly apart from society but it is not able to champion the development of the civil society that Vietnam needs.

Policies on the press have created a sensationalist and intrusive journalism on a par with Western tabloids; at the same time the media provides few of the social or political checks that the society needs. For a brief period after 1986 the Party tolerated a feisty and combative press but it tightened up its controls after seeing what went on in Eastern Europe. While the press has been freed to attract readers with tabloid stories, it is not free to challenge the state. Officials are aware that they cannot control all the information coming into the country, but they are able to keep a firm grip on the domestic media. As newspapers and new television channels proliferate, monitoring their output has become an increasing struggle and a source of anxiety. However, the press remains timid and unwilling to use its power to effect real change in society; journalists are mostly following changes, and reacting to the shifts in their society. Survival is, as always, the priority.

The former priest and editor Nguyen Ngoc Lan said, 'an apparatus press is a useless apparatus' because it is unread and ignored by the majority. The government can control the press and harness it to serve only its ideas, but it cannot make anyone read it or believe it. The media will eventually need to reflect more than the shift from an impoverished Spartan society to one obsessed with consumption. If it is to play a role in dealing with issues of corruption, crime, education, the development of civil society, legal reforms and political change, it will have to stand up for itself. It will eventually have to deal with demands that the Party allow those voices that have been silenced for so long to be heard.

10

Cymbals and Litanies

No sugar and no honey of success
can bribe my tongue
Thunder that crashes overhead
can't strike me down.
And if they seize my paper, seize my pen,
I'll take a knife and write on stone.

PHUNG QUAN
'What My Mother Once Told Me', 1956

Where the deadening hand of state censorship falls across journalism, limiting it as an arena for critical thought and expression, fiction and poetry take on an even greater significance. In the 1980s, literature was one of the most important ways in which Vietnamese aired their frustrations and grievances. In short stories, novels and poetry they challenged official versions of history and politics, and struck out at conventions, both literary and social. This writing did more than just trace a jagged seismograph of changing values and ideas, it provided an unsettling cultural edge to *Doi Moi*. Writers were generating change, not just describing it.

In a few years, a small group of writers, editors and publishers rolled back decades of control and offered fresh views of contemporary and historical Vietnam. Using disguise, analogy and parody, they slid around the censors and published stories that would send ripples of delighted surprise and scandal through the reading public. Readers eagerly awaited their copies of newspapers and magazines to decipher stories and pick out the array of forbidden ideas hidden within the text. Literature was no longer purely the tool of the state; it wasn't just about the edification of the masses. Instead it was clever, critical and slippery. Characters did not just adhere to the same old models – the good peasant, the brave soldier, the wise cadre and the evil landlord – but were as raw-edged and riotously diverse as life itself. For the first time since the 1950s, Vietnamese writing was alive and energetic.

Writers are supposed to be important in Vietnam. It is a country that prides itself on its high literacy rate and its respect for the written word. Streets are named after poets and everyone knows of the great nineteenth-century bard Nguyen Du, whose epic poem 'The Tale of Kieu' is regarded as the country's foremost literary treasure. Newspapers publish short stories and poems daily, bookstores are packed and many streets have small private libraries from which books can be borrowed for a few cents. Literacy, represented by a nation of people with their noses tucked into books, has been touted as a great socialist success story in Vietnam, an expression of their determination to overcome the aftermath of the war.

The veneration of writers in Vietnam has become something of a myth. Certainly literature does matter; it is a vital part of life for many readers, but writers themselves are not treated too well. They have been subjected to stifling political control and censorship. Even if they can get their books published, they rarely make any money. Almost all of the most important literary figures have to rely on second jobs or run their own businesses. A small number have earned some money from translations of their works published overseas, but most writers live in a shocking state of penury. Despite this, Vietnam has in recent years produced some remarkable literature; complex, charged writing that has made people sit up and take notice for the first time in decades.

In October 1987, the Party chief Nguyen Van Linh addressed a group of around a hundred writers and intellectuals to give his official approval to the currents of critical writing that had been trickling out. Linh complained that the literature written since the end of the war had been poor and the Party was in part to blame. Writers and artists needed new freedoms if they were to address the issues affecting Vietnam. He urged writers to infuse their work with a new spirit.

His speech opened the floodgates of criticism, releasing a pressure that had been building since the late 1970s. Speaker after speaker attacked the limits of socialist realism and the controls of the party. Nguyen Ngoc, then editor of *Van Nghe* magazine, talked of a 'lost generation' of artists and writers who had been forced to 'talk only about success, never failure; about achievements, never losses; about correct decisions, never mistaken ones'. There was a widespread rejection of the artistic controls imposed by the Party and a surge of anger against the passivity, self-loathing and artistic weakness it had bred. 'For too long the leadership held artists in great contempt,' the critic Nguyen Dang Manh said. 'People held in contempt end up seeing themselves as small and contemptible.'

Not everyone sprang into action with critical tracts and subversive novels. There were powerful and bitter memories of the oppression of writers in the 1950s when a tense Maoist grip strangled a budding movement known as *Nhan Van Giai Pham*. In 1945 many writers and artists had joined the Revolution, but the atmosphere in the areas controlled by the nationalist Vietnam Independence League – the Vietminh – started to change distinctly after the Chinese Communist Party victory in 1949. Mao Zedong's defeat of the Kuomintang freed up political and military advisors who were sent to Vietnam. With them they brought many new ideas of control and class warfare, including self-criticisms and self-rectification programmes under which people were expected to confess their 'class attitudes'.

Rules on artistic production were laid out by Truong Chinh, the pro-Chinese ideologue who then headed the Communist Party. There was to be no 'art for art's sake', only art that served the Revolution and the masses. Artists and writers were urged to take on the task of 'awakening, mobilising and organising the masses, imbuing them with a spirit, a will, a faith, appealing to them to rise up to carry out the Revolution . . . Just as we have to manufacture bazookas, mortars and guns to fire at the enemy, we must likewise create cultural bazookas, mortars and guns to destroy them.'

What this meant in practice was works of literature in which stereotypes of good peasants, evil landlords and feudalists and colonial foreigners were arrayed against each other with inevitable victory for those who were on the right side of Marxist history. To encourage the emergence of writers with the right class backgrounds, workers were encouraged to submit their writings and those with even a basic literacy found themselves bundled up the official ladder to literary stardom. The army was a particularly fertile ground; while the majority of works were set in a rigid and formulaic mould of socialist realism, the ranks produced some of the most important writers and critics to emerge after 1945.

The restrictions imposed by the Party caused considerable resentment among many writers who formed a movement that resisted some of the demands of socialist realist literature. In this they were influenced by a Chinese writer Hu Feng who, according to the French historian Georges Boudarel, urged a return to 'humanism' rather than rigid obeisance to the diktats of the Party. His ideas were picked by Tran Dan, a young writer sent to China to write a filmscript for a movie about the battle of Dien Bien Phu.

Tran Dan's book about the battle, *Wave upon Wave of Men*, depicted soldiers as human rather than purely fictitious heroes. With its realistic tone, it became a hit in bookstores. A group of like-minded artists, most of them also military men, gathered around Tran Dan and applied some pressure for a less restrictive environment for the arts. Tran Dan prepared a statement delivered to the leadership that denied the Party's idea that it should command the complete allegiance of all artists:

> The highest expression of a writer's responsibility is his
> respect for and his faithfulness to truth. That is the supreme
> measure by which one appraises a writer and his works . . .
> Truth, with its breadth and scope transcends all directives, all
> theories. Revolution needs no apostle to burn incense and
> praise programmes and has even less use for shamans who
> celebrate its cult as they clap cymbals and intone litanies.
> Today one finds in our art much artifice (and even hypocrisy).
> To call it by its rightful name, it's a hackneyed, simplistic,
> elementary literature. The writer sets up a frame and then
> crams reality into it.

All of this was radically opposed to what the Party's cultural czars such as Truong Chinh and the poet To Huu were saying. The Revolution required a merging of the political and artistic. The aim of writing was to create models of the new revolutionary man. At this time the Party was busy in its programme of land reform that would radically change the political and social landscape. Land reform turned into a violent purging of former village leaders. Grudges were taken out indiscriminately and thousands of people were executed. The Party, up to then a diverse group bound together more by nationalism than ideology, was purged of all those who did not hew to a narrow Maoist line.

The backlash to these new artistic and social policies emerged in two journals first published in 1956 – *Giai Pham* (Works of Beauty), and *Nhan Van* (Humanism). *Nhan Van* was published only five times. Its sixth edition was stopped at the printers and the magazine banned. Despite its brief life, its echoes are still heard thirty years later. These two magazines prompted a frenzy of publishing until the end of the next year with half a dozen journals of criticism and literature appearing. There was a demand for debate and openness although these writers, almost all members of the resistance and many from the army, were not trying to overthrow socialism, but to modify its form.

The articles and short stories published in *Nhan Van* and *Giai Pham* were often caustic and directly dealt with the issues that trouble Vietnamese politics and intellectual life to this day – democracy, the rule of law and the role of political institutions and freedom of expression. Indeed the writing that emerged at this time was the most assertive to come out of Hanoian intellectual circles since before 1945.

Land reform had reaped a bitter backlash for the Party, which had become more cautious in the way it dealt with political dissent. But controls were tightened, forcing much of the criticism to go underground or to appear in oblique metaphors that could be decoded by those in the know. By 'talking in shadows and wind' writers could stray far beyond the boundaries.

In January 1958 the machinery of Party control turned against these writers. Magazines were closed and the Party daily *Nhan Dan* ran a series of articles by Ho Chi Minh urging the destruction of 'rightists' as the writers had now been dubbed. The Central Committee met to discuss the problems of the arts and literature, and the poet and politician To Huu began a campaign to crush 'saboteurs on the ideological and cultural front'.

The extent of dissent in the arts at this time is illustrated by the number of people forced to undergo rectification classes by the Party. According to Boudarel, of the 476 people compelled to attend self-criticism meetings some 300 were writers and artists and the rest were 'cultural officials'. Those purged included Van Cao, a musician who composed the national anthem. He would spend much of his life in disgrace. He enjoyed a few years of rehabilitation before his death in 1995, when his obituaries glossed over his troubled life.

Tran Dan, the writer who had kicked off the movement, tried to commit suicide by cutting himself with a razor. He survived, but a jagged scar was notched around his neck in a livid reminder of those days. Artists were sent out to work in factories or in the fields to reinforce their understanding of peasants and workers. It emerged later that much tougher actions had been taken against some who were tried as spies and sentenced to up to fifteen years in jail. The crushing of the *Nhan Van Giai Pham* movement would presage a shift in cultural and political policies after 1960 when Le Duan consolidated his power. There was an increasing emphasis on the ideological and cultural aspects of the Revolution and the creation of a new socialist man. Soon, with the country at war, the emphasis was on survival and fighting and there was little room for intellectual debate. The suppression of the *Nhan Van Giai Pham* movement began three decades of suffocating intellectual subservience in Vietnam. All arts were put to the service of reunification and war, a movement that dominated all culture until the 1980s when the ghosts of *Nhan Van Giai Pham* could be partially exorcised with the arrival of a new generation of writers.

The new writers who emerged in the late 1980s were a marked departure from the tightly controlled world of official cultural associations where most of Vietnam's intelligentsia reside. These supposedly revolutionary groups preferred their art and literature to be stuffily conformist; in one of those paradoxes that Marxist states throw up, their supposedly revolutionary models could have been the worst sort of Victorian sentimental painting and writing. One of the most outspoken defenders of the Party line on the arts was Phan Cu De, Director of the Institute of International Cultures

at Hanoi University and author of a number of volumes on literature. De was an ambitious academic who had long been a cultural
henchman in charge of enforcing the rules that stifled so much creativity. For his decades of unswerving loyalty going back to the
crushing of the *Nhan Van Giai Pham* movement, he had been
rewarded with the usual perks of foreign travel and access to funds
that were used to restrain any critical impulses among academics.

De was an eager voice in defence of cultural controls, always
ready with a shrill attack on a writer. He was quick to step in following an appeal by General Tran Do, a former top ideology and
cultural official who became a vocal critic of the Party, that the
authorities shed 'the concept that "works have problems", meaning
that they must be controlled and examined, even done away with'.
De launched a defence of the critic's right to censor. 'Why shouldn't
managers and critics have the right to "examine" works with problems that have been condemned by the masses and the press?'

'People cannot be allowed to do whatever they want in the way
they are now allowed to eat whatever they want,' he wrote in an
article in the Party's theoretical journal. 'That would be tantamount
to loosening the responsibilities of critics and managers. Creators
have creative freedom but at the same time freedom must also be
given to critics and managers.' In this sinister tangle of words, De
argued that depriving him of the power of censorship would violate
his freedom.

De was particularly aggressive against the writer Duong Thu
Huong. When asked in an interview about her being honoured with
a French cultural award in 1994, the *Chevalier des Arts et des Lettres*,
his face strained into a rictus of loathing, every muscle in his neck
and around his mouth tensed in anger. 'She's not the best, she's not
the best,' he hissed. 'Why has she been honoured with this award?
It is an insult to all Vietnamese writers.'

The flap surrounding the award of this bauble – other honourees
include such luminaries as Sylvester Stallone and Sharon Stone – to
a Vietnamese writer showed how literary and intellectual freedoms
had contracted from the period of relative openness in the late
1980s. The award might have passed unnoticed but for the furious
reaction it provoked in Hanoi. The Ministry of Culture and
Information announced it was suspending all co-operation with the

French government. Professor De jumped at the chance to denounce the writer, spiking his diatribes with renewed accusations that Huong was unpatriotic, an unforgivable sin in Vietnam. The literary magazine *Van Nghe*, no longer a great supporter of fresh voices in literature, denounced the award 'as a political act . . . that is bound to raise legitimate doubts about the aims of France's cultural policies towards Vietnam'. It was certainly a political act as the culture minister, Jacques Toubon, was also mayor of the *arrondissement* in Paris with the largest number of overseas Vietnamese, many of whom were great admirers of Huong.

By the time she was awarded the medal, it had been nearly six years since Huong had published a novel in Vietnam but she was still a focus of rancour and contention. In those years she had been jailed for seven months and become an outcast from official literary circles. Her name was taboo in the official press and her writings were published infrequently and then only by editors willing to risk official censure. General Secretary Linh called her a 'dissident slut', an epithet she wore like a badge of honour. More hurtfully, articles appeared overseas questioning the quality of her writing and one foreign journalist accused her of being an hysteric embittered by the failure of her marriage.

Huong's sin was one of apostasy. She had once been a bright-eyed enthusiast of the Communist Party, indeed she was a proselytising, hand-clapping member of the faith. In 1968 she joined a propaganda team working in Quang Binh province in the centre of the divided country. Her group of performers was part of a movement, motivated by the slogan 'The sound of singing drives away the sound of bombs', that performed socialist works to divert attention from the suffering of a province that was heavily bombed by the United States. 'During that time in Quang Binh, I had the chance to see the tolerance, the suffering and the shortages that people experienced, which were simply unimaginable,' she said. There she witnessed the sight of her country being bombed 'back into the Stone Age', in the immortal words of US Air Force General Curtis Le May. 'They were partly successful in this,' she said. 'With a B-52 everything in a house, even the simplest things like kitchenware and clothing, were lost. People had to use tin cans or coconut shells to cook or eat.'

For seven years, Huong was part of the massive war effort and its sense of excitement, direction and valour. The end of the conflict in 1975 created a short-lived elation and then a creeping disillusionment at what had been won and the price that had been paid for victory. Huong marked the decline of her faith from her first visit to Saigon shortly after the North had taken the city.

The first impression I had was the sight of so many books being sold everywhere on the sidewalks, all these books by authors that I had just heard about like Dostoevsky, Chekhov, Balzac, Stendhal, Anatole France and also many American authors. It really amazed me.

I was amazed that there were so many radios and cassette recorders on sale. In the North people could only listen to a very rudimentary kind of radio. If someone had a radio that could pick up foreign broadcasts they had to have a permit from the police and they had to be considered very trustworthy by the government. When I went to the South what dazzled me was not the luxury of the so-called phoney prosperity but the availability of media and books from around the world. I started to realise that a regime that forces people to listen to just one radio station, that blocks all sources of information and keeps its people in a dark corner must be an inhuman regime. This was the first shock I got about the society I was living in.

As with many Vietnamese, the creeping sense of disillusionment took time to crystallise into anything of substance. Huong carried on as a propagandist, writing filmscripts and short stories. Her writing rarely strayed from the format of socialist realism. In 1979 she wrote a number of furiously anti-Chinese tracts after Deng Xiaoping ordered his forces across the border into Vietnam. She was even part of a cultural troop that went to the northern frontier provinces to make films about the brief but destructive border war.

'When the war was over and we were left with our own reality and society, I started to write for my own needs,' she said. At first she wrote mostly anodyne and sentimental love stories, but her works began to take on a more critical edge. In the story 'Love Story

Told Before Dawn', she started to explore the intrusion of ideology into the lives of ordinary people, a theme that is recurrent in her later writings. A couple marry but the relationship sours. The husband asks for a divorce so he can remarry, but after the interference of an official from the women's union, the wife refuses to end the marriage. The story ends with the woman realising that because of this official intrusion, she has spoiled both her and her husband's prospects for happiness.

In 1980 Huong complained in remarks at a conference of the poor state of Vietnamese writing, but was quickly warned to hold her tongue. In the next few years her filmscripts tested some of the boundaries of what was acceptable. Most of them were not and were rejected.

Her first literary success, *Beyond Illusions*, was published in 1986 just as literature was starting to come alive again. She followed it up with *Paradise of the Blind*, an enormous critical and public success. It broke through the conventions of socialist realism by portraying the miseries inflicted by the Communist Party during the land reforms of the 1950s. The villains were not the conventional class enemies or foreign invaders, but party factotums themselves. Their betrayal of the values of the Revolution was laid out for all to see in a book that told its story in an open, almost cinematic way with little hidden in the allusions that normally disguised the political content of Vietnamese writing.

Huong's background in movies and propaganda shows through in the strong plotting and style of *Paradise of the Blind*. It is the story of a young woman, Hang, who relates the story while working in the Soviet Union in the 1980s. Decades earlier her uncle had led a land reform committee in a northern village. Hang's uncle drove her father from the village and dispossessed her mother; rather than being punished for his misdeeds he rises up through the ranks of the Party along with his ambitious wife. Later the family move to Hanoi, where the uncle and his wife become senior cadres and Hang's mother prospers as a market trader, a lucrative but despised way of earning a living. The dishonesty of the Party and the hypocrisy of its acolytes pervades the book; a society that claimed to be egalitarian is actually highly stratified and kept in check with fear. When it was published, the book was astonishing for its honest depiction of life from the 1950s to the 1980s. What has surprised many readers is that the war is almost absent from this intensely domestic book; politics and history are forces that buffet these characters and leave them struggling to find a small measure of comfort wherever they can.

Huong had become a popular writer of fiction but was soon to emerge as a more politically-charged figure than other writers of this time. She became increasingly outspoken as her works gained in popularity, selling tens of thousands of copies – unusually large numbers in Vietnam. The fires of dissent were fanned by the cracking up of Communism in Eastern Europe and Huong became one of the most important flames, although at first she worked within the confines set by the Party. In 1990 she left the Party – the Party says she resigned, she says she was kicked out – and a year later she was arrested on charges of smuggling 'reactionary' documents out of the country. The documents were her own fictional writings and she had been turned in by an overseas Vietnamese man to whom she had given them to take out of the country. To many it smacked of a trap set by the Party, then engaged in tightening the political and cultural vice. She was held outside Hanoi in a compound run by the Ministry of Interior but was released after seven months. Nearly thirty-five pounds lighter as a result of the prison diet, she was unbowed by the detention or the constant interrogations.

After her release, Huong was kept under close watch and was refused permission to leave the country. She began to regard the years of openness between 1987 and 1990 as something of a trap for intellectuals. In her view it had been a repetition of other closely controlled periods of openness that exposed writers. Once out in the open, they were marginalised and silenced.

Huong's was a difficult voice to keep down. She has maintained her dignity in the face of almost constant attacks on her, some of them from unlikely sources. One of the most extraordinary was by Barry Wain, a former editor of the *Asian Wall Street Journal*. Without actually interviewing Huong and offering no named source for his information, Wain wrote in his newspaper that 'a major factor in Huong's disillusionment is her troubled personal life, particularly her husband's decision in the mid 1980s to leave her for her best friend'. Wain portrayed her as emotionally unstable and promiscuous, two canards that have been levelled against upstart women writers for centuries. She had been 'driven almost crazy by endless tribulations', he quoted 'friends' as saying. This unnamed group of confidantes claimed all that Huong wants is a 'normal home, a proper husband and a peaceful family'.

Wain suggested that Huong was only a second-rate writer and therefore not entitled to political opinions. His accusation that her disillusionment with Communism was caused mostly by her troubled private life was justly attacked for its sexism and irrelevance when the article appeared in 1993.

Wain, who has generally taken a thoughtful approach to Vietnamese writers in his articles, played completely into the hands of propagandists and those figures in Hanoi who cultivate visiting correspondents to spread disinformation. Mostly ignoring her work, he attacked the blurbs on a translation of her book published in the United States and said that she had never been imprisoned for her demands for political freedoms but for sending abroad documents 'detrimental to state security'. It is remarkable that Wain would accept the version promoted by the Vietnamese government. The piece reflected the endless attempts by the government to discredit Huong. In this case, the bitter and gossipy fringes of Hanoi's literati were happy to help. But the writer is actually quiet and contemplative; her warmth and gently subversive humour belie Wain's portrait of her as a neurasthenic and weepy political ingenue.

Huong has been seen as a threat by so many writers and rivals on the sidelines of the intellectual world that many of them have been willing to denounce her. Many, like Phan Cu De, have taken a particular relish in tearing her down, using their cultural power to try to destroy her reputation at home and abroad. She, in return, has been scathing about the petrified intellectual landscape in Hanoi. 'There are only a few single individuals who have the quality of intellectuals. They are aware of the freedom of the mind. They are willing to pay any price to protect their own dignity. All the rest are just civil servants. They are paid by the government so they have to follow its ideology.'

'I'm at the margins of society now,' she said. 'I'm an outsider. I know and accept that.' Her works are rarely published, critics have turned on her and she has been superseded by a new generation of writers who are less explicitly political, but who focus on the concerns thrown up by *Doi Moi*. The harshness with which she has been treated is undeserved. She might not have reached the literary level of writers such as Thiep or Pham Thi Hoai, but her novels are far from pedestrian when compared with the mass of literature in Vietnam. More importantly, she has been a voice of honesty and courage, attributes that are recognised even by the many intellectuals who dislike her writing.

In a matter of a few years, Huong went from Party insider to outcast. In 1987, she was being hugged by the General Secretary of the Communist Party and urged to speak out. A decade later she had won some acclaim overseas but was reviled by the political establishment at home. According to one critic, she had not just attacked the Party but had 'insulted history itself'. Huong had no regrets about the path she had taken, but expressed some degree of cynicism about those in the Party who had kicked off the literary movement. Vietnam, she said, was still a 'feudal Asian monarchy' where rulers like Linh had no respect for writers. 'Nguyen Van Linh just imitated Mao Zedong's dictum about shaking the net to see what fish you can catch.'

Literature has had an extraordinary capacity to needle the government. In 1972 at the height of fighting in Vietnam, Pham Tien Duat, a soldier and poet, wrote a short verse called 'White Circle':

> Bomb smoke rises in black circles
> White circles hover along the ground
> My brother and I walk on in silence
> the silence expected after war
> Friend, there is no loss greater than death
> The white mourning band takes the shape of a zero
> Inside that white circle
> a head burns with fire.

For writing this verse, Duat was thrown out of the Communist Party. Its sadness and sense of loss were intolerable in wartime.

Writers were expected to cheer up the troops and rouse the masses with tales of heroism. Duat's stark, grieving verse with its references to the white turbans worn by those in mourning would not create revolutionary fervour or 'drown out the sound of bombs'.

Eighteen years after 'White Circle' was written, a book was published that recast the war in the eyes of many Vietnamese and became the first major international success by a Vietnamese novelist. *The Sorrow of War*, published in Vietnam with the less contentious title, *The Fate of Love*, would transform writing about the war.

When Bao Ninh went to join the army in 1968 he was a skinny seventeen-year-old. Like all students graduating from his school he went to a football field outside Hanoi and joined the queue of young men. 'At the recruiting station they had singers and poets, working up the spirits of those signing up. There were two types of people – those who really carried torches for the war, full of anti-American spirit, signing their forms in their own blood. And then there were those like me. We were told to go and we went. We weren't particularly afraid as we knew we had to fight.'

The sounds of the poets and performers in the drama troupes would become an enduring memory for Bao Ninh, who spent the next decade of his life in the army. He became one of the heroes that the performers would sing about, one of the many generations of Vietnamese warriors who fought foreigners. He was one of the Glorious 47th Youth Brigade, 500 boys who went off to fight. In 1975, he was one of just a quarter of those men who came back to Hanoi. Moved to a number of different units during the war and its aftermath, he was among the soldiers who fought in the final battle at Ton San Nhat Airport in Saigon just before the city fell and Vietnam was united.

The Sorrow of War was published in 1990 to mixed reviews. For many the complex, dream-like novel was a more realistic representation of the war than anything else they had read before. It was filled with the *Sturm und Drang* of conflict; its shocking scenes of violence and depravity ripped open the wounds of the war. The soldiers are real humans who do not behave like the heroes in most Vietnamese novels. They spend their evenings getting high or desperately scavenging for food. Their return to the world of post-war

Hanoi was a return to bleak disillusionment, not the utopia they had been promised. Like Duong Thu Huong, Bao Ninh writes movingly about the 'fervour fallen flat' that characterised the aftermath of the war.

The book's structure moves rapidly between flashback, memories and the present. Its blurring between the voice of the main character Kien and the narrator, marked it out as much more complex than other literature of the time. This distanced Bao Ninh from the book and its provocative opinions. The structure is also a marked and deliberate contrast to socialist realist literature which preferred straightforward plots. Despite his efforts in some ways to remove himself from the sentiments expressed in the book, Bao Ninh faced some splenetic attacks over the book, not least from some other veterans who loathed his portrayal of fighting men. They were enraged about his suggestion that the war was a civil conflict and not another chapter in the long history of fighting off foreign aggressors.

In 'Wild Wind', a short story published in the late 1980s, he wrote about a village that was 'protected by American forces' and about 'the horrors of brothers killing each other'. These lines sparked a torrent of criticism in the army newspaper *Quan Doi Nhan Dan*. 'Who asked Americans to come and protect a Vietnamese village? When a foreign army comes to another country to occupy the land and kill the people, they should be called "invaders" not "protectors".'

Bao Ninh, the critic said, had 'not concentrated his hatred on the enemy but on our national heroes: Vietnamese soldiers'. His writing in this case reflects his experience. Bao Ninh says he never fought against American infantry, only South Vietnamese. It is this unacknowledged fratricide that leaves some of the greatest legacies of bitterness in Vietnam. His picture of Vietnamese as superstitious and often terrified has proved more recognisable and moving to many veterans than the official version of the war.

But criticism did come from many other writers who had fought and written about combat. The writer Do Kim Cuong, himself a war veteran, complained that *The Sorrow of War* was not realistic, it had not been true to his own memories of the war. He brushed off the idea that it was a novel and not supposed to be true, instead angrily denouncing it as a falsification of history. This is a criticism many American veterans have levelled at other writers or film-makers whose works do not mesh with their own memories of the conflict. Few people who fought are ready to acknowledge that memories of war tend to be unreliable and evanescent, much like the jumble of images in *The Sorrow of War*.

For Bao Ninh the attention went much further than simply *ad hominem* attacks in newspapers. He was closely monitored by the police, he often was forced to spend time in the countryside to escape the pressures of life in Hanoi. His works were not formally banned but were not easy to buy in Vietnamese. After he refused to make cuts in a second novel, the publishing house declined to put out the book. The government denied him permission to travel overseas except for a trip to Sweden with members of the official Writers' Association. Several writers, even those who have not adopted an overtly political voice, find themselves shadowed and monitored in a manner that is tiring and dispiriting. These controls may in the end be more effective than throwing writers into jail; instead the state saps their creative spirit in a less obvious way.

Bao Ninh, himself a relatively apolitical character, says Vietnamese have no interest in ideology or Communism and would never go to war again. He flinches when he sees conflicts on the television news, reminded of the horrors of the past and he talks not of enormous glories of the war or of the repetitive tales of suffering, but often of the ambiguous and clearly unheroic aspects of soldiers' lives. Just after the fall of Saigon, when he was one of the soldiers who fought in the last battle of the war to take Ton San Nhat Airport, he entered the home of a family in the city. He imagined himself as a young hero; to the family he was a terrifying armed intruder. They cowered in a corner and begged not to be killed. Bao Ninh says he left bewildered and shocked that not everyone had seen him as a liberator.

There is often an attempt to make direct links between Bao Ninh's life and the novel, which is certainly drawn from his own vivid experiences of combat. He went off to war as a young man and fought in some of the toughest battles. But his life is not a mirror of the protagonist Kien's anomic existence. His father was not a tor-mented painter but a rather staid academic. His mother had been a librarian and had provided him with a multitude of books, including translations of foreign works, that were generally unavailable in Hanoi in the 1960s. As with many of the most interesting voices in Vietnamese literature, he gives much credit to an education that was allowed to stray from the rigid boundaries of the classroom where literature has until recently been examined only through the prism of class analysis.

After the years of conflict that took him all across the country he returned to civilian life in Hanoi with a deepening sense of resentment at the country's failures in peacetime. He studied biology and worked in a laboratory before he was sacked. He was kicked out of the Communist Party, which he had joined as a soldier. While he was drifting around, a victim of the ennui and economic collapse after the war, the eminent critic and teacher Hoang Ngoc Hien, took him under his wing at the Nguyen Du School, a special training centre for writers modelled after the Pushkin Institute in Moscow. It was there that Bao Ninh wrote a short story that evolved into *The Sorrow of War*.

There is not a lot of room for catharsis in Vietnam; people find what solace they can and many did in Bao Ninh's work. *The Sorrow of War* released the currents of suffering that lie just below the surface lives of many veterans. Bao Ninh, himself, finds escape in the bottle and by fleeing Hanoi to the countryside, not because it is easier to write there, 'but because it is easier to survive'. In the dusty political ambience of Hanoi, Bao Ninh comes off as something of a bohemian but he is fairly careful to avoid confrontations with the authorities and keeps a low profile, despite the success of his book overseas where it has won a number of awards. As he put it: 'Too much success is a prison for a writer in Vietnam.'

He has retained a bluntness that the government does not like, a refreshing honesty, particularly in his clear-eyed views of the mythology that surrounds the war. He suffers none of the self-importance of that generation as they survey young people today who have not known the rigours of conflict. 'I could tell young people that I fought for freedom and independence but the reality is more modest. I was told to do my military service and I was on the winning side. The younger generation is better than ours, ours is too tough, under-educated, conservative and over-fed with patriotism.

Our generation has no right to lecture the younger generation on our great victories. We never reached the goals for which we were fighting.'

Looking back on the day he was drafted, his voice took on an edge when he spoke about the performers cheering on the new recruits. 'I hated the singers and poets. I didn't like the spirit of exulting fighting or war. Coming home was different. Like all soldiers, I came home to see my mother. It was a very sentimental day. And then we went back to a very monotonous banal life. And then despair and distrust.'

Nguyen Huy Thiep came among them, a critic wrote, like a 'quirky wind or a troubling star', a strange natural phenomenon that sent a shiver of consternation through the world of Vietnamese writing. He plunged the desiccated critics and cultural commissars into a state of bewilderment. Critics had played an important role in policing the pages of literary magazines and newspapers with forensic skills that were able to excise any hidden meanings. Their scratchy pens were poised over any potentially troublesome poem or story, ready to seek out the pessimistic or critical, anything that strayed from the numbing cheer of socialist literature.

The only time Thiep came remotely close to the path of socialist realism was to mock the language, tone or characters of the Party's house style. He first caused a stir with a short story called 'The General Retires', published in June 1987. A senior military officer returns home to his village outside Hanoi after years spent on the battlefield to find a senile wife and a mean-spirited, soulless world. Although he imagines himself to be inured to suffering and death from war, he is shocked by what he finds at home. His son is passive and awkward, married to a woman hardened by the post-war poverty. He is horrified by his daughter-in-law's sideline from her job in a maternity hospital, from where she collects aborted foetuses and feeds them to the Alsatian puppies she breeds to supplement their income. When the general confronts her, she is not contrite but scolds a worker for not grinding up the embryos to disguise them.

The world of 'The General Retires' is one of meagre economic calculations and increasingly ostentatious displays from the emerging rich who have made their money from crime or corruption. There is a ribald marriage between a villager and his heavily-pregnant girl-friend. 'The wedding on the edge of the city was a ridiculously vulgar affair. Three cars. Filtered cigarettes that were replaced by roll-your-owns at the end of the dinner. There were fifty trays of food but twelve were left untouched . . .' As a band plays deafening Abba and Beatles songs, the general becomes 'bewildered and miserable'.

The funeral of the general's wife is also a haphazard and dismal affair that further alienates him from his home village and family. Eventually he returns to his army unit, dying during the war against the Chinese in 1979. Thiep's tone is flat and deadening, accentuating the bleakness of those times. His characters describe themselves in the bureaucratic tone of the all-important political dossiers kept on all adults. They rarely connect with each other, remaining inarticulate or ill at ease. A Vietnamese critic wrote of it: 'The world of "The General Retires" is a world where man has no desire, no hope, where society has no future. The general is the only one of Thiep's characters who understands that faith gives us the strength to live and yet he is also the one who lives, and who chooses to die, in the name of an obsolete faith.'

Thiep's historical trilogy of short stories – 'A Sharp Sword', 'Fired Gold' and 'Chastity' – sealed his reputation among his admirers and detractors. In these stories, he tore down the myths of a well known and contentious period of Vietnamese history at the end of the eighteenth century. It did not offer a simple alternative history, but the possibility of many views, questioning deeply-held notions of authority and truth. He broke away from a tradition of didactic writing, allowing readers to make up their minds about his characters. The stories took heroes off their pedestals and added some humanity to the cardboard villains of Communist Party historiography. The sacred legacy of heroism used by the leadership to justify their power was revealed as a sham. 'What the new generation of Vietnamese writers want to say is that "heroism" is not only dead, it is not only boring, it is not only a heavy hand strangling the options necessary for an acceptable way of life but it simply does not exist, either now or in the past,' wrote the historian Keith Taylor. 'Heroes are a fiction.'

The reaction to Thiep's writing was remarkable. By 1988 the Vietnamese press and literary journals had published more than ninety articles about him, according to one of his translators, Greg Lockhart. 'We have to admit he is fantastically talented,' wrote a critic. 'His short stories are unusual in the sense that they always leave a very strong impression on us, they force us to think.' To others he was a pornographer with an artless style that offended the truly cultured. His were not the ideas of 'a healthy and wholesome mind', wrote the historian Ta Ngoc Lien. In the introduction to a collection of his works, the editor reflected on the confusion surrounding Thiep: 'It is as if every new story of his has provoked discussion and debate throughout the country from north to south. There are those that sing his praises until they've run out of words; there are those who disparage and denounce him; and there are even those who call for him to be brought to court and imprisoned.'

Thiep's evasiveness left critics with the nagging fear that they were being mocked, but the writer never quite furnished them with enough proof. The ambiguities of his work protected him, as have some well-placed friends. But his literature has caused some problems. Nguyen Ngoc, the editor of the literary journal *Van Nghe*, was dismissed in 1988, in part for publishing Thiep and championing the new literature. His sacking caused a furore and marked the end of a brief period of openness when Thiep was able to publish works that most obviously challenged the past and the politics of the present.

Thiep portrays himself not as an heroic iconoclast but as a 'pitiful writer'. This posturing as the unorthodox outsider is a little affected now given that his stories have been published in the most prestigious newspapers, turned into movies and gathered together into acclaimed collections. But he does occupy an uncertain place in the system, like many Vietnamese intellectuals. He was himself a former teacher and official in an educational publishing house where he operated around the margins of the law, smuggling goods and trading in the shady grey markets of Hanoi.

To earn a living, he opened a restaurant across the Red River from Hanoi in the suburb of Gia Lam. In an over-developed area clouded with the dust of new construction, he built a wooden thatched house on stilts like those of the ethnic minorities in the remote

northern province of Son La, where Thiep had spent a decade teaching. It's a relaxed, unpretentious restaurant that serves wild game
from the highlands. It is also a place for Thiep to hold court; here he
meets admirers, moving in a slow, rather dour fashion from table to
table to talk about life and literature.

Thiep spent ten years in Son La, enduring the wretched poverty
and obliterating hunger of the region. As well as being a time of
intense difficulty, his years there were a source of inspiration that
provides his writing with a sympathy and understanding of
people's lives. Now he is quite wealthy, although little of it shows in
the worn clothes and rather meagre life that seems to be worked
into the craggy lines of his face. No other writer has attracted the
critical acclaim in or outside of Vietnam, but for many in the established Hanoi literati, Thiep is still the illegitimate son of a banana
vendor who has clawed his way up. Starting a restaurant led to
whispers that the writer had embarrassed himself by selling out to
the unsavoury forces of commerce. Thiep turned the snobbery and
contempt back at them. A critic who vilified him in the official press
became the target of a mocking but cleverly evasive short story.

'Unlike in the West, Eastern political traditions have never shown
proper respect for writers and thinkers. This tradition has stayed
with us to the present,' Thiep wrote in an essay in *Song Huong*
(*Perfume River*), a journal that published some of the most daring fiction and commentary. Vietnam had produced only 'court writers'
who were servile and unquestioning. The whole canon of socialist
writing could be brushed off, Thiep said. None of it was real literature, it purely served political aims and not very lofty ones at that.
'Literature and the arts have become propaganda tools and an aid to
teaching obscene morals,' Thiep wrote. 'People are tired of bogus
moral treatises. The time has come for literature to take correct steps
on its difficult journey.'

Thiep provided a sly commentary on the real esteem accorded to
writers and intellectuals in 'Fired Gold', the second story in his trilogy. A character meets the revered national poet Nguyen Du who is
leading a life of poverty and isolation. 'Before me is a slight man
whose face is creased with misery. This man is a clever and talented
poet. I sense that he understands absolutely nothing about politics
and yet he is an unswervingly dedicated official. His character

is superior to that of other people yet what value does such character hold when real material life is impoverished and luckless?' The poet is compared to the Emperor Gia Long, the first of the Nguyen Dynasty monarchs, who is painted as a monster in official histories, as he is seen as having prepared the ground for French colonialism.

Thiep, however, contrasts the pathetic state of the great Nguyen Du with the competence and immensity of reviled Gia Long to make a number of points that shocked readers when the story was published in 1987. Intellectuals are depicted as weak and held in contempt by the powerful; Nguyen Du is left 'drowning in the soft mulch of life'. Political leaders are depicted as cruel and egotistical, too absorbed in ensuring their places in history to carry out the social reforms necessary to alleviate poverty, while intellectuals like Nguyen Du are too marginal to make any difference.

The Vietnam in 'Fired Gold' is not the heroic and resourceful country of Communist Party lore; it is not the scrappy fighter that has maintained its cultural purity, but the bastard offspring of China. 'The most significant characteristics of the country are its smallness and weakness. She is like a virgin girl raped by Chinese civilisation. The girl concurrently enjoys, despises and is humiliated by the rape . . . Nguyen Du does not understand this. Nguyen Du is the child of this same virgin girl and the blood that flows through his veins is laced with allusions to the brutal man who raped his mother.'

These were shocking words that questioned the roots of Vietnamese culture and identity. In the complex narratives and ambiguous language of Thiep's finely-worked stories, he challenged assumptions about Vietnamese history, identity and heroism in a way that had not been done in decades. History was set by the state, cut up into periods of resistance and periods of foreign domination. Heroes and villains were clear-cut and served useful lessons for the present. By blurring the boundaries of history and fiction and shifting his vocabulary, Thiep could take the reader from a historical fable to contemporary political criticism and yet avoid censorship. His works were much more than purely political; his writing was done with a care and precision for language that startled his readers. Writers like Bao Ninh and Duong

Thu Huong wrote in a lush style that borrowed from French romanticism and even from socialist realism. Thiep referred back to history and legends but used language in a way that was extraordinary and new. His voice is often described as 'flat' and 'effectless' in its deliberate contrast with the sing-song cadences of Party slogans.

Thiep's translator, the historian and critic Peter Zinoman, points to a line in 'Fired Gold' that illustrates the writer's ability to use the language of state propaganda to undermine its message. In one of the multiple conclusions to the story, Thiep writes: 'It [Europe] begins to understand that the beauty and the glory of a people are based neither on war nor revolution nor on ideologists or emperors.' The words 'beauty and glory of a people' is one of the stock phrases of Communist Party slogans and its insertion into a sentence about eighteenth-century Europe immediately brings the reader back to the present. 'After redirecting our attention to the modern state, the sentence rejects revolution, war, ideology and leadership as valid criteria for assessing national "glory",' Zinoman wrote. 'Lacking real economic accomplishments, the Party traditionally points to successes in these fields to justify its exclusive monopoly over power. Thus the form of the sentence openly mocks the state's sloganeering rhetoric, the content bluntly assails its grounds for political legitimacy.'

Just a few years after Nguyen Van Linh had appealed to writers to become a critical force in society, the arc of literary freedom was descending, restrained again by the state. The four novelists who had the greatest impact – Nguyen Huy Thiep, Bao Ninh, Duong Thu Huong and Pham Thi Hoai – are still writing, but none has had much published in Vietnam in recent years. An occasional short story or essay will appear, but they have less impact these days. The illicit excitement of their earlier works could only last so long before the effect wore off.

They have all faced restrictions by the government, administered in a mostly haphazard but nevertheless unsettling way. For a while they would be denied visas to travel overseas and then suddenly the authorities would show a change of heart. Even Huong, the most politically suspect of these writers in the eyes of the authorities, was able to publish the occasional old short story. Her books were not officially distributed. They can be found in English or French, but only with difficulty in Vietnamese. She was not jailed but nor was she completely free. Despite numerous invitations to attend conferences and speak overseas, she has only been allowed out of the country once, to visit France. The best writers have been held in check with restrictions and threats; the rest are cushioned and suffocated by their dependent relationship with the cultural authorities that publish their books and reward their obedience with sinecures and perks.

There was no longer much belief in the transformative powers of writing. Far from encouraging writers to guide the direction of reforms, the government urged them to be more positive, con-demning them to return to their places in a laudatory chorus for the state. Le Mai, a diplomat and Vice Foreign Minister not normally known as a literary critic, wrote in the Communist Party journal *Tap Chi Cong San* in February 1995: 'Life as reflected in the pages of these recent works is dull and gloomy. The image of Communists is distorted. Some writers view the recent war as a cause of "grief" that they will carry for ever . . . Occasionally, Communists are por-trayed as heartless and violent people who simply live in the certainty of mythical and outmoded values.'

He had a prescription to remedy the situation: 'Finding new and wonderful features, discovering the creative potential and great capabilities of those who can forget themselves for the sake of the fatherland and for socialism and creating Communist characters for the renovation period are requirements. This is the responsibil-ity of Vietnamese writers today.'

What the government wanted to see was a 'national' literature, a heart-sinking prospect in which all works would be formed within a template modelled by a handful of Party officials. Inevitably this would mean a return to a tooth-aching wholesomeness, a panorama of young girls in white *ao dais* and conical hats, cheery red-cheeked peasants, banyan trees, summer evenings, fireflies, and little boys on buffalo playing the flute. A short memoir by Nguyen Khac Vien, a doctor, historian and propagandist, published in an American journal presaged this with a dreamy look at his rural youth, of play-ing under a banyan tree in a landscape of silver and green paddy fields. Like most honey-dipped rural nostalgia, it comes across as overwhelmingly forced and false.

Pham Thi Hoai is a writer whose nihilistic streak and pungent vocabulary places her far from the fictive rural idylls of Vien and at odds with the many advocates of a return to a tendentious tradition. She has become discouraged by what she called a 'Vietnam fever' overseas that has given considerable attention to its fiction. Sloppy, unimaginative works have been praised, elevating them to a position they don't deserve, she said. Hoai believed the literary world has become debased, like that of artists who now mostly paint a saccharine image of Vietnam for tourists.

Some of the works published in anthologies overseas are now 'more Communist than the Communists', she complained. Most of the writing, she said, were by Communist hacks and did not reflect the state of literature in Vietnam in the 1990s. The best writers, she said, kept their works in a drawer, waiting again for an environment that might allow free publication.

Hoai made her biggest impact with the novel *The Crystal Messenger*. The work is narrated by a woman trapped permanently in the stunted body of a young girl. She casts a desolate eye over the landscape of modern society, politics, manners and sexuality. Her twin sister is enormously beautiful and vain, her brother, an army deserter, is criminal and violent. Figures of authority are all emblematic of the absurdity of power in Vietnam. The local Communist Party official is a priggish, self-important dwarf who is wildly mocked but clings to his position with the backing of the police. A foreign ministry official who marries the narrator's sister represents a new consumerist urban élite, with his neurotic obsession about hoarding his stocks of imported lavatory paper and his endless boasting of foreign trips. Even intellectuals, in the form of a weak but ultimately murderous poet, are portrayed with withering scorn.

The Crystal Messenger is set in a world of numbers rackets, criminal gangs, official corruption and frenzied greed, and yet the novel is surprisingly funny and refreshing. As a commentary on modern Vietnamese life, it is unmatched. Nothing is sacrosanct for Hoai; the family, the Party and the state all come under her acidic gaze. Although influenced by European writing, Hoai's novels and stories are strongly Vietnamese; she captures all the incongruous details and brittle contradictions of life in a socialist country where everyone is obsessed with money and status.

The writer now lives in Germany with her husband and despite her misgivings that leaving Vietnam might affect her writing, she has been able to continue producing controversial and interesting work. Her latest work, *Marie Sen*, shocked readers with its story of a Hanoi prostitute and her many clients. Hoai's use of a rich and bawdy slang has aroused particular ire among some critics. The Ho Chi Minh City Police newspaper has kept up a barrage of attacks against Hoai because in her writing 'the purity and refinement of the Vietnamese language is degraded into filth and vulgarity'.

Writing in the paper about a collection of short stories by Hoai, a critic asked why she had not been prosecuted for her works. 'If this was a pornographic film, the producer and consumer would be punished by law. This book has not only sex stories but is politically opposed [to the Party] so why has it not been punished by law?'

This was only one of the many attacks against Hoai, who was accused by a reviewer of writing a jumble of 'half-European, half-American ideological statements mixed up with "quotations from the street"'. Hoai, who studied to be an archivist in East Germany, has often been damned for the range of foreign influences on her writing. Her novels and short stories confront so many of the rigid ideas that Vietnamese officials, and particularly men, have about their country, their language, and perhaps most shockingly their sexuality, that most of her stories are simply unintelligible to them. Translations of her work, she says, diminish it enormously as much of the impact comes in the juxtaposition of street slang, neologisms and phrases plundered from the Party's dated lexicon. Hoai admits her more recent works have little for the reader to grasp on to for hope; they are irredeemably bleak stories of poverty, lust and power, but they capture much in the Vietnamese experience that has been shut out of literature for too long.

It is no longer possible in Vietnam to close off vast areas of human experience from literature. The government still tries to control writers, but it is losing its battle against freedom of creativity and expression. Writers no longer play quite the role they did in the process of reforms; those first heady days of breaking down barriers and invading the hallowed ground of history are already over. Literature, however, remains a potent critical force. It is an important arena in which individuals have fought the state to claim their cultural space. It has been one of the few ways Vietnamese can challenge the state's versions of history, of morality and identity.

11

A Mirror of Things Past

Why did the maker stage such drama here?
Since then, how many stars have spun and fled!
Old horse and carriage paths – faint autumn grass.
Once splendid towers and mansions – setting sun.
Rocks stand stock-still, unawed by time and change.
Waters lie rippling, grieved at ebb and flow.
From age to age, a mirror of things past:
the scene from here can break the viewers heart.

LADY THANH QUAN
'Remembering the Past in the City of the
Soaring Dragon'
Translated by Huynh Sang Thong

Nguyen Van Huan sat down outside Hanoi town hall on the edge of
Hoan Kiem Lake on a grey Sunday afternoon in January 1996. He
pulled a bottle of petrol out of his jacket pocket, poured it over his
clothes and set himself on fire. Hours later when Huan's corpse lay
in a morgue in a nearby hospital, the ragged children that earn their
living selling postcards around the lake were helpfully pointing out
to journalists the scorch marks on bushes near where the 36-year-
old man had died.

His death had tragic echoes of the self-immolation of Buddhist
monks in Saigon during the war. But the suicide had not been an act
of political protest nor a self-sacrifice to the cause of religious or
political freedom. It was a sign of the rumblings that were building
up in the city over what has always been the most basic source of
conflict in Vietnam – land.

Huan took his life to protest against a decision by a court in
favour of his neighbour who wanted to take back some land in the

suburb of Gia Lam. Huan wanted to keep the 600 square metres of land, which had been leased by his family for decades, but the court ordered him to hand half back to his neighbour. His court appeal had not even been heard when in frustration and rage he killed himself outside the offices of Hanoi's bureaucrats.

After years of socialist controls, the freedom to use, purchase, rent, inherit or sell land set in motion the gears of speculation, and slowly the attendant wheels of elation and fear began to turn. Land has again become almost everything, a source not just of wealth but of identity, marking entry into a new class for the first time since the Communists marched into Hanoi in 1954 and shared out its elegant homes amongst themselves. Conversations turned to mysterious measures of land and gold, the two things intimately connected in the language of money. Sales, allocations and registrations developed their own armies of bureaucrats, middlemen and agents. Property developers appeared out of nowhere. Plaster and pilasters went up in an orgy of architectural excess and a low fog of scandal and deceit settled over the city.

Hanoi can appear to be history itself, an emblem of everything Vietnamese and colonial embalmed for so long in a sticky lacquer of poverty. It captures much of its time and of its past, blending the lush, romantic side of Vietnam with the drab and austere. The warp and weft of the past appear exposed and little changed by the decades since the French left.

But economic reforms have begun to have a profound impact. A colonial city that is nevertheless entwined with the whole idea of national identity has in the space of forty years seen two almost complete reversals. In 1954 the Hanoi that symbolised French control as the capital of Indochina was remade as a symbol of the Vietnamese revolution. That process was nearly halted by war, but as new monuments to victory rose, the economy collapsed and poverty became a constant reminder of failure. In the 1990s Hanoi was again remade by new economic forces, returning far back to its millennium-old roots when the area by the Red River was populated by the *Ke Cho*, or 'market people'.

Underneath the surface are a myriad stories of how the city was built, of the political and social forces that shaped it and the people

who encouraged or resisted those changes. Hanoi has defied any
steady urban evolution. It has had periods when it lay almost dormant, sidelined as a political centre or constrained by poverty. At
other times the city has given an unpleasant glimpse of what the
future might hold as it took an unrestrained lurch forward.
Vietnam's identity lies in the layered cosmologies of the city, in its
archaeology and its hidden histories of conflict and change.

Hanoi changes markedly with the weather. In winter a soupy
grey mist hangs over the city, a penumbra of dampness that leaves
puddles on stone floors and chills the bones. The French called this
tiring cloud that hangs between rain and fog *crachin*, or a 'spitting
rain', to distinguish it from the summer monsoon. In January and
February, Hanoi looks like the set of a damp film noir, all furtiveness
and smoky shadows with a soundtrack of slowly turning *cyclo*
wheels. Just a few years ago, when most Hanoians still rode bicycles
and blackened steam trains hooted and chuffed through the city
centre, it was still possible to imagine oneself in Europe half a century ago.

But the winter months weigh heavily; they are a wearying time of
spattered mud and sodden raincoats, of impermeable grey skies
that never lift. The air is tinged with dust from the charcoal used for
cooking; an aural reminder of winter comes in the hawking and
snuffling of an entire city afflicted with colds.

The first colour arrives with *Tet* when the streets of the city are
filled with markets selling flowers and kumquat bushes covered
with bright orange fruit. From the countryside convoys of bicycles,
pedalled by young men in the military olive clothes worn there,
their faces half hidden by their green helmets, bring in branches of
pink peach blossom, a colourful mobile forest offering the promise
of spring in the unopened buds.

The weather changes precipitously at the end of winter; snuggled
down under heavy quilts, one would wake in a malarial sweat to
discover that summer had come overnight. Almost immediately
the city takes on a more languid feel, windows and doors are flung
open; life moves out on to the streets. There is something
Neapolitan about the street life. Noisy arguments build up in
sudden flurries and just as quickly are gone. Shouting matches,
often over the gambling that is ubiquitous on street corners, erupt

without warning, filling the air with blistering and imaginatively foul language. The streets are crammed with vendors, people washing clothes, idling families, sleeping babies, angry neighbours and old friends.

It is easy to find the glimmer of romance in the almost operatic drama of the streets. But as more city-dwellers have the opportunity to find some peace and privacy, they are doing so. A retired teacher, who with much relief moved out of his crowded family home filled with dozens of children, nieces, nephews and cousins of all ages, into a small house of his own, slyly paraphrased Ho Chi Minh's dictum that 'nothing is more precious than independence and freedom'.

Summers are even longer and damper than the winters in Hanoi. Life spreads out around the parks and lakes; particularly in the evenings when a syrupy light touches off the ochre and cream of the crumbling colonial buildings. Air conditioning – increasingly common in richer households – has brought some relief from temperatures that can go as high as 40 °C. During the day the crush of traffic, the pollution that is intensified by heat and the almost unbearable noise flood the senses. Late at night, when the streets are empty except for a few *cyclo*s and some night workers crouched at tea-stands dimly lit with ten-watt bulbs, when the blossom perfumes the night air for a few months of summer and when the heat dips, it is easier to appreciate the extraordinary beauty of Hanoi. Old trees create tunnels of foliage along streets lined with colonial villas. In the old city, narrow streets and narrower houses create a sense of a maze, festooned with power cables, like jungle creepers swarming over an ancient monument. The street-plan disorientates, the street names confuse but in its meandering and organic way, the old city delights.

What makes Hanoi remarkable nowadays in a world of increasingly homogenous urban landscapes are its varied patinas and forms. There is no corporate city centre bereft of life after working hours, there are no silent, soulless dormitory suburbs. Hanoi hums all of the day and most of the night. There are a few brief hours after midnight when the city stills, but by four in the morning cocks start crowing in backyards or from balconies and bloodcurdling screams of pigs being slaughtered can shatter sleep. Soon there is a persistent clanking of pans from soup stalls preparing for the breakfast rush. By five, the city is up; old people exercise by the lakes, slowly tracing out in the air the invisible calligraphies of *t'ai chi* or paddling shuttlecocks back and forth. During the cool hours just after dawn, even Ba Dinh Square fills up with people. Families are out washing or collecting water from street wells. By seven it is hot and the traffic is thick and noisy, the hooting of horns harsh and incessant.

Long before the colonial transformation of Hanoi, the city was at the centre of Vietnamese identity, near the sacred site where the first Hung king mythically merged nature and culture to found a people. It is the place where 1,000 years ago a golden dragon is said to have risen through the clouds showing Ly Thai To, the first emperor of the Ly Dynasty, where to establish his capital. Hanoi was founded in 1010 when it was known as Thang Long, City of the Ascending Dragon. It consisted of a citadel and some temples surrounded by a small village of traders that evolved by the fifteenth century into what is now called the Old City or the Thirty-six Streets district. The street plan of this area dates from that time, but most of the buildings are much newer; flooding, the pervasive damp of Hanoi, nearly constant remodelling of the city by rulers and attacks by pirates, such as the Chinese Black Flag bandits in the nineteenth century, meant few buildings in this area are more than a century old. But even if the structures are relatively new, the sites and the designs often date back much further.

In the seventeenth century imperial administrators taxed the width of shop fronts. The response was to build narrow buildings that evolved into the 'tube houses' found in the Thirty-six Streets district. The houses were low, kept to just one storey and a windowless attic, supposedly to prevent any attempt on the life of the emperor as he was carried around in a palanquin. This district dates back to a time when merchants and craftsmen moved in from the countryside to service the court. The old city was once crossed with narrow canals that connected the lakes that dot the city and allowed sampans to bring merchandise down from the Red River. The area evolved around different guilds and trades, some of which still occupy the same streets.

The Thirty-six Streets were named after the trade or product, starting with the word *Hang*, or merchandise. Tin makers hammered out their wares on Hang Thiec and the silversmiths that came in from Hai Hung province continue to occupy Hang Bac. Each of the trades built a temple of which dozens still remain, including the White Horse temple, the oldest in the city, built in honour of a horse that showed the Emperor Ly where to build the city walls so they would not fall down. In the two square kilometres of the city there are more than fifty temples still in use, while dozens of others have been converted into schools, day-care centres or government offices.

Nowadays few people have the resources to renovate old houses, which have decayed alarmingly. As the population has soared, houses have been divided, further complicating who should pay for maintenance. The houses are now extraordinarily crowded; shops and storerooms are packed with inventory. Further back the roofs rise up and under them platforms have been built to provide sleeping areas for entire families. There is a sharp chiaroscuro between the tiny dark interiors and the bright courtyards filled with plants, birds and aluminium cooking pots.

The Thirty-six Streets area is one of the most crowded urban districts on earth, with each resident living in only one and a half square metres, less than half the average for the whole of Hanoi. Half of all houses have to share a kitchen, 95 per cent share bathrooms and all share courtyards and access points. As the Thirty-six Streets returned to their role as the centre of Hanoi's commerce and adopted a new role as a tourist attraction, many families accumulated enough money to rebuild. The tiny houses were far more charming for tourists than they were for residents who had to endure their leaking roofs, flooded floors and ancient plumbing.

When the French took effective control of Hanoi in 1882, the city was a prosperous town of around 120,000 people. It made its money through the manufacturing of a range of goods from the pottery that had been made in the village of Bat Trang since the fifteenth century, to silk in the lakeside area of Nghi Tam. There had been a vibrant trade in goods that were brought up the Red River by boat. By the time the colonists arrived there had been several centuries of contact with the West, starting with Dutch traders in 1638.

The French forces occupied a small area next to the river and built a barracks there in their first act of remodelling Hanoi to their design. A grand city was an important part of the French *mission civilisatrice*. The French required that the city reflect their vision of imperial grandeur. Work started on the inevitable cathedral and offices for the governor. This was not just to cow the natives with the splendour of French architecture, but in some ways to justify the colonial enterprise in Indochina, which had not met with universal approval in France. The power of the colonial authorities was under constant challenge, not just from the Vietnamese but also from French business interests and opponents of colonisation. Dozens of different governors were appointed during those unsettled early years. 'In Indochina even more than in metropolitan France, the instability and weakness of political authority encouraged grandiose and vain acts of assertiveness,' wrote the architectural historian Gwendolyn Wright. 'Civic architecture tried to convey the impression of authority and continuity when there was none.'

Following a devastating fire in 1888, the French stepped up the pace at which they were to build their monumental city. The gates of dozens of small villages were demolished and new streets designed south of Hoan Kiem Lake in the city centre. The ramparts surrounding the Citadel were torn down, ostensibly to create more space but doubtless also to remind the Vietnamese of who was now in charge. It was a period of rapacious vandalism by the French, who destroyed one of the city's largest temples on the banks of Hoan Kiem to make way for a post office, a town hall and other buildings, including the Metropole Hotel. Only a small gate remains from the Pagoda of Nguyen Dang Giai built in the 1840s. The vast complex that covered thirty hectares was decorated with carved wooden reliefs depicting the gruesome punishments awaiting the faithless in hell. The temple had never been popular in Hanoi as its construction had been paid for with higher taxes, prompting a verse quoted by the nineteenth-century Vietnamese writer Petrus Ky, that is one of the earlier examples of Hanoians resisting new construction and objecting to outrageous spending:

> What virtue, Giai, in all this mad expense?
> In every quarter starving crowds are dense

> Vo De's lesson is still before your eyes
> Whom can Buddha save if everyone dies.

Vo De was a sixth-century emperor whose devotion to Buddhism drove him to be lenient to his enemies. They took advantage of this and laid siege to his citadel, causing the deaths of many people. His story was a warning against piety. By the time the French demolished the temple, it was in an advanced state of disrepair having been vandalised by the monks, who sold bricks and tiles to make enough to live.

Another site demolished by the French was the Thi Huong Examination Hall, where scholars had sat their Confucian exams. At the time the French policy was to break the back of the Chinese-influenced mandarinate which had spawned opposition to their rule. The site became a French military camp and later a new chamber of commerce building was put up there, reflecting the real French interest in the country. The military swept away archaic rituals and made the world safe for commerce. The area is now the site of Vietnam's National Library, a more suitable use for this intellectually hallowed ground.

In 1900 the French declared Hanoi the capital of Indochina and the centre of French colonial administration of the region, returning it to a position of political importance after nearly a century in the wilderness. The Emperor Gia Long had moved his capital to Hue in 1802 and Hanoi, as it was known after 1830, was reduced to the status of a provincial administrative centre. It had been eclipsed politically and culturally by Hue and economically by Saigon and Haiphong, but as the new French colonial capital it would make something of a comeback.

Saigon at the turn of the century was a vastly more developed centre than Hanoi, and its French commercial élite was increasingly powerful. Expanding the administration in Hanoi and turning it into the capital of all of Indochina was a way to diminish the power of the colonial traders in Saigon and return it to the bureaucrats sent in from Paris. To reinforce this message, Governor Paul Doumer started work on a large palace, which now houses the offices and ceremonial rooms of the presidency.

Not long after the start of these grandiose projects there was to be a shift in the way architects and town planners worked in Vietnam. The appalling conditions created by colonialism in Indochina had stirred some outrage in France, and in 1909 the Chamber of Deputies ordered colonial authorities to pay attention to the traditions and cultural needs of locals. The French started to push on their sceptical subjects the idea that colonialism really served the Vietnamese. A symbol of the supposed new respect for the indigenous population was the increasing incorporation of local architectural motifs in colonial buildings. Across the country, treasury offices and schools were built in a style that merged colonial architecture, elements of French design and local flourishes, particularly on the roofs.

Governor-General Albert Sarraut began reforms to the education system and ordered the construction of a massive *lycée* next to his palace. This complex, nowadays the headquarters of the Communist Party, looks like a vast colonial barracks well-suited to the regimenting of young minds. Other buildings were more self-consciously 'Asian'. The treasury building and the *Ecole Française d'Extrême-Orient* designed by Ernest Hebrard are fanciful oriental melanges. Although Hebrard criticised architects for tacking dragons or mythical snakes on to their buildings purely as exotic decoration, his own approach was not much different; his conservative buildings were enlivened by flourishes he pilfered from a range of Asian cultures.

As Wright put it: 'His buildings usually resemble a pastiche of exotic details superimposed on a *beaux-arts* plan.' His building for the *Ecole Française* 'constituted a hodgepodge of architectural motifs: the polychrome façade evoked Japanese Shinto temples, steep, tiled porch roofs recalled Hindu temples in India, while the two-tiered roof of the central core alluded to Siamese, Cambodian and Laotian temple structures'. Hebrard's aim was to develop 'a Vietnamese style' although he imperiously denied any Vietnamese a voice in the creation of this new architectural language. Much later Hebrard's architecture did influence the emergence of an eclectic Vietnamese style in the 1990s when buildings threw together gaudy mixes of French and oriental design.

Cities such as Hanoi – Wright and other historians have argued – were not attempts to recreate European urbanism in the colonies, but places of experimentation where planners were able to develop policies that were later adopted at home. Numerous architects and planners saw the colonies as blank slates where ideas could be tried out before being applied back in the Metropole where there was less room for running roughshod over city-dwellers in the name of experimentation. New ideas of urban design, planning and zoning were developed outside of France before going back. Cities across North Africa and in Indochina were not simply nostalgic recreations of the home country, but crucibles of modernism producing new ideas on design, housing and hygiene.

This comes across in Hebrard's work in Hanoi, where he attempted to separate residential and industrial zones. He even tried to save some local monuments, but was generally unconcerned about how the Vietnamese might want to live or what they regarded as important. Under his plan for Hanoi, the Vietnamese were to be moved to a residential area outside the city centre. Hanoi was remade to reflect the demands of French colonialism. There was a large administrative sector and zones for French and Vietnamese housing. Commercial and industrial districts were also kept apart. Hebrard's aim was to defy the organic growth of these cities with their emphasis on the individual, and promote a sense of aesthetic, social and racial organisation.

The essential rules of French colonial building were laid out by a congress of architects and planners that met in Vincennes outside Paris in October 1931. Their conclusions were that one should never mix European and native populations – strict segregation was necessary for good order. Cities should be built to encourage European immigration and to maximise their advantages over the natives. Although French and locals were kept apart, a *quartier indigène* was necessary as a reservoir of servants and coolies. Ordinances were established to maintain the separation of the races and were justified on the grounds that proximity to Asians 'constitutes a real danger because of the ignorance of the most elementary rules of hygiene', according to a municipal report. The French were only worried about hygiene when it came to maintaining their distance from the Vietnamese, otherwise it was not a top priority. Seven per cent of Hanoi's budget in the early years of the century went on public buildings, only 2 per cent was spent on sanitation. Wright points out that the city administrations in Vietnam were never too concerned about the corrupt and negligent water monopolies that regularly poisoned French and Vietnamese alike.

Hebrard's vision of Hanoi was an imposing and well-organised city of sturdy government buildings set in parks along wide boulevards. The Vietnamese population figured little in his thinking and fortunately for them only a small part of his design was ever completed. The scheme was also disliked by many colonials who wanted distinctly French buildings to remind them of home; they did not want faux Vietnamese designs. Hebrard's far-sighted zoning laws were also enormously unpopular among the powerful business interests whose belief in keeping commerce unfettered in the colonies outweighed any concerns about pollution. Hebrard's plans for Hanoi were mostly ignored, and they became the first of a great many grandiose schemes for cities in Vietnam that have not been completed.

For Hebrard, colonial architecture was not a weak imitation of European forms but something that could hold its own. He wanted to 'direct the natives along a path that accords well with their traditions, their temperaments and their attitudes, making them evolve normally towards a modern art that will be particular to them'.

Despite Hebrard's patronising statements about steering his natives, he did little to help them. The French trained only a handful of locals and by independence there were just ten Vietnamese architects in Hanoi. This group, who mostly worked as draughtsmen, had been given an orthodox training in the *beaux-arts* style and as such they were ill-equipped to design the 'modern socialist architecture' that the new Communist government wanted. As the capital of the Democratic Republic of Vietnam, Hanoi demanded a fresh style of architecture and a distinctive vision of urbanism to replace the racial divisions and capitalist impetus of French colonialism.

The French packed up their belongings and fled. The Communists took over, sweeping through the city and into every building. Thousands of wealthy Vietnamese families fled to the South while others were evicted from their homes to make way for new socialist heroes. Those who had left the capital since the start of the war in 1946 returned to demand housing and jobs that were now doled out not by virtue of wealth or colonial position, but through new rankings set up by the Party.

The new government did not abandon the spatial arrangement of Hanoi that had placed those in power along the widest boulevards and next to parks and lakes. Top officials and socialist embassies took over the large houses around Ba Dinh Square where the top colonial officials had lived.

Middle-ranking cadres were allocated three square metres of space per family member. Villas once occupied by a single family were shared out among half a dozen families. If the original residents had stayed on, they were evicted or shunted into a single room. Some houses in Hanoi still crackle with tensions between the impecunious original owners and the mass of people who moved into their homes. This system had a devastating impact on the houses themselves. As a central office was responsible for maintenance, little work was ever done; the government had almost no money and spent what it had on senior officials. As families expanded new additions were built on to the old villas; coral-like crusts of shacks grew on their sides and façades. Once glorious buildings are now hidden behind corrugated metal and plywood additions. Now there is a huge demand for shops on the streets, so a new layer of shanty additions has been tacked on to many houses.

There were a number of subtle alterations in the political symbolism of architecture in the years after the Communist takeover of Hanoi. Ho Chi Minh did not occupy the large wedding cake Governor General's Palace but lived in a modest house in the grounds, although most likely not the one that now exists as a well-preserved memorial. The Communist Party took over the former Lycée Sarraut, the austere barracks-like building that dominates one side of Ba Dinh Square. The treasury became the foreign ministry and the large houses that once belonged to the élite of the Indochinese administration were handed over as embassies for friendly socialist countries. The Soviet Union occupied a large former school close to the square.

It had taken the Communists eight years to win Hanoi, which had been badly damaged in the first battles in 1946. Once they had taken control they were determined to leave their ideological mark. Urban planning was one of the essential tools of socialism that would supposedly turn cities from parasitic centres of bourgeois consumption to highly productive areas of manufacturing and industry. Hierarchies of wealth and class were to be ironed out through the state's provision of housing and services to all areas of the city equally. But the newly independent state had no money; the socialist paradise would have to wait.

Ba Dinh Square in the city centre was redesigned but remained much the same size as it had been under the French. There was no attempt to imitate the massive and alienating space of Tiananmen Square that had been carved out of the crowded centre of Beijing. Hanoi was spared the Pharaonic schemes that blighted other socialist capitals, but the new rulers immediately started to leave their mark on the city. The most obvious manifestations of colonialism, the statues of former governors and the names of streets, all changed. A French statue of a farmer and a buffalo that was emblematic of a superior colonial attitude was removed. Nearly three decades later it was replaced with a large bronze statue of Lenin.

Hanoi was a city of religious diversity, with everything from a Cao Dai temple to the small green-and-white mosque that still stands as a cool Islamic oasis in the midst of the dancing dragons and other gaudy embellishments of the Thirty-six Streets. There was a profusion of Buddhist and animist temples, clan houses and other ceremonial buildings that made up the important public spaces of the city for the Vietnamese population. Roman Catholic churches occupied important sites across the city and dotted the suburbs with incongruous European spires. Many of these buildings were closed or converted to other uses such as granaries, kindergartens and government offices. Restaurants, bars and many cafés were closed. The emphasis was on creating public spaces that served political needs while closing down private arenas that could breed dissent and danger.

Change even swept through the interiors of government buildings. French flamboyance was discarded and replaced with more suitably austere designs. Over the years rooms in government buildings gathered the feel of Communist countries; armchairs with antimacassars, pictures and busts of Ho Chi Minh and the institutional smell of green tea and camphor that was never dispersed by the slow ceiling fans. These interiors changed again in the 1990s when government offices splurged their money on flatulent plastic sofas, air-conditioning and gaudy back-lit pictures of beaches at sunset.

The first priority after 1954 was housing for the flood of people coming into the city. Cash shortages meant that only 5,000 apartments were built in the first five years after independence; the first buildings were put up on the site of a French cemetery as the new era literally buried the architectural past of Hanoi. The real building boom took off in the early 1960s with the construction of new suburbs. The low-rise buildings gave each family one private room; they shared kitchens and bathrooms with others. Each person in theory had four square metres of space, in reality they each had far less as the population soared. The number living in the inner city rose from 120,000 in 1943 to 740,000 by 1974.

Buildings were thrown together from slabs of concrete, not out of any regard for Corbusian aesthetics, but because it was the cheapest means available. Even when these buildings, supposedly a triumph of socialist planning, were going up there were rumblings of discontent at their ugliness and poor quality of construction. 'Architects are not at all satisfied,' a journalist wrote in an article on the city's building programme. 'They have tried, using all means, to make these buildings more aesthetically beautiful but everything – bricks, paint, panes, qualified personnel – are in short supply and people are always telling them to work faster.' What the journalist failed to mention was that the buildings began their rapid disintegration almost as soon as they were built. The pilfering of cement had left the concrete soft and prone to Hanoi's pervasive damp.

The housing paid no heed to the way Vietnamese lived; there were no courtyard spaces in which to relax, grow plants, raise fish or keep birds. Architects felt no need to accommodate these bourgeois pleasures. There was not a lot of emphasis on natural light or ventilation either; the result was apartments that soon turned into suffocating, penitential hovels.

Although Vietnamese villages were densely crowded to provide protection and enable the maximum amount of land to be used for farming, they also had clearly developed private and public spheres. Houses had small walled courtyards and distinct entrances. Private facilities were not shared. Public places, such as *dinh* or 'clan houses', were clearly marked out as communal, indeed they were there to reaffirm village cohesion. The new housing blocks had almost no breakdown between private and public space, almost all facilities were shared, resulting in almost constant under-currents of tension.

The appeal of public housing was illustrated by the failure of a government plan to sell off the buildings in the 1990s. Many of the blocks were in an advanced state of disrepair with the soft, leprous concrete flaking off in dangerous chunks. The stairwells with their disconcertingly uneven treads and cracked ramps for bicycles often stank of urine or rotting food. Outside, the public areas had been taken over by impromptu markets, while ground-floor apartments had been expanded and turned into shops or karaoke bars. Trees and gardens disappeared under the pressure of commerce or were cut down to provide more room to park motorbikes. To create a sense of individuality and get more space, residents caged in bal-conies, covering the buildings with accretions of rusting metal. Like housing estates across the world, they have become places where few people would choose to live.

A handful of people purchased their apartments but most saw little need. They paid only peppercorn rents that allowed them to save incomes to buy land elsewhere. The blocks had little provable resale value and lacked the emotional and financial security of a small plot of terra firma. Apartments were valued at between 100 million dong ($9,000) and 800 million dong ($70,000) but the gov-ernment was forced to cut these initial prices by half. This, of course, actually deterred many buyers. There was little point in owning an asset that the authorities could arbitrarily devalue. The city's efforts to create a home-owner class from its tenants was doomed to fail-ure.

Hanoi authorities originally wanted to follow the model of Soviet planning, under which cities were organised into mostly self-suffi-cient communities called *mikroraiony* or 'micro-regions'. These would have merged housing, industry and recreation to ensure short commutes. This was not an alien idea in northern Vietnam where villages were densely built to maximise farmland and pro-vide protection. Villages often specialised in a certain trade or handicraft. But the *mikroraiony* in Hanoi were designed on too large a scale to replicate village life and never completely got off the ground. The major impact of this policy was to break down the zoning system set up by the French that separated industry and housing. City authorities would deeply regret the abandonment of zoning because of the problems of pollution and crowding. By the 1990s, planners were trying without much success to relocate belching factories outside of the city.

After 1960 all resources were sucked up by the war and almost nothing was built in Hanoi for fifteen years. An article written in 1984 by the city's mayor to mark thirty years since liberation had little to say about new buildings or improved living conditions, but instead concentrated almost entirely on what Hanoi had contributed to the war effort in the way of mobilising men and supplies.

In 1965 the United States began bombing Hanoi to eradicate the city's industry and hobble the transport networks supplying the war in the South. The bombing was aimed at increasing the psychological pressure on the Vietnamese leadership. The city's population, which had soared since independence, once again slumped with the evacuation to the countryside of children and unessential workers. The bombings, which continued until the infamous Christmas bombings of 1972 that badly damaged the Bach Mai Hospital, had a huge impact on the city. The US claimed it did not target residential areas although its bombs hit the French High Commission, the Indian Embassy and an inner-city street called Kham Tien that became an emblem of the horror of the war. A plot of land razed by the bombs has been turned into a memorial for the dozens who died there.

The suburbs of Hanoi were pounded with high explosives; outside the city centre the B-52s really did make the rubble bounce, as American pilots used to joke. According to the Vietnamese government, two thirds of suburban villages were destroyed along with 108 factories and industrial buildings, ninety-seven schools, fifty-four hospitals or clinics and 100,000 square metres of housing, or around a quarter of the total stock in the city.

The slogan of those days was that Hanoi would be 'rebuilt bigger and more beautiful than before'. In 1973, the Leningrad Scientific

Research Centre for Town Planning and Construction began work on a master plan that, in the words of the historian William Logan, 'was totally divorced from both the local culture and the economic realities of an impoverished government'.

This vision of Hanoi was based on the expectation that after years of war the city's economy would boom. Vast factories and industrial estates were part of the plan, but it did not consider the lack of capital available to fund this explosion of large-scale industry.

Sketches of this new Hanoi have an otherworldly quality; they resemble those 1950s plans for permanent settlements on the moon. They are imbued with a cheery utopianism aimed at erasing any suggestion of randomness or diversity from city life. Chinoiserie flourishes abounded in the flying eaves and cut-out concrete screens, but the overall motif was 1960s Moscow with miles of identical and soulless housing blocks set in lonely windswept plazas and linked by heavy concrete overpasses.

A new city centre was to be built by West Lake, the 500 hectare oxbow lake next to the Red River. New boulevards – vast, pompous and obliterating – would radiate out from there. Each was to be lined with housing and high-rise public buildings. The model was to be the Stalinallee in East Berlin, the extension of Unter den Linden that cuts a wide and alienating gash out to the suburbs. A similar highway would go through the old city and run across a bridge to Noi Bai Airport which was located forty kilometres from the city to allow for a massive expansion of population. Five special industrial zones were planned, each housing about 60,000 workers and specialising in a certain trade. It was a design for a creepily anonymous city, the architecture was the same heavy-set construction that went up across the Soviet-influenced world. Like Le Corbusier's design for rebuilding Paris, the plan offers up a vision of social control and uniformity completely at odds with the spirit of the city it was to replace.

The plan was approved by the government in 1976 but economic realities and yet more warfare, this time with Cambodia and China, meant it would never be realised. Hanoi escaped another brush with the urban planners. The Soviet influence did leave a mark on Hanoi, ranging from the housing blocks that, in the words of the novelist Le Minh Khue, 'had sprung up to imprison both human bodies and souls', to the ugly concrete extensions that ruptured the façades of a number of more elegant colonial buildings such as those housing the Ministry of Culture and Information. The largest building of this period was the Vietnamese-Soviet Cultural Palace, a large, dingy slab, weakly adorned with stained marble lotus motifs and set back behind an ugly plaza. Used as the city's main theatre, it was supposedly a gift from Moscow, although its costs were included in aid money that Vietnam was now struggling to repay.

Ba Dinh Square was radically changed as the socialist necropolis of Uncle Ho was built between 1969 and 1991. The redesign dramatically changed the nature of the public space. The curved pathways and roundabout were ironed into two straight boulevards that are more suitable for military parades. Over the years security in a number of government buildings was tightened and fences went up. The colonial Botanical Gardens became part of the Palace Grounds and now surround the necropolis. The honour guard and heavy police presence around the government buildings do not make the area relaxing, and it is often closed to the public for ceremonial events. But it has not been stripped of all its soul. The French buildings and the trees balance the socialist design and the Ba Dinh Club, a sports centre for senior cadres, has a certain raffish 1930s charm. Its white curves dappled with the reflections of the pool and the diving board that peeks over the wall bring a touch of the Riviera to the centre of Hanoi.

The designs of emperors, the French and the post-colonial government have all come up against constant resistance from people whose ideas of urban planning were very different from the centralised controlling instincts of the state. This tension has shaped the cityscape; planners design and impose, residents subvert and change from within. The imperial, colonial and Communist states all had the capacity to impose their political vision on the city, although none ever reached their ideal of perfectly representing their power and controlling the population at the same time. Now the state has only a limited capacity to impose its will and it lacks a clear vision for the city.

The conflicts have grown sharper since people were given the freedom to build their own homes and to make money from their properties without being cast with the dread label of landlord. Across the city there was a surge in construction that created what a Vietnamese architect described as 'gilded slums'. Millions of dollars of savings went into creating these dripping worlds of dark alleys and randomly scattered houses that are a planner's nightmare, but in many ways reflect old designs of Vietnamese villages. There are no straight roads, only tortuous narrow lanes. Austere modernism and Soviet bombast have given way to gaudy indulgence. Sewage goes straight into the ground or any nearby lake, water is pumped illegally from the nearest well and electricity tapped off from the mains without paying.

In a short story 'Scenes from an Alley', Le Minh Khue described the extraordinary rapidity with which Hanoi started to change. An impoverished woman bribes an official to allow her son to go and work in Germany. 'Five years later he returned and turned their miserable hut into a two-storey villa. Western money could perform magic more powerful than a fairy's. If you wanted a multi-storey house, it would instantly materialise. If you wanted a guard dog or ornamental plants, they'd be yours in the blink of an eye.'

With the explosion in new building, came an explosion in land conflicts. Without a detailed land registry, these alleys of Hanoi became a battleground of rival claims over what are often tiny plots of land. Few disputes end in a claimant self-immolating, but the feverish property market of the 1990s has left its scars.

Now that disputes erupt over a few centimetres of land, Hanoians speak fondly of a time when neighbours helped each other more, and when community spirit was stronger. They tend to forget that social controls were also much tighter and everyone was much poorer, but most agree that Hanoi has become a less civil place. It is hard to measure these changes as in the 1960s and 1970s complaints about civility, noise, teenage delinquency and overcrowding were commonplace in the Hanoi press. But by one measure the city has changed dramatically. Average housing space has declined from 5.1 square metres per person in 1954 to 2.3 in 1983 and 1.2 in 1992. Hanoi is the most densely populated area of the country with 2,161 people per square kilometre.

Crowding on this level has meant a very flexible division between private and public space. When most of the population still draw their water from wells in the street, wash in shared bathrooms and cook in shared kitchens, there is little chance of anything going unnoticed. Life in Hanoi is subject to almost constant intrusions although this is diminishing. Loudspeakers attached to poles on almost every street still squawk into life at dawn to chastise wrong-doers, promote a new government decree or announce the lottery numbers. People no longer have to go to ward meetings where they would be given instructions in the 'new habits of life', but the state still maintains a close and claustrophobic presence.

Life in Hanoi sprawls widely out on to the street, indeed it is often hard to know where the pavement ends and a house or business begins. Commerce spills out from the shop-houses that may just have a small platform where the whole family sleeps. Children watch television in a room that houses three generations, their motorbikes, several businesses and an altar. Almost every activity that in the West would only take place in private, takes place outside, demanding that it is the voyeur rather than the actor who feels shame for viewing anything too closely.

As people want houses that have a shop front, most buildings have followed an age-old pattern of tiny narrow plots that extend back sometimes as much as 100 metres. Now that steel rods have replaced foundations of bamboo, and cement has taken over from lime and sugarcane juice, people have been able to build upwards as well, creating extraordinary towers up to eight storeys high but only three metres wide. As each family demands its own property, land has been constantly divided into plots of ever-diminishing size. The architect Le Hiep attributes this to deep-seated notions about land among Vietnamese. 'No one has been able to solve the problem of the peasant mentality of Vietnamese – if some land in the city is to be split between three brothers they cannot share it out by splitting three storeys of a building, they each have to have their own bit of land so the area gets divided into smaller and smaller segments.' There is more to it than tradition; the complexities of the land law and the lack of trust that permeates the world of Hanoi real estate keeps families clinging doggedly to their own plots.

With only a few controls over the style and size of buildings,

landowners have been free to create a world of crazily dispropor-
tionate buildings. Bavarian turrets, Swiss chalet roofs, onion domes
and minarets have sprung up around West Lake. This nearly apocalyptic Legoland, alternatively swirling with dust or sticky with
polluted mud, replaced what had been an area of small villages,
temples and market gardens around the massive ox-bow lake that
dominates one side of the city. The disparate styles, the hurried and
cheap construction and the determination of each designer to be as
different as possible from anyone else, has created a chaotic vision
of what happens when the state loses control of its cities.

Just next to this area runs a long dyke that protects Hanoi from
the Red River, a wide and turbulent gully of silt that often threatens
to break its banks. Without this dyke, Hanoi would be devastated
with each monsoon. In 1993, there was a rash of building, fuelled in
part by the magical money sent home from Vietnamese traders and
gangsters in Eastern Europe. On both sides of the dyke people
squeezed houses right up on to the one-storey-high barrier. Cracks
started to emerge in the barrier as people built houses and apartment buildings facing right on to the road that tops the structure.
Despite the obvious folly of this construction and the fact that most
builders had encroached on to public land, work was allowed to go
on, unhindered by the city's planning office.

The area was a favourite for officials who were putting their ill-
gotten gains into houses to rent to foreigners. With rentals paid up
front for as much as two years, skilled investors could build a
house, rent it and have enough to buy two more plots. In this frenzied market, designs for a public park that would have circled the
lake were quickly jettisoned and instead the once picturesque and
quiet area was submerged by developments. But all this conspicuous construction soon aroused a backlash that illustrated how, when
political will is strong enough, the government can still act to control the design of the city.

After Vietnam Television broadcast a documentary on the dangers posed by construction on the dyke, Prime Minister Vo Van Kiet
ordered all those who had built on the barrier to tear down the
front of their houses. More than 1,100 houses along the dyke were
found to have been built illegally. The escalating scandal of mismanagement and corruption in the planning was gleefully taken up

by the press and the government was forced to issue a denial that any ministers had houses on the dyke, which was technically true although their wives and children were suspected of owning buildings there. The Interior Ministry began an investigation and several middle-rung officials in the Chief Architect's Office were questioned and suspended from duty. Bulldozers moved in and tore off the façades of the houses, leaving people to live for several months in rooms missing their front walls.

Now that there is a widespread belief in personal ownership of property, the stakes are much higher and protests over evictions more vocal. Hanoians began in the 1990s to demonstrate noisily when removed from their homes to make way for new office buildings, hotels, golf courses or roads. These protests occasionally erupted into violence, with the police forcibly dispersing villagers who tried to block projects.

Pitched battles with rocks and tear gas were fought in 1996 over a golf course being built by the South Korean conglomerate Daewoo Corporation in Kim No village in the suburbs. A woman drowned in a pond in mysterious circumstances during the fighting when soldiers arrived to clear the land. She was alleged by the authorities to have been chased into the lake by angry villagers, four of whom were arrested and jailed.

At the end of the year, violence erupted again at Kim No when workmen built an access road out to the site and began to fence off the area. Villagers had held out for more compensation. At first the local authorities refused, but then they raised the offer. Instead of appeasing the villagers, this made them suspicious that officials were holding back most of the compensation paid by the foreign investor and not passing it on to the villagers. Once again the villagers refused to leave and piled up armories of stones around the village to deter any intruders.

When the police arrived to remove them from their land, the villagers sent out their first line of defence – children marching in a line and carrying pictures of Ho Chi Minh. Even evoking this near sacred emblem did not stop the police. They smashed the pictures and shoved the children aside. One of the police told the villagers: 'This isn't Ho Chi Minh's time any more, its Vo Van Kiet's time now.' The village elders went out to talk but were beaten, precipitating a pitched battle. The police finally retreated under a hail of rocks having stirred up the villagers into a state where compromise was no longer possible. From the muddy battlefield, villagers gathered an arsenal of electric stun weapons, truncheons as well as shields and helmets that had been dropped by the fleeing police. Another battle broke out when trucks turned up to drop off building supplies. Soon the access road to the site was littered with burned-out trucks and incinerated machinery.

When the villagers initially agreed to hand over their land, *Hanoi Moi*, the city's Communist Party newspaper, praised them for displaying their 'traditional revolutionary fervour' in making way for a golf course. There was less praise when they went back on the deal. Newspapers were banned from reporting on the dispute and foreign correspondents who visited the village were dressed down by the Foreign Ministry. Inside the village, tensions boiled up between village leaders who wanted to go ahead with the deal and those who were now determined to cling on to their land. Some men killed pigs that belonged to the village chief who was widely regarded as corrupt. Both sides seemed to stoop to new lows. Officials negotiating the compensation deal had the irrigation system cut off, damaging the fields. They then cut their offer of compensation on the grounds that the fields were no longer as productive.

The dispute raged for more than a year, resulting in many clashes and severe economic losses for the villagers. They were victims of a system of land tenure that fools people into believing that they really own their property when in fact it is the government that has control. Instead of buying land for a fair market price, foreign developers end up paying officials vast sums of money for the right to use a plot. Much of the money is usually skimmed off before it reaches the people who have farmed the land for generations.

Villagers who had legitimate complaints about the process had no way to raise them with the authorities. At one stage, a number of villagers even held a Vietnamese journalist who had gone to the village and lectured her on their side of the story, which the local press had completely ignored. Later, when asked about rumours that they were planning to take a foreign reporter hostage, a farmer dryly replied that they didn't 'have enough rice to feed a hostage'.

Officials were almost entirely unsympathetic. Their stock response was that all land belongs to the state and that farmers were merely granted rights to use it temporarily. Those rights could also be taken away with no consideration for the wishes of the villagers. But Hanoi officials had not given the farmers at Kim No village any concrete assurances about replacement land or compensation. Their ancestral roots in the land were wrenched out by force to make way for a powerful investor known to have paid millions of dollars in kick-backs to city officials.

Land prompted most of the handful of demonstrations that have occurred in recent years in Vietnam. A group of elderly men and women who were being evicted to build a road in Hanoi staged vigils outside the office of the head of the city's Communist Party Committee. They were complaining about the corruption that has pervaded the ill thought-out procedures for the government to take over land or to evict residents. Most money allocated to compensate residents seldom reached their pockets, instead it was siphoned off to local officials. Demonstrations are very rare in Hanoi and often provoke the jittery police into brutal overreactions. At these protests, no rocks were thrown, no buildings set ablaze, there was not even any chanting. But simply by organising against a government and publicly expressing their discontent, this group had taken a major step.

Evictions have become probably the greatest source of social discontent not just in Hanoi but across the country. Land is in extremely short supply in Vietnam. The average population density is twice the Asian average and most people are squeezed into two narrow river deltas and along the narrow coastal plain. Many people have already been pushed on to marginal lands so promises of compensation or relocation offer little hope. Some have been holding out for larger sums of compensation more in the spirit of greed than need. Many people have flocked to areas targeted for foreign investment, hoping to be paid large sums to leave again. Some have ended up disappointed with their share and there have been attacks on building sites. A number of reports on trials of those involved in violent land disputes emerged in the press, giving some way to judge the extent of the problem. In May 1997 riots in Thai Binh province to the south of Hanoi caused a spasm of anxiety in the government; farmers from more than 100 villages attacked local government offices. Several people were said to have been killed by a massive mob of irate peasants, driven to rebellion by burdensome taxation and corruption. A report by the NGO Oxfam showed that farmers were paying eight different taxes managed by Hanoi and another six types organised by local officials. These included a salt tax, fees on houses and gardens and a slaughter tax for any animal killed. The protests sent a tremor of consternation through the government. Pham The Duyet, a member of the Politburo in charge of mass organisations, was sent to calm the situation as rebellious villagers refused to pay any more.

After a five-month news blackout, some sketchy reports emerged in the official press, which pinned what the Party newspaper *Nhan Dan* called 'the complicated events' on troublemakers, but did acknowledge a problem with corruption. *Nhan Dan*'s bland report apportioned blame broadly, but it is clear that not only were local officials rapacious and unrelenting in their extortion of money from villagers but that the reaction against them was extremely widespread. *Nhan Dan* blamed a handful of people who lack 'cultural background, professionalism and sense of moral values', but did not comment on a system that bleeds farmers white with an array of grossly unfair taxes. These protests have become like brush fires; as soon as one is put out, another erupts elsewhere.

There is a Vietnamese saying, often ignored by the government to its great cost, that 'trying to stop a market is like trying to stop a river'. Hanoi was merely marked by decades of Communism but it is being remade by the market. After a century in which governments had built the city around the needs of administration and political symbolism, the 1990s saw shopkeepers and foreign developers become the main forces in its transformation. City planners became almost irrelevant as these forces changed the landscape without any reference to the few rules that did exist. New masterplans were drafted and abandoned; by the time they were approved they had been overtaken by events. In 1986, the government stopped the socialist housing programme that had created large areas of Soviet-style concrete buildings in the western and southern suburbs. People now had to build their own homes.

Foreign money began to have an impact on a city that had been untouched by the market for four decades. Developers put up buildings on some of the most sensitive sites in the city, including the Hoa Lo jail, a powerful symbol not just for the US prisoners of war who dubbed it the Hanoi Hilton, but for the many Vietnamese held there by the French before 1954. A Singaporean developer built offices and apartments on the site, eventually leaving a small area of the prison to be turned into a museum after veteran revolutionaries protested against the destruction of what is almost a sacred site.

In the wave of development in Hanoi in the early 1990s, several buildings, hugely out of scale with the surrounding city, were thrown up. Some were so alien in this low-rise city they might have been spaceships that had mistakenly landed there. They were something of a parasitic force on the surrounding neighbourhoods, sucking up the water and electricity supplies. These gaudy over-lit palaces often sat surrounded by a moat of darkened houses enduring yet another power loss and water cut-offs.

These changes started to threaten the most cherished images of Hanoi that are a central part of the Vietnamese national mythology. A popular song about the city recalled its 'dormant streets' and cicadas at noon, 'the blue waters of the Sword Lake' and parks 'where the young grass, is not yet marked by traces of your steps'. The placid image of a refined and peaceful Hanoi has survived the arrival of various urban blights – the chaotic new buildings, the angry swarming traffic and the polluted lakes. The popular conception of Hanoi derives from centuries of celebratory poetry and art. Hanoi 'gathered the finest flowers of the four provinces', in the words of the fifteenth-century scholar-king Le Thanh Ton. People from Trang An, a term of Chinese origin meaning eternal tranquillity that was used to designate the capital, were better mannered and more industrious and intellectual than the rabble from the surrounding countryside, the emperor wrote.

The self-congratulatory tone lives on. A newspaper article in 1994 said Hanoians 'reflect new socialist qualities and virtues; have inherited the fine tradition of the citizens of our capital, a capital that has been civilised for 1,000 years; are rich in patriotism and love socialism, possess a rather high cultural standard and aesthetic talents; are courteous and hospitable, lead a style of life that is simple and wholesome and possess the socialist international spirit'.

A more recent image of Hanoi that has sunk into the national consciousness has come from the paintings of Bui Xuan Phai, an artist whose cityscapes were often intended as a rebuke to socialism but have now been adopted as almost the official image of the city. His paintings show Hanoi in miniatures of desolation, his palette of greys and browns recalls the city's dank Februarys. The streets are devoid of commerce, bustle or any activity. In one of his famous city scenes, a hand-painted sign hangs outside a shop with just the words 'Boiled Water'. It is a pitiful scene, an emblem of the poverty that blighted Hanoi during and after the war years. Phai lived as an outcast from the official art world as his paintings were too nega-tive, they lacked the cheer demanded of socialist art. He only really gained recognition after his death when he was elevated to a place as Vietnam's foremost modern master. Today he holds the dubious honour of being a favourite of Hanoi's burgeoning group of art forgers.

Phai's melancholic views of Hanoi, once attacked for failing to reflect the glories of socialism, have now come to represent an imag-ined past that was peaceful and romantic. This is Hanoi before the rapacious advance of capitalism, before advertising and karaoke bars, before Honda Dreams turned the traffic into a daily night-mare and commerce transformed Hanoi into a giant souk. Phai's paintings have now become the prism through which artists see Hanoi. Dozens of painters now churn out scenes resembling Phai's paintings even though the streets no longer look the same. These purely nostalgic visions have none of the power of Phai's almost obsessive and critical depiction of Hanoi under socialism.

Hanoians are starting to wake up to rapid changes that might destroy much of what they hold dear about their city. The need for better policies of conservation and urban planning have become an obsession for the press, with attention focused around Hoan Kiem Lake. The lake, surrounded by low shop-houses and some larger public buildings, lies between the old city of the Thirty-six Streets and the newer colonial district to the south. This lake is central to the myths of Hanoi; it is here that a turtle is said to have given the emperor Le Loi a sword with which he smote the Chinese. Some turtles still live in the lake although it is something of a miracle that

they survive amid the sewage and litter. Their occasional appearances on the surface of the green water are said to be auspicious;
huge crowds quickly gather to ogle the small leathery heads that
poke out of the murky water looking as if they're gasping for fresh
air. The day after any apparition, newspapers would run blurred,
long-lens photographs that look like pictures of the Loch Ness monster.

'As a result of recent urban activities, the great spirit of Hoan
Kiem Lake at the heart of Hanoi, the thousand-year-old capital and
national pride of Vietnam, may cease to exist,' warned an architect
writing in a Saigon publication. The area has been altered significantly since 1954. A large post office, built in a Marxist municipal
style favoured by designers of Chinese railway stations, was con-
structed. Next to this, the graceful French town hall was demolished
and replaced with a drab modern box clad in cracking and stained
marble. In more recent years, a Vietnamese developer put up a spec-
tacularly ugly office building at the lake's northern end and the
department store at the south-west corner was demolished. The
final straw for many came with the development of a hotel that
would have loomed over the northern end of the lake. Even though
the Hong Kong developer had already won planning permission for
the hotel, the government stepped in and ordered them to cut a
few floors from the building.

The battle over this hotel became emblematic of a struggle to protect Hanoi from foreign developers that stirred up a rancorous
debate in the press. Foreign investors were said to be tearing the
heart out of Hanoi and turning it into a soulless wasteland of tower
blocks and offices. There was more than a hint of xenophobia in this
attitude as the most egregious abuses of the planning rules and the
most horrible architecture were the responsibility of Hanoians
themselves, who believed in preserving the character of the city
only as long as they themselves did not have to make any sacrifices.

In the crowded Old City, people wanted more space and dry
buildings with modern plumbing. There was also the driving force
of rising prices. In 1992 land prices in the old city went from $240 a
square metre to more than $700. The economic gains of rebuilding
higher and bigger were irresistible. Many put up boxy concrete
shop-houses that stand several storeys over the traditional height of

buildings. These glitzy 'minihotels' went up in a 'Lego Deco' style with a profusion of classical pilasters, Chinese motifs and rococo plasterwork that makes the most eclectic post-modernism seem restrained. These decorated sheds of concrete, plaster and neon sprang up in violation of building codes that existed only on paper. Fines were not high enough to deter landowners from rebuilding, and officials from the various overlapping offices that tried to control construction could be easily bribed.

Few residents of the old city were too disturbed by the loss of their damp and collapsing houses even if it did mean an erosion of the heritage of Hanoi. Some even argued that as there is little genuinely Vietnamese architecture in the city, that they should not spend money on preserving what is mostly Chinese or French in origin. Preservation policies have been criticised as simply serving tourists and the government élite without much reference to the city's population. This attitude has only been strengthened by officials such as Hoang Dao Kinh of the Ministry of Culture and Information who said that once restored, the old French opera house, a glorious tropical copy of the Palais Garnier in Paris, would be reserved for 'elegant people who wear suits and ties to enjoy the arts'.

In 1994 Hanoi celebrated the fortieth anniversary of the fall of the city to Vietminh forces. The anniversary evoked a nostalgia for the Hanoi of the past, which was no longer seen as a parasitic construction of French colonialism but had been remade into an elegant intellectual city of mythology, the realm of mandarins and poets rather than rough peasants. 'People without shirts and in shorts roam the city streets as if they were walking through paddy fields,' sniffed the historian Nguyen Vinh Phuc in a newspaper article. What was needed, he believed, was a return to 'a civilised urban way of life'.

What has undone the supposedly civilised way of life has been a massive influx of rural Vietnamese seeking work in the city. Migration from the countryside to cities had been held in check until the late 1980s by bureaucratic controls under which all people required residency permits and permission to travel. When this system broke down, the exodus to the cities began from the poor, crowded provinces around Hanoi, particularly following the demobilisation of more than half a million soldiers after the end of the conflict in Cambodia in 1991. Squalid hot-bunking dormitories filled up with men who came to the city to work on building sites or to pedal *cyclos*; a new complex sub-culture of recent migrants appeared in a city that had not seen such an influx since 1954.

Each morning a steady stream of people cross the Long Bien Bridge weighed down with goods to sell in the city. Most find a patch of pavement from which to work, setting up what are known as frog markets because when the police try to catch them, they quickly jump away. The city is full of little flurries as police arrive and dozens of women scurry off, carrying their goods in baskets on the front of a bicycle or on poles balanced across their shoulders. The police seem to favour carrying out these raids before lunch, the confiscated evidence, one surmises, probably does not last long.

In July 1995, the city authorities tried to 'restore order' to the streets of Hanoi by clearing out market traders and enforcing regulations on vending. The result was a more furtive trade, not better organised streets. The campaign handed more power to the ever-present police, a group of brutal and corrupt men, puffed up with a sense of entitlement. The police normally stole any produce or destroyed it by running over the baskets. The vendors could do nothing but stand forlorn and powerless, their livelihoods crushed on the pavement.

Hanoi is increasingly marked by a nasty and insistent snobbery against those from the countryside. Posturing urban sophisticates spit the words *nha que* (literally country-dweller) at each other as an insult. There is a brazenness about the contempt for the rural intrusion which is quite startling in a Communist country. In her study of urban migration, 'Peasants on the Move', Li Tana quotes a report from the Party newspaper *Nhan Dan* in which an official complains that the Hanoi People's Committee was 'right wing and impotent' and did not dare 'chase the migrants out of the city with a free hand'. 'We have the instrument of dictatorship at hand, we have the police, army and the concourse of people's force. Yet you do not sweep those wandering people out of Hanoi.'

The government craved a city that could be kept pristine and well organised without the supposed problems created by either peasant migrations or foreigners, another source of official displeasure. There were several attempts to resegregate Hanoi and force foreigners into certain areas of the city. This was done once again on the grounds of political hygiene. In an editorial the *Nguoi Lao Dong* newspaper called for the establishment of special zones for foreigners. 'To be frank, we must say that foreigners should have the right to live anywhere they want,' the labour union newspaper said. 'But we should also consider other factors: the safeguarding of security, discrimination and some anxieties on both sides.' A special area for foreigners would help maintain 'normal co-existence between the foreign and Vietnamese communities'.

Foreigners were often refused permission to live in areas of the city or on the same streets as senior officials, military officers or sensitive installations, which in the paranoid world of Hanoi bureaucrats could mean buildings as banal as post offices. An order that meant foreigners would not be able to rent properties owned by the state would have created an effective re-segregation, as foreigners would have had to move into new property developments. This rule, however, caused outrage among the many senior cadres who were earning huge sums renting out the villas they had been given by the government. These officials were a powerful lobby and the rule was never implemented.

Hanoi's changing and rising population, its strained infrastructure and its anarchic planning have forced discussion about the meaning of architecture into the background, but there are concerns about how the country can modernise and maintain a sense of identity. Most architects admit that the current situation is dire. In a recent competition for young architects from Southeast Asian nations, entries from Thailand, Laos and Cambodia could immediately be identified, according to Nguyen Hong Dao, a professor of architecture in Ho Chi Minh City. The entries from Vietnam were all bland modernist blocks that could have come from anywhere.

One of the problems is that Vietnam does not have much of an architectural tradition to build on. Le Hiep attributes this to a Taoist sensibility that preferred nature to grandeur. 'In China the buildings are taller and larger. They try to build up to the sky to challenge nature whereas Vietnamese build lower structures that are more in harmony with their environment.

'Vietnamese don't need mansions or towers,' Hiep said. 'At the corner of Nguyen Thai Hoc and Van Mieu there is a place where there used to be a temple. There is no temple there now but there is a tree. People still go there to worship, leaving incense and offerings by the tree. They don't really need a temple – architecture is just not important to Vietnamese.'

Vietnam has a richer tradition that Hiep acknowledges, but architectural students are taught next to nothing about their own heritage. Younger architects are only now starting to pick up on the importance of numerology and the form of geomancy known as *feng shui* that enriched the meaning of buildings. They are starting to ignore the equalising political imperatives of socialist architecture and think again about how people want to live.

One of the best examples of the richness of meaning encoded in Vietnamese buildings is the Chan family chapel in the old port of Hoi An in the centre of the country. This old building that dates from the eighteenth century is an example of Confucian, Taoist and Buddhist influences at work. A front garden representing the future unfolds in a large and spacious area; the house represents the present; a small garden at the back of the house, with a raised area in which the family buries the umbilical cords of its children, represents the past. The garden is also planted with symbolic plants to represent prosperity and health. The house has two roofs, representing yin and yang. Lamps are shaped like pomegranates which, with their profusion of seeds, are a symbol of fertility. Five pillars hold the eaves, representing a hand that protects the family.

Dragons, a symbol of power and fortune, decorate the beams but are carved so that the entire beast cannot be seen. Dragons must never be shown in their entirety, they must always disappear into clouds or water. Almost every aspect of the design of the house has some readable meaning. It is an enormous challenge to translate this heritage into successful modern design, but it does offer a path for Vietnamese architects to follow if they want to do more than produce cities of bland modernist boxes given a veneer of local charm with a chinoiserie roof of flying eaves and coloured tiles.

Just as great a challenge will be to preserve the treasure trove of architecture that already exists. The colonial heritage of Hanoi has not been wiped out, but it may yet disappear. The city has gone from being too poor to change much to being just rich enough to wreck everything without putting in place the policies that could safeguard its heritage. The spectre of other Asian cities, megalopolitan nightmares of traffic, pollution and overcrowding, should haunt Hanoi. The complicated web of interests that have hindered the coherent development of other cities is emerging. Large developers tied to local government through links of patronage and corruption, officials more interested in private affluence than alleviating public squalor and planners insensitive to the needs of people are all jostling for power. It does not bode well for the city as it approaches its first millennium.

12

Social Evils

Virtue cannot separate itself from reality without becoming a principle of evil.

Albert Camus
The Rebel, 1951

In the humidity of a Saigon summer the guitar defied tuning but the man plucked on nevertheless, sending out a warped melody that barely made it over the syncopated beeping of motorbike horns coming in from the street. Around him three dozen men sat cross-legged on the tiled floor of the ramshackle villa, each clutching a sweating bottle of soya milk, all of them sucking on their straws with an unsettling intensity. The men started to sing, their voices dampened by weariness and perhaps a little bit of embarrassment. The song was about their attempts to give up drugs, a battle a good many of these men, their bodies and faces aged well beyond their years, will lose.

Most of them will go back to drugs to smooth the edges of lives harried by a myriad problems, finding escape in the thin residues of burned opium or in the stronger rush of heroin as it surges into their clotted veins. This gathering offers no miracle cure for their addiction, but the mere fact that the group is meeting at all is something of a miracle in itself.

Outside the villa were dozens of pairs of plastic sandals, arrayed in lines along the steps and across the courtyard. There was something troubling about this profusion of cheap footwear. The sandals brought to mind memorials for the Holocaust, or for the tens of thousands killed by guns each year in the United States whose shoes were once lined up on the steps of the Capitol in Washington

DC. After the meeting, all the men finished their soya milk, scuffled around, heads bowed, to find their sandals on the steps and pedalled off home. Almost all of them will be dead within a few years, killed by the human immuno-deficiency virus that around 70 per cent of all injecting drug users in Ho Chi Minh City carry in their blood.

Every day the villa that houses the group is filled with the sort of people the Vietnamese government detests. This is as far away as one can go from the sunny picture of family life that appears on posters. Downstairs the emaciated smack addicts, many of them former South Vietnamese soldiers, sing and yearn for another fix. Upstairs a former prostitute camps it up with two young gay men in tight black jeans and muscle T-shirts. There are piles of papers and old computers stacked on desks, doors fly open as different groups look for a room where they can hold a meeting. Vietnamese state offices are normally afflicted with a fly-blown torpor. Gravity seems much stronger and the air thicker in government buildings as heads loll on desks and work is carried out with a painful slowness. But at this HIV/AIDS awareness group, a hothouse of degeneracy in the eyes of many Vietnamese, there is a rare energetic buzz that comes with the enthusiasm of volunteers, believers, people with a genuine attachment to what they are doing.

The centre is a base for a group of mostly young Vietnamese who train people to go out into the community and teach them how to avoid infection with HIV. There are three main groups dealing with drug users, prostitutes and gay men. Each group presents its own difficulties of how to reach its target audience and how to give them assistance in ways to avoid infection with a virus that will have a devastating impact in Vietnam.

HIV has become one of the many pressing issues testing the government by pushing the boundaries of what it can accept as policy and by testing whether it can deal with a vastly complex social problem without resorting to the knee-jerk response of authoritarianism and control. It is also proving how far the government will tolerate the emergence of civil organisations outside its direct control that demand a voice in government policies and actions. HIV presents Vietnam with an array of economic, political, social and moral issues that it has never dealt with before.

So far Vietnam has received good marks for the way in which it has handled the HIV pandemic. There has been less official denial of the problem than in many Asian countries, even than in Thailand, which is seen as more politically and socially open. The government has no religious constraints as is the case in some Islamic countries or in predominantly Roman Catholic nations such as the Philippines. Advertising of condoms is widespread and open, unlike in many Western countries, and the government has allowed some needle exchange programmes. After some initial hesitancy and insistence that AIDS was a purely foreign problem, the issue was recognised early on at the highest level of government, which in October 1992 established a national committee to co-ordinate policies.

The virus has not yet got into its stride in Vietnam and few people have died so far. By 1996, around 2,000 people had succumbed to diseases that their failing immune systems could no longer fight off. The number of deaths is expected to rise to 20,000 by the end of the century. Another 330,000 people will be infected with HIV by then, according to figures from the agency UNAIDS. At least 100,000 people a year will join the list of those infected and some 6,000 will develop AIDS. Another 8,000 will die each year, a figure that will rise sharply in the early years of the new millennium. Hospitals will fill up with huge numbers of patients, many of them abandoned by families and friends. They will mostly die from tuberculosis, the opportunistic infection that has made a dramatic comeback across the world in recent years in a morbid partnership with HIV.

It is not yet clear what pattern HIV will follow in Vietnam but the likelihood is that it will mimic the development of the pandemic in Thailand. The first to be hit are injecting drug users and sex workers. Migrant workers and truck drivers will spread the virus outside the major cities and it will slowly burn its way through the countryside. Wives will contract it from their husbands, children from their mothers. Heterosexual sex will eventually become the main means of transmission. Young people are already being hit hard with most of those infected aged between fifteen and twenty-five. With Vietnam's generally poor levels of nutrition and health care, the development of AIDS is likely to be quicker than in the West with most people succumbing within a few years of infection. The complex drug treatments that are changing the patterns of the disease in the West and prolonging lives will remain out of reach of countries such as Vietnam for some time to come.

Vietnam has almost no way at the moment to deal with the issue of AIDS treatment. They have built some specialised hospitals, but these have filled up too rapidly and will not be of much use. The Dong Da Communicable Diseases Hospital in Hanoi is the main AIDS unit for the city – there is no sign outside, as patients want to remain completely anonymous. The unit is bare and ragged but fairly clean, there are open lavatories and wash places that smell of antiseptic. The beds are basic, the paint mottled with damp. Most patients are treated at home where they can remain private, often they prefer doctors to visit them there, some have not even told their families, their fear is so great. Similar units in areas of higher infection in the South have become dumping grounds for the dying; demand for beds massively outstrips the government's capacity to provide care.

HIV is already starting to change Vietnam's government and social systems. Officials in Hanoi realised early in the trajectory of the disease that they needed to change the way they viewed the sensitive social and political issues that surround HIV/AIDS. The Ministry of Health only began testing for HIV at the end of 1990 when the first person was discovered to be infected – a thirty-year-old woman who was said to have contracted the virus through sexual contact in Germany. Most of those who first showed up as HIV positive were foreigners – mostly Thai fishermen imprisoned for illegally working in Vietnamese waters – or Vietnamese who had contact with foreigners.

This cemented into place a belief that it was a 'foreign disease' that could easily be avoided by avoiding contact with outsiders. Awareness of the illness was high – a survey in 1990 found that nearly 93 per cent had heard of it – but there was little understanding of its means of transmission. Most people thought it could be caught through casual contact and few understood that condoms were a vital part of safe behaviour. Fewer than a third of those surveyed had ever used a condom. Among many there was a fatalistic view of the disease that meant few people were willing to change their behaviour. Others felt it could be avoided as long as one steered clear of foreigners and washed after sex.

With its large numbers of sex workers and growing population of drug users, Vietnam was ripe for an explosion of HIV infections. As the virus had arrived in Vietnam later than in other parts of Asia, there was a greater awareness of what to do. The government was more responsive than many Asian governments and started to put into place a mechanism through which it could respond to the disease. While it has generally won plaudits for its willingness to acknowledge the potential devastation of HIV, the record is mixed.

HIV requires an openness about social problems such as prostitution and drug use, but the government has generally favoured a harsh response to what it calls 'social evils'. As the changes brought about by *Doi Moi* unsettled the leadership, they harked back to methods of social control they used in the past, but the changing nature of Vietnamese society has rendered these methods unworkable and outdated. The panoptic society that the Communist Party desired was always unworkable; it simply drove people to hide in the crevices and fissures of life. What has emerged is a system that fails to create the tight social order the Party desires and yet still hinders the development of a sustaining, tolerant civil society. Now there is a range of social pressures, from HIV to emerging labour and environmental movements, that are starting to have a profound effect on the way the state uses its power.

Vietnam is starting to see first buds of an emerging civil society that buffers the individual from the power of the state, serving the interests of a group rather than the government. A whole variety of associations, clubs, religious groups and organisations centred around an issue like HIV are starting to appear outside of the control of the state. In a Communist country like Vietnam, this has been troubling for a government that has always sought to deny the worth of civil society. These organisations were either dismissed as the legacies of feudalism or simply bourgeois affectations through which a ruling élite bedazzled the working classes to keep them subjugated. With the arrival of the Communist Party, none of these institutions would be needed. There was a certain resilience in organisations that had often been around much longer than the

Party, so they were most often co-opted and controlled rather than completely eradicated.

While officially scorning the need for the mass of institutions that make up civil society, the Party has actually been a force behind its emergence. The economic crises of the late 1980s that pressured the government into reforms led to a situation where the government could not afford to maintain its role in every sector of life. Large areas of the economy, transport, education and healthcare were effectively hived off into the private sphere. This growing sector that has remained mostly outside the control of the state has been a warm and nutritious Petri dish on which the varied fauna of civil society has started to grow. Villages have set up special funds for education or have started private schools, healthcare has been taken over by doctors, pharmacists and other healers who charge for their services, and economic reforms have thrown up countless private companies and small traders.

But the government's tendency to resort to control and incarceration as a way to handle social problems is also proving durable. The Marxist and Confucian legacies mean that there is little room for the idea of problems arising not just from individuals but from broader social issues. The experience after the end of the war in 1975 reinforced this strong thread of political action. Prostitutes and drug users were rounded up and sent off for re-education along with those with connections to the South Vietnamese government or military. They were seen as a product of the dissolute and corrupt Southern regime that had been physically and morally ravaged by foreigners. The cure was isolation and the ascetic regimen of social-ism. Many 'degenerates' were sent off to New Economic Zones, one of those terms whose bland optimism hides a grim reality, in this case a stark internal exile.

Nguyen Khac Vien, a French-educated doctor and long-time pro-pagandist for Hanoi overseas, wrote in the late 1970s about programmes set up to treat the hundreds of thousands of addicts. 'At the centre, people refrain from all resort to violence and doors are unlocked. Drug addicts find here an atmosphere of comrade-ship, a cordial support from doctors and responsible cadres, a community life, a political and ideological education that helps them take an interest in social problems, in short, many factors which could not be found in the former society. A Communist Youth Union member with his revolutionary convictions, his frankness [and] his dedication often succeeds better than an eminent specialist.'

That isn't quite how many drug users remembered the years after 1975. Banished to camps or villages in the central highlands or the bleaker, least fertile sections of the Mekong Delta, many struggled not just with their addictions but with malaria, hunger and poverty. Policies have rarely been that benevolent, indeed today drug addicts are routinely rounded up and sent off to closed centres where they are expected to get clean largely on their own. According to a doctor who works in a rehab programme, addicts are offered almost no treatment except perhaps vitamins and an occasional massage. With as many as 70 per cent of injecting drug users now HIV positive, these centres have become dumping grounds for the abandoned and sick who have nowhere else to go.

Drugs were an initial preoccupation of the Revolution in 1945. In his litany of horrors imposed by French colonial rule that Ho Chi Minh read out in the Declaration of Independence, drugs featured prominently. 'To weaken our race they have forced us to use opium and alcohol,' he told the crowd. The French had used a state monopoly on opium sales to finance the colonisation of Indochina; addiction was widespread as both the cause for and a means to escape from poverty. For decades the government in Hanoi pinned drug use on colonialism and then the decadence of the United States. But its idea that drug use was concentrated in the south of the country because of the area's greater exposure to foreign influences has been challenged by figures showing that some of the highest levels of drug use are in the mountainous provinces along the borders with China and Laos. The government's conservative estimate puts the number of users at 200,000. It is now having to face the reality that the use of opium and heroin are firmly anchored in poverty and Vietnamese life.

The tradition of punishment also runs deep in the government's attitudes towards prostitution. After the war, tens of thousands of women were rounded up and re-educated, although this did not on the whole mean giving them skills they could use instead of working the streets. Neither did prostitution vanish under Communism, although it did become less obvious and more fiercely punished. After 1986 it surged again and now there are around 300,000 sex workers according to official figures although the real number is probably higher; some estimates put it as high as 600,000. Officially the government fervently disapproves of the sex industry; in reality its officials and agencies are active participants as brothel owners and clients. The Interior Ministry, which runs the police, owns the VIP Club in Hanoi, where a bevy of women in sprayed-on tight dresses shuffle unenthusiastically around the dance floor each night as they wait for foreign men.

The rise in prostitution is often pinned on tourism, but foreigners play only a marginal role; prostitution in Vietnam is a mostly home-grown industry. There are sex workers in high-class establishments that cater solely for foreigners, and the sex tourism industry has eyed Vietnam with interest, but it has not been the dominant factor. The press has shown justifiable outrage at cases where women have been sold into prostitution overseas, but there is much less noise over the much larger number of women who go from the country-side to city brothels. A line in the 'Story of Kieu', Vietnam's national poem that traces the life of a woman eventually forced into prosti-tution, reflects a common acceptance of prostitution if it provides sustenance for a family or village: 'What does it matter if the flower falls if the tree stays green.' Prostitution is acceptable as part of the sacrifices women must make for their families. Prostitution is often driven by harsh economic forces. If floods hit the Mekong Delta, as they often do, the number of women working the streets of Saigon and Phnom Penh rises sharply.

Prostitution does not necessarily attract the social opprobrium it does in many countries; attitudes vary widely. A survey by the youth newspaper *Thanh Nien* in 1988 found that only 20 per cent of young people believed prostitution was wrong. Official corruption and 'repression against the masses' were seen as much worse offences.

It is a diverse industry ranging on the low end to street walkers who cater to *cyclo* drivers and rural migrants, up through to the high-class call girls working the lobbies of five-star hotels. It per-meates the hotel and restaurant businesses where few would identify themselves as sex workers and yet often take money for sex. Visiting prostitutes is part of male bonding and growing up; it marks a transition from adolescence to adulthood. Paying for sex is not the furtive, hidden pursuit that it has become in the West, but a social activity, often done with friends. A survey of sexual attitudes carried out by the aid organisation CARE International found that men often shared sexual partners and male promiscuity was at extremely high levels among the urban population. According to the CARE research, around half of the men questioned had slept with two or more partners in the previous two weeks. Many men said they felt a strong need to explore sexual relations outside marriage. Almost all of them saw this as a natural instinct.

There were no velvet drapes to ensure a permanently crepuscular interior. There was no welcome from an obsequious bowing servant or hostess. There were no coils of incense smoke winding up past antique porcelain and scroll paintings, no lacquered bed with a canopy of crimson silk, no art deco fantasy of an opium den. The squat concrete house just off one of the main streets in Hanoi's French quarter was a 1990s reality check on the old Oriental image of 1930s narcotic chic.

Two children sat by a screeching television showing videos of Doraemon, a marsupial cartoon cat that invaded the consciousness of Vietnamese children stirring consumer cravings as powerful as any narcotic addiction. The house was neat and clean although the air was a thick mix of the sweet, slightly putrefied odour of opium and damp dog from a litter of white fluffy puppies crowded into a cardboard box. These dogs, briefly a favoured accoutrement of middle-class households in Hanoi, were bred by the woman, who padded around cheerfully cooking dinner in a tiny kitchen while her husband lay on the floor and glowered at his nervous ingenue customers.

To smoke the pipe, a long tube of wood – not some antique silver and ivory creation but a simple bamboo bong – was filled with the sticky resin and set alight; the smokers sucked in the fumes and held them deep in their lungs. The pipe was filled again, accompanied by constant grumbling from the owner who was more interested in satisfying his all-consuming, dawn-to-dawn, fifty-pipe-a-day habit than catering to his clients. He shouted at his young wife, who cowered away from her malevolent, opiated husband as if repelled by his thin limbs and grey-green pallor. After a few more pipes, he curled up on a thin mat, his head resting on a small plastic stool and the muttering subsided. The children fixed their attention on Doraemon, ignoring everyone around them with an intensity that suggested much practice at blocking out the world.

Even with its currents of domestic abuse and malice, this scene was much better than the insalubrious lives of most drug users in Vietnam, whose days are often scheduled around the demands of stealing enough to get a hit of blackwater, the diluted residues of opium that can be bought for a few dozen cents a shot and is often stretched out with the sedative diazepam. It's a hurried, tense life, alleviated only for a few brief moments with each hit. In a world where everyone lives in fear of the police and of informers, addicts can still visit shooting galleries but remain anonymous. In some galleries the users bind their upper arms to plump up a vein and then put their arms through a hole in a screen. The hidden owner then shoots them up and both sides remain unknown to each other. Clients have no way of knowing whether they have been shot up with a clean needle or how the drug has been cut.

If you are not dealing or running a shooting gallery, you have to steal to feed a habit. Crime, particularly in Ho Chi Minh City, has exploded along with the drug problem. The manager of an ice-cream shop was stopped by two young addicts on his way home late one night. They cut open his face and stabbed him repeatedly. Across his cheek was the brutal, puckered scar of the new hole they tore in him in order to rob him for their next fix. Violent muggings and burglaries, crimes most often fuelled by drugs, have soared along with drug use.

In December 1995, the government began to respond to what it saw as these ruptures in Vietnamese society by organising a mass campaign against 'social evils'. It wasn't an isolated spasm of state action, but the latest in a long line of campaigns launched against everything from bourgeois pop music to prostitution. There was something of a pattern to this ebb and flow of social control; the government was forced by a lack of resources, or other diversions such as a failing economy, to loosen the reins. A few years later the media would whip up a storm about a surge in behaviour that threatened the nation's 'good traditions and moral values'. There would be a sudden crackdown that would sweep the problems underground for a few weeks. But inevitably they always came back, indeed the main targets of the campaign – prostitution, drug use, pornography – appeared to be on a constant rise.

The way HIV figures were gathered has hastened the cycle and exaggerated some of the responses. Most testing in Vietnam is done forcibly, so when police carry out raids and round up those in high-risk groups, the incidence of HIV appears to rise rapidly. Local authorities panic and order crackdowns on drug use and prostitution, producing another jump in the figures and so on. Officials rarely look at broader trends in the development of the pandemic. Government figures also indicate that almost all HIV carriers are drug addicts, but they are much more likely to be caught and tested than any other high-risk group and therefore show up more in the figures.

The decrees issued at the end of 1995 – known as 87/CP and 88/CP – were aimed, the government said, at 'consolidating the management of cultural activities and services and promoting the bans of some serious social evils'. The origins of the campaign remain obscure. It appeared to be launched by Prime Minister Vo Van Kiet who was under pressure on his reform programme. Many members of the Party believed these reforms had spawned the social problems they claimed troubled them. Certainly the loss of control over society troubled the Party and the government and their response was to launch the 'social evils' campaign. Nothing much happened until February 1996, when, in a whirlwind of raids and photo opportunities, the police began scrubbing society clean.

The first target was foreign advertising, which has been suddenly added to the list of social evils. Crack teams armed with ladders and paint fanned out over Hanoi to remove the scourge of Coca-Cola signs and Kodak advertising. Shop owners watched in dismay as their expensive signs were given a coat of white paint for not complying with a rule that the Vietnamese name of a product must be in larger letters than the English words. This obscure regulation was widely regarded as moot for most products as Vietnamese use the same brand names, but there was no stopping the police.

While owners of bars were hurriedly hiding their illuminated advertisements for French cognac, the police were moving on to their next targets. According to the Ministry of Culture and Information which was leading the fight, in just two weeks in Hanoi alone police raided fourteen music stores, 144 video rental stores, 253 karaokes and a dancing hall. All this industry netted nearly 15,000 illegal video tapes and 3.4 tonnes of books. The ministry also listed 362 'negative posters' and 153 'incidents' that had been uncovered, although it was tantalisingly vague about the nature of these crimes. None of these raids was hindered by anything as limiting as due process. Many video store owners said the police raided them purely to earn bonuses from bribes ahead of the *Tet* holiday.

Soon there were flag-waving parades through the streets and an almost incessant white noise of new rules and regulations broadcast across the street loudspeakers. Party officials and youth union activists went door-to-door through public housing blocks requiring that people sign pledges not to indulge in social evils. Posters of a massive fist crushing such evils as porn movies and prostitutes went up along with banners with the less than pithy slogan: 'Preventing and fighting against social evils and building an advanced culture of national identity is the task of each citizen.'

Many people in Vietnam, as in all countries, are genuinely concerned about these social problems, but it is hard to whip up enthusiasm these days about old-style mass campaigns with their intrusiveness and hectoring tone. The openly xenophobic tone of much of the campaign that pinned the blame for the deterioration of morals on the West didn't generate much interest. 'I think economic reasons, more than an invasion of Western culture, are where the deterioration of morals started,' said Nguyen Thuy Hanh, a 27-year-old secretary in Hanoi. 'This campaign is necessary but it seems that the authorities don't have a clue where to apply it.'

As usual most social evils went deeper underground for a while. The neon lights outside the karaokes and bars were switched off, but nothing much changed inside. The streetwalkers and roving pimps on their Honda bikes were less in evidence on the city streets. The public, inured to all this windy propaganda, indulged in all the evils it desired but more discretely than usual. Only a few were unlucky enough to get caught; a group from Hanoi Polytechnic, the country's most prestigious science university, were caught watching pornographic videos under the guise of a 'cultural activities club'. Police discovered seventy students and three staff members watching the films just days after the college had distinguished itself by winning a national student quiz on the 'social evils' campaign.

For all the talk about the never-ending fight to eradicate these scourges, what was remarkable about the 'social evils' campaign was its restraint in comparison to earlier cultural cleansings. There were no parades of criminals through the city streets, no house-to-house searches or mass settlings of scores by intrusive neighbours. The government even felt a rare compulsion to explain its activities, calling a news conference at which officials denied any anti-foreign intent behind the eradication of advertising and said some police might have gone a little too far in painting out signs.

There was also a realisation that the 'social evils' campaign was working against efforts to control the spread of HIV. There was a wide split between the 'eradicationists', who believed that HIV could be controlled by wiping out prostitution and drug use, and those pragmatic officials who felt education and so-called 'harm reduction' programmes, that aim to minimise transmission through needle exchanges and condom distribution, were the way to lower the soaring infection rates. The latter group had quietly condoned the establishment of peer education networks, HIV support groups and special help for patients using non-governmental organisations. Able to win only the broadest consensus for action against HIV, these officials quietly gave the nod to other institutions to step into the breech. The women's and youth unions, both tightly linked to the Party, began innovative peer education programmes even before it was possible to mention condoms in government documents. Their work was supplemented by other emerging NGOs who started not just to work in these areas but also attempted to influence government policy by calling for more openness and tolerance.

Vietnamese working with these organisations to change ideas and encourage innovative policies were privately dismayed or cynical about the 'social evils' campaign. When asked what the impact of the campaign had been on HIV education programmes, three counsellors immediately responded that it had been a huge setback

for their work and had not had any impact on the number of sex
workers or drug users.

'These so-called social evils are on the rise and HIV is on the rise
as well,' said Thanh, a former sex worker who had become one of
the leading peer educators in Ho Chi Minh City. 'The "social evils"
campaign just makes it worse. Now people are anxious, they have
to have sex in a hurry because they are frightened of the police
turning up. They don't have time to take any measures.'

The problem was the same for drug users, who were shooting up
in fear that the police might raid the galleries. In these conditions
there was no way to persuade them to use clean needles and to
avoid sharing, said a drug educator called Nghi. Programmes to
distribute clean needles were closed down by the police who felt
that they were encouraging drug use.

Aids educators themselves had been caught up in the campaign
when police arrested them for doing their work in brothels and
drug dens. The Ho Chi Minh City Police newspaper launched one
of its noxious campaigns against the peer education programme,
saying it was being used as a cover for people to sell sex or drugs.
Officially peer educators were supposed to be ex-drug users and ex-
sex workers, but not all had put their past lives behind them. They
were also supposed to urge sex workers and drug users to try to
stop what they were doing, but most educators saw their role as
stopping infections with HIV not salvaging every life or putting
every person back on the right track.

The 'social evils' campaign also meant a tougher line in the press
and not just in the police newspapers. 'Some are more critical now
as they have to follow the government line but others have recognised the work we can do,' said Thanh, who has even been
honoured by the city government for her work with prostitutes. It is
a tough job; she has to encourage the women to go for health checks
by showing them grim photos of sexually transmitted diseases.

The level of education of most sex workers is very low and many
have difficulties dealing with the information about HIV. 'They
don't see the dangers of HIV now, but they do feel the dangers of
not having any money or being hungry,' said Thanh. 'Police are not
so much a problem for us but they are a problem for HIV education.
Initially when we make contact there are difficulties reaching

people. You have to build up trust, ask them about their health, tell them how to take care of themselves and explain that in the past you were in the same situation and that you want to do something to help them. I always say that they are much luckier than us as no one helped us in the past, we had to go to the STD clinics by ourselves. It is less of a problem nowadays.'

HIV has even sparked debate in the press and among officials over the efficacy of policies of social control. With its omnipresent police trained in East German techniques by the Stasi and the voluminous files said to be kept on many people, the state might be expected to do a better job at monitoring those who test positive, but so far there has been a massive failure to keep a check. The state's intrusion here is not all bad; organisations such as the Women's Union try to provide support, comfort and some financial help. The problem is that officials are just not trusted and the fear of isolation and intolerance among those with HIV remains intense.

By mid 1997, 5,200 people had tested positive for HIV, but the authorities only had addresses for 2,390, according to figures from the National AIDS Committee published in the *Lao Dong* newspaper. More than half of all people who had been tested had evaded further contact with the authorities. Of those whose whereabouts are known only 16 per cent regularly attend health check-ups and meetings with officials. Only 9 per cent had received any material benefits from the state. *Lao Dong* queried why so few people with HIV were being 'managed' – a euphemism in Vietnam for intrusive state control. 'Can we manage all the people with HIV?' the paper asked, an unusual step as social policies are rarely questioned in public. 'How can we manage them? What is the management for? Is it really necessary?'

HIV has forced the government to question whether it can really carry out national campaigns in a society that is becoming increasingly diverse in attitudes and mores as well as increasingly divided between rich and poor, rural and urban. 'Social evils' campaigns play well to a fairly small and ageing group shocked by what they see as a society in decline, but they have little appeal to a growing urban middle class that is young, individualistic and increasingly driven by consumption. HIV/AIDS education has shown up the failure of state propaganda in a country that is being inundated with increasingly slick advertising and marketing campaigns. The standard mechanisms of state control and information – the mass rally, poster campaigns, the visit by the neighbourhood women's or youth union official – are unlikely to cut it against the froth of consumer information out there.

With some hesitation and considerable assistance from foreign NGOs the government has opened itself up to new ways of informing people and has allowed discussion of what in Vietnam are relatively new ideas, such as the right to privacy. In fact many of these means are not that new, they were part of the inventive repertoire of propaganda that helped bring the Communist Party to power, but they have become ossified and stale when commanded by the Ministry of Culture and Information. Peer education has been among the most controversial means of getting the word out on HIV, but in some ways it mirrors the youth units that once recruited new Party members. The cartoon books introduced by an Australian NGO are not much different from the travelling exhibitions of pictures of French colonial exploitation that the Party once used to communicate their message to a mostly illiterate population.

As in most countries, the first wave of HIV advertising stressed that AIDS was fatal and incurable, creating an attitude that there was nothing that could be done against it. It was also tinged with an anti-foreign sentiment. One respondent told an NGO researcher: 'Nobody dares to say that 100 per cent of foreigners have AIDS, but at least 50 per cent of them might have the disease.' Another quoted by a CARE report on HIV said: 'I think there are two types of people that may catch AIDS: first of all, government staff who work in the tourist service and other economic agencies and those who are involved in joint ventures; second, girls who work in dancing halls and restaurants.' One man was more specific about which types of foreigners were at risk: 'I used to say that Spaniards could most easily get AIDS . . . The Iraqis should be the ones most at risk from AIDS.'

A study by the Ho Chi Minh Academy, the Party's think-tank and training ground for top cadres, found that HIV education was too narrowly focused on issues such as drug use and prostitution. This encouraged a sense of immunity and complacency among many people just as the virus was starting to appear in an increasing number of pregnant women and soldiers, two broad groups that are subject to tests. The government itself has remained particularly complacent in the area of controlling blood products. Aware of the scandals that brought down bureaucrats in Japan and France over tainted blood, few officials have been willing to tackle the issue.

Research by CARE found that people disliked government campaigns and had not absorbed much information from them. Posters of prostitutes and emaciated drug addicts reinforced ideas about who could get the disease and heightened the concept that it was possible to tell if someone had HIV by the way they looked. People did not want to be told not to have sex. Sex was one area where the government had almost no voice, where bureaucracy and the censorious state could no longer intrude. Many Vietnamese have remarked that getting contraceptives or having an abortion were some of the few activities that did not require a plethora of paperwork and hassles. The martial images and language used in AIDS campaigns also turned people off, it was all too close to the aggressive Party propaganda that most people spend their lives tuning out.

A recent attempt to reach people in a less hectoring manner was through a soap opera for Vietnam Television that wove issues raised by HIV into its plot. The drama series, backed by the European Commission and CARE International, was aimed at breaking down ideas established by earlier HIV campaigns. Soaps were a relatively new introduction to Vietnamese television, but the poorly dubbed Mexican and Brazilian telenovellas imported via Russia were hugely popular.

The new series, which goes by the poetic if confusing title *The Wind Blows through Light and Dark*, was written by a number of well-known writers in an uneasy collaboration. The series followed several families in rural and urban Vietnam as they cope with the strains of the country's rapid economic and social change. The message on HIV was kept deliberately low-key and woven through with other plot lines in the thirty episodes that were under production. 'We want to change the idea that AIDS is something that only

exists in cities or that it only affects those who associate with foreigners,' said Thuy Linh, a short story writer who worked on the
series. 'Our message is that even if you lead a simple life you can get
AIDS,' said Linh. 'We're telling people to be faithful, have one wife,
one husband, use condoms when you have sex.'

Two main characters, a young woman from the countryside and
a middle-class professional man, are infected with the virus, giving
the writers the chance to break down stereotypes and encourage
compassion. Linh said that as Vietnam had no social activists or
celebrities who had acknowledged being HIV positive, there were
no role models to whom people could relate. Few people with the
virus have spoken out and press coverage of the illness has tended
to focus on drug users and prostitutes.

The writers, who struggled with their divergent views of what
should happen to the characters, were careful not to overload the
show with social messages. 'It's a very normal soap, with love, hate,
jealousy, all those things,' said one of the film crew.

Having failed to change many minds with a single megaphone
voice of disapproval, the Party appears to be allowing the development of a more tolerant outlook and a less monolithic approach to
social issues. There is a basic awareness among policy makers that
the urge to control and monitor closely often ends up driving a
problem underground.

The Party is not yet ready to give up its rhetoric on these issues.
The army and Party dailies fire off regular broadsides against
deviants, foreigners and other enemies of the state, but at the same
time the government is allowing the development of networks and
associations that not long ago would have been unthinkable. Drug
users gather in self-help groups and are not rounded up for re-education. Prostitutes counsel other sex workers without too great a
fear of arrest. HIV activists lecture senior army and police officials
on the danger of the virus by reminding them that their men are
among the most at risk from commercial sex and drug use. It is a
small but significant step towards a real civil society that might
limit the coercive capacity of the state and tilt the balance of power
towards the people.

There is a widening belief in the government that punishment and social control have become mirages to distract people from the real problems that afflict the country. These heavy-handed responses become a poor substitute for more realistic and less facile solutions to social problems. As the state's powers of coercion become less effective, officials are increasingly looking at the mechanisms of a civil society to provide the channels of information, debate and problem-solving that can no longer remain in the Party's monopoly. A number of outspoken and forward-looking individuals have challenged the government on issues such as HIV, the environment, labour conditions and other social issues; they are beacons of hope in a political landscape that is less than inspiring.

The trend is doubtless going in the right direction, but the path towards a more open and inclusive society has not been straightforward. Each move forward requires a bone to be tossed to those who still favour firm state control. For each needle exchange programme, there must be a 'social evils' campaign, for every peer educator, there must be a round-up of sex workers. Only by doing this odd dance of one step forward, one step back, can consensus in the government be maintained.

The government is still suspicious of ideas about civil society; many feel the Party should control all organisations through the Fatherland Front and not allow the development of any alternative arenas for discussion. The state still fears NGOs, indeed it has been intent on controlling and limiting their sphere of influence. Any organisation outside the remit of the Party can find itself a focus of political repression. A revealing, and somewhat pathetic example, is that the scout movement is still banned. Once popular in the 1930s, scouting has returned in recent years but has had to remain underground because it is still officially banned. There are no uniforms and meetings are held covertly. In a country where criminal gangs operate almost with impunity and corruption is rarely punished, scout troops live in fear of the authorities as they secretly learn to tie knots and light fires.

If Vietnam can deal with HIV, an issue fraught with social problems in every country, it will likely open up on a whole range of other issues in which an inclusive, open attitude will foster better policies. The development of a civil society will ease an almost inevitable transition to a more open political system. The nations of the former Soviet Bloc have struggled to establish these institutions in a short time, but in many cases have been remarkably successful; they have shown that civil society can emerge rapidly when the bonds of Communism are broken. These countries have developed, in the words of the British philosopher Ernest Gellner, societies 'in which polity and economy are distinct, where polity is instrumental but can and does check extremes of individual interest, but where the state is checked by institutions with an economic base; it relies on economic growth, which by requiring cognitive growth, makes ideological monopoly impossible.'

13

Faith

*The Vietnamese religion (if indeed one can use the singular)
produces an impression like that inspired by a foray into the
great forests of the Annamite Cordillera: On all sides are great
tree-trunks, their roots penetrating to unfathomable depths,
supporting a vault of foliage lost in shadows; branches stoop
down to the earth and take root; seemingly endless creepers
run from tree to tree, their origins undiscoverable; there are
inextricable thorns, and fronds of surpassing elegance and delicacy; expansive flowers of outlandish appearance bestrew the
ground, or deck a treetop with a fiery dome or ensconce themselves in the fork between two boughs; the bark of the tree is
black, or gnarled, or slimy and one cannot touch it without a
shudder; there are dead branches upon a thick carpet of mould
and decay; on all sides sap thrusts up and life abounds in overwhelming profusion.*

LEOPOLD CADIÈRE
The Religion of the Vietnamese

Just before *Tet* in 1997, workers were sprucing up the Ba Chua Kho
temple in Ha Bac province near Hanoi, creating two new pavilions
from wood and concrete, with flying eaves curving upwards at each
corner and walls painted with colourful scenes from the life of the
woman who had inspired the pagoda. Two men in shorts and green
pith helmets skilfully smoothed stucco over the walls while other
villagers tiled the ornate roof. Outside, stall owners were setting up
along the road leading up to the temple from a small lake in preparation for the tens of thousands of people who would shortly
descend on the temple.

For a few weeks each year, thousands of people from Hanoi and
across the Red River basin swarm to the Ba Chua Kho pagoda.

Newly prosperous merchants and officials, dressed up for the trip, came carrying elaborate trays of fruit and shiny lacquered suckling pigs. The temple has become the place to pray for prosperity, the essential urge in the 1990s. Crowds are sometimes so large that people would queue for hours before placing their offerings on the altar and bowing with incense sticks clutched in their hands. Attendees regularly complained about the crush of people, saying that pickpockets and the grasping vendors arrayed outside were spoiling the atmosphere of this once peaceful temple.

Ba Chua was a wife of an eleventh-century emperor who spent much of his time battling the Chinese. She was put in charge of organising provisions for his forces and she did this with considerable energy and success. Marginal lands were tilled and planted with rice. All free hands were put to the task and enough food was grown to feed the troops who were defending Vietnam against the northern invaders. Another version of the story has her hiding the keys to the granaries from the Chinese, enabling the food to be taken by Vietnamese soldiers fighting a rear-guard action. Yet another has her burning the granaries and killing herself to stop the enemy taking the supplies. As with so much of Vietnamese history from that time, there are a number of versions, but all contain the central theme of providing for troops who were battling Vietnam's eternal enemy. When she died in 1077, her husband dedicated this temple to her memory.

Those who visit the temple nowadays have more modest requests for Ba Chua than feeding an army. For city residents it is to ask for success for a new karaoke bar, food stall or photocopying stand, for farmers it is to pray for good crops. 'In spring, after the new year, there is not much work to do on the land so people come to the pagoda to pray for fortune,' said Nguyen Van Lien, a retired soldier who helps look after the temple. 'At the end of the year, they come back if they have been successful and prosperous during the year.'

For Nguyen Van Nguyen, a 71-year-old farmer who spent much of his life fighting in the army, even serving a spell in the prison on Phu Quoc Island, the temple is about more than just wealth. 'This is the place where our national identity is expressed,' he said. It hasn't always been that way. The temple only reopened to the public in 1990. Before that it was in the middle of an army base and was used for storage. Even during the war, soldiers serving in the base would climb into the temple to pray, Lien said. Much of it was destroyed during the war, the caretaker said, although he refused to say whether this was by the Vietnamese themselves or by US bombing. Others in the village said the temple was unused and fell into a state of neglect after the 1950s. In the early 1990s the Ministry of Culture and Information designated it a site of national importance and paid for renovations and new buildings.

In just a few years, the temple went from being derelict and mostly ignored to becoming a centre of pilgrimage for tens of thousands of people caught up in the new national pastime of money making. Its pavilions were rebuilt and its message of national independence reinforced. Its themes were brazenly capitalist, indeed it was a sort of spiritual bank that offered one-year loans of good fortune that had to be repaid in offerings. Yet it was seen as an intensely spiritual place. 'It is very sacred here,' whispered a civil servant from Hanoi who had come to repay a year of prosperity for his wife, a rich trader.

Ba Chua Kho is just one of thousands of pagodas across the country that have been revived as centres of spiritual life. After 1986, shuttered village temples were opened up; those converted to granaries or schools returned to their original use. Rituals and festivals were revived and temples in their multiplicity of forms regained their importance in life. Many catered to new spiritual needs: temples that brought prosperity to farmers now do the same for an urban middle class, those connected with fertility are now said also to extend the lives of those living with HIV. Religion in all its forms in Vietnam has been unleashed and Vietnamese have returned to their faiths in extraordinary numbers. Roman Catholic and Protestant churches are bursting at the seams; those attending mass in the big city cathedrals often spill out into the surrounding streets from where they follow the services over loudspeakers. Altars to ancestors and household spirits had been quietly tolerated over the years, although any elaborate worship was normally quickly condemned as counter-revolutionary and wasteful. The Party's attempt to replace all civil institutions with government bodies under its strict control left people feeling atomised and as a result many have embraced religion. Faith has become a way to intensify bonds of community that had been weakened not just by Marxism but in recent years by the market.

This religious revival is a phenomenon that has aroused mixed feelings in the Communist Party. On the one hand, promoting the multitude of faiths and festivals as part of traditional culture has filled the ideological void. Allowing this to happen has been a great success for the Party; the policies have proved an enormously popular part of *Doi Moi*. There is however a lingering distaste among many Party officials for the mysteries of faith. Organised religions are still seen as a potential source of problems. An article in a theoretical journal, *Tap Chi Quoc Phong Toan Dan*, laid out the fears that demands for greater religious freedom had stirred up:

> What is the real nature of so-called 'human rights violations and violations of freedom of religion' in Vietnam that enemies inside and outside the country are talking about? In their plot to carry out peaceful evolution to change the political system in the remaining socialist countries, they are giving particular attention to the banner of religion in order to deceive and arouse the masses. They say that in Vietnam, there is no party or political organisation with the capabilities, discipline and spirit equal to that of religious groups. Only believers have the spirit and courage to sacrifice themselves for their beliefs because their faith helps them ignore hardships and dangers. They say the end of the Communist system in Vietnam will be decided primarily by religion.

For many officials, ideologists and intellectuals in Hanoi, this popular explosion of religion is not really about faith but superstition, something the cleansing rationality of Communism was supposed to have eradicated. The Vietnamese word for superstition, *mi tin*, is a recent derivation from the Chinese term *mi xin* and has only been used since 1949. In a country where many people follow personal and localised faiths that combine elements of Buddhism, Taoism, Confucianism and village customs, it is impossible to draw a line between religion and superstition. Attacking supposed superstitions was a useful way of undermining traditional power structures in order to replace them with the Party's influence. Damning religions as superstition became one of the tools of domination; now the resurgence of religion has become a way of contesting that power.

It is still commonplace for those in power to question the very nature of religious belief. In an article on Buddhism, the Communist Party's theoretical journal *Tap Chi Cong San*, complained that few people seemed to have any real understanding of the religion:

> They do not know how to use the rational factors of Buddhism to benefit themselves, other people and the country. Moreover they serve the Buddha only in order to gain good fortune and ward off bad luck and some do so for temporary material purposes. At many pagodas, near the altar you can see people using divining sticks, drawing on their horoscopes, consulting mediums and so on. There are even people who go to the pagoda in the hope the Buddha will help them cover up their improper deeds. In front of the altar they ask the Buddha to strike the public security forces and tax collectors blind, deaf and dumb in the hope that they will not be prosecuted for their crimes . . . Such things reduce an intellectual religion to the level of a vulgar and common creed.

Most Vietnamese describe themselves as Buddhist although that can mean a multitude of things ranging from branches of Mahayana and Therevada Buddhism to local variants of Zen. The official Buddhist church estimates that 60 per cent of Vietnam's 75 million people are Buddhists. Others put the figure as low as 15 per cent. These figures are simply guesswork – it is nearly impossible to define who is a Buddhist in a religion with so many permutations. Leopold Cadière, a Jesuit priest whose decades in Vietnam were spent in intense study of local religions, wrote in 1944:

> Many Europeans who live in Indochina are deluded about the importance of the Buddhist religion among the Vietnamese population; for them the Vietnamese are Buddhists, pure and simple and some writers have not known better than to subscribe to this generalisation . . . The Buddhist religion has

formulae designed to win happiness for a man during his life and especially after his death, but few Vietnamese have recourse to these formulae; further when they go to the monks, they go to them not as official representatives of their principal religion but only as providers . . . of one more guarantee against the afflictions of a baleful destiny in this life or the next. Buddhism is a philosophy, a conception of man and of the world; but the number of Vietnamese who understand something of this philosophy is totally nugatory.

Vietnam's true religion, Cadière wrote, 'is the cult of spirits. This religion has no history because it dates from the origins of the race'. A belief that spirits are all around people, concealed in nature and made known through daily mundane actions still pervades much of life, but the worship of these spirits is not always elaborate. 'A prayer may be offered up in elevated language, in verses accompanied by music and dance, but, equally, the devotee may mutter his request as he passes before the little pagoda which he holds in awe or again he may simply express his heart's desire within the recesses of the spirit.'

It is the worship of ancestors and spirits that dominates religious life, but this type of faith is highly individualistic and has not led to mass organisations. Consequently the Communist Party has seen these diverse beliefs as less of a threat to its power. Indeed these faiths, with their emphasis on cultural identity, history and locality, usefully reinforce many of the Party's ideas about nationalism without throwing up challenges from an organised hierarchy.

The other main faiths are Roman Catholicism with about 7 million followers, according to the Church (and about 5 million according to the Communist Party), the modern Cao Dai sect with about 2.5 million adherents, Hoa Hao with 1.5 million followers and about half a million Protestants of a variety of denominations.

The Vietnamese constitution supposedly protects the right to freedom of religion but this strange document offers much but delivers little. The reality is that the Communist Party has only permitted degrees of freedom of religious activity when it has suited them. Between 1945 and its eventual victory over the French in 1954, the Party courted all religious groups that opposed colonialism. After independence the Party stepped up its repression, particularly in Roman Catholic areas in the North where the religion was briefly a potential threat to their power. In the South, they once again linked up with religious groups opposed to the Saigon government. After 1975 the Party rounded up many of the same religious leaders and sent them off for re-education.

Roman Catholics have rarely had an easy time in Vietnam. A group of Portuguese missionaries expelled from Japan arrived in Vietnam in 1612 in what was the first contact. The Imperial Court banned Catholicism in 1631, a prohibition that was reiterated many times over the next two centuries. Those early years of contact between Vietnam and the West were marked by *autos-da-fé* of bibles and persecutions of those who carried them. In 1712, the Trinh dynasty ruler came up with a powerful deterrent to the adoption of Christianity by his people: he had the words 'student of Dutch religion' – the Dutch made up a large proportion of the foreigners who visited Vietnam – carved into the foreheads of converts.

It wasn't just the Confucian élite who opposed the intrusions of Catholic missionaries. Alexandre de Rhodes, the Jesuit from Avignon who devised the system of romanisation for the Vietnamese language and is today one of the few foreigners honoured with a street name, complained that Vietnamese peasants tended to blame the 'new sorcerers' for droughts and floods. Converts were often cut off from their families, stirring up much resentment. Catholics also refused to join in or pay for important village festivals; instead they often set up their own villages, a process that heightened disputes over land and water. The religion was seen by a majority of Vietnamese as an uncivilised intoxicant that sucked people in and broke their familial and social ties. It must have seemed as alien and dangerous as some of the stranger cults appear today.

Even in this hostile environment, Catholicism became the first Western import to take hold. A missionary, Bertrand Reydellet, estimated that in 1756 there were 300,000 converts, meaning that about one in twenty Vietnamese were Christian. Most Catholics came from rural areas where the influence of Confucianism did not run as deep as it did among the élite. Christianity had the appeal of salvation as well as ritual and community in a country that had often endured civil conflict. Catholicism showed a surprising adaptability to Vietnamese village life, meshing well with some local beliefs. Catholics often justified their faith by saying their ancestors had been followers and therefore they must continue the faith to honour them. As even illiterate peasants were loved and saved by the faith, it drew its most intense adherents from the disenfranchised and poor.

The imperial élite remained suspicious that Catholicism might undo their power structures, a sense that was heightened in the 1830s when a French missionary took part in a rebellion against the Emperor Minh Mang. The missionary was captured and tortured to death. His execution was vividly described in an Imperial circular aimed at discouraging similar events. In 1847 the Emperor Thieu Tri ordered Catholics to be branded on their faces with the characters for infidel. Foreign priests were to be drowned and Vietnamese priests sawed in half lengthways. This assault on Catholicism would provide a pretext for French intervention and the eventual subjugation of Indochina.

The role of Catholics in the early stages of colonialism rankles with some Vietnamese even today. Catholics acted as spies and guides for French expeditionary forces whom they believed would protect them from the anti-Catholic pogroms that occurred throughout the nineteenth century. Followers of the faith were seen as a fifth column for the French and were the focus of a number of acts of resistance against the encroachment of the colonialists. One of the best known was the rebellion led by Truong Dinh from 1859 to 1864. This Mekong Delta rebel went by the title of 'Western Pacifying, Heretic Exterminating Generalissimo' and was known for his massacres of Christians. The Scholars Uprising of 1874 had a similar theme; its battle cry was 'Pacify the Westerners, exterminate the heretics and serve the Nguyen Dynasty'. They swept through the central provinces killing, according to the French, more than 4,500 Catholics in one month alone. Many of those who survived had their noses or ears cut off or their feet smashed. A decade later in Thanh Hoa province in the north, rebels herded Catholics into churches and burned them alive. A French officer who visited the province after the rebellion had been put down reported finding

2,000 Catholics with their throats cut. It is hardly surprising that Catholics lived with a strong awareness of political threats.

In 1949, five years before the war against the French would end, the atmosphere in the zones of North Vietnam under Vietminh control changed. The creeping influence of Maoism led to the unsettling imposition of self-criticism sessions and self-rectifications under which people were forced to admit their class backgrounds. Land reforms became increasingly brutal. In many villages they were an excuse for the poor to exact vengeance against the rich, for personal vendettas to be worked out in a febrile political atmosphere. Even some enthusiasts for the Revolution began to have their doubts, some slipped out of the liberated zones and back into areas of French control to escape the increasingly tense atmosphere.

Among Catholics, who were concentrated in the Red River delta provinces, there was a growing anxiety about what Communist rule would bring. In 1952, the Vatican began preparing for the possibility of victory by the Vietminh; three years earlier when Mao had taken over in China, most clergy there had fled to Taiwan with Chiang Kai-shek, leaving millions of people without religious leadership. The Vatican ordered Vietnamese priests to remain in their parishes if the Communists took over. Only those attending or teaching at seminaries would be allowed to leave.

As defeat for the French became increasingly inevitable, thousands fled south. The Geneva Accord allowed a period of two years during which there would be freedom of movement between North and South Vietnam. Despite the Vatican's order to stay on, few clergy were willing to continue their work under Communist rule. They argued that as their flocks were fleeing to the South, they had to go as well. At the same time they were encouraging members of their parishes to move. Much has been made of rumours that circulated of an impending US nuclear attack and of apparitions of the Virgin Mary ordering the faithful to move south, but these ignore the impact of what Vietnamese themselves knew about what was happening in Vietminh controlled zones. Many had legitimate fears of Communist rule, which they had been fighting for some time. They knew that a powerful, intrusive and atheist Vietnamese state would not be friendly to Catholicism.

Around half a million Catholics went south, among them almost all the clergy from the northern provinces. According to figures gathered by a French-Vietnamese historian Tran Tam Tinh, around 40 per cent of all Catholics fled the North and more than 70 per cent of priests were among them. In those dioceses such as Phat Diem where priests took it on themselves to encourage and even organise the exodus, nearly 60 per cent of the laity and 85 per cent of priests fled. In Hanoi, the archbishop followed the Vatican's orders and stayed while only a quarter of the city's lay population went south.

Under President Ngo Dinh Diem, the refugees got special attention in the South and were often settled on some of the most fertile land, a source of resentment among the majority of the population. Diem came from a deeply Catholic family; one of his brothers was Archbishop of Hue, a nephew would become Bishop of Nha Trang. Diem introduced new family laws – only the President could grant a divorce – and his government launched campaigns to convert Buddhists to Catholicism. His zealous religious life, much-influenced by the fierce Spanish and Irish Catholicism that had once prospered in the North, led to comparisons with Torquemada and the Spanish Inquisition. Diem's brutal suppression of peaceful demonstrations by Buddhist monks, some of whom burnt themselves alive in protest at his policies, was one of the factors that led to his overthrow and assassination in 1963.

In the North, Catholics did not fare so well. The land reforms after 1954 particularly targeted potential political opponents to the Party who might have challenged them in the elections planned for 1956 under the Geneva Accord. Provinces with large Catholic populations were a particular focus of land reforms and the brutalities that accompanied them. Many priests were put under house arrest while churches across the North were closed. Most of them would not open again for more than thirty years.

The sites of Roman Catholic pilgrimages are not generally known for their solemnity. The hardships of long journeys often ended with bacchanalian festivals that mixed a hefty shot of the profane in with the sacred. With pilgrims come souvenir stalls piled with rosaries, pictures of the Virgin and other gaudy paraphernalia of Catholicism. Vietnam's holiest site has none of the busy commerce of pilgrimage, only bleak reminders of the church's troubled history.

Not much remains of the basilica at La Vang; just part of the tower and one end of the large Romanesque church stand in a flat area of farmland just off Highway One in Quang Tri province. The rest was destroyed in 1972 in what was among the most ferocious battles of the war when North Vietnamese troops took the province. Shells decapitated the church tower and fire ripped through its roof. Its solid brick walls and their buttresses collapsed leaving only jagged broken arches standing in the swampy landscape.

There is a small group of buildings to receive visitors and a shrine, a forest of massive Gaudiesque concrete banyan trees that look more like mushrooms, built in 1961, on to which visitors bolt stone plaques carved with messages of thanks to the Virgin Mary. Leading up to the crumbling remains of the basilica is a long grassy area lined with statues of the Stations of the Cross with the heavy square musculature of socialist statuary. It is in this esplanade that every three years, pilgrims gather to honour the Virgin, who is said to have appeared here in 1798. A group of Vietnamese Catholics, fleeing from the troops of the Emperor Canh Tinh, sheltered here and were given guidance by the Virgin. At the end of the nineteenth century, when the area had been colonised by the French, a church was built on the site to commemorate the apparition and those who had died at the hands of the Vietnamese court. Later in 1928, the larger basilica was built.

Since 1901, there had been a celebration here every third year on August 15th, the day of the Assumption of the Virgin Mary, except for a hiatus between 1975 and the resumption of the festival in 1988 when the Archbishop of Hue defied threats from the police and led pilgrims to the church. By 1996 it had become one of the largest gatherings in Vietnam. Officially 65,000 people attended the three days of the 24th Marian festival, but some of those who attended said thousands had gone without permission and that up to 100,000 people went to hear the Cardinal Archbishop of Hanoi give mass.

La Vang is connected in the minds of many with the government of Ngo Dinh Diem, a passionate Marianist who led the pilgrimage in 1961 that attracted a quarter of a million people. At the site of the church, just thirty kilometres from the line dividing North and South, he declared the sanctuary to be 'a tiny fortress of the free world shielding itself against Communism'. La Vang was not just a sacred place for Catholics, it was a shrine to anti-Communism close to one of the most contested and volatile frontiers of the Cold War.

Given its past role, it is hardly surprising that the government is unenthusiastic about the revival of La Vang as a site of pilgrimage. A plan to build a new basilica, a vast edifice in the shape of a conical hat, was blocked on the grounds that the faithful should be focusing on helping the poor, not building new churches. When a church choir in Ho Chi Minh City asked for permission to film at La Vang to make a music video for fund raising, it was refused by the government. Even though the pilgrimage to La Vang is the biggest religious gathering in Vietnam, it is rarely reported in the press, indeed it remains almost invisible and unknown.

Along with economic reforms has come a new response to religion, aimed at relaxing some of the Party's restrictions. Many of the priests who had been incarcerated since the 1970s were released and church festivals were allowed to resume. Slowly the government began to return some religious property it had confiscated, although it only got around to publishing a decree on this in 1993. The new liberalism has only gone so far in alleviating tensions between church and state. In an interview with the *Saigon Giai Phong* newspaper, Archbishop Binh, who had generally avoided confrontation with the authorities, said openly that he was 'still afraid of the government'.

Most people can worship more freely, but the Party is determined to limit the power of the church hierarchy and its capacity to organise its followers. The church has fewer than 2,000 priests for its 7 million parishioners. Some areas, particularly those in the North had so few priests that each Sunday they would cycle for hours along the paths between the paddy fields to give mass at a dozen different churches. At Phat Diem around 2,000 people cram the dark wooden cathedral for the morning mass, with hundreds more spilling out into the paved courtyard that surrounds the church. Three thousand people come each week to worship at the large church at Ton Dao, just north of Phat Diem. Father Hunyh, the parish priest, serves mass to a packed church and a huge crowd standing outside in the hot sun. Later he pedals around some of the other four large churches and twenty-six village chapels that make up his parish. In all, he single-handedly ministers to 10,000 people. It leaves him no time for pastoral care or education; he can barely keep up with the minimum of rites for deaths, christenings and marriages.

It is not that there is any shortage of men wanting to become priests. At the cathedral in Phat Diem, a group of young men mill around waiting for tourists to guide around the grottoes and church buildings. Most of them speak fluent English and French which they learn from the older priests in preparation for joining a seminary. Paul, a young man from a nearby village, has been waiting five years to start classes. The seminaries are only allowed to admit a new class every two years and each applicant must undergo a thorough vetting by the local government and provincial religious authorities to ensure he has a sufficient allegiance to socialism and will not present any political threat. Officials can arbitrarily deny people the right to join a seminary. Those without the correct political background are condemned to long and often fruitless waits during which time they can only study by themselves.

In 1975 the seminaries in the South were emptied and many of the men were sent to re-education or as 'volunteers' in new economic zones. Peter, the eighteen-year-old son of a Southern military officer, had just entered the seminary in Danang in 1975 when it was closed and he was sent off to the countryside. When he returned to the city, his father had been taken away to a re-education camp and his mother and siblings were living in poverty. He worked as a *cyclo* driver, still harbouring some hope that he might be able to become a priest. By the mid 1980s his parents pressured him to abandon his vocation and marry. Finally he did so, giving up any chance of joining the priesthood. Now he works as a tour guide, using the languages the priests taught him so well at school. For him the years between 1975 and 1986 were lost, along with so many opportunities and hopes.

Only around 400 priests have been trained in Vietnam since 1975, while many of those who were close to being ordained were refused the chance to become priests. In 1995 when a new group of priests was ordained, many of them were already middle-aged and had been waiting decades to join the priesthood. Many priests have spent years in prison or under house arrest, including Paul Cardinal Pham Dinh Tung. He was appointed Bishop of Bac Ninh in 1963 but spent most of the next thirty years under guard in his residence writing a life of Jesus in the form of mnemonic rhymes. Cardinal Tung was born in 1919 and most of the priests in the Hanoi diocese are of a similar age. At the small church on Ham Long Street in the city centre the priest was so elderly it was painful to watch him serve mass. He was so frail he could hardly stand and frequently lost his place or stumbled over the words.

The Catholic Church still arouses an intense suspicion in the Communist Party. The Party ranks Pope John Paul II as second only to Mikhail Gorbachev in its demonology of those responsible for the collapse of Communism in Eastern Europe. Roman Catholicism is also connected closely with colonialism. In 1988 Pope John Paul canonised 117 martyrs from Vietnam in the largest ever mass elevation of people to the sainthood. Nearly one hundred of the new saints were Vietnamese who had been tortured or executed between 1745 and 1862, while the others were Spanish Dominicans or French priests who had worked in the country. The Pope used the ceremony at St Peters to highlight the state of the Vietnamese Catholic Church and to reassert its patriotic as well as religious identity. 'Vietnamese Catholics feel themselves to be authentically Vietnamese and faithful to their land,' he said.

But the reaction in Hanoi to the elevation of the men and women to the sainthood was one of complete fury. 'Among those Vietnamese to be canonised are some honest worshippers of God but others were implicated in political crimes . . . and were condemned for high treason,' said Nguyen Quang Huu, then head of the Religious Affairs Commission. The Pope's actions were 'a violation of national sovereignty' and would be 'an obstacle to the Vietnamese desire to have friendly relations with the Vatican'. Churches in Vietnam were banned from celebrating the event, the most important act of recognition of Vietnamese Catholicism. The canonisations had fallen on the day Vietnam honours its army. Priests were ordered to celebrate that instead and bishops were refused permission to attend the ceremonies in Rome.

Party policy is to disconnect priests from their parishioners and to prevent the church from acting as an organised force outside the control of the Fatherland Front, a gathering of social and religious groups that is under the complete control of the Communist Party. Priests are expected to restrict themselves to saying mass, they are forbidden from adopting any role as a political or social conscience. Those who want to continue as working priests know that they cannot openly oppose the government, even on such issues as birth control and abortion for which there are firm instructions from the Vatican. The government has also tried to keep priests isolated from the Holy See. Bishops were regularly denied permission to leave on *ad limina* visits, the regular trips to report to the church authorities in Rome.

Nguyen Van Ly, a priest in Hue who sent out a widely circulated letter of complaint about restrictions on the church commented on the situation: 'In the entire 255 years that the church was being persecuted (1630–1885) although bishops, priests and seminarians had to be in hiding, sometimes they were arrested and killed but the sacred rights (to appoint bishops, to ordain priests and to confirm children) were never lost. The church was always in control in ordaining and appointing personnel within its discretion. Today although the church is said to be free, it is indeed very passive. It has to open its palms to ask for the government's grace; it cannot ordain or appoint the personnel that it thinks deserving and needed.' The government, Ly wrote, was only interested in turning the church into 'a flexible instrument, a loyal servant, an obedient subordinate'.

In July 1989 official contacts between the Vatican and Vietnam resumed with the first visit to Hanoi by a Papal envoy in thirty-five years. Pope John Paul II sent his close advisor Roger Cardinal Etchegaray to broach the possibility of a thaw in relations and a Papal visit. Etchegaray celebrated mass at the cathedral in the centre of Hanoi as thousands of people gathered in the small square outside. A loud cheer went up when Etchegaray told the crowd that the Holy Father wanted to visit Vietnam.

Premier Do Muoi's face is said to have frozen when Etchegaray made the same remark in a brief meeting. Later the Cardinal visited Phat Diem and Ho Chi Minh City where tens of thousands of people ringed the cathedral as he said mass. None of the vast public gatherings were reported by the media which only remarked on

Etchegaray's meeting with Do Muoi. A few days after the Cardinal left, state television ran a foreign movie on its evening broadcast, an unusual event at the time. Its choice was *The Thorn Birds*, an Australian film about a lecherous Catholic priest.

Nearly a decade later there is no sign that the Pope will be kissing a scrubbed section of the tarmac at Noi Bai Airport any time soon, although he is said to yearn for a visit to one of the few countries denied him. Vietnam has mended its ties with dozens of nations, even its former battlefield enemies in China and the United States, but it has not patched things up with the Pope. For Hanoi, the breach rests on issues of sovereignty, for the Vatican, on issues of freedom. Hanoi is unwilling to compromise on its insistence that all social groups, including religions, come under the control of the Fatherland Front. The Vatican says that Vietnam does not meet even the minimum standard of religious freedom that it wants to see. While it has applauded a relaxation on the restrictions of personal worship, rules that control the appointment and activities of priests, restrict educational and charity work and a ban on publications by the church are still a heavy burden.

A lingering sore point has been the post of archbishop in Ho Chi Minh City, the most populous and important diocese. When the city fell to Northern forces in 1975, the Archbishop, Paul Nguyen Van Binh, stayed on in the city and called on Catholics to co-operate with their new rulers. His activities were almost completely circumscribed and hundreds of priests were taken off to re-education camps or fled abroad. Binh's deputy, and most likely heir, was François-Xavier Nguyen Van Thuan, who was a nephew of the former President, Ngo Dinh Diem. Thuan had been appointed to the post on 24 April 1975, just six days before the city fell to the Communists. It looked to Hanoi like a plot by the Vatican to impose a nephew of Diem on the city and ensure opposition to Communist rule by Catholics. Diem and his family had been devoutly Catholic but were despised by many Vietnamese for their zealous persecution of other religions. For Hanoi, it was completely unacceptable to have a member of this family take over the most important Catholic position. The government refused to accept his nomination and placed Thuan under house arrest in his former diocese in Nha Trang.

Bishop Thuan was taken to the North and held in a re-education camp until December 1988, more than twelve years after he had been arrested. Even then he was not able to take up his post but was eventually allowed out of the country to travel to Rome. After he left, the government declared him *persona non grata* and refused to let him return. The Vatican's protests at what it called 'this manifest injustice' were not heeded in Hanoi. The Holy See was left with no choice but to back off from its failed attempt to appoint Thuan deputy archbishop. Instead the Pope appointed him as the deputy to Cardinal Etchegaray on the Pontifical Council on Peace and Justice.

That only stirred up the hornets' nest further. Hearing that Archbishop Nguyen Van Binh was near to death, the Vatican appointed the Bishop of Phan Thiet, Huynh Van Nghi, as a supervisor for the diocese but not as deputy archbishop, which would have ensured that he replaced Binh. The government in Hanoi rejected the appointment, saying it was illegal and calling on him to step aside. Officials were furious that they had not been consulted and had no intention of letting just anyone fill the position. They were also suspicious that the Vatican had not appointed him deputy archbishop so that the post could be kept vacant for the eventual re-appointment of Thuan.

The chief negotiator from the Vatican has been Archbishop Claudio Celli who served as Deputy Secretary of State, a position equivalent to a vice foreign minister. Celli had visited Hanoi numerous times to iron out problems of appointments. About a quarter of all Vietnam's dioceses have no bishop and many of those priests who are still serving are too old to carry out their duties. The situation in many parishes was critical. To overcome the problem, the Vatican very reluctantly agreed to get approval from Hanoi for any appointments, something it has refused to do in most countries.

Celli arrived in Hanoi in April 1995 expecting the smooth approval of four new bishops. Instead of this thawing of relations, he was given the brush off by Vu Quang, head of the Religious Affairs Commission, who rejected the appointments. Celli was left trying to disguise his rage under his cool Jesuitical manner when he announced the setback. He described it as 'an accident on our journey' but said dialogue with the Vietnamese would continue. The reasons the Vietnamese had given for refusing to appoint the bishops were 'unacceptable' Celli said. It appeared that all appointments were to be held hostage until the Vietnamese government had its way in the appointment of the Archbishop of Ho Chi Minh City.

The Vatican and Vietnam are something of a match for each other diplomatically. Officials on both sides favour an opaque language and an evasive negotiating technique making progress very slow. 'All problems stem from the Vatican,' said the head of the Religious Affairs Commission in Ho Chi Minh City, displaying the unbending attitude that has hampered the development of better relations. The Vatican was only mildly less rigid in its view of the Vietnamese government.

The country's bishops have pressed the government for more freedoms and have been repeatedly rebuffed. In 1992 the bishops addressed a petition to Vo Van Kiet demanding to be able to meet whenever they chose, the right to freedom of movement in their dioceses rather than having to inform the police every time they travelled. They also wanted to be able to take part in church activities in Rome without seeking permission, to distribute an internal newsletter and to have a greater say in the publication of religious works.

To boost training they asked to be able to open new seminaries and to start teaching new pupils each year rather than every second year. The number of candidates for the priesthood needed to match the requirements of the diocese and should not be set by the government. They also wanted to open more religious schools to prepare seminarians and the right to ordain priests on the basis of their religious vocation, not their political suitability. Church buildings should be returned to the church which also wanted to be able to renovate its properties without first seeking permission from the government. These, as several priests had pointed out, were freedoms that the Vietnamese church had enjoyed for most of its history and had not even been denied by the Nguyen Dynasty. The response was a stony silence and then a new set of regulations on religion. Another letter was sent in 1997 by the Cardinal Archbishop of Hanoi requesting the same limited freedoms. Again, there was no reply.

The vitriol directed against the Catholic Church does not reflect a real threat from the church to Communist rule. Many senior church figures want good relations with the state and are fully aware of their faith's adage about giving unto Caesar. Catholics at most make up only about 8 per cent of the population. As many of these are among the poorest people in Vietnam it is hard to see how they might present such a menace. But the level of mistrust is intense and has barely diminished. Even such figures as Mother Teresa, who was normally courted by leaders eager to bask in the reflection of her supposed saintliness, have been shunned. In 1996 she was denied a visa to visit Vietnam and seven sisters of her Missionaries of Charity were told they could no longer run the children's homes they had set up in Hanoi and Ho Chi Minh City. The government said they were trying to spread religious beliefs; the nuns replied that they were just trying to help the poor.

Antipathy towards the church is usually phrased in terms of national sovereignty, ignoring the fact that Catholics fought the French as well as the Communists. Vietnamese Catholics are seen as outside the mainstream and irredeemably tainted with foreign ideas. A newspaper article about the cathedral in Hanoi described it in its first sentence as 'a mark of foreign domination'. Most articles in Vietnamese newspapers about Catholics stressed their 'solidarity with non-Catholics', a point that never has to be made between Buddhists and non-Buddhists. Government leaders are constantly urging Catholics to join the push for national development, insinuating that they are somewhat outside it. At the same time the government closed down many Catholic groups and refused to allow them a role in education or charity work.

An article written by a Communist Party Secretary in Thai Binh province and published in a Party theoretical journal made no secret of the imagined dangers posed by Catholicism in the province. The whole region had become a hotbed of anti-Communist activity, wrote Nguyen Xuan Lai, before urging the Party to take additional measures 'against the destructive plots and stratagems of the enemy'. Indeed as the widespread rioting in Thai Binh in 1997 showed, there was much opposition to Communism, but mostly from farmers worn down by graft and abusive taxation. Catholics are caught in a constant bind – they have to prove themselves to be good socialists while at the same time their membership in the Catholic Church by definition makes them agents of peaceful evolution and imperialism.

Not all Vietnamese have displayed this knee-jerk anti-Catholicism. Phan Boi Chau, the writer whose views influenced a generation of Vietnamese nationalists, appealed early in this century for Catholics to be brought into the anti-colonial struggle. He argued that although some of them might have aided French colonialism, they had not benefited later as the new rulers regarded them with disdain. Their faith, Chau wrote, should be channelled into anti-French nationalism.

One only has to go to mass to see how much a part of Vietnamese life Catholicism has become. At St Joseph's Cathedral in Hanoi, men and women are still segregated on either side of the aisle. The tones of the Vietnamese language lend a beautiful lilt to the sung responses and the plainsong of the choir. Most of those attending mass in Hanoi are dressed in the green drab shirts and trousers worn by peasant farmers. The pith helmets introduced by the French but turned into a symbol of resistance and national identity sit on the floor next to each man.

She huddled deep in a long coat and wrapped a scarf over the grey stubble that was growing out over her head. Through the thin partition came the caterwauling of a love song being belted out in the depths of the grimy catacomb of a karaoke bar in a new suburb of Hanoi. Her fingers rubbed together involuntarily in the pill-rolling movement that is a sign of Parkinson's disease. The woman was a Buddhist nun in hiding since she had fled the Long Tho Pagoda in Dalat after police came in with hired workers and destroyed the compound of flimsy wood shacks.

The pagoda had been the religious centre of a monk called Thich Minh Dao who in 1960 had set it up as a place of meditation and withdrawal from the world. The sect merged the otherworldliness of Zen Buddhism with Vietnamese traditions as a way to find peace in a troubled time. Its simple pagoda in the pine forests outside Dalat became a place of refuge.

This world of silence and meditation collapsed on 30 October 1996, when Thich Minh Dao was arrested for 'abusing superstitions causing serious consequences'. Police had raided the compound of the religious group, rounding up Thich Minh Dao's followers and questioning them. 'They came and made me hold up a can of beer and a calendar with women on it. They said that the monk used these things,' the nun said. The police also planted garlic, which is not supposed to be eaten by devout Buddhists, and other 'evidence' of Thich Minh Dao's wrongdoing.

Ten days after Thich Minh Dao's arrest, the police came back with several hundred hired labourers. Armed with stun weapons and guns they herded out the two nuns and a man who helped farm, and began destroying the wooden buildings. Within a day the pagoda was gone.

When asked about this, a government spokesman in Hanoi would only say that 'the pagoda does not exist'. This was true enough, as after thirty-six years it had just been destroyed. The press had already begun the character assassination of Thich Minh Dao, portraying him as a deviant who presided over a mysterious cult in a compound surrounded by high fences and guarded by fierce dogs. *Thanh Nien*, normally one of the better newspapers in Vietnam, printed completely unsubstantiated accusations of rape and other abuses. Thich Minh Dao was described as a 'big man who was filled with sexual energy'.

'He forced all people in the pagoda, both men and women, to strip off their clothes and walk about in the moonlight for him to watch,' the newspaper said. 'He would even call young girls to his room to have candies and drinks and then . . .', the journalist wrote, leaving the central accusation against Thich Minh Dao unsaid but obvious.

Cases of sexual abuse and rape by Buddhist monks are not uncommon in Asia and the accusations against Thich Minh Dao might have been plausible, except for the fact that in the only specific case offered by the newspapers and the police, the alleged victim vociferously denied she had been raped. The young woman from Nha Trang had gone to stay at the pagoda to escape pressure from her mother to enter into an arranged marriage. Her mother followed her to Dalat and complained to local officials about the pagoda. They didn't act immediately, but later the story was leaked to the press who wrote it up in vivid terms.

When the young woman read these articles, she was furious. She denied having been raped but said the reports in the newspaper had left her feeling violated. She wrote letters demanding the retraction of these 'absurd and completely false' reports. The journalists who wrote them, she said, deserved to be punished for fabricating interviews with her. None of her letters was published by the newspapers.

Lao Dong newspaper said that local religious authorities had received complaints of sexual abuse by Thich Minh Dao dating back to 1981 and yet they only decided to act in 1996. If this was true, it did throw up the question of why they had not stopped him fifteen years earlier. The authorities undermined their credibility further by charging Thich Minh Dao with the meaningless crime of 'abusing superstitions', and not the far more serious sexual offences.

The nun drew a picture of rising tensions between the isolated sect and the local authorities over money and land. Many of the Buddhist temples in Dalat had become rich in recent years from donations. The area attracted large numbers of tourists and overseas Vietnamese who were generous donors to pagodas. Most monks ensured they were left alone by sharing some of this wealth with the police and local officials. The Long Tho Pagoda, which observed strict rules of poverty and self-sufficiency, did not accept donations and did not pay off the police. 'They didn't like the pagoda because it was secretive and a bit unusual,' the nun said. 'Before, when they [local officials] came for money they were refused or only given small sums that insulted them.' The pagoda was also on a large area of land that was coveted by the local authorities who were in a frenzied land-grab as Dalat's tourist industry grew.

The actions of the provincial authorities in Lam Dong even sent a ripple of shock through government circles in Hanoi. The sect's intellectual and meditative bent had attracted a fair number of high-level people in Hanoi among its 1,000 followers. The former Premier Pham Van Dong was said to have visited the pagoda on several occasions. Certainly there was some shock at the vindictiveness of the campaign against the monk and his followers.

Thich Minh Dao's case represents an extreme example of the difficulties faced by all religions in Vietnam. While the Party wins plaudits for allowing greater individual rights to worship, abuses by the local and central government persist in the current lawless environment. All faiths are under constant threat from corrupt officials and the security forces that are unrestrained by law. Where religions compete with local officials for resources or the allegiance of people, the state uses its Draconian regulations to crush the faith. Those religions or groups that have a history of political opposition to the Communist Party – the United Buddhist Church of Vietnam, the Roman Catholic Church and the Southern religions of Cao Daiism and Hoa Hao – have all been the focus of attempts to separate the faithful from their spiritual leaders. The hierarchies that could form some organised part of civil society to moderate the power of the state have been placed under intense scrutiny and control. The faithful are left atomised, without priests or monks to lead them, and thus are less of a threat to a Communist system that is fearful of opposition and the mystery of religious belief.

By far the toughest response to the religious resurgence of the years after 1986 has been to the United Buddhist Church of Vietnam, an organised group of monks and nuns that traces its history back to the arrival of the faith in Vietnam nearly 2000 years ago. Buddhist groups had been a nuisance, although rarely a direct political threat, since the 1950s. After 1975, the Communist Party wanted to merge all sects into a single, state-controlled organisation under the Fatherland Front. As early as 1960, the Party was said to be concerned about the potential threat from organised Buddhism if it developed outside of their control.

In 1995, the former government official Do Trung Hieu, who had been tried and jailed along with the dissident Hoang Minh Chinh, released a document describing the Party's policies towards the Buddhist church. Hieu had been a political organiser for the Viet Cong in Saigon before 1975 and afterwards was appointed head of a group tasked with merging the Southern Buddhist groups with the compliant and broken Northern church. He became the principal architect of a process to destroy the United Buddhist Church of Vietnam by bringing it into the Vietnam Buddhist Church, a government-controlled group officially started in November 1981.

According to Hieu, the aim was to split monks and nuns from the laity by organising a church that would be in charge of Buddhist ritual and worship but would not have any social role. The official churches would not allow participation by lay followers, only those monks and nuns that met official guidelines on patriotism and respect for socialism. The laity would not be allowed to become an organic base of support for the church.

Do Trung Hieu said that Party control over the merging of the churches after 1975 was almost complete, although great efforts were made to present it as a natural merging set up by the monks. 'To preserve appearances, the task of unification was handled by monks, but the Party's control and its determination to transform Vietnamese Buddhism into a puppet of the CPV was obvious throughout the reunification process.'

Hieu, who served fifteen months in jail for making these criticisms, has in recent years attacked the jailing of the remaining hierarchy of the UBCV, who are mostly in jail or under 'pagoda arrest' and are unable to see their followers. Foreign diplomats, human rights monitors and journalists have not been allowed to visit them. In response to requests to meet them, the government would either claim security problems or say that as they were common criminals they had no right to meet with foreigners.

One of the most serious acts by the state against the UBCV was the arrest of its members as they were carrying out a flood-relief mission in the Mekong Delta. Thich Quang Do, the Secretary General of the church and the senior figure who was not under arrest, was jailed for five years for his role in the mission. The group had been charged with 'sabotaging the policy of solidarity' and 'taking advantage of freedom and democratic rights to infringe upon the interests of the state, social organisations and citizens'.

According to a report in the *Nhan Dan* newspaper, Thich Quang Do and his followers 'took advantage of a mission to take relief goods to flood victims to introduce their illegal Buddhist organisation to the public, earn credit with political organisations overseas, demonstrate their strength and help their self-proclaimed organisation acquire prestige'. In the zero-sum game of Vietnamese politics, any organisation that built up prestige detracted from that held by the Communist Party and thus had to be controlled or destroyed.

The only way to silence men like Thich Quang Do has been to jail them. Mai Chi Tho, the former Interior Minister and brother of the powerful Party figure Le Duc Tho, is said to have attempted to buy

Do's acquiescence to government policies by offering him the post of abbot at the Quan Su Pagoda in Hanoi. He refused and continued to campaign for the independence of the Buddhist faith from government control until he was locked up.

The UBCV has become a major irritant for the government, mostly because of a Paris-based organisation run by Vo Van Ai, an indefatigable and noisy advocate for religious and human rights in Vietnam. The mere mention of Vo Van Ai's name sends officials in Hanoi into spasms of rage because of the way he has been able to keep the issue of the Buddhists on the agenda at international meetings on human rights. Former Vice Foreign Minister Le Mai frequently tried to discredit him, referring in a voice crackling with scorn to 'that man and his American girlfriend'. His 'American girlfriend' is actually a British colleague called Penelope Faulkner who works with Ai to publicise cases of religious persecution. The other accusation frequently levelled against Ai is that he was a supporter of the South Vietnamese government before 1975 and therefore has no place criticising human rights abuses. In fact he was strongly critical of the Saigon government, enduring their harassment over his stance on human rights.

Ai and others in the Buddhist movement have, however, undone some of their work by over-dramatising the issues. Most Vietnamese do not know about men like Thich Quang Do nor do they appear to care that much; these monks do not necessarily represent the spiritual or political aspirations of the population at large. Except for certain communities in Hue and Ho Chi Minh City, the organised Buddhist church wields little real power. Its influence in Hue is strong, as shown when police raided the Tien Mu Pagoda there in 1993 and were met with demonstrations from the many Buddhists in the city.

The visceral reaction to religion by the Party and its constant vigilance over the hierarchies of various faiths is out of proportion to the potential threat to their power presented by the fragmented religious establishment. The Roman Catholic Church is never going to have the same impact that it has had in Poland or the Philippines. At most it commands the loyalty of less than 8 per cent of the country and links between the Vatican and the faithful have been much weakened. Although most Vietnamese describe themselves as

Buddhist, few worship in any organised way and the pagodas and organised churches of monks have little political heft. Yet religion remains a matter of tension because the government cannot resist interfering with strong-arm tactics.

In November 1997, riots broke out in Xuan Loc Diocese, just outside Ho Chi Minh City after Catholics protested against the local government's plans to confiscate some church land. The diocese is home to 800,000 Catholics, the largest group in the country. Most came from Thai Binh in 1954. Tensions had been brewing in Xuan Loc since April 1997 when the provincial government ordered all Catholic social groups to be closed down. Associations for young Catholics, mother and children groups and even Catholic music groups were disbanded, stoking up resentment that burst into violence later in the year.

The Party is haunted by a past when religions ran private armies, amassed vast properties and commanded extraordinary loyalty. It still remembers the religious role in the fight against colonialism and later the symbolic power of self-immolating monks and the way those appalling suicides galvanised opposition to the South Vietnamese government of Ngo Dinh Diem. Those times are over; those extreme acts were mostly reactions to colonialism and the aggressive anti-Buddhist policies of Diem, but the Party cannot let go of its exaggerated fears of the impact of religion on politics.

14

China Lite

*The Southern emperor rules the Southern land
Our destiny is writ in Heaven's Book.
How dare ye bandits trespass on our soil?
Ye shall meet your undoing at our hands!*

LY THUONG KIET, A VICTORIOUS GENERAL,
ADDRESSED HIS TROOPS WITH THIS POEM IN 1076

Along the narrow trails left slippery with the summer monsoon, porters wend their way across the border, through the landscape of soaring limestone outcrops and down to the town of Lang Son. At the frontier crossing, trucks are backed up for about half a mile, waiting their turn at customs while motorbikes zip past, precariously laden with everything from bales of cloth to crates of beer. In a thin convoy the bikes follow the winding road down to the nearby town to unload their goods at the market. Each of these journeys, repeated hundreds of times every day, adds to a growing sense of unease among Vietnamese about a perennial problem: their neighbour, China.

The official reopening of this border in 1991 after years of tension, unleashed a wave of commerce that threatened to undo Vietnam's struggling state industries. With each motorbike-load of consumer goods that crossed the border a measure of hope died for the state sector whose shoddy and over-priced products could not compete. Exports to China were on the rise, but they could not keep up with the goods coming in from factories in Guangdong province. With each Chinese economic sneeze, Vietnam would catch more than a cold. A currency devaluation in China sent exports across the border soaring; to ease an overload of inventory in Chinese warehouses, the goods were dumped on the Vietnamese market. When China banned satellite dishes, the price of a Chinese-made dish in Hanoi fell by half as companies shipped them across the border.

The impact goes far beyond the area along the border. In 1995, China suffered a shortfall in rice production in its southern provinces and began importing large quantities of smuggled rice from Vietnam. Although this was illegal, many state firms, even the navy, got in on the act of taking rice from the Mekong Delta. Prices soared and farmers, expecting greater profits, planted high-yield, low-quality strains that would make them money in the Chinese market. By the time the next harvest came around, China had solved its shortage and prices plummeted. Farmers were left holding large stocks of poor-quality rice that could not be exported anywhere else. Whether Vietnam likes it or not, its economic fate is inextricably linked to its powerful neighbour.

Commerce resumed in 1988 on a small scale with porters carrying goods along paths through an area sown with land mines. For most of the previous decade the area had been the site of skirmishing between border patrols who glared across the line drawn up by the French and Chinese governments in the nineteenth century. This was where the two countries had slugged it out in a border war in 1979 when the relationship between the fraternal socialist neigh-bours, described as being 'as close as lips and teeth', turned from the fixed smiles of socialist solidarity into open hostility. Chinese leader Deng Xiaoping, who had long regarded the Vietnamese as ingrates under the control of the Soviet Union, wanted to teach Vietnam a lesson for its invasion of Cambodia to oust the Beijing-backed Khmer Rouges. This pedagogic war taught both sides a lot: the Vietnamese were reminded of how little they could trust their northern neighbour. The Chinese learned that their peasant army was poorly trained and ill-equipped; Mao may have written the books on guerrilla warfare but it was the Vietnamese who had spent decades practising it. Their soldiers had even picked off Chinese tank commanders who, lacking radios, had to communicate by semaphore.

Economic links were the first ties to be re-established. Following a discreet nod from the government in Hanoi, trade soared ten-fold in just a year. The flood of goods into Vietnam was useful for the government at first. The economy was doing badly, there was a rising sense of political discontent and Hanoi's Communist allies in Eastern Europe were collapsing. Chinese-made consumer goods coming into Vietnam gave an impression of improving conditions and eased economic tensions even if in the long term they competed with Vietnamese products. By 1990 the trade had expanded beyond the small-scale operations of residents of the northern provinces. Border towns like Lang Son were growing apace, their markets filled with Saigonese packing heavy money-clips to buy up anything they could ship south. Twenty-eight Chinese provinces and cities opened trading offices in Dongxing, the main town on the other side of the border.

China had captured Lang Son in the 1979 war, dynamiting nearly every building in the small town of 60,000 people. The Vietnamese rebuilt the town but it remained an impoverished and anxious armed camp until border trade resumed; only then did this phoenix rise from the ashes. Tu, one of the wealthiest traders, once fought against the Chinese; he was part of a local militia that hiked the surrounding hills laying ambushes for the invading troops. Now he cheerfully bargains with Chinese traders in fluent Mandarin. Along with his eleven brothers, he built a small empire in just a few years of trading everything from herbal medicines to electronic goods. The family share three large houses, one of them topped with a tiled chinoiserie pavilion where Tu spends hot afternoons drinking expensive imported rice wine, breaking off occasionally to shout down instructions at labourers unloading trucks at a neighbouring warehouse.

Lang Son is not shy about its new wealth or how it makes its money. There is a glitzy new hotel decorated with Chinese characters and a panda mosaic; most shops and restaurants take the Chinese currency. The rising skyline of four-storey houses is serrated with hundreds of satellite dishes and the muddy streets are lined with a growing number of cars and motorbikes. The market is filled with a cornucopia of mostly illegally imported products, almost all made in China. After initially turning a blind eye, the central government now disapproves of this lucrative trade that has blossomed beyond its control. Meanwhile local cadres have grown rich on the trade. One woman who had recently spent $50,000 building herself a marble and wrought iron palace admitted that the secret to her wealth was her daughter's marriage to the province's top Party official.

Trade has raised living standards in what were some of the poorest and most isolated provinces, but this has come at some cost. According to Brantly Womack, an American political scientist who has studied the border trade, Chinese imports contributed to an overall decline in production of many consumer goods between 1986 and 1992. Particularly hard hit were Vietnamese textile mills, pottery factories and shoemakers. The Vietnamese bicycles – almost a national emblem since they were used to carry rice to the battle of Dien Bien Phu and supplies down the Ho Chi Minh Trail – were pushed out of the market by lighter, better-made Chinese bikes. It wasn't just the state sector that hurt; small private manufacturing also contracted.

While Vietnamese markets filled with Chinese goods, Vietnam did not make much of interest to consumers on the other side of the border. A Chinese trader, poking in a desultory manner through stacks of Vietnamese porcelain, said: 'Chinese people don't want to buy Vietnamese products. Their quality is no good.' Chen Rufang, the representative for a trading company in neighbouring Guangxi province concurred: 'Vietnamese porcelain is ugly and poorly made.' There were a few things of interest to the Chinese: rice, rubber, and luxury cars stolen elsewhere in Southeast Asia and shipped to Vietnam before being driven over the border. Weapons were also widely traded; the Hong Kong police complained that an increasing number of robberies there were being carried out with weapons originally from Vietnam. There was, according to the Vietnamese media, a rise in the smuggling of women across the border either as brides or to work in the brothels of southern China and Macau.

The government's ardour cooled when it realised the impact the trade was having on its own economy. In 1992 it banned the import of seventeen categories of goods including bicycles, light bulbs, porcelain, glass, paper, cosmetics and batteries. The new rules were widely flouted by traders, indeed if they had been enforced they would have had a chilling impact on commerce in Vietnam which had grown massively, centred on Hanoi's Dong Xuan market in the north and Ho Chi Minh City's Cholon district in the south. A string of import bans, tariffs and new trading regulations failed to control the commerce; the border is too porous and the profits are too great. In 1995, the government warned that 'cultural pollutants' were the latest wave of imports from China; what they were referring to were the compact discs, laser discs and CD-ROMs that had been flooding in when China briefly clamped down on pirating at home. 'This trade is posing a real threat that demands immediate action if the government is to strengthen itself on the ideology and cultural fronts,' warned *Saigon Giai Phong*, the Party newspaper in Ho Chi Minh City.

The issues were taken up at talks between the governments. Vietnam wanted more trade between state companies and less of the private commerce that had exploded to more than a billion dollars a year by 1995. By then trade with China made up around 10 per cent of Vietnam's total imports and exports and accounted for a large chunk of the growing deficit. For the Chinese, however, Vietnam accounted for only a tiny part of its trade, similar to the amount of business it did with Brazil. In Beijing there were more pressing issues than controlling the border provinces which were prospering from this exchange. Vietnam, in any case, was no longer an ideological little brother to be kept in check with aid and preferential deals; it was now a competitor for export markets and investment in an increasingly aggressive economic world.

Both sides believed that they could arrive at pragmatic solutions to economic issues that were less inflected with historical and ideological tensions than their border disputes or diplomatic differences. Instead they added a new element of unease, particularly for Vietnam which has lived for centuries constantly aware of China's hot breath on the back of its neck. Hanoi had to decide how to build links with China while maintaining its own economic independence and security. Economics has now joined the list of sensitive issues. Officials in Hanoi have been growing irritated by China's failure to sign off on a $170 million loan to refurbish the Thai Nguyen steel works, built by the Chinese in the 1960s and now outdated and unproductive. In mid 1997, a joint fishing venture was cancelled by the Vietnamese who were annoyed by what they describe as the plunder of their territorial waters by Chinese trawlers.

It hasn't been easy for China either to work out a new *modus operandi* in this relationship. As Brantly Womack points out, since the founding of the People's Republic in 1949, Vietnam has been a test to the limits of Chinese power. Vietnam has been a proving ground for China's capacity to influence its neighbours militarily, economically and ideologically, and Beijing has not always come off well. During the Vietnam War, China sent thousands of advisors to Vietnam and gave the equivalent of $20 billion in aid (Vietnam put the figure much lower but has not said exactly how much it received. In 1979 it churlishly suggested it had only received some light weapons and a little food from China, but this was a massive understatement), and yet shortly after the end of the conflict, the two countries were at each other's throats.

As the more developed economic power, China has a definite upper hand in the working out of a new relationship. Vietnam now faces a complex decision on how far to integrate its economy with China. Should it hitch its wagon to the powerful economic locomotive of southern China, the fastest growing economic region on earth, or should it resist? Vietnam may not have much choice. The Red River delta has not grown as fast as southern Vietnam and has fewer links to the rest of Southeast Asia. Given the country's poor transport links and difficult geography, it is easier to link the area to southern China than to the rest of Vietnam. Potentially lucrative businesses include the transhipment of Chinese goods and the sale of coal and electricity to the power-hungry manufacturing centres of Guangdong province.

Officials in the border province of Quang Ninh, the centre of Vietnam's coal industry, have already begun illicitly selling electricity across the border. Trucks also cart coal to China, but the trade is small-scale. What is needed is an integration of the power networks that would enable Vietnam to sell electricity to China, but any agreement is a long way off. Such arrangements require a high degree of trust and binding, long-term contracts.

Hanoi has probably missed the boat on transhipments of Chinese exports. Haiphong, the main northern port, is the nearest harbour to much of both Yunnan and Guangxi provinces and could have emerged as a major centre for trade. Unfortunately the port is already at capacity and its harbour is heavily silted. Likewise, the French-built railway that connects Haiphong to Yunnan is of too narrow a gauge to be useful for carrying large volumes of goods. The province is now building a number of connections with China, Burma and Laos to serve its growing trade.

Vietnam has been hesitant to weave together more complicated economic links with China. It does not yet have the confidence to make such moves. Officials make ritualistic appeals for more investment and aid, but neither side has any expectation of blossoming links in the near future. Eventually, closer ties may be inevitable as Vietnam needs to find a way to engage China economically beyond selling it drugs, women, guns and smuggled Mercedes sedans. So far the government has been unable to come up with effective policies on trade, so it has lost control of the issue to smugglers and local officials. Even in the arena of economics, where both Marxist-Leninist governments have shown considerable pragmatism, the fog of anxiety and rivalry precludes a long-term vision.

Not only are there security concerns over the land border but the countries have rival claims to much of the South China Sea, a flashpoint because the area is believed to have large reserves of oil. There are also deeper cultural concerns of how to deal with Confucianism and other Chinese influences; how to live with a Chinese community and overseas Chinese investment that have been vital factors in improving the economy; and how to keep up political ties with China while not getting too close for comfort.

When Lee Kuan Yew, the Singaporean leader and sage of Asian values, visited Vietnam in 1995, he told journalists that the country 'had a certain something' that he believed would ensure its future economic success. What he meant was that Vietnam fitted in cultural terms into a group of Asian nations that had seen their economies take off since the 1960s, propelling them from colonial backwaters to models of development. Looking around for a uniquely Asian explanation for this success, they hit on Confucianism. The teachings of Confucius – respect for family and authority, the emphasis of the community over the individual, a moral bureaucracy selected by merit – were the Asian equivalent of Max Weber's Protestant ethic that had transformed the West.

This was an important turnaround in the perception of Confucianism, which had been derided as an unchanging system of feudal values that had held China back, keeping it poor and weak and creating the environment for Western colonialism. Now Confucianism was touted as the source of economic strength in Asia. It was always a strain to shoe-horn the theory and reality together. None of the Southeast Asian countries were purely Confucian and there was little in Confucianism that could account for their success. Three success stories – Indonesia, Malaysia and Thailand – did not have any Confucian background and yet still prospered. Singapore was even quite hostile to the philosophy during much of its startling growth, encouraging people to learn English and limiting the scope of Chinese education. China and Vietnam, where the Confucian ethos is stronger, lagged far behind in economic development, their countries stuck in a morass of Marxist central planning. Confucianism even seemed quite hostile to business, with its clear disdain for the merchant class and its emphasis on elevated intellectual pursuits.

Simplistic explanations of Confucianism as the motor for Asian success have largely been discarded. Policies that encouraged savings and education, kept inflation and budget deficits down had more impact on economic growth than any close reading of the Analects. Governments that encouraged foreign investment, kept wages low and maintained political and labour stability could hitch their countries to the forces of international business and rise with them. Asian prosperity is better explained by classical economic theory than Confucianism.

Governments, however, were less keen to abandon Confucianism as a shorthand explanation for their successes. It lent some legitimacy to authoritarian regimes and justified minimal attention to the rights of the individual; at best it has influenced the centralised, reformist democracies of South Korea and Taiwan, at worst it has been a fig leaf for despotism. Confucianism gave some historical depth to nations that had emerged out of colonialism and were looking for ideas around which they could crystallise this nationalist sentiment. It was a useful political tool in countries undergoing breakneck social and economic change as it tapped into nostalgia for an imaginary, simple and well-ordered past.

Vietnam has come a little late to the idea of resurrecting Confucianism. Its connection with the philosophy and its degree of influence in different historical periods is one of the central subjects for debate among historians. It is central to ideas of Chinese influence in Vietnam, raising the problem of whether Vietnam slavishly followed the Confucian model even after it had won its independence from China, or whether its indigenous traditions and those imported from other Southeast Asian countries have carried more weight. It is a debate that is fraught with anxieties in Vietnam, which has had periods of intense hostility towards China. Relations have been at best lukewarm and tentative since the thawing in 1991 of the diplomatic permafrost of the 1980s. Even today emphasising Confucianism is problematic for Vietnamese scholars whose aim – as set by the government – is to create indigenous traditions that promote nationalism, not dilute it by suggesting yet more links to China.

The Temple of Literature in Hanoi, a complex of buildings dedicated to Confucius, is, as many Vietnamese proudly point out, older than any similar temple in the Chinese capital Beijing. It dates from 1020, but as a centre of Confucian learning reached its peak in the fifteenth century. Confucian examinations continued until they were stopped by the French early in the century as the mandarins emerged as an increasingly hostile force to colonialism. The nineteenth-century court at Hue mimicked the structure of a Chinese court with its basic Confucian precepts, but historians are increasingly finding the differences between China and Vietnam are greater than the similarities.

Nguyen Quang Loc, a writer who heads the Van Mieu Institute in the Temple of Literature, maintains that Vietnamese Confucianism was not at all close to the Chinese model but had been adapted and shaped by Vietnam, which has emphasised issues of morality and faith over other aspects such as discipline. 'It is not just a copy of Chinese Confucianism,' he said. Vietnam had followed the faith 'in a fragmented and confused way'. In his opinion, Vietnam has a greater emphasis on the individual than the community and women were always treated better.

Keith Taylor, one of the foremost Western historians of Vietnam, has expressed deep doubts about the nature of Vietnam's Confucian tradition, seeing it as a construction of French colonial scholarship. 'Confucianism came to bear the burden of representing the essence of Vietnamese tradition when the idea of, and the demarcation of, "a Vietnamese soul" or cultural identity became important to the French.' French scholars and administrators emphasised Confucianism over Buddhism and Taoism even though these had a greater influence over the lives of most Vietnamese. The Confucian models of family life were privileged over other forms; ideas of social behaviour were based on a narrow archetype from areas of the Red River, the mythical primordial cradle of Vietnamese culture where life was very different from the rest of the country. Confucian bureaucrats only had minimal control over areas infested with warlords and rival clans. Even during the Nguyen Dynasty, supposedly a model of rigid Confucianism, officials were not selected and promoted entirely on merit but on other factors. After the southern Nguyen Dynasty won their civil war against the northern Le, few mandarins were chosen from the north of the country. Clan loyalties, spirit worship and patron-client relations all muddied the waters of Confucianism.

The official position on Confucianism has shifted considerably. For many years it was denounced as feudal and morally bankrupt, an insidious Chinese influence that weakened the country and prepared the ground for colonialism. It could be countered by the scientific nature of Marxism and Ho Chi Minh Thought. The latter, always a hazy belief system at best, is now being given a gloss of Confucianism. Both Loc and Professor Nguyen Tai Thu of the Institute of Philosophy link Ho Chi Minh's emphasis on personal virtue to Confucianism. Indeed in an important speech in 1951, Ho quoted, without attribution, from a definition of great men by the Confucian disciple Mencius to explain what it was to be a 'worker' – the most esteemed level in the Marxist class system. Workers, Ho said, were those 'who cannot be tempted by wealth and honour, worried by poverty or subdued by force or power'.

Historians of Confucianism have refocused their energies to finding a new relevance for it rather than simply attacking it as feudal. Now the doctrines are seen as a potential way for Vietnam to build up a sense of community and create the same disciplined image as Singapore or South Korea. Confucianism might offer the resources to cope with the moral dislocations of Market-Leninism that have bred corruption and individualism. There seem to be moves to turn

Ho Chi Minh into what Taylor described 'as an enabling and legit-
imating figure for a Confucianism' that would be blended with
Marxist-Leninism to come up with a uniquely Vietnamese ideology.
Ho Chi Minh is being cast not as the person who overthrew colonialism and feudal vestiges, but as an heroic figure who introduced
a modern and distinctly Vietnamese version of Confucianism. One
of his most quoted aphorisms of late has been about the dangers of
'individualism'. The emphasis is no longer on the Marxist criticisms
of individual economic pursuits but on individual lapses from
Confucian rectitude.

'Modern Vietnamese nationalism found success in its alignment
with a global Communist community,' wrote Taylor. 'Post-modern
Vietnamese post-nationalism may find success in alignment with a
global Confucian community at the forefront of international economic development.' Confucianism is a way to build ties with other
Asian nations, almost all of which have a history of hostility with
Vietnam. The emphasis in relations with South Korea nowadays is
not the brutality of their troops who fought alongside the South
Vietnamese during the war, but on ancient links forged at the imperial court in China where both sent envoys to pay tribute. Much has
been made of the links created between the Korean Lee and the
Vietnamese Ly clans by the exiling of a Ly Dynasty prince to Korea
hundreds of years ago. The ideological gulf between the former
enemies has been happily bridged by fictive bonds of Confucianism
and ancient ritual. Likewise Lee Kuan Yew, once a bitter opponent
of Vietnam who orchestrated the country's isolation over its invasion of Cambodia, is now welcomed in Hanoi to advise on how to
blend the brisk discipline of neo-Confucianism with investment by
Western multinationals.

Confucianism has gone from being part of the French idea about
its colonial subjects to being part of the manufacturing of nationalism by Vietnamese trying to win independence. But any adoption of
a Chinese model is contentious. The writer Nguyen Huy Thiep
struck a chord when he wrote of the country's national poet as
being 'a child of rape through whose veins courses the blood of his
Chinese father'. Nguyen Du's epic poem 'The Tale of Kieu', which
is central to how many Vietnamese see their cultural identity, is
based on a Chinese poem and the constantly victimised but plucky

Kieu is nowadays taken as representing Vietnam. In Thiep's stories, Confucian mandarins are incapable of ameliorating the poverty that afflicts Vietnam; their world is abstract and obsessed with China. 'The great tragedy for Vietnam,' said Thiep, 'is that we have spent so much time absorbing Chinese culture and so much time resisting it.'

The overwhelming emphasis of official Vietnamese history is on resistance, almost always against China. The fear of domination has been constant and has crossed every ideological gap, it has created the brittle sense of anxiety and defensiveness about Vietnamese identity. Foreigners may have imagined Vietnam as a 'China Lite', but the Vietnamese have long been determined to see themselves as distinct, never wasting a chance to mark themselves as different from the Chinese. Even Ho Chi Minh, fluent in Mandarin and so friendly with the leadership in Beijing that he spent his vacations in China, had strong reservations about getting too close. Discussing whether it would be better in 1945 to be under Chiang Kai-shek's Nationalist army or to have the French back, Ho came up with the famous but often bowdlerised remark that he 'would rather sniff a little French shit for a few years than eat Chinese shit for the next thousand years'.

But the relationship is about much more than hostility. Ho had spent many years in China and was profoundly influenced by Mao's Revolution. In 1950, the Vietminh launched a study campaign of Mao's writings, which were translated into Vietnamese and distributed to all Party cells. Ho himself translated Mao's works 'On Practice' and 'On Contradiction'. When asked why he did not write much himself, Ho was said to have replied that 'Mao had said it all'. The official line nowadays on this comment was that Ho was being sarcastic, but certainly in the early years of the Revolution there was a considerable reliance on the Chinese leader's theoretical vision. Around this time there was a shift in emphasis from fighting for independence to ridding Vietnam of feudalism. The pro-Chinese Truong Chinh gained in prominence as a Party ideologist. In 1952 and 1953 more than 16,000 cadres underwent 'thought reform', an education process that was aimed at raising revolutionary consciousness and effectiveness. Thought

reform was as sinister as its name suggests and caused some supporters of the Vietminh to leave liberated zones, disillusioned with
the shift in political emphasis.

Land reforms based on a Maoist model of class warfare began in
earnest in 1953 and continued for three years until they led to a
peasant revolt in Nghe An province, Ho Chi Minh's birthplace.
Village land reform units were set up to sniff out landlords, confiscate their land and redistribute it to poor peasants. This process
soon disintegrated into a vicious settling of scores in many villages;
poorer peasants were put on trial and farmers were condemned as
landlords and executed even though they may have held only a
few hectares. A process that had started out boosting support for the
Party by providing land to peasant farmers, backfired when it
ripped apart village life.

Throughout this period, China also provided considerable military aid to Vietnam. By 1952 there were 8,000 Chinese advisors in
the country and another 1,000 medical personnel, according to
reports from the time and documents later released by the Chinese.
The Vietminh controlled the entire border area and were able to
bring in weaponry, in particular artillery, that was critical in their
final battle against the French at Dien Bien Phu in 1954.

Ho described the relationship in those years as being like 'one
hundred favours, a thousand loyal affections and ten thousand
loves'. No praise was high enough for the Chinese; Marxism and
the support of Beijing to win independence had overwhelmed the
centuries of antipathy between China and Vietnam. Mao never
deigned to visit Vietnam but he sent President Liu Shaoqi in 1963.
Ho greeted him with a speech rippling with hyperbole in which he
described the friendship as being 'eternal, like the rivers and mountains of our two countries'. By that time, Vietnam had edged away
from the Soviet Union and was close to China although it had
refused an offer by then Party General Secretary Deng Xiaoping to
come completely into the Chinese camp in exchange for $1 billion in
aid. Having decided in 1960 to fight for reunification with South
Vietnam, Hanoi knew it needed to keep its supply lines to China
open and the government in Beijing friendly.

Mao had considerable charismatic appeal as an Asian leader and
China seemed to offer a more applicable model of development

than the vastly distant and different Soviet Union. The drift towards Beijing halted in 1966 when the Cultural Revolution began. Hanoi had to keep up an appearance of enthusiasm for this maelstrom that Mao had unleashed to build up his waning power, but it wanted no part in this permanent revolution. Thousands of Vietnamese students were caught up in the chaos that particularly affected universities; many were hurriedly recalled to Hanoi. The late Deputy Foreign Minister Le Mai, then a junior diplomat in Beijing on his first posting, recalled the massive demonstrations by Red Guards in support of North Vietnam's fight against the South. 'We had to attend and act enthusiastic but actually the protests were very disconcerting; we couldn't afford to have that sort of disruption at home while we were fighting a war.'

Officials in Hanoi quietly backed off their embrace of China. Little Red Books of Mao's quotations were not universally distributed; the few groups that espoused a Vietnamese Cultural Revolution were warned off doing anything to disrupt a well entrenched leadership. Although Vietnam needed Chinese support in the war, it also needed Russian weapons, particularly air defence systems. That required a position of neutrality in the Sino-Soviet split, which by the late 1960s had entered some of its most tense years with several serious border clashes.

The announcement in 1971 that Henry Kissinger, then National Security Advisor, had been to Beijing to plan a visit by President Richard Nixon was a stunning blow to Hanoi. Vietnam's closest ally and most reliable partner in the fight against US imperialism had without warning got into bed with its enemy. Vietnam would later paint this as part of an attempt by China to delay reunification, another betrayal by Zhou Enlai who had pressured the Vietminh to accept the division of the country at the Geneva talks in 1954. The Chinese had 'great nation expansionist and hegemonist designs' on Vietnam and the rest of Asia, the government said in a bitter litany of complaints against Chinese behaviour released in October 1979. The White Book, as this document is known, revealed that tensions had been building since the late 1960s. In 1976, Vietnam signalled its growing hostility by cleansing the Politburo and Central Committee of all officials who were seen as pro-Chinese, including three former ambassadors to Beijing.

Cambodia provided the tinder for the relationship to flare up. Since the early 1970s, Vietnamese forces that had fought alongside the Khmer Rouge increasingly found themselves fighting against the Maoist guerrillas who were torn with a nationalistic loathing of their neighbour. After Pol Pot took power in April 1975, he repeatedly sent his forces into border areas that Cambodia claimed. His forces killed thousands of Vietnamese villagers but for some time the government in Hanoi kept quiet. After repeated invasions and massacres, Hanoi could tolerate it no longer and counter-attacked several times. Planning began for a full-scale invasion; the troops crossed the border on Christmas Day 1978 and by 7 January Pol Pot and the Khmer Rouge had been ousted. A few weeks later, on 17 February 1979, 200,000 Chinese troops swarmed across the northern border.

The lips and teeth are no longer drawn back into a snarl but the smiles of Chinese and Vietnamese officials are still a little fixed. Relations have improved, a process that was hastened by a settlement in Cambodia and by the retirement of Deng Xiaoping who never lost his visceral hatred of the Vietnamese. The Chinese leader punctuated his diatribes against Hanoi by noisily hoicking phlegm into a spittoon placed next to his chair. Deng's policy of 'bleeding Hanoi white' by keeping up tension on the northern border and enmeshing Vietnamese forces in a guerrilla war in Cambodia was a success; by the late 1980s, the Vietnamese economy was in a perilous state, damaged by war and Hanoi's own ineffectual policies.

In July 1990, Beijing agreed to a long-standing Vietnamese request for a high-level summit meeting. In September, General Secretary Linh and then Premier Do Muoi met their Chinese counterparts Jiang Zemin and Li Peng in Chengdu, capital of Sichuan province. Pham Van Dong, by then retired, also attended. Foreign Minister Nguyen Co Thach was conspicuously left out as the Chinese had demanded.

Isolated after the Tiananmen massacre and with Communism collapsing in Eastern Europe, China decided it needed to mend relations and could do so on its terms. In November 1991, General Secretary Do Muoi and Prime Minister Vo Van Kiet went to Beijing to complete the process of normalisation.

Vietnam had made a major concession by getting rid of Thach as Foreign Minister. Thach had been one of the most passionately anti-Chinese figures in Hanoi throughout the 1980s, his distrust of Beijing constantly reinforced during the tortuous negotiations over Cambodia. One of the prices of normalisation was Thach's replacement with the bland and inoffensive ambassador to Moscow, Nguyen Manh Cam. Hanoi got little in return for more normal relations; China was not much interested in settling any of the contentious issues such as the border, the repayment of old debts and the status of 200,000 ethnic Chinese who had fled Vietnam. China could not resist toying with Vietnam's weakness, doling out high-handed slights such as signing an agreement with an American company to explore for oil in a contested area of the South China Sea during a visit to Beijing by former General Secretary Linh.

By the mid 1990s, the two sides were back to a guarded friendship born not of affection but of the shortage of reliable Communist countries and their convergent national interests to maintain stability while focusing on economic development. First to be resuscitated were the exchanges of folk dancers and army choirs so beloved of socialist culture ministries. Later there was an enormous expansion of contacts at all levels of the Party and government. By 1996 there were about 300 meetings a year between officials of the two countries. After the Vietnamese leaders had paid the necessary respectful visit to Beijing, the Chinese leadership came to Vietnam. President Jiang Zemin visited in November 1994 in an attempt to recreate the past friendship. His visit glossed over the troubling territorial disputes and Vietnam's anxieties about China's economic power; instead Jiang visited a cigarette factory built in the 1950s with Chinese aid and spoke of a time when the countries 'sympathised with and supported each other and cultivated profound friendship in our struggles'.

When President Liu Shaoqi visited in the 1960s around 300,000 people lined the streets of Hanoi to welcome him. Ho Chi Minh's hyperbolic rhetoric fluttered off to new heights of praise for China. But more than three decades later neither side could dismiss all that had passed between them. Jiang's visit was cordial but austere and more than a little stiff; the differences between these fraternal socialist countries were plainly visible behind the thin covering of diplomatic protocol and language.

Chief among the problems that were papered over were the territorial disputes over the land border and the islands and atolls that pepper the South China Sea – which the Vietnamese insist should be called the East Sea. China claims the whole of the sea, demarking its territory with what it calls its 'historical line' that loops down towards Indonesia and encloses the entire area. It marks out China's old claim of suzerainty over the area, which is enough in a country obsessed with its primordial claims of ownership for the government in Beijing to insist it now has full sovereignty. Vietnam's claim, regarded as stronger by international lawyers, comes from the administration of the islands during French colonial times.

Within China's 'historical line' are hundreds of tiny islands, many of them coral reefs that are often submerged and could not support human life. Only thirty-three of them are permanently above water and these are tiny arid sand banks threatened by typhoons. They are claimed not just by Vietnam and China but at least in part by Taiwan, Malaysia, the Philippines and Brunei. It is not land that is at issue but what might lie under it and what currently sails between these specks.

Almost all of Japan's oil imports sail through the area, as does a rising proportion of its other trade. The area is possibly rich in natural resources; oil may lie in the complex and folded layers of rock beneath the sea, but so far only a tiny area has been explored. With China set to become a major oil importer within the next few years, it needs to find its own energy resources. The Tarim basin in north-western China has proved a disappointment; the South China Sea may be the place to slake its thirst for fuel.

China's historical claims to the area are dubious at best; they should hold as much weight in the modern world as the Papal Bull of 1493 that divided the world's oceans between Spain and Portugal. China has not just stopped at this historical fiction. Aware that occupation is nine-tenths of international law, China has slowly consumed the Spratly and Paracel Islands, taking advantage of inattention or weakness of rivals to snatch up a few of the atolls. As South Vietnam crumbled in 1974, Chinese troops took over the Paracel Islands. Hanoi, then a close ally of Beijing, could only stand by in mute rage.

In 1988, Vietnam and China fought a brief naval skirmish near the Spratlys. Vietnam came off worse, losing more than eighty sailors and two vessels. Since then the battles have been mostly diplomatic and economic as the rivals try to reinforce their claims and step up exploration for oil. Since the early 1990s both sides have been expanding their presence on the islands, building up infrastructures such as docks, barracks, communications antennae and even air fields. Anything that buttressed claims to the islands has been given maximum publicity; the construction of new buildings or a jetty on one of the far-flung archipelagos was often front page news in the official press. Even archaeologists have been busy trying to establish an earlier historical claim than that of China by pointing to shards of pottery found on the islands. Even if these fragments were actually found on the Spratlys, to present them as evidence of sovereignty or even occupation beggars belief; on that logic China and Japan could equally lay claim to vast swathes of mainland Vietnam because of the ancient ceramics found there. Such remnants are only proof of contact and trade.

Vietnam and China have been holding talks on the future of the islands but without much progress. China is willing to allow joint development of the area as long as rival claimants first acknowledge its sovereignty. In an imperious manner that has rattled Vietnam, China has refused to discuss the issue in international forums, saying it will deal with it only in bilateral discussions. Vietnam has sought the backing of its fellow members of the Association of Southeast Asian Nations (ASEAN) who share some of the anxieties of an increasingly powerful China that has slowly expanded its territorial claims. Most Southeast Asian nations have had to balance their security concerns with a need to maintain relations with China; Vietnam has had to do all of this while also handling considerable historical baggage.

So far it has tried to do this by separating out the toughest problems and agreeing to postpone any search for a resolution. Talks are held on the Spratlys but neither side expects progress; outside of the negotiations they attempt to gain minuscule advantages without upsetting the whole game. There is little confidence in Hanoi that talks will stop the Chinese pushing for more territory in the South China Sea. 'The Chinese have kept on expanding their claims since

World War II,' said Le Minh Nghia, chairman of Vietnam's Frontier Committee that handles territorial claims. 'They have executed their strategy step by step. History shows that they won't stop until there is a force there to stop them.'

Tensions have been reduced to a background hum but occasionally a loud and discordant note can unsettle the whole region, such as when China took over Mischief Reef in an area claimed by the Philippines. None of the players in the South China Sea has much room for manoeuvre. China lacks the military capacity to control the South China Sea; Vietnam lacks much of a defensive ability but has the advantage of holding around twenty of the largest islands. Taiwan has an air base on an island but rarely pushes its broader claims for fear of alienating Asian nations in which it has major investments. The Philippines, Brunei and Malaysia are unlikely to resort to force.

The hope among these nations is that the future may bring an environment that is more conducive to a comprehensive settlement; in the meantime the best that can be done is a series of confidence building measures on marine safety and the environment that could eventually lead to joint exploitation of resources. None of these schemes has made much progress; China is often tagged with being the biggest dog in the manger, handing out oil exploration concessions in what Vietnam says are its coastal waters but blocking moves towards collective exploration. Oil exploration has become a focus for a nervous diplomatic dance with both sides testing the other's reactions to an expansion of its activities in the area. When China awarded an American company exploration rights in a zone claimed by Vietnam, Hanoi protested furiously. When that had no effect, it sent its own exploration vessels into the area and began negotiations with another American oil firm, Conoco Inc. Having beaten their swords into ploughshares, the two countries have started poking and jabbing at each other with these new weapons.

Much of the talk of oil development is premature. Exploration has barely begun and the South China Sea presents one of the toughest environments for extraction of petroleum, with its frequent devastating storms. Vietnam has several oil fields off its southern coast but the area has not lived up to initial expectations; the geology is more complex than expected and the reserves have proved lower than first estimates.

Despite this, all eyes are going to be on the area, long identified as a potential crucible of conflict in Asia. In the past, Vietnam and China have only been able to hide their grudges for so long; the slow smoulder has always flared up violently. Vietnam knows that China has rarely been a benign and unobtrusive neighbour. Now their relationship is similar to what it was in the early 1970s; neither side is completely happy but neither is willing to provoke the other. The focus for both countries is for the moment domestic stability, not regional expansion, but it may only be a matter of time before something goes wrong, pushing the countries from cautious accommodation into confrontation.

'You are now entering the Independent Republic of Cholon,' said a Foreign Ministry official as our taxi crossed into District Five of Ho Chi Minh City, the city's Chinatown. In truth Cholon's four square kilometres are no longer a purely Chinese enclave, the geographic and demographic boundaries now blur into Ho Chi Min City's urban sprawl. But officials still suspect the area of marching to a different drum. Home to 500,000 people descended from Chinese immigrants who arrived between the eighteenth century and the 1950s, Cholon is one of the largest concentrations of overseas Chinese in the world. Around another half a million live elsewhere in the city and another one million across Vietnam, mostly in the Mekong Delta. The Viet Hoa, as they are known, make up the country's largest minority.

They also make up the richest minority in Vietnam. Cholon's impact on the economy of Ho Chi Minh City is staggering; an area that has about a tenth of the city's population accounts for around 40 per cent of its output and most of its recent growth. The city is one of the fastest growing economic centres in Asia with double-digit annual growth in the past few years. Viet Hoa have drawn in much of the legitimate foreign investment; they have also sucked in huge amounts in under-the-table funds from family overseas. Two thirds of ethnic Chinese in Ho Chi Minh have family connections with the West or other Asian countries. Even those who don't have family abroad often have the advantage of being fluent in the languages of the overseas Chinese: Mandarin, Hakka, Hokkien, Cantonese and money.

Vietnam's largest private company, Bitis, is owned by a family of Viet Hoa who have used family ties, business acumen and an appreciation of the value of close government connections to get rich. The company is Vietnam's largest shoemaker and seller; it has more than 400 shops and is the best known local brand. It was the first Vietnamese company to open a representative office in the United States. Apart from shoes, it also has investments in property, factories and trade.

Bitis represents a model for how the private sector has emerged in Vietnam. Overseas Chinese money and connections combined with government contacts in highly bureaucratised countries have produced formidable economic blocks in Indonesia, Thailand, Malaysia and the Philippines. In exchange for political and financial support, ethnic Chinese have been granted monopolies on certain trades, reaping huge rewards. The diasporic Chinese in Asia are estimated to have upwards of $500 billion in capital which they have been able to move rapidly into emerging economies like Vietnam. By mid 1997, Taiwan, Hong Kong and Singapore had pledged more than a third of all the investment in Vietnam. Including the considerable amounts of overseas Chinese money coming in through tax havens such as the Virgin Islands, total pledged investment from overseas Chinese had reached upwards of $13 billion.

Considerable sums have also come in under the table; the property boom in Ho Chi Minh City in the late 1980s that saw hundreds of new hotels, houses and restaurants open was fuelled by large numbers of overseas Vietnamese, many of whom are of Chinese origin, investing through family members still living in the city. 'The strength of the Chinese is that they have the networks to get hold of capital,' said Tran Tuan Tai, head of the Viet Hoa Bank, one of the most successful of the new joint stock private banks that opened in the 1990s. While many Vietnamese companies, including state firms, have been held back by the difficulties of raising capital, those with links into ethnic Chinese financing networks have profited. With this money, Cholon has boomed into a dense area of traders and small-scale manufacturers; new markets and apartment buildings have sprung up. Karaoke bars, restaurants and brothels cater not just to Asian executives but to a *nouveau riche* who have slipped right into the fast-paced conspicuous consumption that has become a sign of modernity in Asia. The rush of overseas Chinese money is remaking the physical, economic and social landscapes of Ho Chi Minh City.

For those who remember the anxieties of the 1970s when the visceral hostility against the Chinese came out into the open, the re-emergence of a rich and showy class of Viet Hoa is both heartening and disquieting. The official compliance with the businesses shows that the government no longer harbours such a deep loathing for people once derided as being a 'Fifth Column' for Beijing and accused of maintaining 'the capitalist heart beating in a socialist body'. Few Vietnamese saw the contradiction in describing the Chinese as simultaneous tools of Communist Beijing and world capitalist forces.

There are concerns that too much wealth concentrated in the hands of a minority may stir up old resentments. The Viet Hoa are not a very conspicuous minority; they speak, look and act in much the same ways as other Vietnamese, they have Vietnamese names and speak the language. Their exclusion is quite subtle: since the late 1970s they have been banned from joining the army and hold few posts in the bureaucracy; their access to education and other state-controlled opportunities is also limited. While a number have been elected to local councils, they have steered clear of political roles.

For an older generation of Chinese, the emerging prominence is worrying; there are lingering fears of a backlash, of a resurgence of old resentments that are a source of quiet concern for overseas Chinese across Southeast Asia. Vietnamese are tolerant of the Chinese minority as long as they behave in certain ways. They need to know their place and remain silent, apolitical, supportive of the regime, not too rich, not too well-connected and on the surface Vietnamese in name, dress and language. If they want to express their culture it has to be within the constraints of minority cultures set by the government. They are allowed their festivals and dragon dancing but little else.

Cuong, a seventy-year-old trader who arrived in Vietnam from the Chiu Chow area of Southern China aged two, is concerned that the Viet Hoa are pushing their luck in the current economic free-for-all in Ho Chi Minh City. 'We still need to keep a low profile,' he says. 'We should stay out of politics, concentrate on important things like family and business.'

Since 1954 the Viet Hoa have been living under the threat of being drafted into armies, forced to take Vietnamese nationality or sent off to New Economic Zones, but they always managed to find a way of getting around the problems. Before 1975, their economic power had enabled them to keep their sons out of the army and by sharing their wealth with Saigon's kleptocratic élite they could maintain their political influence.

When the Communists took over Saigon in 1975, the only recourse of Chinese traders such as Cuong was to flee the country. As Saigon fell, Cuong and his family burned all their documents to disguise their connections with the élite and then planned to flee. Cuong attempted to leave eleven times; on each occasion his escape was foiled. Finally he gave up and decided to stay, prospering as a middleman in various deals and running his trading company.

Nearly half the 1.3 million Chinese living in Vietnam in 1975 left. Tens of thousands of Chinese working in the port in Haiphong and in the coal mines of Quang Ninh province fled across the border. As relations between China and Vietnam deteriorated, both sides traded accusations over the Viet Hoa community. China accused Vietnam of discrimination, of forcing the Chinese out and demanding huge payments to let them go, accusations that are all borne out by the testimony of those who fled. Vietnam said Chinese spies were encouraging people to leave.

After 1975 it is clear that there was a campaign of ethnic cleansing that resulted in tens of thousands of deaths as many Viet Hoa fled by sea. Estimates of the number who died at sea, either drowned or killed by pirates, vary from the low thousands to hundreds of thousands, but given the violent storms that afflict the South China, the crowding of boats, the difficulties with navigation and supplies, it is not unreasonable to believe as many as 40,000 died. Meanwhile Vietnamese officials, flushed with victory, grew rich as they pocketed the gold that refugees were forced to pay to escape.

There is no doubt about the discriminatory policies of those times. The government banned the hiring of ethnic Chinese, students were removed from colleges and schools, and businesses owned by the community had to be turned over to the state. In September 1975, the government started rounding up 'big capitalists', mostly Chinese from Cholon. Chinese were forced to take Vietnamese nationality, something that many had avoided up until then. In March 1978 as relations with China spiralled downwards, the campaign, known by the sinister appellation 'X2', began to nationalise the wealth of all Chinese. Many had already lost their savings in currency reforms, now their businesses were confiscated. Soldiers counted out the chopsticks in restaurants that now belonged to the government.

Ethnic Chinese in northern Vietnam, a well-settled and integrated community, were essentially told that they had a choice between relocating to New Economic Zones – impoverished areas mostly in the highlands where migrants often received no assistance in establishing farms – or they could leave the country. Those who could afford it paid the ten taels of gold and left (a tael is an Asian measurement for precious metals equivalent to 1.08 ounces or 36 grams). The fact that they had to pay to leave has created a myth in the West that many boat people were rich, that they were flush with gold and jewels. Almost all of them left with nothing; forced out of the only country they had ever called home in one of the most shameful policies ever enacted by the Vietnamese government.

The impact on the economy was severe. Coal production slumped, the ports in the north of Vietnam ground to a halt for lack of porters. Thousands of traders and craftsmen left. While keeping up a barrage of lies abroad about the Viet Hoa, the government revealed its real attitude in a pamphlet that described the Chinese as 'intelligence agents, torturers, cooks and maidservants' for forces from the United States. Foreign visitors to Hanoi were reassured that the Chinese were leaving because of Beijing's campaign of disinformation. And yet the Chinese population in the North fell by half in a matter of months. In Hanoi the number of Viet Hoa fell from around 20,000 to just 2,000. The lies that tripped so easily off the lips of men like Nguyen Co Thach at that time are reminiscent of the dissembling of Serb leaders in the conflict in the former Yugoslavia. Thach, for example, told a journalist that the fact that ethnic Chinese were paying to leave showed that they were not being coerced to go. In reality they were being coerced to pay and to leave.

Life was particularly tough for the nearly 300,000 refugees who fled to China. Most were semi-skilled urban workers. There were few opportunities for them in China, which had yet to launch its economic reforms and was still suffering from the aftermath of the Cultural Revolution. Most new arrivals were sent to state farms, some of which saw their populations double overnight. The United Nations High Commissioner for Refugees tried to provide assistance in China, but most Viet Hoa had considerable problems adjusting to life in a country their forebears had left long ago. The UNHCR estimates more than 10 per cent of resettled refugees left the state farms almost immediately.

Those refugees now present a serious difficulty in relations. China says some want to come back to Vietnam, which has replied in general that they are not welcome. For this reason Vietnam has refused to take back ethnic Chinese boat people from camps in Hong Kong for fear of setting a precedent for the much larger population of refugees in China. There are many other legacies of those days. Vietnam was impoverished culturally and economically by its policies against its Chinese minority; the loss of so many well-educated and trained people continues to be a drag on development.

Throughout the 1980s, there was a state-sponsored process to encourage discrimination against the Chinese, even to the point of trying to weed out words of Chinese origin from the language. This goes on even today. Censors at the English-language *Vietnam Investment Review* routinely strike references to China or Chinese influences from stories. Photographs that showed Chinese characters on signs or temple gates were replaced with images that were 'more Vietnamese'.

Academics were encouraged to find the roots of Vietnamese Buddhism not in China but in India, which was a reliable ally. Chinese communities in rural areas were left out of development plans and sidelined in ghettos of unrelenting poverty. This has become particularly stark in Dong Nai province, Ho Chi Minh City's booming neighbour, where Chinese villages are lacunae of stark deprivation in the midst of a rapidly expanding economy.

The campaigns against the Chinese have nourished prejudices

that are still strong. Many Vietnamese, particularly in the North, are openly hostile to Chinese. In Hanoi, there were frequent scares about the poisoning of Chinese produce and fruit; newspapers regularly jumped on this bandwagon and urged readers not to buy foodstuffs from China. It was completely plausible to people that Chinese farmers would have an interest in killing off the consumers of their fruits and vegetables.

China is still a convenient scapegoat for all manner of complaints. Consumer reports jumped on the dangers of Chinese-made toys. Chinese beer was said to contain birth-control pills that would render Vietnamese infertile. Even a plague of rats and mice was blamed on the fact that all the rodent-eating snakes were being caught and shipped to China for food.

The suspicion and fears are a lasting legacy of Vietnam's ethnic cleansing of its Chinese population. Ultimately almost everything can be pinned on China and its looming presence. A Vietnamese historian summed it up with a bleak utterance: 'China is always just there,' he said, gesturing northwards, 'and it will always be dangerous.'

15

Melancholy Tribe

There is no sorrow above, the loss of a native land.

EURIPIDES
Medea

When Buu Chanh last saw the Saigon River, the great rope of silted water that loops through the city, he was being pushed into the dank hold of a fishing boat heading out to international waters and escape from Vietnam. Twenty years later, he saw the river again as a glinting trail of mercury thousands of feet below the Business Class cabin of a Malaysian Airlines jet. Chanh's departure in 1975 was hurried and terrifying, a dangerous journey with no known destination. His return in 1995 was almost as fraught with anxiety. 'I saw the immigration officers in their uniforms and I was terrified. I thought they were soldiers. I was sure they were going to arrest me, that they would shake me down for money. My hands were sweaty; I could hardly talk but the next thing I knew I was outside the airport and there was all my family climbing over the barricades.'

The scene at Ton San Nhat Airport in the weeks before the lunar new year celebrations was the Fall of Saigon in reverse. Outside the terminal huge expectant crowds jostled and scuffled along the barricades near the arrivals hall, clutching children and cellophane-wrapped bouquets of roses for relatives arriving from Los Angeles and San Francisco. As the dazed and jet-lagged passengers emerged there were sudden eruptions of recognition and emotion as families were reunited; standing in the steamy car park they began the process of bridging decades of division as well as sometimes wide and awkward gaps in culture, wealth and ideas.

But you can never really go home again. The Viet Kieu, as overseas Vietnamese are known, are a diverse group that defy any easy summation but once they go back to Vietnam they find themselves compressed into a narrow range of stereotypes. For most Vietnamese, they are a confusing blend of familiar and foreign; on one hand they appear Vietnamese, on the other they are generally richer, better educated and more cosmopolitan. They are envied and scorned for their imagined wealth, held in respect and contempt for their sophistication and familiarity with the West and sometimes regarded as traitors for leaving. The ambivalence is constantly reflected in the government's attitude to Viet Kieu; on the one hand they are considered part of the nation and officials have urged them to bring their capital and expertise back home, while on the other they are often treated with contempt and suspicion. The official line is that they must have 'goodwill' – what this means is that they can come back if they avoid any political role. They must become quasi-citizens without any memories of, or opinions about, the past. They must subscribe to the state's brittle and enforced amnesia if they are to be accepted again in their homeland and that is something many cannot will themselves to do.

The journeys they faced to reach the countries of asylum were often harrowing. Women and young girls were taken from boats and sexually abused for days on end by Thai pirates before being dumped alive into the sea; others were shipwrecked on the sandy atolls of the South China Sea, surviving on rainwater and by eating raw sea birds and fish. Those who reached countries such as Malaysia faced hostile governments. In the chaos of escape, families were divided and children and parents separated, often forever. Michael, an Australian Vietnamese, saw his young sister dragged off by pirates. She was never seen again. Her image, like that of thousands of others, is frozen; she will forever be a terrified eleven-year-old girl wrenched from her family in the most brutal fashion.

Given the way most Viet Kieu fled, that many wish to return is testament to powerful urges to maintain identity or to re-establish some roots. Despite their bitter memories, Viet Kieu have been coming back in ever increasing numbers since the government in Hanoi signalled its willingness to allow them to return. Around

400,000 a year returned for visits and some moved back permanently. Links between Vietnam and the overseas communities, almost entirely ruptured since 1975, resumed. There are around two million overseas Vietnamese around the world, mostly in France, the United States, Germany, Australia, Canada and the United Kingdom.

They had lost a war, lost their country and many would lose their families. They lived in communities inflamed by these losses, often in countries they had not chosen, doing jobs they did not want – and for which they were often over-qualified. But their lives were infused not just with the melancholy of exile but also with drive and ambition, the desire to recover from the stunning defeats. The stories of Viet Kieu often trace a descending parabola of suffering followed by extraordinary achievement, an ascent into a world of material and intellectual success as the 'model minority' in Western countries.

Their model minority status in the United States is however something of a myth; there is a successful middle class but many more recent arrivals from Vietnam are trapped in housing projects and mired in poverty. In the minds of many Americans, the Vietnamese community is emblematic of their generosity in receiving so many refugees. This whole notion is wrapped up in the confused memories of the war, but the reality is that most Vietnamese arrived in the late 1970s and early 1980s when a conservative backlash against immigrants was beginning. In 1979 a number of Gallup polls showed that more than 60 per cent of Americans opposed the admission of Vietnamese refugees. Those who did make it to the United States were often seen as rivals for scarce jobs; those who arrived during economic downturns would find it extremely difficult to get work. A survey in San Diego in 1984 was illustrative of the economic situation for the majority of Vietnamese soon after they arrived: 22.4 per cent were unemployed and 61.3 per cent were below the poverty line. Those who did have jobs were in the lower income rungs; 29.2 per cent said they got no benefits at work and 48.7 per cent said they had no possibility for promotion.

The image in Vietnam is that all Viet Kieu are enormously successful and wealthy; when they return they are expected to come back laden with gifts, particularly with designer clothes and the latest gadgets that cannot yet be found in Vietnam. Viet Kieu stoke these cargo cult images by sending back photographs of themselves with their trophies of success – trips to Disneyland, massive cars and sprawling suburban homes. To return without evidence of success can be a huge loss of face. Jimmy Nguyen, a jeweller in Seattle who spends several months a year in Ho Chi Minh City, rents returning families heavy gold and diamond jewellery. They leave their cars with him as collateral and return the jewellery and a rental fee when they return. 'When they go back to Vietnam they say they own a restaurant but of course they just work in one; you can't go back and say you are just a waiter in a *pho* restaurant,' he said.

It puts enormous pressures on those who do go back to show that they have been a success. It has also built up the expectation in the government that it could look to the overseas Vietnamese to return with cash and Western business savvy in the way the overseas Chinese have helped China. An oft-repeated figure in the media was that there were 40,000 Viet Kieu professionals working for organisations such as NASA and the World Bank who were longing to return home to help the Fatherland. It was never questioned why these people should give up their jobs and professional respect to return to a country from which many had fled under terrible circumstances.

Whilst Viet Kieu have swarmed back for visits, they have not returned in large numbers to live or invest. So far Viet Kieu account for only a trickle of the authorised foreign investment and few people have been convinced by the tax breaks and preferential treatment on offer. From 1988 to 1996, the government has licensed $127.6 million of projects from Viet Kieu with only $6.3 million from the United States, home to around half of the 2.7 million-strong overseas community. 'Viet Kieu investment is minimal, not even 1 per cent of foreign investment capital,' acknowledged Nguyen Ngoc Ha, President of the Ho Chi Minh City Committee for Overseas Vietnamese. The government has offered a 20 per cent reduction in taxes and a flat 5 per cent tax on profit remittances. Viet Kieu are given the same rights as domestic firms to lease property and hire staff unlike other foreign investors.

These concessions have not proved enough. The *Saigon Times*

Weekly, a business magazine, described laws on Viet Kieu investment as containing 'vague, ambiguous and unrealistic provisions',
such as one that required overseas Vietnamese to provide proof
that they were of sound mind. The magazine urged the government to revise its policies. 'They need to take some more significant
steps,' said Nguyen Binh, who returned to Vietnam as country manager for Federal Express after fourteen years in the United States.
'Lots of people want to come back but they need further measures
they could accept as a gesture of open arms.'

Many want their property back. Thousands of houses and businesses were confiscated after 1954 in the North and after 1975 in the
South, but proving ownership is an onerous task for those who
come back. Houses were split among dozens of families and businesses wrapped into state enterprises. Few have been able so far to
reclaim property. If many Viet Kieu were able to do this it would
certainly result in another massive disruption of the lives of many
city dwellers.

Vietnam does not recognise dual citizenship; those who fled may
have taken foreign passports, but unless they formally renounced
their Vietnamese citizenship to the President's office in Hanoi they
remain Vietnamese in the eyes of the law. That means they get little
in the way of consular protection if they do run into trouble. The
irritation people feel about this is compounded by a dual pricing
system under which foreigners, including Viet Kieu, pay sometimes
as much as twice the price for transport and hotels. Overseas
Vietnamese, it seems, are Vietnamese when it suits the government,
and foreigners when it does not. Responding to the irritation this
caused, the government tried to end dual pricing for Viet Kieu in
1997.

These were among the many mixed signals that come from the
government and hinder the development of closer relations with
the Viet Kieu. For overseas Vietnamese to return and live permanently in Vietnam, they have to follow regulations that include the
clause: 'Vietnamese expatriates wishing to come back home must
not participate in or support any organisations conspiring against
the country or take any action against the Vietnamese government
and the Vietnamese community abroad.'

No definition is given of these organisations – they could include almost every Vietnamese association outside of Vietnam. Even the least politically active Viet Kieu is likely to have some contact with overseas groups that are opposed to the government in Hanoi. For most of those who want to go back, this clause is unlikely to create any problems. But for some Viet Kieu it is emblematic of the lack of trust and reconciliation and of the disdain for the overseas Vietnamese that lingers in Hanoi more than two decades after the end of the war.

There are still strong political suspicions in Hanoi about some Viet Kieu; they were all tarred with the brush of extremism even though only a tiny number are still actively opposed to the government. Ahead of the Party Congress in 1996, Do Muoi told cadres in Ho Chi Minh City that the metropolis was a seething bed of opposition and hostility towards the government and that particular vigilance was required. The coded message was that the overseas Vietnamese who had returned to the city represented a serious threat. Around the Congress many Viet Kieu living in Hanoi were called in for questioning in what has become a routine heightening of surveillance around major political events.

Many Viet Kieu were suspicious of being taken for a ride by unscrupulous officials. Customs and immigration officers at Ton Sun Nhat Airport were notorious for shaking down Viet Kieu on arrival and departure, feeding off their understandable fear of officialdom. Viet Kieu were frequently the target of police raids and often had to pay bribes. Most of those who returned to Vietnam had some sort of scuffle with the bureaucracy; they nearly always ended up paying.

'There is a lot of fear among people who go back,' said Truong Quang Luu, head of the Special Broadcasting Service Radio in Australia. 'The fear is there because of a lack of transparency and a sense that the officials can be capricious in the way they treat people. Some people still fear that they could just disappear.' Luu, one of the most prominent Viet Kieu in Australia, had his own taste of the way the government views overseas Vietnamese. A former South Vietnamese diplomat, he fled to Australia in 1975 and became a lawyer. He was chosen in 1994 to visit Vietnam as part of an Australian parliamentary delegation looking into human rights conditions. Just before the visit, he gave an interview to the Vietnamese service of the BBC in which he discussed human rights. It was too much for the Vietnamese to bear; they cancelled his visa and the Australian government was forced to call off the visit. 'I was just an excuse,' Luu said. 'The Vietnamese government was never enthusiastic about the visit.' Officials in Hanoi simply could not bear the idea of an overseas Vietnamese standing in judgement of their rule.

By 1996 Viet Kieu were sending back around $600 million a year to help their families and to invest under the table. Spotting a potential source of revenues, the government slapped a tax on remittances and so the flow of cash through banks dried up; instead people sent cash or found others ways to get money into the country. None of this helped encourage investment. Disappointed by the slow inflows, the government blamed foreign countries for stifling the ambitions of overseas Vietnamese. Reports quoted Deputy Foreign Minister Nguyen Dy Nien, chairman of the Central Committee for Overseas Vietnamese, as saying that only 10 per cent of businesses started by Viet Kieu had succeeded in their adopted countries. The reports did not say how the minister arrived at the figure, but newspapers attributed the failure rate to racism and businesses 'being hindered by the current laws in the resident countries'. It was a line that caused some ironic chuckles among Viet Kieu trying to set up shop in Vietnam. In 1997 the remittance tax was dropped after the government realised it was a stifling restriction on the inflows of capital.

There were other factors in the reluctance of many Viet Kieu to return and invest. Until the mid 1990s many Vietnamese communities, particularly those in the United States, were vociferously opposed to anyone returning to do business. They saw investments in Vietnam as propping up the Communist government. Investors were seriously discouraged from returning. One Vietnamese-American who returned in the late 1980s to advise the government on investment policies nearly lost his family when his home in Chicago was burned down. The culprits were not found, but the executive believed that he had been targeted after an article about his return appeared in a newspaper in Vietnam.

To add insult to the occasional harassment of Viet Kieu by the authorities, the media tended to portray them as gaudy, unscrupulous parvenues who have somehow disturbed the refinement of

Vietnam. Cases of fraud and other crimes involving Viet Kieu received front page treatment in the press and the message was often made clear that they could not be trusted. The most prominent case was that of Nguyen Trung Truc, managing director of Peregrine Capital Vietnam, a branch of a now bankrupt Hong Kong investment bank. Truc, who had fled to Australia before 1975, was one of the first high-profile Viet Kieu to return to do business, setting up not just the Peregrine branch but a number of other companies trading everything from Johnson & Johnson baby products to Mercedes-Benz cars. His flamboyance and reliance on political connections backfired on him when he was arrested for tax evasion. His companies were closed and he was fined large sums after city authorities rounded on him.

The Vietnamese, particularly in Australia and the United States, are unusual immigrant communities. Most hastily fled their country; few had any time to prepare for their move. Few spoke English on arrival, few had many contacts or ties to the communities to which they moved. There are considerable differences between those who arrived in the immediate aftermath of the fall of Saigon and those who went later. The first evacuees had left in a rush, but most arrived in the United States quite rapidly and without enduring long waits in refugee camps. Many had worked with the Americans, spoke English and were generally well educated; Vietnam lost a good proportion of its educated élite in that first wave of 180,000 people taken out by the United States.

Later arrivals were a very different story; they had often endured years in re-education camps and prisons. Many had a horrifying time fleeing the country only to spend years in camps in Hong Kong or in Southeast Asian countries. Many were just foot soldiers in Saigon or petty traders; they had little in the way of language skills or qualifications that would be useful in the United States. The final group to leave in the late 1980s were mostly northern farmers and fishermen, driven out by poverty. This group had the most difficult time adapting to life abroad. Often crammed into public housing in violent areas of big cities, they had few economic prospects. Their children faced the pressures of urban adolescence. Some, like Dat Lu, a young Vietnamese-American who grew up with his mother and siblings in New York, went from a grim high school in the Bronx to brilliant academic achievements at Harvard. Lu was a rarity; not only did he achieve considerable success at college but on graduation went back to New York to set up a community centre for young Vietnamese. Many more young Vietnamese ended up in violent inner-city gangs or trapped in fast food service Mcjobs.

The myth of the model minority needs to be put in perspective, but at the same time many Vietnamese went from being impoverished migrants to middle-class suburbanites in remarkably little time. Cities like Westminster in Orange County, San Jose in the Bay Area of Northern California and Houston, Texas, all have vibrant communities of increasingly wealthy and settled Vietnamese.

These people had remade their lives in the United States and few had any intention of going back to Vietnam. Their children were different. Many had grown up experiencing the land of their birth vicariously through the festivals of Viet Kieu communities and stories told by their parents and grandparents. For them there was a desire to return to Vietnam to find part of their identity which many had spent their teenage years trying to hide. In college, it seemed, the desire to find out more about their place as Vietnamese and Asian-Americans drew many to return to Vietnam as students, to work or just to visit family.

This generation has started to bring a new perspective to Vietnamese-American identity; they saw themselves primarily as Americans, not exiles in America. They had few memories of Vietnam and although they had grown up with the sadness and nostalgia that ran through their parents' lives, they generally had a fresh, uncritical view of Vietnam. Many felt they had to adopt a different view of the United States from their parents'. It was a source of some tension in the United States that Vietnamese did not always share the bright, optimistic myth of the American Dream. For many, the United States was not home, it was a place of exile. They were supposed to shed their longing for their homeland and become good Americans but many could not. They had come from a country with little tradition of migration and most had left in a sudden traumatic manner.

The younger generation had less choice; it could not remain aloof from mainstream America in the way some of the older Vietnamese tried to do, closing themselves off in Vietnamese communities and pining for home. They were forced to assimilate and develop hybrid identities as Vietnamese-Americans. For some this has meant Ivy League colleges and a fierce professional ambition; for others membership in the violent urban gangs that have developed in poorer Vietnamese neighbourhoods. Some 41 per cent of Vietnamese residents of Orange County told pollsters from the *Los Angeles Times* that gangs were the community's main problem, not only creating a climate of violence but adding to the burdens of prejudice as Asians were increasingly linked to crime. With names like Oriental Boyz, Scar Boyz and Orange Boyz they run drugs and protection rackets. There are even gangs for teenage girls with names like Innocent Bitch Killers and Banana Girls. Crime is woven deep into these communities; American and Vietnamese traditions of prostitution, drugs and violence all mix together.

Young Viet Kieu tended to take their identity as Vietnamese less seriously than their parents. They were not so much inheritors of a priceless historical tradition dating back thousands of years, but half spawned by a culture that could be laughed at as well as revered. In an short memoir of his childhood, the Vietnamese-American author Khoi T. Luu wrote:

> Even now I startle my friends, Vietnamese and non-Vietnamese alike with my ability to crack jokes; it's as if I'm violating some secret code of behaviour inflicted (or self-inflicted) on the Vietnamese people: we're not supposed to laugh, not this heartily. We can only study, over-achieve, invade the hallowed halls of overpriced and overrated colleges. We can only cry – cry for our lost nation, our slaughtered brothers, deceased fathers, exiled status, our food stamps, our garage-sale clothes, our language barriers and so on.

Although his own family had 'experienced the burden of that collective pain', Khoi made the point that life does go on. 'As for me I have lost my father, my homeland, my roots, my childhood innocence and parts of my sanity – all because of the war. But what I do have left – and I thank my family for teaching me this – are my dignity, an ironic sense of hope and, believe it or not, my sense of humour.'

Like many Vietnamese who grew up in the United States, Khoi felt the strain of being caught between cultures, of occupying an area between their parents and the mainstream of America. Humour has long been part of the process of cultural integration in the United States; a way of softening the blows of immigration and ethnic exclusion. Jewish, Italian, Irish and Polish immigrants all had their jokes; ethnic humour has played a huge role in the popular culture of the last century. Khoi, a student at Harvard in the early 1990s, has covered much of the same ground, laughing at the habits of Vietnamese families in America and settling some scores in the battles of the sexes – one of the greatest areas of tension for many Viet Kieu because of the differences between Vietnam and the West in the treatment of women. A favourite joke of young Viet Kieu: 'Why did the Vietnamese woman cross the road?' The answer: 'It doesn't matter, what is she doing out of the house anyway?'

Hung Le, an Australian comedian and musician, now earns a good living as one of a tiny number of Vietnamese entertainers who have made it in the West. He takes no prisoners and concedes nothing to political correctness in his monologues on life in Vietnam, his family's flight from the country and his life as a Vietnamese-Australian. Hung and his family left Saigon just hours before its fall and were picked up by the US Seventh Fleet off the coast. They were taken to a refugee camp in Guam ('Club Med with barbed wire') and later ended up in Australia because an uncle was living there. Hung was one of the first Vietnamese migrants to arrive in the country and at school in Melbourne he was the only Asian.

His father, an artist, had encouraged the children to play music and Hung became an accomplished violinist. He started busking to earn money, spicing up his act by clowning around and playing famous pieces of classical music at very high speed. Performing at the Edinburgh Fringe Festival, Hung saw stand-up comedians for the first time and was inspired to combine music and humour in a new routine.

'At my first performance I was heckled constantly by this Aboriginal woman. She kept saying things like "My husband was there in Vietnam, he fought there. Fuck off you Vietnamese," etc . . .

First I wanted to say to her: "Sorry I don't speak alcoholic." But I couldn't. Then I thought about pretending to shoot her but wasn't sure if that would go down too well either. In the end I just ended up getting down on my knees and begging her to shut up.'

Hung, who has shaved off his straw-coloured dreadlocks in favour of a stubble-headed look, has shocked many by playing up to stereotypes, but in fact his act undermines them. His jokes are typically about his experiences or are based around ideas of Vietnamese, but his own manic personality belies them; he is living proof to his mostly white audiences that Vietnamese do not fit their stereotype. On stage, dressed in tails with his comically mobile face and the musical punctuation he provides with his violin, he can get away with telling jokes that would be lame or offensive elsewhere. 'How can you tell when a Vietnamese teenager has broken into your home?' Answer: 'Your children's homework has been done and your dog has disappeared.'

His routine is mostly about his family's experiences in Vietnam where they lived just opposite the Presidential Palace in Saigon which was bombed in a coup attempt against President Ngo Dinh Diem and later attacked just before the fall of the city. 'They always said that Vietnam brought war into people's living rooms. Certainly did with ours.' He successfully juxtaposes the stereotypes of Vietnam with familiar Australian experiences – his is part of a long tradition of comedy in which stereotypes are built up only to be ultimately demolished.

But Hung has been quite prickly about shows that have set up stereotypes about Vietnamese that he did not like or that lacked some redeeming comic power. He was offered a role in *GP*, a very popular evening soap opera set in a surgery of general practitioners. The part was loosely based on his real-life character; it was about a young Vietnamese violinist. The plot centred around a violent argument with his father who eventually burns his son's violin. 'Vietnamese just don't behave like that. I told the script-writers so they changed it from the father to the uncle; they completely missed the point.' He turned down the part and another actor got what was a great break in Australia.

'He is the most ocker of all the comedians I represent,' said his agent, Michelle Wild, using the word to describe a certain type of working class Australian. 'He says he is over-assimilated and that's right.' Hung can tear down Australian ideas about Vietnamese because he is so Australian. He was kicked out of Melbourne University for drinking too much; a considerable feat in a country where drinking is an honoured national pastime. He doesn't have much appeal in the Vietnamese community in Melbourne but through his humour he has told a lot of young Australians about what it is like to be Viet Kieu. His humour broke down barriers at a time in Australia when debates on race and immigration were boiling up again. Hung noted with some irony how his own career had been aided by the outspokenly racist comments of an independent member of parliament Pauline Hanson, whose anti-immigration views sparked off a sometimes rancorous national discussion. 'Since she started, I've been on the radio all the time.' Hung has emerged as an unlikely but refreshing spokesman for minorities in Australia.

Hung and Khoi represent an important shift in Viet Kieu culture. Viet Kieu once maintained all the romantic and melancholy ideas that are important for diasporas. There was a homeland that could not be visited, that was portrayed as utopian and threatened. For those struggling with life in alien countries, there was some comfort in the notion of going back; of recovering the homeland. The Viet Kieu, particularly those in the United States, kept up their governments-in-exile and other pretences; they were defined as a group by their myths of return. They refused to accept the idea that their years outside the country might have altered them to the degree that they could never go back and be fully accepted. 'Political refugees are always haunted by a sense that they might be able to go back to their countries and that does not foster a settled or productive environment,' said Truong Quang Luu. 'Look at the White Russians who settled in France after 1917 and faded into oblivion. Many Vietnamese are just like that.'

The Vietnamese faced some difficulties fitting in with the myths of their home countries. In the United States they were expected to give up their nostalgia on arrival; it was unseemly to hanker too deeply for the old country when one should be striving for the American Dream. But many Vietnamese did not feel hugely grateful; many felt the US had destroyed their homeland and then abandoned it to Communism. America was not necessarily a land of opportunity but a place of harsh cultural dislocations.

Viet Kieu have become a distinct group separated from Vietnamese who lived in the country all their lives, although it is not clear how long it took to become Viet Kieu once one left Vietnam; Ho Chi Minh wandered the globe for thirty-five years before coming back to lead the Revolution. When he arrived in Hanoi to declare independence it was the first time he had ever set foot in the capital. Today he would be classified as a Viet Kieu and forced to submit to some humiliating notions to establish his credentials as Vietnamese.

Today a younger generation is coming back with less historical baggage; they have generally returned without political agendas but on journeys of self-discovery or to find work. Their reactions were mixed. Diane, who returned to work for an American multi-national, hated it. 'I had some memories of the place but they were about a life that no longer existed. I remember getting ice-cream with a maid and a big house in Vung Tau where we spent vacations. I was horrified by the poverty when I came back. I ended up very disillusioned by the state of the country and the corruption.' She returned to the United States after eighteen months.

Many young Viet Kieu complained of the restrictions their families in Vietnam imposed on them; it was shocking for many women to feel a stronger sting of sexual discrimination and limitation than they were used to at home. Many felt a loss of self-sufficiency when caught in the smothering embrace of Vietnamese families. Those that grew up in the United States often felt their culture was ignored there; Vietnam meant only the war and all the horrors associated with it. They expected to find in Vietnam a richer appreciation of their own identity and culture, but often faced a hurtful rejection or indifference.

Theodore Nguyen, whose family had settled in Houston, was one of the first of the twentysomething generation to come back to Vietnam in the early 1990s, setting up a housing renovation business and an antiques store. Returning heightened a sense of not belonging completely in either the United States or Vietnam. 'It's as if I go through some sort of X-ray machine and in Vietnam it accepts my body but not my brain, while in the United States its accepts my brain but not my body.' Viet Kieu who do go back find themselves a focus of curiosity but also occasionally resentment and exclusion. 'The stigma of being Viet Kieu can be quite strong,' said Nguyen. 'You are a member of the group but not a full member. You didn't go through what the rest of your family here went through. They tell you about the hardships, about the times they had to eat animal feed from Eastern Europe which really humiliated people. You try and explain the difficulties of living in the United States, but it really doesn't cut it compared to what they have been through. Here I am always slightly excluded. I have a passport, I can leave any time I want.'

Throughout most of the 1980s, the government viewed Viet Kieu with almost relentless hostility. The Museum of War Remnants, formerly the US War Crimes Museum, has an entire hall devoted to what the government views as attempts at subversion by overseas Vietnamese. There are photographs of trials at which dozens of people were sentenced to long terms for their involvement in alleged plots to overthrow the government. Hanoi is still terrified of the Viet Kieu opposition movements abroad even though few have much real political impact; they are divided into hundreds of often mutually suspicious movements that seem unable to organise a coherent opposition to Communist rule. Opposition groups were embroiled in a series of scandals; in the Californian city of San Jose, the National United Front for the Liberation of Vietnam tried to hitch itself to the bandwagon of Reagan-era hostility to Communism, and attempted to organise funding for an army modelled after the Nicaraguan Contras. The Front raised millions of dollars in the 1980s but it channelled the money not into subversion but into the restaurants owned by its leadership.

Some extremist groups in the United States are believed to be behind a number of murders and violent attacks in the late 1980s and early 1990s as they tried to eliminate prominent figures who were softening their stance against Vietnam. Nguyen Dam Phong, a newspaper editor who wrote about scams against Vietnamese by political groups in the United States, was gunned down in what was believed to have been a politically-motivated crime.

The sensitivities of these groups were extraordinary. A delivery truck belonging to the Los Angeles newspaper *Nguoi Viet* was fire-bombed after a cable show presented by the paper's editor Yen Do inadvertently showed the Communist flag in a scene of Saigon that was accompanying a music video. On the van was scrawled the message: 'If you are VC, we will kill you.'

According to the New York-based group, the Committee to Protect Journalists, five Vietnamese journalists were killed in the United States between 1981 and 1990 in what are suspected to be attacks by right-wing groups. The murders were believed to be the work of a sinister death squad of former Southern soldiers that called itself the Vietnamese Organisation to Exterminate Communists and Restore the Nation. The crimes remained unsolved; most Vietnamese were scared to talk about them and had little trust in police departments.

The extremism on both sides has eased; contact has brought with it greater understanding and time has healed some of the wounds of war and division. Many Viet Kieu who vowed they would never return have been lured back by the chance to see their families and homeland again. They have realised that it is safe to return and that they will not face much hostility. In Vietnam the novelty of Viet Kieu is starting to wear off; they are no longer seen as rich cousins and benefactors to be milked as much as possible. The gaps that divided them politically have narrowed and the cultural divide is getting smaller. Some Vietnamese now find Viet Kieu somewhat rigid in their views. 'They are often very conservative, they have a very fixed idea about Vietnamese culture,' said Ly Qui Chung, who has many family members who live abroad. 'Many of their ideas about Vietnam were frozen in the 1960s and haven't changed at all. All they want to see is that culture come back.'

Most Viet Kieu want reconciliation, not conflict, but feel the government is not yet willing to shed the suspicions and hostility that linger on from the war. Certainly there is nothing to suggest that Hanoi is ready to give up its rigid version of history that almost refuses to acknowledge that South Vietnam ever existed. Hanoi was never magnanimous in victory; instead it determinedly tried to erase the very existence of South Vietnam. There are signs that those policies may be ending. Duong Van Minh, the last President of South Vietnam was given permission to return to the country. A former South Vietnamese army doctor, famous for being the first surgeon to separate conjoined twins in Vietnam, was elected to the National Assembly in 1997. The volume of attacks against the overseas Vietnamese in the official press has been turned down and many officials do genuinely want the Viet Kieu to contribute what they can to the country's development. But the only real reconciliation that has been forged so far is between Viet Kieu and average citizens in Vietnam.

16

Young and Restless

As to our generation, what great feats await us?

PHAM THI HOAI
The Crystal Messenger

Patricia Kaas loped out on to the stage to a roar from the crowd, her second-skin dress already scorched with sweat in the 35 °C temperatures inside the Giang Vo Exhibition Hall. It was the first rock concert to be held in the airless building, indeed in 1994 it was the first appearance by a Western popular performer in Hanoi. Kaas, a full-throated, sinuous Edith Piaf for the 1990s, had been brought in by the Alliance Française as part of their programme for promoting French culture. The show sold out immediately, aided by the subsidised tickets and the rarity of the event. Billboards had been put up around town but the Ministry of Culture and Information soon ordered them removed. In small letters in the corner were the words *Rock Phap* (French rock). The word 'rock' was still too inflammatory to be used in Vietnam. The posters were taken down and the word was painted out.

As Kaas' band struck its first chord, the crowd of young Vietnamese charged forward, overturning chairs in a section reserved for the French community and sending the crowd of diplomats, aid workers and teachers scuttling to the side. With Kaas stepping up the pace of the music, the crowd at the front became more boisterous. The grinning teenage boys stripped off their shirts, danced wildly and chanted up at the singer: 'I want to fuck you.'

Ho Chi Minh always let it be known how much he liked children. Unlike Mao or Stalin, Ho genuinely seemed at ease in the official pictures and newsreels of him meeting with Youth, the supposedly uniform collection of earnest young people in Communist societies. In one famous and endlessly replayed loop of film, Ho is seen sitting on the steps of the Presidential Palace laughing while children fondle his wispy beard. One wonders what he would make of young people today; the first generation raised in a unified, Communist Vietnam. Would he have understood adolescent rebellion, a force he channelled to spectacular effect to win power, or would he have sided with the Hanoi police who eventually stormed the Kaas concert? As the singer launched into an encore of her song 'Come into the Light', the power was cut, plunging the hall into darkness. Riot police equipped with masks and shields burst through the doors, flailing around with their clubs to disperse the exuberant crowd cranked up on their first taste of live rock.

Since that concert, Vietnam has become a fairly regular stop on the world tours of performers such as Sting and the Canadian Bryan Adams, both of whom performed in Ho Chi Minh City. Plans to bring James Brown to the city were nixed by the government; the concert was going to clash with celebrations for Ho Chi Minh's birthday. Vietnam, with its Rip Van Winkle popular culture that had skipped the years after 1975, became the place for faded stars to enjoy a fleeting revival. It was one of the few countries where the likes of Boney M, Leo Sayer, John Denver or Lobo would be able to attract even a glimmer of public attention, yet alone packed venues and flower-waving groupies.

With radio stations pumping out an insipid diet of easy-listening melodies and karaoke encouraging a new respect for such artistes as the Carpenters, Vietnam was suddenly awash with performers. During his shows in Hanoi, John Denver paid tribute to the restorative effects of karaoke on his career, claiming he had heard his country and western numbers drifting from bars across Vietnam. Denver, the first American singer to perform in the Vietnamese capital, packed them in for two nights, although at $30 a seat many Vietnamese were reluctant to fork out to hear another foot-stomping rendition of 'Take Me Home, Country Road'.

The dated feel, quite charming to outsiders, didn't last long. By the mid 1990s Vietnam was sucking in popular culture from around the world at such a pace that clubs were playing the latest techno dance music from London or New York within a few weeks of its release. The transmission of music, fashion and dance steps was as fast as MTV; the young Saigonese in Gossip, the hot club for a while, took only a few hours to become proficient hip-hop dancers. Fashions took a little longer to reach the city as they had to be copied in sweatshops and sold in the markets.

Through magazines, television, music videos and contact with foreigners, young Vietnamese absorbed and remade trends that originated half a world away. Lyrics to songs were published in newspapers, the grim social commentary of black rap artists about American inner cities was translated for an eager Vietnamese audience. Such was the demand for this service that people wrote to papers requesting the words to their favourite songs.

Even what are considered subcultures in the West have permeated the increasingly porous membrane around Vietnam. In Ho Chi Minh City, at the Phuong Cac café, hundreds of gay men gather on Sunday mornings. The air shimmers with expensive cologne as the young show off their designer clothes and buffed bodies. Logos of designers like Versace and Calvin Klein abound and most are real, not the fakes that are common in Asia. Everything from the clothes, the pumped-up muscles, the haircuts – many had a Caesar cut with a short shaggy fringe that was ubiquitous for a while in the mid 1990s – to the attitudes and confidently open manner had been sucked in from a gay culture that had transcended all borders; the café could have been in Soho or in San Francisco's Castro District. Just a few years ago this level of spending, never mind the openly declared sexuality, would have been unthinkable, but by the 1990s urban Vietnam had truly found a place in the world culture of youth and public consumption.

The parents of this new extravagant generation grew up during the war; few of them had much contact with the outside world and even most people in the South had little to do with the Americans before 1975. In the North their exposure to other cultures was limited to occasional East European movies and a limited array of approved Russian novels translated into Vietnamese. It was a time of endless campaigns such as the 'Three Readies': 'Ready to join the armed forces, to fight and to fight well; Ready to overcome difficulties and step up work production and studying; Ready to go anywhere and do anything required by the Fatherland.'

For the young, it was a stultifying environment of duty and obligation; youth was celebrated for its sacrifices and martyrdom and was always overlaid with the spectre of death. A typical animated children's cartoon made in Hanoi in 1968 had the following synopsis in the studio's catalogue: 'US aggressors spray noxious chemicals to kill the flora and fauna. Little Set is angry so he throws his axe into a minefield. The enemy post is completely destroyed.'

Not everyone fitted the heroic, self-sacrificing model. War sometimes had a liberating effect on social and sexual mores; if one is going off to die in battle, it is hard to care about convention. In 1971, teenagers were being bombarded with a campaign known as the 'Three builds and two Antis': 'Build up working attitude, respect and good behaviour, Anti theft and unwholesome behaviour in boy-girl relations.' If it was necessary to have a campaign against it, unwholesome behaviour in boy-girl relations was obviously not entirely unknown.

In South Vietnam, the sinister Madame Nhu, the sister-in-law to President Ngo Dinh Diem and official first lady, had also tried to deal with the pressing issue of unwholesomeness, but with considerably less success than the puritans in the North. Her strict Catholic family rules outlawed divorce, adultery and dancing. She was even said to have proposed a ban on padded bras until the problems of police enforcement were made clear.

After Diem and Nhu's husband were assassinated during a coup in 1963, the rules were lifted almost overnight; the middle-class youth of Saigon was free to take everything that America could give in the 1960s: the frug; high, lacquered beehives and eye-popping mini-dresses; The Beach Boys, The Doors and Bob Dylan; flares and love beads. Life in the South was far from hedonistic; the war was as much of a constant presence as it was in the North. The more serious side of 1960s popular culture also infected the country. They even had their own Dylan and Joan Baez: Trinh Cong Son, a poet and songwriter whose works were banned in the South and Khanh Ly, the singer intimately connected with Son's mournful songs of war.

In 1975, all this came to an end. Khanh Ly left for California where she remains a star in the Viet Kieu community. Son stayed on in

Vietnam. He was sent to work on a farm for four years and when he returned to the city he was banned from performing songs written before the fall of Saigon. Only in 1989 was he allowed to perform them again, but even to this day the most controversial songs about the civil war and Viet Cong attacks on civilians are banned. Son still has a vast number of fans for his mournful, romantic melodies, but it was his piercing lyrics that attacked both sides of the conflict that earned him the suspicions of all the governments.

Bans were a serious issue. A young singing star, Pham Ngoc Son, was arrested for performing pre-1975 songs at a private birthday party in Ho Chi Minh City in 1994. He later received a one-year suspended sentence for 'abusing the rights to freedom and democracy by disputing the benefits of the state and social organisations'.

Fearful of the insidious influences of popular music, the government has tried to establish some controls. Rock bands must register with the Ministry of Culture and Information, which has a list of what the official in charge of the controls called 'good cultural products'. This largely meant syrupy love songs or those with titles like 'The Brigade Departs', 'The Driver's Song' and 'A Moment for the Fatherland'. Only about 250 songs dating from before 1975 were on the approved play list; anything that mentioned peace, the collapse of Communism, the Berlin Wall, sex or violence was banned.

A young Hanoian musician whose band played mostly Beatles' covers laughed off the restrictions, saying they were not very onerous. He took a ministry official out for a drink every six months, showed him some lyrics he didn't understand and paid a bribe. John Lennon's 'Give Peace a Chance' was heard another day in Hanoi.

Hanoi in the early 1990s felt a little how the United States must have felt in the 1950s. War and economic depressions were over, people had more money and more access to consumer goods that took on almost totemic value as symbols of a new open social order. People no longer shopped in the drab state department store on the corner of Hoan Kiem Lake that was stocked with a limited range of dusty and undesirable goods. Markets exploded in size, shops were filled with new and varied fashions and many city-dwellers had enough money to buy things that would have been luxuries a few years earlier.

Dressed in smarter clothes and better fed than they had been in a generation, the young of Hanoi took to cruising the streets on their motorbikes. On Saturday nights they would parade around Hoan Kiem Lake on their Honda Dream II bikes, which were snapped up despite a price tag of more than ten times Vietnam's per capita GDP of $250.

Promenading soon evolved into racing the bikes at high speeds through the city streets. The races began in Ho Chi Minh City but soon spread to Hanoi. Racers would wait until the early hours before starting the high-speed chases through the narrow streets of the Old City and around the wide boulevards that ring Hoan Kiem Lake. Large crowds gathered at the lake on public holidays to wait for the races. As the whine of under-powered engines being pushed to their very limits grew louder, the crowd would wait in silence until the racers burst into view and screeched their way around the lake to loud cheers from spectators.

Tan, a 22-year-old who now works for a foreign publisher in Hanoi, used to join the throng of racers vying to win up to 20 million dong (about $1,800) in the shorter races around Hanoi. 'I loved the speed and freedom, I loved the bikes,' he says, already dreamily nostalgic for a pastime he says he gave up when he left college. For Tan, as for thousands of other young people, speed meant liberation from the family and other forces of control; it provided a new view of life outside of these constraints. A whole sub-culture developed around the races, with organisers who secretly plotted out weekends of motorbike duelling. There was a special vocabulary, high stakes gambling and women skilled in riding side-saddle in perilously short miniskirts. As if the races were not already dangerous enough, special variations were added to spice them up; a favourite was to race with the brake cables detached.

Much of the thrill came from evading the police who tried desperately to stop the races, without much success. Early on Christmas morning in 1994, dozens of racers zipped around the lake, suddenly changing directions and darting down a side street to avoid the police. As a police jeep came around the lake, a large crowd of spectators launched a fusillade of rocks that smashed its windows and sent the driver fleeing.

The police did get better at stopping the races; barricades were set up at key junctions and officers were equipped with high-powered motorbikes, stun weapons and indelible paint sprays. Two police-men would single out a weaker-looking racer on the edge of the pack and hunt him down, like lions picking off a lame gazelle. Once they got near to the racer, they would often tap him with a cattle prod, a jolt of blue light sending him skidding off the bike. Once caught they would be roughed up a little, handcuffed and their motorcycles confiscated. Only a few ever received jail terms; rumours constantly circulated in Hanoi that most racers were chil-dren of the city's powerful political élite who could easily keep their embarrassing offspring out of the newspapers and out of jail.

In a futile attempt to blunt the youthful sense of immortality that contributed to the racing craze, the police put up displays of autopsy photographs of people killed in bike accidents, including a gruesome series of a young woman nearly decapitated when she came off the back of her boyfriend's bike during a race. None of this had much effect, although the races did diminish in frequency over the years and the authorities turned to other new social problems involving the young, such as drug use and football hooliganism. These stories came to dominate the anxious news reporting on the misbehaviour of youth. Meanwhile, according to some riders, the former 'professionals' who had earned good livings by racing turned their biking skills to drive-by purse snatching.

In the surge of consumption that took over the city, a motorbike was an essential purchase. Top of almost everyone's wish-list was a purple, $2,800 Honda Dream II that has reached cult status as a symbol of success. 'If you want to do business and you ride a bicy-cle, no one will believe you have the money to do anything,' said Nguyen Viet Hong, the owner of a motorbike wash shop, one of the many spin-off businesses generated by the rush to buy motorbikes. There are 600 motorbike wash shops in Hanoi alone, employing 3,000 people. Repairs and spare parts provide work for thousands more.

Just a few years previously, entrenched poverty and tight controls on consumption meant few could afford even a whole chicken. The handful that could afford a motorbike faced a lengthy battle with bureaucracy for permission as well as some suspicion about how they obtained their money. Now dealers say wealthy urbanites think nothing of buying several Hondas in one go, equipping each member of the family with one. More than three million motorbikes now throng Vietnam's streets and around 500,000 are legally imported every year at a cost of more than $1 billion a year, or about 7 per cent of its gross domestic product. Add in around 500,000 motorbikes that have been smuggled in and the total figure spent in the past five years reaches nearly $8 billion, more money than the country has received in actual inflows of aid and foreign investment in the same period.

The biggest impact has been on Vietnam's savings rate, which according to figures from the World Bank stands around 16–18 per cent of GDP, half of that in the Asian tiger economies such as Taiwan or Singapore. In the early 1990s it was better to hold wealth in a motorbike rather than in risky banks or in cash during a time of inflation; Honda Dream IIs held their value. Dream IIs were at the centre of some complex financial transactions; businesses in need of loans would buy them on hire purchase and then resell them immediately, usually for a small profit. They could then invest the cash in their businesses and pay back the dealer over the next year.

Dream IIs are on the decline as fashion items; they have become ubiquitous and thus devalued. Now in Hanoi the richest consumers buy massive copies of Harley-Davidson bikes that actually have tiny 100cc engines that are under the 175cc limit set by the police. With their huge chopper handlebars, leather seats and chrome accessories they have become a display item for some flashier types, while the Dream II becomes the workhorse of the respectable middle class.

John Lennon may have been responsible for one of the first tremors in the youthquake that is shaking up Vietnam. In December 1993, a concert to mark the anniversary of his death turned into a brief protest against the police. A group of young men started an impromptu march around Hoan Kiem Lake carrying a poster of the late Beatle and singing 'Hey Jude'. When the police tried to stop them, they hurled bottles and burnt furniture. The crowd was dispersed after several arrests, but it was an eye-opening event for the authorities who were starting to deal with a rise in rebellious behaviour. For most young Vietnamese this meant staying out a little late or perhaps a few furtive gropes in the dark recesses of Lenin Park. Rebellion sometimes went further than this; since the mid 1980s there has been a marked rise in reports of juvenile crime. The peace generation that grew up after the war has become the consumption generation. Profoundly apathetic towards politics and sometimes hostile to authority, they are unashamedly more interested in their personal welfare and achievement than broader social issues.

The peace generation represents a challenge to a system that conflates national identity with morality and political beliefs. For years Vietnamese were told that to be patriotic, to have a sense of national identity, they also had to behave in a certain way and believe unswervingly in the system. Decadent, consumerist behaviour was an affront to socialism and the nation. Nationalism and social order have been closely linked; politicians and the media generally blame 'foreign influences' for any breakdown in their social order, even though the West has had only a limited impact in Vietnam in the past two decades. There is a fear that the country is losing its roots, that the myths that have sustained it are losing their appeal. This was brought home in the movie *Please Forgive Me* by the director Luu Trong Ninh which explored the different response to the war of a younger generation. The movie, which is about the making of another movie, shows the tensions between the older generation who feel their children do not understand their sacrifices, and a younger generation who feel their elders have bequeathed them a bankrupt and morally dislocated nation. Ninh was forced to cut a number of scenes, including one in which a group of people mock the Ho Chi Minh Youth League, the training ground for future Party members.

Former Party chief Nguyen Van Linh expressed views shared by many of his generation when he said young people 'have lost their sense of self-restraint and now indulge in opportunism, the cult of money and the pursuit of leisure. Some of them derive pleasure from drinking parties and places of fun and enjoyment, while others seek consolation in saints and gods at temples and pagodas to relieve personal sorrows or detach themselves from life'.

A newspaper headline bleakly summed up the options that the government saw for young people: 'Misguided, Selfish or

Obedient? Who are Today's Youth?' Many young people have refused to accept the narrow definitions of order and identity that Party rule has tried to impose, and have been less inclined to swallow its arguments against foreign influences. They see no contradiction between their identity as Vietnamese and an enjoyment in new forms of popular culture that takes not just from the United States, but also from a range of countries in Asia and from Viet Kieu communities around the world.

In the mid 1990s those artists who somehow crossed the borders between cultures were increasingly popular. Jimmii Nguyen, a law graduate from California turned Viet Kieu heart-throb, was the first overseas Vietnamese singer to be allowed back to tour. Another huge star was Elvis Cong, a pompadoured magician who brought a little Las Vegas to the Vietnamese-Soviet Cultural Palace in Hanoi. His shows were hugely popular; tickets cost $5 but were scalped for up to $30 each outside his shows. He did twenty shows in one month in Hanoi and all sold out.

Cong's show blended the cute with just a hint of sexuality. He had the required magician's assistants in skimpy sequined outfits and performed with several singers in figure-hugging lycra outfits, but he was careful never to cross the line. After tying up his lithe assistant in a cage, he made her disappear but diffused the sexual tension of the scenario by covering the cage again and magically filling it with small girls in ballet tutus.

The 37-year-old Cong lived a strange dual life. He was hugely famous in Vietnam and a constant feature in the tabloid press. Surrounded by a rather seedy entourage, he toured the country almost constantly, playing to packed theatres even in the furthest backwaters. At home in Orange County in California he led a more banal existence as the owner of a pizza restaurant. Success in Vietnam did not come easily due to the suspicion of overseas Vietnamese. 'At the beginning it was terrible, it was very hard to take the first step,' he said of his efforts to bring his act to Vietnam in the early 1990s. 'I'm Vietnamese but I live in the United States so that was a big problem,' he said. 'For a foreigner, it would have been nothing.'

Initially Viet Kieu entertainers were scorned; now they are appreciated for livening up the rather stagnant local entertainment scene with new methods and some glitz that can still pass as sophistica-tion. Cong says that now officials understand his shows, there are no problems even in the more conservative provincial towns, where he has been known to fill a 15,000-seat stadium. He attributes his huge success to an understanding of how 'to blend American styles for Vietnam', such as his opening act in which he arrives on stage in a puff of smoke dressed in tight black leather and jeans astride a Harley-Davidson bike. The opening is a direct rip-off of the American magician David Copperfield's stage entrance.

Many Vietnamese, particularly intellectuals, loathe performers like Cong; newspapers questioned the cultural value of his shows and suggested that he was unemployed in America and just taking advantage of Vietnamese gullibility to make a buck. Others have sneered at any attempt by Viet Kieu to participate in the cultural life of the country. A common line was to suggest that Viet Kieu could not possibly understand Vietnam nowadays. The rather snide cov-erage he received didn't stop Cong selling out dozens of performances a year as people paid to see a figure who combined some foreign glamour with a close connection to his audience.

Another popular star of the 1990s was Phung Thao, the daughter of an American serviceman and a Vietnamese woman. Instead of leaving like most Amerasians, Thao endured years of taunts from classmates and worked her way to success as a singer, becoming a familiar face on television and in the cafés of Ho Chi Minh City. In 1996 the *Tuoi Tre* newspaper named her album *Café Alone* the best of the year. Thao says she was treated terribly when she was young because of her mixed heritage, although 'when Amerasians started getting out of Vietnam suddenly they became very popular'. Other Vietnamese would pay Amerasians to say that they were parents or family to enable them to emigrate to the United States.

Now there is a certain cachet in being mixed. Thao's looks and her wavy hair are emulated, not scorned, and her slightly husky voice, different from the chirpy sopranos of so many Vietnamese, is widely admired. Thao satisfies a growing demand for entertainment that bridges the gap between Vietnamese and Western popular culture. It is part of a growing acceptance and enjoyment of a wide range of cultures and influences and an appreciation of 'fusion cultures' that blend elements from overseas and Vietnam.

The post-war generation tends towards greater diversity of opinion; they have been moulded by broader influences and are less inclined to accept authority. They have grown up in a world of both greater opportunities and greater disenchantment. Asked about who were Vietnam's heroes, many young people simply looked blank; a handful would name a football star or entertainer.

In 1996 an eye-opening event illustrated the extent to which figures from popular culture had replaced those from politics or the military as central figures of heroism or tragedy. Le Cong Tuan Anh, a young actor known for his sweetly melancholy film presence, committed suicide by taking an overdose of anti-malarial pills after becoming distraught when his girlfriend's family refused her permission to marry him because of his poor background. Anh, who was twenty-eight at the time, had grown up in an orphanage and endured a tough childhood until he became famous in 1990 with a breakthrough role in the movie *The Bitter Taste of Love*. As an actor he tore down traditions in a similar way to Marlon Brando and other method actors of the 1950s. Before playing a role in which he had a breakdown and went mad, he spent time in a hospital studying the mentally ill; a routine move perhaps in Hollywood, but still unusual in Vietnam. Anh's background, the poverty and hardship of his life and his innocent demeanour in his movies were powerful ingredients that combined into stardom.

On hearing the news of his death in a hospital in Ho Chi Minh City, sobbing teenagers gathered to mourn the star whose luminosity had been greatly enhanced by his tragic and youthful demise. Newspaper reports competed in the extent of detail they gave about his death; the articles were in such demand that street traders photocopied them and sold them on the streets. His funeral was attended by tens of thousands of fans in what was one of the largest gatherings of recent decades in Ho Chi Minh City.

References to the past are pervasive in newspapers, movies and other media in Vietnam, but a survey of 1,800 young people in Ho Chi Minh City found the majority were ignorant of much of their own history. According to the historian David Marr, the survey showed that more than a third could not recognise the name Hung Vuong – the legendary founder of Vietnam's first dynasty.

Two-thirds could not recognise the name Truong Dinh, the nine-teenth-century anti-colonial rebel leader. More than 80 per cent could not tell their questioners anything about the origins of the street name where they lived, even though most streets are named for important historical figures.

More than 85 per cent could identify the Argentinian football star Maradona and the singer Michael Jackson. These figures would be no great surprise in the West, but for some Vietnamese they were profoundly troubling. The country's very identity as defined by the Party was tied to figures that were unknown to many young people. Propaganda just did not reach them over the din of other entertainments; the survey revealed that only 3 per cent of university students and only about 10 per cent of young people in general enjoyed movies with revolutionary themes. These accounted for a significant proportion of Vietnamese movies produced each year.

For some members of the older generation, the failure to absorb this history threatens the very survival of Vietnamese identity; indeed the young are now seen as something of a problem. The younger generation is probably no more likely than their parents to find a consensus on national identity, social mores, political values or economic direction. But they do seem to agree on a few things; the limited amount of data released from a 1992 government-sponsored survey of young people showed strong support for further reforms but also limited interest in democracy. This may have been a reluctance to discuss politics with those carrying out the survey, but it also probably reflected a feeling among young people that material benefits come first. Eighty per cent of students and three-quarters of young people in general put work as their most important issue in their lives and indeed there was a remarkable drive for self-improvement in this generation with many young people attending language and computer classes after work.

The survey showed a widening gap between the interests and aspirations of university students, mostly middle-class and urban, and youth in general, who are mostly from the countryside. Students were more interested in foreign movies and music, whereas in the countryside, where their is less penetration of other cultures, there was a strong interest in more traditional forms of entertainment.

The very image of youth has changed in the past decade. Once celebrated as heroic and optimistic as they marched off to war, young people have started to be viewed by their elders as disturbing, even potentially dangerous. Stories abound of teachers killed by their students, or rising juvenile crime, of young people becoming almost predatory. In 1989, more than 5,000 people gathered in the southern province of Dong Nai to hear the trial of sixteen-year-old Huynh Phu Son who had seriously injured a teacher. The boy was jailed for seven years for the attack, which stunned a public that had become fearful for the survival of its treasured value of respect for education.

Given the paucity of statistics on crime, it is hard to say whether there has been a dramatic increase in delinquency or whether it is now reported more often by the media. Juvenile crime is said to have risen 150 per cent between 1991 and 1995, according to Nguyen Xuan Thuy, a researcher at the Institute of Criminology. The press has said teenagers commit four out of five of all crimes in Ho Chi Minh City, but this figure is certainly overstated. Drug use is said to have soared, attendance at school slumped. But newspapers that once only celebrated Party successes now make their money by selling sex and scandal. These are ingredients best spiced with youth, hence the prominence of reports on underage hookers and teen crime sprees.

Changing values, particularly in a society that has been so tightly controlled for so long, are bound to raise anxieties and these are coming out in the changing image of young people. Young Vietnamese defy categorisation. There are 40 million Vietnamese under the age of twenty-five; more than half the population were born after 1975. Their world and ideas are much more diverse than those of their parents and they tend to be more outspoken. They are often portrayed as feckless and cynical, but younger Vietnamese often have a more vigorous response to the injustices of their society than the rather more cowed generation above them. At a conference of youth organisations in 1988, several speakers directly confronted the government's record of failure in providing for young people, accusing them of failing an entire generation.

Mai, a young soldier, told the conference: 'We army youth are a great force standing on the front line of combat, enduring every hardship and sacrifice for the Fatherland, but we are constantly worried and concerned for our future. We don't know how we will live after we complete our military obligations and return home. What will we do? Is there a place in society for us? How can youths be prepared to join the army and have peace of mind in taking up arms in combat to protect the Fatherland when going to work or study in foreign countries are this son and that nephew of someone holding position and power? The power of those who have money in their hands?'

By 1992, disaffection with the political system saw a decline in membership of the Ho Chi Minh Youth Union to fewer than 2 million members, down from 4.7 million in the late 1980s. Membership in the Union had once been a requirement for entry into university and it was the route to all-important membership in the Party. With its political role diminishing, the Union took on pressing social issues and became a channel for discontent. Its newspaper *Tuoi Tre,* was one of the most outspoken in its criticism of government policies. 'Young people have been badly served by their families, schools and by society. Their basic needs such as employment, study, recreation and health have not been attended to,' it said in an editorial.

One of the sorest points is the failure of Vietnam's education system, sometimes still mistakenly touted as a great success story. The Party had once placed much emphasis on literacy; Vietnamese used to joke that they were all given the skills of reading but then banned from reading any books. Supporters of the government in Hanoi often made much of their education programmes; officials themselves seemed to give a more realistic assessment. Vu Mao, a former youth leader and now a senior official in the National Assembly, wrote of his dismay at the education system in the journal *Tap Chi Cong San.* Complaining of the failure of schools to instil moral lessons, he unusually blamed not foreign influences or consumerism but the Party's education restrictions. 'School lessons usually lean towards generalised political sentiments such as revolutionary heroism, comradeship, companionship and patriotism which are presented in an extremely vague and superficial way.' Mao complained that the number of children attending school was too low and that illiteracy had re-emerged as a serious problem.

'Moreover, the quality of instruction at schools is very poor.'

By 1996, the Minister of Education, Tran Hong Quan, had admitted that education 'is experiencing a quantitative stagnation and a qualitative decline'. The country was short of more than 100,000 teachers and was using shift systems in some towns because it lacked enough classrooms. Fewer than half of all university professors actually taught the subject in which they had earned their own degree; only about three-quarters actually had a degree and only 13 per cent had a doctorate. Colleges lacked books, schools were almost completely bereft of facilities. The schools that foreign visitors had marvelled about were mostly Potemkin colleges or those reserved for the children of the élite.

Only 12 per cent of Vietnamese older than fifteen were illiterate, better than the average of 24 per cent for Asia and the Pacific. But Vietnam had only 33 per cent of its students in secondary school compared with 54 per cent across the region. The numbers going on to secondary school declined by around a third between 1986 and 1989 and the number of girls being sent to school has declined sharply. Students receiving tertiary education are few in comparison with other countries in the region. Vietnam sends twenty students to college per 10,000 people, Thailand, which has a severe problem of under-education, sends 166 per 10,000 and the Philippines 266 per 10,000. Vietnam's economic competitiveness in the region is likely to be severely constrained by its failure to educate beyond the primary level, and little is being done to improve the situation. In 1996 spending on education per pupil declined 20 per cent in real terms.

In the cities, richer parents now compete ferociously to get their children into the best schools. A high rank in the Party helps but money will now also get results. It is, however, a creeping source of resentment. Teachers have to be paid off so that children will be taught. Salaries in education are miserable; in the cities teachers earn $20 to $30 a month. They have to demand extra payments to survive. Private schools were legalised in 1988 and since then parents were asked to 'contribute' to state education. Children from poorer families are being forced to drop out earlier, particularly girls in the countryside, creating a new illiterate underclass whose economic opportunities are going to be seriously limited.

Each year more than a million young people join the job market; now they are doing it with almost no preparation. What is emerging is a lumpen-youth, a vast group with few skills and little education whose vision of the world has been formed in ways that are little comprehended. Popular culture has been a vast influence on their lives; it has recast their views on sex, violence, masculinity, femininity, heroism and national identity. While their parents grew up with the idea that fighting foreigners was heroic, a younger generation of men have been more marked by martial arts movies which are watched avidly in almost every home and café across the country. Young women have been shaped not by the demands of war that freed women from many societal constraints, but by re-emerging images of femininity in which women are heavily made-up, trussed up in tight *ao dai*s and always ready to serve their demanding menfolk.

The state no longer controls ideas about what it is to be heroic. While the Vietnamese media still harks on about security and national independence, central aspects of the Communist Party's legitimacy, the subject arouses little interest among the young; asked what they cared about in a poll, only 20 per cent said the nation's security, the least important item on a list of twelve. Work, economic status, education and corruption all ranked significantly higher. Encouragingly for the Party, democracy and social equality were a concern of only 21 per cent of young people.

The enriching of popular culture has also heightened a sense of individualism. Previously 'culture' existed mostly in the public sphere – it was broadcast over loudspeakers, seen on televisions or enjoyed in stadiums or cinemas. Movies were shown in factories, people watched a single channel of television amid a crowd at a café or at the home of a neighbour. Nowadays people listen to music on personal stereos or watch their choice of videos at home; people make individual choices, they no longer have their entertainment imposed on them. This is bound to lead to a degree of stratification as people mark themselves out by the choices they make; it is another aspect of the unravelling of the imagined equalities of Vietnamese life.

A state that once firmly set the boundaries of consumption by forcing mass choices on people has lost control; a new generation of young people have grown up with the pulsing beat of international pop culture. This is not the overwhelmingly American force that many suspect. There are inventive local producers of all types of popular culture. Taiwanese and Hong Kong singers are as popular as Western performers. Japanese *manga* – often intensely violent cartoon books – are better known than Superman. Doremon, a marsupial cat from Japan, was one of the biggest hits of the 1990s, his round face plastered everywhere. After a diet of stodgy and humourless Eastern European cartoons or drab social realist literature, the simple, whimsical comics have evoked a deep response from Vietnamese. At the height of its popularity, the publishers of the *Doremon* comic book were churning out more than 160,000 copies a week – more than a hundred times their normal print run – while sales of videos and cassette tapes featuring the cat broke all records.

Ever vigilant against the evils of 'Western values', the cultural commissars were more relaxed about the import of Asian popular culture, particularly that from Japan, which is generally seen by officials as a modern and moral nation. This was encouraged with a careful campaign by the Japanese to build up their acceptability. They started with the television series *Oshin*, a serial that depicts the harsh life and struggles of a village woman in nineteenth-century Japan. 'All the young and old in my family watch *Oshin* because for the older ones it reminds them of when life was so difficult here, while for the young ones it explains how things used to be,' said Nguyen Thi Mai, a secondary school teacher. *Little House on the Prairie* has also been hugely popular as a replacement for Oshin.

Oshin was useful in improving Japan's image and dispelling myths about a country that until recently had very few links with Vietnam since its troops were there during World War II. 'The first thing the Vietnamese think of when they see Japanese people is money, so it's good for them to see in this programme that we weren't always rich and that things were difficult for us once,' said a Japanese businessman.

There has been some resistance among an older generation who remember the Japanese occupation. 'Japan is popular here just for its goods, not for its culture,' said the academic Phan Cu De.

'Although in Vietnam by the beginning of the century some revolutionaries talked about the similarities between our two countries
and two races, Vietnamese remember the atrocities committed by
the Japanese in 1944 and 1945,' he said. 'Even now, the Japanese
don't have a perfect image here. There are issues of sexual harassment of workers, their harsh attitudes towards other Asians. I think
the Japanese are laying the foundation for a strategy to conquer the
Vietnamese market. As we all know, Vietnam and Southeast Asia
are the most promising markets for Japan. We know how the
Vietnamese love, even worship Japanese consumer goods.'

Consumption is taking on an ever increasing role in life, mostly in
the cities where incomes are significantly higher than in the countryside. The US embargo had kept out many goods, although
Coca-Cola and other products were smuggled in from Thailand
and China. Immediately after the embargo was lifted in February
1994, Coca-Cola and Pepsi began bottling their drinks in Vietnam;
Pepsi's joint venture bottling line and a blitzkrieg of advertising
were ready to go as soon as President Bill Clinton lifted the trade
ban. When American companies held a trade show in Hanoi
during April the response was overwhelming. A crowd of thousands stampeded into the Giang Vo Exhibition Centre, nearly
knocking over stands in their desire just to look at American goods
even though nothing was actually on sale. When one company
started handing out small sachets of potpourri, their stand was
nearly submerged beneath the waving hands reaching out for the
free gifts.

The economic impact of consumption has become clear; the
Vietnamese are importing too much, sucking in consumer goods
that they cannot afford. Part of this is the result of pent-up demand,
but it is also about new forms of social competition. This is particularly strong among the young and has been widely noted. The
children of the middle classes in Hanoi and Ho Chi Minh City are
becoming important consumers. They demand their own motorbikes, their own pagers and cellular phones, extra tuition and
English classes as well as clothes and spending money. All this conspicuous consumption can only aggravate the emerging class
tensions; passers-by in Hanoi watching a small plump child on a

tiny but working motorbike looked daggers at the parents. Was it envy or contempt?

The ambivalence towards consumption and the open market comes across in the world of advertising, an industry geared to young people. Before 1986 there was no commercial advertising; now cities are covered with billboards and the media is mostly financed by advertisement sales. The government has allowed more than two dozen advertising agencies to open in Hanoi and Ho Chi Minh City, while thousands of small businesses make signs and provide other services. Advertising billings rose twenty times between 1990 and 1996 to more than $120 million. The government welcomed the economic benefits but there was a clear distaste for this most capitalist of businesses.

Advertising agencies followed the big international companies into Vietnam in the early 1990s but were working under difficult conditions with no clear regulations. A government crackdown in 1996 during which advertisements were torn down and signs painted over signalled a change in the diffuse regulatory environment. Local cultural offices began insisting on checking advertisements before they went to press or were put up, a process that led to some almost comic misunderstandings. The German lingerie company Triumph was stopped from advertising its underwear with the slogan 'Fashion and so much more'. The Ho Chi Minh City cultural office wanted to know exactly what 'so much more' really meant. Shell ran into trouble with its line 'You can be sure of Shell'. A bureaucrat decided that nobody should be allowed to put such confidence in an oil company. J&B Whisky faced problems because its colours – red and gold – were too close to those of the Vietnamese flag. Sony had to stop a television advertisement after many complaints; the ad showed a cute puppy watching television, an image that might seem harmless enough, but some viewers took it as an offensive suggestion that Vietnamese were like dogs. Advertising, it seemed, was a minefield of cultural sensitivities. The crackdown on advertising coincided with the official first day of its 'Three Nos' campaign against pornography, prostitution and gambling. While foreign advertising has never been explicitly labelled as a social evil, executives said the timing of the crusade was a case of guilt by association for the industry.

The political ramifications of consumption and popular culture are less easily measured than the economic impact. What is certain though is that the state is not good at producing its own entertainment in competition with the private sector. Up until 1986 all cultural production in Vietnam was state-controlled and subsidised; much of it was aimed at having a political impact. The money that once funded film-makers, dance troupes, opera companies and popular singers has dried up, but the market has not yet completely filled the gap.

The film industry has suffered more than any other area from the loss of subsidies. Movies have captured the imagination of Vietnamese since colonial times; Charlie Chaplin and the Three Stooges were enormously popular as they transcended any language barrier. The country's own film industry varied enormously between North and South; in the North, output centred on propaganda and the style owed much to Soviet cinema; in the South the emphasis was on flashier, Hong Kong-style direction and romances or adventures. After 1975, all film-makers came under the control of the state with a national company in Hanoi and the Giaiphong Studio in Ho Chi Minh City.

A rusting helicopter carcass and mounds of decrepit equipment littering the sound stage of the Giaiphong Studio are testament to the sorry state of the movie industry. Adjacent rooms that look like sets from a bleak apocalyptic thriller turn out to be workshops for lighting equipment, and offices are cobwebbed and dirty; it is all a long way from the glitz normally associated with film-making.

'The facilities are some of the oldest in Vietnam,' said the studio chief, Tran Thanh Hung, who has worked for the 'Liberation Studio' since its early days. 'Our equipment was mostly made in the 1950s. Only the promise of more state funds and increasing interest in making films in Vietnam by foreign companies, mostly from the United States and France, is offering a glimmer of hope.

Two co-productions received strong international attention – *Cyclo*, by French director Tran Anh Hung won the Golden Lion at Venice and a Vietnamese-Algerian film called *The Dust of Life* was nominated for an Oscar for best foreign film. The studio was also trying to line up a number of projects with American film-makers.

Paramount was planning to shoot Graham Greene's *The Quiet American*, and the government had given the green light to a movie of André Malraux's *The Royal Way*, starring Kiefer Sutherland.

But the hope of salvation from abroad almost always was dashed by the collapse of projects or the government's refusal to allow foreign directors to shoot in Vietnam. A plan to film *Fields of Fire* – the war book by former US Navy Secretary James Webb – came to nothing. *Cyclo* did raise the profile of Giaiphong overseas but the controversial movie has not helped much at home. The intense and surreal vision of crime in Ho Chi Minh City was too violent to be shown in Vietnam, said the Giaiphong Studio chief Hung, who was furious at the director for making such a controversial movie.

Giaiphong Studio, like almost every cultural organisation in Vietnam has its roots in the war. It was founded in 1962 by Viet Cong guerrillas fighting the South Vietnamese government and began by producing newsreels and propaganda films to be shown in villages controlled by the National Liberation Front. 'The golden era of Vietnamese film-making was back then during the war,' said Hung, who began his career as a battlefield cameraman shooting newsreel footage.

After 1975 Giaiphong took over the Institute of Cinematography in Saigon and several of the private studios that had flourished during the 1960s producing sugary musicals and dramas that were banned when the Communists took over. Up until the end of the 1980s, the studio employed 400 people and enjoyed subsidies that enabled it to produce about twenty documentaries, features and animated cartoons a year.

But few people, particularly among the young, nowadays want to see the weighty socialist genre films now that illegally imported videos offer up a range of Hong Kong martial arts movies and Hollywood action heroes. There has also been a dramatic decline in the number of cinemas; there were 300 across the country in 1993 but fewer than seventy remain, and movies are no longer shown in state factories or on communes.

Aware that it has lost control over popular culture, the government has been saying it will fund more movies, but old habits die hard. The scripts that are approved by the Ministry of Culture and Information are barely different from the old propaganda fare during the war. Films ordered by the state, often on historical or social subjects, cost up to $180,000 – three time most other productions – but they 'have no social or economic impact' because of their low quality, according to Dang Nhat Minh, the country's leading director and chairman of the Cinematographers' Association of Vietnam. Films on the battles of Dien Bien Phu and the Ho Chi Minh Campaign for Saigon in 1975 were ignored by the public; these movies, pricey to make by Vietnamese standards; played to almost empty houses for a few days before being replaced with more commercial fare, most often 'Instant Noodle' martial arts flicks made on the cheap in Ho Chi Minh City.

At a conference of the Association in 1995, a deep malaise permeated the air. The industry was in a state of complete crisis, said Thanh An, Vice Chairman of the group, 'and there is nothing that could likely help it'. Most of the budgets for films go on salaries and hiring equipment so little is left for sets and other costs; salaries for actors and directors are around $20 a month. Cameras and other equipment 'would have been thrown away thirty years ago in other countries,' said Huu Muoi, a trainee director and graduate of the Moscow Cinematography Institute.

But Tran Van Thuy, a documentary maker who has worked with Britain's Channel Four, said the biggest problems 'were not about money but about the way we make films'. Film-makers lacked skills as well as a willingness to be creative, he said. Censorship generates frustrations as films must be submitted several times to committees that can cut 'inappropriate' scenes or scrap entire projects.

A small island of optimism emerged in VTV3, the country's third television channel that was set up to provide entertainment rather than just folk dancing and martial music. Since the start of broadcasts in the late 1970s, the state channel had offered mostly programming from Eastern Europe and some locally-produced shows. One young Hanoian recalled the excitement over a Bulgarian detective series in which the raffish Eastern European had a different girlfriend every episode; it was chaste by today's standards but in the early 1980s it was the raciest, most exciting entertainment around.

VTV3 broke through some of the barriers by focusing on entertainment rather than edification. Its most popular programmes have been SV96, a student quiz show, and *Van Nghe Chu Nhat* (Sunday Culture), a programme that mixed news and advice with a short, locally-produced movie, mostly somewhat tacky melodramas shot on the tiniest of budgets. Lai Van Sam, the director and presenter of SV96 said the programmes were the first in Vietnam specifically aimed at the young. 'We've never paid enough attention to entertainment, it was all just propaganda,' he said. 'The biggest problem was persuading VTV to take the risk, they are still afraid of addressing a younger generation.' The programme is a light-hearted mix of quiz show and obstacle course not far from *Jeux Sans Frontiers*. It attracts more than 10,000 spectators to each filming and is made on a tiny budget of around 20 million dong ($1,600) for a two-hour show.

Sam himself is emblematic of the new Vietnam. He is the host of a cheesy game show who throws out phrases from Communist Party documents and mixes his high-speed entertainment-industry patter with meaningless official mantras about 'Industrialisation and Modernisation'. At ease with money and commercialism, he is searching for a new vocabulary for the state's propaganda – he calls it 'information about life' – through which the Party can reach young people. 'I think we've done something right as young people love the show while old people hate it. They write in complaining that it is only entertainment, that it is too commercial, that it is all about advertising.' Not all young people saw it that way. Even VTV's relatively fresh offerings were still too bound with official rhetoric for the cool youth of Hanoi who were not taken in by skits on social evils or calls for young people to work harder.

VTV3's novel approach – putting on shows that people might actually want to watch and packing the schedules with cheap schlock from the 1970s such as *Charlie's Angels*, has been a tough act for the other more politically worthy channels to follow. VTV1 is supposed to focus on political and national culture, while the organisation's second channel covers science, technology and education. Major urban areas also have their own channels, mostly showing entertainment and sports. Several of these channels signed up with foreign companies including those owned by the media tycoons Kerry Packer and Rupert Murdoch, but nothing came of the deals. The 'social evils' campaign intervened and close relationships with foreigners were considered suspect. In changes to the investment law in 1996, foreign investment in television was put off-limits as the state tried to close off another door.

Television has emerged as the most powerful means of communication in the country but it presented formidable difficulties for the state. It had to be entertaining but at the same time reinforce the values the government wanted to promote; it had to entertain and inform across a widening generation gap; it had to strengthen a sense of national identity while accommodating a hunger for foreign programming. Juggling these contradictory demands has been tough; those working at VTV say the organisation is under constant close scrutiny from ideologues and that its managers have grown increasingly timid. But if VTV is unable to provide entertainment, people will find alternatives. Nowadays choice is unavoidable.

Choice breeds diversity and diversity is still a problem in Vietnam where the state has devoted considerable energy to presenting a unified vision of national identity, culture and politics. It is hard to reconcile the national mythologies of a Spartan and non-consumerist people to the grasping reality of a poor people who desire to be rich. Consumption is bound to raise certain ideological problems. Popular culture has been an urban phenomenon in a country bound together by a rural identity; for decades the Communists cast the cities as dens of greed and indulgence and tried in vain to iron out the differences between urban and rural.

To the ideologues of Hanoi, Western popular culture has a distasteful stench to it. Mass culture has become, for the Party, a sign of societal decay to be bracketed together with other social evils. In fact the emergence of a complex and syncretic mass culture is a sign of the decay of the Party's power. They are unable to control its messages. Even when they try to co-opt it, as in the case of using the martial arts series about Judge Pao as a focus for their corruption campaigns, they are not completely in control. Martial arts movies serve up mixed political messages of Confucian respect for authority and for the idea of the individual challenging unworthy rulers. The élite may be remaking their ideas of politics in part through literature, but the masses are more likely to remake their notions of legitimacy, morality and politics through television in a way the Party does not understand and cannot completely control.

The rapidity of change in the arena of popular culture and consumption shows how much control the state has lost in the past decade and how much choice people have gained. In a decade, Vietnam has gone from a state of isolation from popular culture to seeing itself threatened from outside. The Party's desire to keep a lock on cultural decisions has left it even weaker than many other Asian countries in its capacity to maintain a unique identity in the face of globalisation, because its state sanction output of movies, music and other entertainment is so weak and unpopular, its artists and writers so hobbled by controls. Other Asian countries have shown that a vibrant and open cultural environment is often the best way to remain distinct.

What is emerging in Vietnam is a complex, hybrid culture with a multitude of messages, some of which reinforce what the state sees as traditional values, others that seriously undermine them. The reality is that this process has been going on for centuries; there is no pure set of Vietnamese values to undermine. Popular culture will not erode Vietnamese identity, it will remake it and keep it in a state of constant flux.

17

Conclusion

More than a decade into their new revolution, Vietnamese are wondering where the journey is taking them. When reforms began stripping away the burden of Communism, they created an unalloyed sense of hope about the future. The country had put behind it the worst failings of socialism in the 1980s, a time many Vietnamese, even senior officials, recall with some embarrassment. Vietnam would become rich, catch up with its neighbours, resume a place in the world community. Now this optimism is tainted with anxieties about what economic progress will mean in a society that must face the problems it once ignored. *Doi Moi* has torn off the veil under which Communism tried to force conformity on an atomised and diverse people. Vietnam can no longer hide difficult issues of national identity, history, religious faith, civil society, freedom and dissent.

The rhetoric of growth and change has awakened fears among conservatives who worry about the erosion of the Communist Party's power. There are concerns about the widening gaps in society between rich and poor, young and old, urban and rural. Vietnam once had a near equality of outcome in its economic policies – everyone ended up horribly poor. Now it has neither equality of opportunity nor equality of outcome but a state of intense competition muddled by the continuing intrusion of the state and the divisive forces of corruption.

The process of shedding all but the symbolism and language of Communism has been easy in comparison with coming up with a fresh vision for the country. Creating new ideas about government and identity that can cope with a diversity of economic, political, national and social views has stirred anxieties among the 2 million members of the Communist Party who rule over the other 74 million Vietnamese. This narrow political élite has not found it easy to cope with change; all the simple things have gone. The world can no longer be boiled down into classes, revolutionaries and counter-revolutionaries, progressive friends and imperialist enemies.

Before his death, the philosopher and anthropologist Ernest Gellner, a long-time opponent of Marxism, wrote in the British magazine *Prospect* of his dismay at the collapse of Communism in the Soviet Union and its empire. These societies had seen their moral order collapse, stripping their people of dignity. 'They had either believed, and now stand exposed as fools; or they had not and are now revealed to have been opportunists, hypocrites or cowards.' Communism had disestablished itself almost overnight in Europe, a first for such an important faith. This tumultuous abandonment of a major creed, Gellner wrote, 'may come to be seen as a disaster comparable with only the revolution itself'.

What Gellner preferred was a gradual transition in ideology and institutions that 'would preserve the idiom and ritual of the past, but empty it of content, or make its content adjustable to taste or occasion'. Red flags and statues of Lenin were fine, the economic and political controls of Marxism and its control over society were not. Communist parties should keep up appearances while dumping ideas about class conflict, central planning and communal ownership. The Party, in Gellner's words, 'would concern itself with the fight against enthusiasm; ensure that no one took Marxism with undue seriousness'.

The Vietnamese Communist Party has taken on that role. It barely bothers to scratch around for a coherent ideology nowadays, acknowledging that its aim is to keep its monopoly on power, not carry the country down the path to some Marxist utopia. Within its ranks it guards against overenthusiasm and, indeed, it has converted its once fevered members from Marxism to Market-Leninism without much resistance. It can still put on a show, although the Vietnamese were never really masters of pageantry; their festivities were always frayed and cheap. Nowadays the Communist Party goes through the motions and so do its members. If, like the former leaders Pham Van Dong or Nguyen Van Linh, officials are inclined to rail at the evils of capitalism or lust for a little class warfare, they are gently led away and told to be quiet. When Pham Van Dong, Prime Minister for a third of this century, said in an interview that he feared that the 'dangerous two-edged sword of capitalism' would destroy Vietnam, his aides later told the journalist that these criticisms of reforms were not to be reported.

Vietnam may yet test the idea that Marxism's slow drift into senescence is better than its precipitous collapse. Party cadres often refer in smug tones to chaos in Eastern Europe and use this as a justification for their continued power. But despite its economic growth of recent years, Vietnam shares many of the problems of the former Communist countries of Eastern Europe. It has its corrupt officials entangled in a growing web of organised crime. There is drug addiction and prostitution, poverty, malnutrition, declining educational standards, a worsening environment and sagging infrastructure. The banking system is on the edge of collapse. State-owned businesses are in poor shape and have not yet felt the invigorating slap of open markets. In the name of 'stability', the Communist Party has put off many of the changes that it will eventually be forced to make. Its vision of stability is to preclude any change in those who hold power. It cannot envisage it as the complex balance of views and opinions, government and institutions, new ideas and old values that sustain nations and political systems.

Under *Doi Moi*, Vietnam's economy and society have changed radically, creating small gatherings and associations, unfocused and diverse pockets of alternative power and individual ideas that can only grow. An economy unshackled from the state has been the breeding ground of an incipient civil society. *Doi Moi* has not just been about the Party stepping back from power; it has also seen people actively move into areas previously dominated by the state. The emergence of a web of institutions and organisations that might limit the power of the state over the individual is beginning, even in the hostile environment created by the Party. A new generation, freed from the bitterness of war and brought up in an environment of peace and growing freedom, are starting to make their mark and have started to challenge the fixed notions of their elders.

Much may have changed already but much remains to be done. New ideas get sucked down and lost in the mud of Hanoi's bureaucracy. New minds don't work freely without the fear of official intrusion. New opinions are circumscribed and information controlled. The process of reform has not been a linear progression from a closed economy and society to a more open version. *Doi Moi* has been marked with digressions and backtracking, a loss of direction and sometimes a hankering for the imagined simplicities of the past. The Communist Party has been forced to relax economic restrictions but it has not liked some of the results. Unable to regain the control or respect it once commanded, its response has been to clench and release its grip on the economy and society in an increasingly desperate manner as its power slips slowly away.

Chapter Notes

Chapter 1 WITHOUT HEROES
The quote is from Pham Thi Hoai's novel *The Crystal Messenger*, translated by Ton That Quynh Du.

Chapter 2 IMAGINING VIETNAM
Quotes from Jean-Jacques Annaud appeared in Norindr Panavong's book *Phantasmatic Indochina*. Michael Paterniti's article on Ho Chi Minh City appeared in the *New York Times Magazine* on 12 January 1997. Stanley Karnow's portrait of General Vo Nguyen Giap appeared in the *New York Times Magazine* on 24 June 1990. Christine Courtney's profile of Ngo Ba Thanh appeared in the *Los Angeles Times* on 24 November 1992. Oriana Fallaci's interview with Giap first appeared in Italian in *L'Europeo* and was reprinted in English in her book *Interview with History*.

Chapter 3 REMEMBERING VIETNAM
Tran Huy Quang's story 'A Prophecy Fulfilled' originally appeared in *Van Nghe Magazine* in Hanoi and was translated for *Vietnam Forum Number 14* (1994) by Sheree Carey. 'Ho Chi Minh: New Perspectives from the Comintern Files' by Sophie Quinn-Judge also appeared in that issue of *Vietnam Forum*.

Chapter 4 FAMINE
Nguyen Chi Thien's poem appears in *The Flowers of Hell* translated by Nguyen Ngoc Bich. Bang Ba Lan's poem appeared in *Vietnam Forum Number 5* (Winter–Spring 1985), translated by Huynh Sanh Thong. Details of the famine come in part from interviews and David Marr's book, *1945*, and from 'La famine de 1945 au Nord

Vietnam' by Nguyen The Anh in *Vietnam Forum Number 5*. The Giang's story 'The Blessed Alms' appeared in *Vietnam Forum* (No. 5) as did Nguyen Ngoc Ngan's story 'The Two Ducks'. The Aurora Foundation Report on the Vietnamese Gulag was published by the foundation in 1989 as 'Report on the Violations of Human Rights in the Socialist Republic of Vietnam April 1975 to December 1988'. Tuong Nang Tien's story 'Communism and Guigozcanism' appeared in *Vietnam Forum Number 7* (Winter–Spring 1986).

Chapter 5 FEAST
The quote about hog's haslet comes from *Vietnam Forum Number 2* (Summer–Fall, 1983), 'Nhat pham phong, nhi long lon'. Details of Tue Tinh come from David Marr's 'Vietnamese Attitudes Regarding Illness and Healing', *Vietnam Forum Number 10* (Summer–Fall, 1987). The story of the origins of Banh Chung comes from Nguyen Dong Chi, a scholar of folklore and is quoted in the *Vietnam Review* (Autumn–Winter, 1996). Quote from Tam Lang comes from *The Light of the Capital: Three Modern Vietnamese Classics*, translated by Greg and Monique Lockhart.

Chapter 6 EMPTY BOX
The quote from Ho Chi Minh's *Letter From Abroad* is from David Marr's *1945*. Most other details come from interviews in Hanoi or Party documents.

Chapter 7 EXCOMMUNICATED
Most of this chapter was taken from interviews or from documents that circulated in Hanoi and abroad in the mid 1990s. Some of these have been published as *Vietnam: The Unheard Voices*. As well as his personal recollections, some details of Bui Tin's life come from his autobiography. My thanks to Judy Stowe for sharing some of her research on the Anti-Revisionists movement.

Chapter 9 PENDULUM
Phung Gia Loc's 'The Night of that Day, What a Night' first appeared in *Van Nghe*. It later appeared in *Manoa* (Winter, 1995) translated by Birgit Hussfeld and Hans Schodder. The responses to it also appeared in *Manoa*.

Chapter 10 CYMBALS AND LITANIES

The quote from Phung Quan's poem 'What My Mother Once Told Me' comes from Huynh Sanh Tuong's anthology of Vietnamese poetry. I am grateful to Peter Mares of the Australian Broadcasting Corporation for sharing transcripts of interviews. Georges Boudarel's article appeared in *Vietnam Forum Number 13* as did Hoang Giang's article 'La Revolte des intellectuels au Vietnam'. Pham Tien Duat's poem 'White Circle' appeared in *Manoa* (Winter, 1995) translated by Nguyen Quang Thieu and Kevin Bowen. For details on Thiep's work see the introduction to a collection of short stories translated by Greg Lockhart. 'Declassifying Nguyen Huy Thiep' by Peter Zinoman appeared in *Positions* (Fall 1994) published by Duke University Press and 'Nguyen Huy Thiep's "Vang Lua" and the Nature of Intellectual Dissent in Contemporary Vietnam' in *Vietnam Forum Number 14* (1994). Translations of Thiep's stories by Peter Zinoman also appeared in *Vietnam Forum Number 14*. 'Duong Thu Huong and the Literature of Disenchantment' by Hue-Tam Ho Tai also appeared in that issue of *Vietnam Forum*.

Chapter 11 A MIRROR OF THINGS PAST

Poem by Lady Thanh Quan from Huynh Sanh Thong's anthology. Details of Hanoi history from works by Gwendolyn Wright and William S. Logan. Quote of poem about Vo De from Petrus Ky, 'Voyage to Tonkin in the Year At Hoi', translated by P. J. Honey.

Chapter 12 SOCIAL EVILS

Details of HIV/AIDS from report by CARE International called 'The Risk of AIDS in Vietnam' by Barbara Franklin, published in 1993. Also HIV/AIDS strategy report published in 1986 by CARE and written by Paula Kelly and 'Targeting Young Men' by Barbara Franklin published by CARE in 1994. Quote from Ernest Gellner from *Conditions of Liberty: Civil Society and Its Rivals*.

Chapter 13 FAITH

Quote from Leopold Cadière from 'The Religion of the Vietnam' translated by Ian Mabbet. Details on Catholic relations from reports published in the French journal *Eglises d'Asie*.

Chapter 14 CHINA LITE
Poem from Huynh Sanh Thuong's anthology.

Chapter 15 MELANCHOLY TRIBE
Quote from Khoi T. Luu first appeared in 'A Heart of Sorrow? Exposing the Lighter Side of the Vietnamese American Experience', *Vietnam Forum Number 14* (1994).

Chapter 16 YOUNG AND RESTLESS
Details from David Marr's paper 'Vietnamese Youth in the 1990s'.

Bibliography

Anderson, Benedict, *Imagined Communities* (1983, Verso, London).

Andrusz, Gregory, Harloe, Michael, Szelenyi, Ivan (eds.), *Cities After Socialism* (1996, Blackwell, Oxford).

Balaban, John and Nguyen Qui Duc (eds.), *Vietnam: A Traveller's Literary Companion* (1996, Whereabouts Press, San Francisco).

Bates, Milton J., *The Wars We Took to Vietnam* (1996, University of California Press, Berkeley).

Borton, Lady, *After Sorrow: An American Among the Vietnamese* (1995, Viking Press, New York).

Bui Tin, *Following Ho Chi Minh: Memoirs of a North Vietnamese Colonel* (1995, C. Hurst and Co. Publishers Ltd., London).

Cadière, Leopold, *The Religion of the Vietnamese* 1944. Translation by Ian Mabbet (working paper) (1989, Centre of Southeast Asian Studies, Monash University).

Chanda, Nayan, *Brother Enemy: The War after the War* (1986, Collier Books, New York).

Chen, King C., *Vietnam and China, 1938–1954* (1969, Princeton University Press, Princeton).

Christopher, Renny, *The Vietnam War. The American War. Images and Representations in Euro-American and Vietnamese Exile Narratives* (1995, University of Massachusetts Press, Boston).

Clifford, James, *Routes: Travel and Translation in the Late Twentieth Century* (1997, Harvard University Press).

Davidson, Phillip B., *Vietnam At War: The History 1946–1975* (1988, Oxford University Press, Oxford).

Diller and Scofidio *et al*, *Back to the Front: Tourisms of War* (1994, Princeton Architectural Press, Princeton).

Dissanayake, Wimal (ed.), *Colonialism and Nationalism in Asian Cinema* (1994, Indiana University Press, Bloomington and Indianapolis).

Doling, Annabel, *Vietnam on a Plate: A Culinary Journey* (1996,

Roundhouse Publications, Hong Kong).

Duara, Prasenjit, *Rescuing History From the Nation: Questioning Narratives of Modern China* (1995, University of Chicago Press, Chicago).

Duiker, William J., *Historical Dictionary of Vietnam* (1989, The Scarecrow Press Inc., Metuchen, N.J. and London).

Dumont, Rene, *La Culture du Riz dans le Delta du Tonkin* (1995, Prince of Songkla University, Bangkok).

Duong Thu Huong, *Novel Without a Name* (Trans. Phan Huy Duong and Nina McPherson), (1996, Penguin Books, London).

Duong Thu Huong, *Paradise of the Blind* (Trans. Phan Huy Duong and Nina McPherson), (1993, William Morrow and Co. Inc., New York).

Epstein, Michael, *Vietnam: A Book of Changes* (1996, Doubletake/W.W. Norton and Co., New York).

Fallaci, Oriana, *Interview with History* (1977, Houghton Mifflin Company, Boston).

Fforde, Adam and de Vylder, Stefan, *From Plan to Market: The Economic Transition in Vietnam* (1996, Westview Press, Boulder, Colorado).

FitzGerald, Frances, *Fire in the Lake: The Vietnamese and the Americans in Vietnam* (1972, Random House, New York).

Franchini, Philippe, *Saigon 1925–1945* (1994, Editions Autrement, Paris).

Freeman, James M., *Hearts of Sorrow: Vietnamese American Lives* (1989, Stanford University Press, Stanford).

Gaiduk, Ilya V., *The Soviet Union and the Vietnam War* (1996, Ivan R. Dee, Chicago).

Gellner, Ernest, *Conditions of Liberty: Civil Society and Its Rivals* (1996, Penguin Books, London).

Gellner, Ernest, *Culture, Identity and Politics* (1987, Cambridge University Press, Cambridge).

Gilks, Anne, *The Breakdown of the Sino-Vietnamese Alliance, 1970–1979* (1992, University of California, Berkeley).

Gleason, Abbott, *Totalitarianism: The Inner History of the Cold War* (1995, Oxford University Press, Oxford).

Grey, Jeffrey and Doyle, Jeff, *Vietnam, War, Myth and Memory* (1992, Allen and Unwin, Australia).

Havel, Vaclav, *Living in Truth*, (ed.) Jan Vladislav (1986, Faber and Faber, London).

Hendrickson, Paul, *The Living and the Dead: Robert MacNamara and Five Lives of a Lost War* (1996, Alfred Knopf, New York).

Ho Chi Minh, *Selected Writings: 1920–1969* (1994, The Gioi Publishers, Hanoi).

Hobart, Mark and Taylor, Robert H. (eds.), *Context, Meaning and Power in Southeast Asia* (1986, Southeast Asia Program, Cornell University).

Huynh Sanh Thong, *An Anthology of Vietnamese Poems from the Eleventh through the Twentieth Centuries* (1996, Yale University Press, New Haven).

Jamieson, Neil L., *Understanding Vietnam* (1993, University of California Press, Berkeley, California).

Karnow, Stanley, *Vietnam: A History* (1983, The Viking Press, New York).

Kerkvliet, Benedict J. and Porter, Doug J., *Vietnam's Rural Transformation* (1995, Westview Press, Boulder, Colorado).

Kibria, Nazli, *Family Tightrope: The Changing Lives of Vietnamese Americans* (1993, Princeton University Press, Princeton).

Kolko, Gabriel, *Vietnam: Anatomy of a Peace* (1997, Routledge, London and New York).

Ky, Petrus Truong Vinh, *Voyage to Tonking in the Year At Hoi* (trans. P.J. Honey) (1982, School of Oriental and African Studies, London).

Lacouture, Jean, *Vietnam: Between Two Truces* (1966, Vintage Books, New York).

Lauras, Didier, *Saigon Le Chantier des Utopies* (1997, Editions Autrement, Paris).

Le Duan, *Selected Writings: 1960–1975* (1994, The Gioi Publishers, Hanoi).

Le Minh Khue, *The Stars, The Earth, The River* (1997, Curbstone Press, Wilmantic).

Lewis, Norman, *A Dragon Apparent* (1951, Jonathan Cape, London).

Lin Hua, *Chiang Kaishek, De Gaulle contre Ho Chi Minh* (1994, L'Harmattan, Paris).

Linh Dinh, *Night Again: Contemporary Fiction from Vietnam* (1996, Seven Stories Press, New York).

Lockhart, Greg and Lockhart, Monique, (trans), *The Light of the Capital: Three Modern Vietnamese Classics* (1996, Oxford University Press, Oxford).

Logan, William S. and Askew, Marc, *Cultural Identity and Urban Change in Southeast Asia* (1994, Deakin University Press, Geelong).

Logan, William S., *Russians on the Red River: The Soviet Impact on Hanoi's Townscape, 1955–1990 Europe-Asia Studies*, Vol. 47. No. 3. 1995. 443–468.

Luong, Hy V., *Revolution in the Village: Tradition and Transformation in North Vietnam, 1925–1988* (1992, University of Hawaii Press, Honolulu).

Mangold, Tom and Penycate, John, *The Tunnels of Cu Chi* (1986, Berkley Books, New York).

Marchetti, Gina, *Romance and the Yellow Peril* (1993, University of California Press, Berkeley and Los Angeles).

Marr, David G., *1945: The Quest for Power* (1995, University of California Press, Berkeley and Los Angeles).

Marr, David G., *Tradition on Trial, 1920–1945* (1981, University of California Press, Berkeley and Los Angeles).

McCarthy, Mary, *Hanoi* (1968, Weidenfeld and Nicolson, London).

McNamara, Robert S., *In Retrospect: The Tragedy and Lessons of Vietnam* (1995, Random House, New York).

Morley, James W. and Nishihara, Masashi (eds.) *Vietnam Joins the World* (1997, M.E. Sharpe Inc., Armonk and London).

Ngo Vinh Long, *Before the Revolution* (1973, MIT Press, Boston).

Ngoc Quang Huynh, *South Wind Changing* (1994, Greywolf Press, St Paul).

Nguyen Chi Thien, *The Flowers of Hell* (1996, To Hop Xuat Ban Mien Dong Hoa Ky).

Nguyen Huy Thiep, *The General Retires and Other Stories* (trans. Greg Lockhart) (1992, Oxford University Press, Oxford).

Nguyen Khac Vien, *Vietnam: A Long History* (1993, The Gioi Publishers, Hanoi).

Nguyen Qui Duc, *Where the Ashes Are: The Odyssey of a Vietnamese Family* (1994, Addison Wesley Publishing Company, New York).

Norindr, Panavong, *Phantasmatic Indochina: French Colonial Ideology in Architecture, Film and Literature* (1996, Duke University Press).

Porter, Gareth, *The Politics of Bureaucratic Socialism* (1993, Cornell University Press, Ithaca, New York).

Quang Thai Trung, 'Collective Leadership and Factionalism: An Essay on Ho Chi Minh's Legacy' (1985, Institute of Southeast Asian Studies, Singapore).

Rutledge, Paul James, *The Vietnamese Experience in America* (1992, Indiana University Press, Bloomington and Indianapolis).

Shawcross, William, *The Quality of Mercy* (1984, Andre Deutsch, London).

Sheehan, Neil, *After the War was Over: Hanoi and Saigon* (1991, Vintage Books, New York).

Sheehan, Susan, *Ten Vietnamese* (1967, Alfred Knopf, New York).

Shiraishi, Takashi and Furuta, Motoo (eds.), *Indochina in the 1940s* (1992, Cornell Southeast Asia Program, Ithaca).

Smith, R. B., *An International History of the Vietnam War* (1983, St Martin's Press, New York).

Stern, Lewis M., *Renovating the Vietnamese Communist Party: Nguyen*

Van Linh and the Program for Organizational Reform 1987–1991 (1993, Institute of Southeast Asian Studies, Singapore).

Ta Van Tai, *The Vietnamese Tradition of Human Rights* (1988, Institute of Southeast Asian Studies, University of California, Berkeley).

Tana, Li, *Peasants on the Move: Rural-Urban Migration in the Hanoi Region* (1996, Institute of Southeast Asian Studies, Singapore).

Tham Seong Chee, *Literature and Society in Southeast Asia* (1981, Singapore University Press, Singapore).

Tran Tri Vu, *Lost Years: My 1,632 Days in Vietnamese Reeducation Camps* (1988, University of California, Berkeley).

Trinh Van Thao, *Vietnam du Confianisme au Communisme* (1990, L'Harmattan, Paris).

Truong Chinh, *Selected Writings* (1994, The Gioi Publishers, Hanoi).

Truong Nhu Tang, *A Viet Cong Memoir* (1985, Random House, New York).

Tu, Wei-Ming, *Confucian Traditions in East Asian Modernity* (1996, Harvard University Press, Cambridge).

Turley, William S. and Sneldon, Mark (eds.), *Reinventing Vietnamese Socialism: Doi Moi in Comparative Perspective* (1993, Westview Press, Boulder, Colorado).

Vo Nguyen Giap, *Selected Writings* (1994, The Gioi Publishers, Hanoi).

Vu Ngu Chieu, *The Other Side of the Vietnamese Revolution* (1996, Van Hoa, Houston, Texas).

Warner, Denis, *The Last Confucian: Vietnam, Southeast Asia and the West* (1963, Penguin Books, London).

Wolff, Tobias, *In Pharoah's Army: Memories of the Lost War* (1994, Alfred A. Knopf, New York).

Woodside, Alexander, *Vietnam and the Chinese Model* (1988, Council on East Asian Studies, Harvard, Cambridge).

Wright, Gwendolyn, *The Politics of Design in French Colonial Urbanism* (1991, The University of Chicago Press, Chicago).

Index

Agriculture and Rural
    Development, Ministry of
    61
Ai, Vo Van 281
AIDS 6, 239–40, 252–3
Allied
    bombing (1944) 49, *see also*
        United States, bombing
        raids
    victory (1945) 50
An, Thanh 348
Anh, Le Cong Tuan 337
Anh, Nguyen Thi Van 175
Anh, President Le Duc 81–2, 86,
    90–1, 100, 173–4
Anh, The 50
Anh, Tran Hung, *Cyclo* 21
Annaud, Jean-Jacques 12
Anti-Corruption and Smuggling
    Committee 132–3
Anti-Revisionist Movement 103,
    105, 108–10, 112
Anti-Soviet exhibitions 108
Army Museum, Hanoi 33, 97
Arnett, Peter 19
Asia
    cities 236
    economy 7, 140, 333
    HIV 239
Asian Wall Street Journal 143, 187
Asian-Americans 317
Association of Southeast Asian
    Nations (ASEAN) 300
Association of Vietnamese

Journalists, Sixth Congress
    (March 1995) 159–60
Aung Sang Suu Kyi 127
Aurora Foundation 53
Australia
    human rights 127, 314–15
    minorities 321
    NGO 252
    Special Broadcasting Service
        Radio 314
    Viet Kieu 123, 310–1, 314–16,
        319–21

Ba Chua Kho temple, Ha Bac
    province 257–9
Ba Dinh
    Club 221
    Hall 81–2, 95
    Square 110, 208, 215–216, 221
        Ho Chi Minh mausoleum
            40–3, 45, 84
Ba Dinhology 81
Baez, Joan 329
banh chung 73
Bat Trang village 209
BBC, Vietnamese language service
    120 , 124 , 165, 314–15
Beijing
    Khmer Rouges backing 284
    Moscow rivalries 107, 113–14
    student protests (1989) 135
    temples 291
    Tiananmen Square 216, 297
Berlin Wall 87, 330

Binh, Archbishop, Paul Nguyen
    Van 268, 272–3
Binh, Nguyen Duc 89, 163, 313
Bitis company 303
Boudarel, Georges 180, 182
Brazil 253, 287
Brezhnev, Leonid 96, 151
Britain
    Channel Four 348
    Viet Kieu 311
Brown, James 327
Brunei, South China Sea 299, 301
Buddhism 211, 216, 260–2, 275,
    279–80, 282, 292, 307
    Catholic converts 266
    church 88
    images 29
    influence 235
    monks 204, 266, 277–8
    nuns 276
    temples 278
Bulgaria 52, 348–9
Bun thang 70–1
Buon Ma Thuot 75–6
Burma 127, 135, 289

Cadière, Leopold 261–2
    The Religion of the Vietnamese 257
California
    University of 10
    Viet Kieu 122–3, 317–18, 329–30,
        335
Cam, Nguyen Ky 132–3
Cam, Nguyen Manh 298
Cam, Phan Luong 79 , 150–1
Cambodia 1, 119, 155, 234, 297
    invasion 284, 293
    Khmer Rouge 63, 85–6
    Viet Cong base 30
Canada, Viet Kieu 122, 311
Cao Dai 262, 279
    Temple 216
Cao, Van 182
capitalism 2, 11, 144, 353–4
CARE Internat ional 245, 252–3
Catholicism 263–5
Ceausescu, Nicolae 159

Celli, Archbishop Claudio 273–4
Central Committee 80, 82, 92–3, 95,
    107, 112, 141, 144
    arts and literature 181
    cleansing 296
    colonial prisons 86
    Ideology Commission 161
    journalists 163
    for Overseas Vietnamese 315
    purged members 110
    Security and Protection
        Department 110
Central Intelligence Agency 23,
    119
Central Research Institute of
    Economic Management 143
Chan family chapel, Hoi An Port
    235
Chang, Chung-Ching, *Treatise on
    Ailments Caused by Cold* 66
Chaplin, Charlie 346
Chau, Phan Boi 276
Chengdu, Sichuan province 297
Chevalier des Arts et des Lettres 183
Chiang, Kai-shek 265, 294
China 100
    advisors 288, 295
    aid 58, 69, 288, 295
    anti-Soviet exhibitions 108
    Black Flag bandits 208
    brothels 286
    Buddhism 307
    Communist Party 179
    conflict (1979) 1, 155
    Cultural Revolution 103, 296,
        307
    culture 17, 294
    economy 283–5, 298
    education 290
    100 Flowers Movement 107
    Long March 118
    Mao Zedong 107, 265
    medicine 66
    Nationalist army 294
    overseas
        Chinese 312
        languages 302–3

population 75
presence of 153
railway stations 231
refugees 307
relations with 53, 272, 283–308
rice production 284
smuggled goods 344
state industrial complex 146
summit meeting 297
war (1979) 114, 195, 285
Wei Jingsheng 127
China Beach near Danang 31–2
Chinh, Hoang Minh 102–10, 121, 124, 128, 279
Chinh, Truong 107–8, 179–81, 294
Chiu Chow, Southern China 304–5
Christopher, Warren 77
Chun, Do-Won, South Korean President, 174
Chung, Ly Qui 79, 155, 164, 324
Cinematographers; Association of Vietnam 348
Clinton, President Bill 344
Club of Former Resistance Fighters 115–17
Cold War 153
Communism 3, 5, 13, 55, 62, 90, 96, 107, 110, 116, 120, 352
capitalism collision 11
collapse of 89–90, 152, 159, 330
countries, famines 50, 68–9
Hanoi 221
Party Youth League 164
Communist Party 6, 31, 34, 37, 75, 80–100, 102–3, 118, 128, 130, 352–4
Congress 95, 98, 100
corruption 6, 87, 120–1, 132–45, 150–2, 162, 168–9, 172–6
discipline 125
economic restrictions 355
Economics Commission 90–1
Eighth Congress (1996) 80–3, 87, 92–4, 106, 112, 138, 172–4, 314
External Relations Committee 85
hardliners 22

Ho Chi Minh's image 40
members 99, 114, 122, 139, 155–6
miseries inflicted 186
nationalism 262
Ninth Party Plenum (1963) 107
Organisation Department 86, 92, 108, 120
personality cult 38
power 81, 159–60, 352
purges 109–11, 113, 125, 128
religious revival 260
revolt (1945) 83
Sixth Congress (1986) 3, 123
state sector 144
top leadership 121
Con Dao Island, French colonial prison 30
Confucianism 18, 25, 83, 137, 260, 263–4, 289–94
examinations 211, 291
influence 235
legacies 242
mould of society 14–15
systems of bureaucracy 137
world 138
Confucius 3
The Analects XII.1 153
Cong An Thanh Pho Ho Chi Minh City (the *Ho Chi Minh City Police Weekly*) 172–3
Cong, Elvis 335–6
Conoco Inc. 301
Continental Hotel 13
Control Commission 139
Council of Ministers 116
Cu Chi 26–30
tunnels 26–9
Cuba 163
Culture and Information, Ministry of 21, 121–2, 171, 175, 183, 221, 232, 248, 252, 259, 326, 330, 346–8
Cuong, Do Kim 68, 191–2
Cyclo 21, 173, 346–7
Czechoslovakia, laws 105

Daewoo Corporation 143, 225

Dai, Emperor Bao 8–9
Dalat, Indochina 8–10
  Buddhist temples 278
  Long Tho Pagoda 276–8
  Palace Hotel 8–10
  tourist industry 278
Dan, Tran 180, 182
  Wave upon Wave of Men 180
Danang
  seminary (1975) 269
  War Remnants Museum 31
Dao, Nguyen Hong Dao 234
Dao, Thich Minh 276–9
De, Emperor Vo 211
De, Professor Phan Cu 182–4, 188,
  343–4
de Rhodes, Alexandre 263
Declaration of Independence 50,
  243, 322
Defence, Ministry of 32
democratic centralism 87
Deng Xiaoping 185, 284, 295, 297
Deneuve, Catherine 13
Diem, President Ngo Dinh 115–16,
  266–7, 272, 282, 320, 329
Dien Bien Phu (film) 12
Dien Bien Phu
  battle of (1954) 22–3, 31, 33, 69,
    121, 180, 286, 295
  films 348
Dinh, Truong 338
  'Western Pacifying, Heretic
    Exterminating
    Generalissimo' 264
Disney, *The Lion King* 82
Disneyland 312
Do, General Tran 183
Do Son 150
Do, Thich Quang 280–1
Doan, Bui Bang 124
Doan Phu Tho 18, 37
Doanh, Le Dang 143
Doanh Nghiep 159–60
Doi Moi 3–4, 93, 144, 177, 189, 241,
  260, 352, 354–5
Don, Ly Quy 56
Dong Da Communicable Diseases

  Hospital, Hanoi 240
Dong Nai province 307, 339
Dong, Pham Van 30, 278, 297,
  353–4
Doremon comic books, Japan 343
Dostoevsky, Fyodor 185
Doumer, Governor Paul 211
Du, Nguyen 197–8
  'The Tale of Kieu' 178, 244, 293–4
Duan, Le 86, 107–8, 116, 123, 182
Duat, Pham Tien, 'White Circle'
  189–90
Dung Quat 147–8
Duong, Phan Que 111
Duras, Marguerite, *The Lover* 12
Duyet, Pham The 132, 228

East Germany 58, 251
Eastern Asia, political traditions
  197
Eastern Europe 83, 100, 176
  animal feed 51
  broadcasts 166
  cartoons 343
  chaos and anarchy 121, 354
  Communism collapse 120, 159,
    162, 175, 187, 270, 285, 297
  Communist governments 90,
    100
  dissidents 104, 125–6
  Hungarian Uprising 106
  jobs 58
  Marxism 96
  movies 328
  state industrial complex 146
  television programmes 348–9
Education, Ministry of 149
environmental movements 241
Etchegaray, Roger Cardinal 271–2
European Commission 149, 253

Fallaci, Oriana 23
Farewell Saigon 39
fashion magazines 175
Fatherland Front 255, 271–2, 279
Faulkner, Penelope 281
Fields of Fire 347

Finance Ministry 149
FitzGerald, Frances 16–21
  Fire in the Lake 16, 19
foreign
  advertising 247
  broadcasts 185
  business licenses 170
  correspondents (reporters) 6, 25
  diplomats 280
  exchange 59
  investors 135, 148
  lawyers 24
  NGOs 252
Foreign Ministry 133, 166, 226
France 21, 50
  ambassador 166
  built railway 288–9
  Chamber of Deputies 212
  colonialism 9–10, 48–9, 100, 158,
      198, 205, 210–14, 216, 232,
      243, 264, 270
    agricultural policies 50
    architecture 26
    exploitation 252
    Hanoi 208, 213, 235–6
    picture 17
    prisons 30, 86, 118, 140
    scholarship 291
    and war memories 21–2
  culture 42, 183–4
  departure 205
  designs 221
  famine 50
  film awards 13
  forces 210
  Gia Lam air base 106
  grain taken 48
  Hanoi control 209
  Ho Chi Minh 38
  independence from (1954) 24, 44,
      83, 86, 161, 262
  Indochina 9–10, 210, 212, 264
  jails 108, 112
  military camp 211
  missionary 264
  navy shipyard 116
  political prisoners 119

  priests 270
  rice sales 49
  rule 49–50
  Viet Kieu 311
  Vietnam film locations 346–7
  Vietnamese communities 123
  war against 67, 265
  White Russians 321
Fred Hollows Foundation 150
Frontier Committee 301

Gaiduk, Ilya 108
Gellner, Ernest 256, 353
Geneva Accord 265–6
Geneva talks (1954) 296
Germany, Viet Kieu 311
Giaiphong Studio, Ho Chi Minh
    City 346–7
Giang, The, 'The Blessed Alms'
    52–3
Giai Pham (Works of Beauty) 181
Giap, General Vo Nguyen 22–4, 30,
    106, 121, 123–4
Giay, Tu 66–7
Gorbachev, Mikhail 89, 151–2, 156,
    270
Great Victory Day 53
Greene, Graham, *The Quiet
    American* 14, 347
Guangdong province 283, 288
Guangxi province 286, 288
Gulf of Thailand 63

Ha Bac province, Ba Chua Kho
    temple 257–9
Ha, Le Hong 109, 112–3
Ha, Nguyen Ngoc 312
Haiphong port 95, 211, 288–89,
    305
Halberstam, David 19
Hammett-Hellman Award 119
Hanh, Nguyen 248
Hanh, Vu Kim 163–64
Hanoi 4, 129–30, 205, 218–19, 260,
    354–5
  advertising agencies 345
  Archbishop 266

Hanoi – *contd*
architects 214, 217, 234–5
Army Museum 33
Arts and Literature Association
159
Bach Mai Hospital 219
Bohemian circles 2
Botanic Gardens 42, 221
buildings 216–17, 222–24, 228,
231
Cardinal Archbishop 267, 274
children 275, 329
Communists 214–15, 227, 285
demonstrations 135
Dong Da Communicable
Diseases Hospital 240
Dong Xuan market 286
foreign money 229
French
cemetery 217
colonialism 208, 213, 235–6
High Commission 219
Giang Vo Exhibition Centre 326,
344
Hilton 142
history 204–36
HIV 240
Hoan Kiem Lake 154, 210, 230–1,
330–3
Housing Department 45
ideologues 260, 350
income of population 142
Indian Embassy 219
intellectuals 188, 197, 260
investors 2
Lenin
Park 334
statue 216
Lycée Sarraut 215
Marxist Mandarins 95
Metropole Hotel 210, 213
mikroraiony 219
musician 330
National Institute of Nutrition 66
1990's, early 330–1
Noi Bai Airport 220, 272
Old City 153, 208, 231–2

Pagoda of Nguyen Dang Giai
210
painters 230
Palace Grounds 221
People's Committee 233
pho stalls 71
Polytechnic 248–9
population 234
preservation policies 232
Presidential Palace 30, 42–3, 215
President's office 313
public housing 218
Quan Su Pagoda 281
restaurants 75, 77–8
Roman Catholic, churches 216,
273
St Joseph's Cathedral 52, 275–6
sainthoods 270
sanitation department 47
Soviet
control (1954) 205, 215
planning 218–19
Temples 2–3, 37–8, 209, 216, 291
Thirty-six Streets district 208–9,
216, 230
trade show 344
Treasury building 42, 212, 215
University, Institute of
International Cultures 182–3
Urban planning 215–16
Viet Kieu 323
Vietnamese-Soviet Cultural
Palace 221, 335
West Lake city centre 220
youth 331
Hanoi Moi 226
Hanson, Pauline 321
Harley-Davidson bikes 331–3, 336
Harvard 317, 319
Havel, President Vaclav 102, 105
'The Power of the Powerless' 100
Health, Ministry of 133, 148–9, 240
Hebrard, Ernest 10, 212–14
'Heroic Mothers' 30–1
Herr, Michael, *Dispatches* 11
Hien, Hoang Ngoc 193
Hien, Vu Thi 129

Hien, Vu Thu 39–40
    Darkness at Noon 40
Hiep, Le 45–6, 223
Hiep, Ninh 61
Hieu, Do Trung 102, 104–5, 279–80
Highway One 33, 267
Hillblom, Larry 8–10
HIV (human immuno-deficiency
        virus) 238–41, 243, 247, 249–56,
        259
HIV/AIDS awareness group 238
Ho Chi Minh 101
    Academy 252
    China 294
    City 13, 21, 26, 75, 84, 328, 330,
        336
        advertising agencies 345
        Archbishop 272, 274
    City (Saigon)
        Buddhist church 281
        Cholon district 286
        Committee for Overseas
            Vietnamese 312
        Communist Party 99, 117
        court house 131
        crimes 246, 339, 346–7
        cultural office 345
        District Five 302
        Giaiphong Studio 346–7
        hierarchy 115, 117
        injecting drug users 238
        jail 84
        Papal envoy 271
        Pasteur Institute 64
        property boom 303
        War Remnants Museum 166,
            323
    Political Academy 89
    Trail 67–9, 286
    Youth League 334
    Youth Union 340
Ho Chi Minh, President 23, 37–9,
        50, 91, 108
    birthday celebrations 327
    busts 216–17
    Campaign for Saigon (1975) 348
    Central Committee 86

cult 40–2, 292–3
Declaration of Independence 50,
        243, 322
Hanoi temple 37–8
'Letter from Abroad' 96–7
Liu Shaoqi, President 295
Mausoleum 40–3, 45, 84
museum 43–5
Nhan Dan articles 181
personality cult 126
pictures 225
Presidential Palace, wooden
        house 43, 215
Prison Diary 117–18
Revolution 322
speech (1951) 292
Thoughts 120–1, 207, 292
Trail 22, 32–3
will 41, 162
wives 39
Youth 326–7
Ho, Dieu 72
Ho, Nguyen 88, 90, 115–19, 121,
        125, 128
Hoa Hao sect 262, 279
Hoa Lo prison 95, 103, 112, 229
Hoa, Truong Van 64
Hoai, Pham Thi 1, 4, 189, 199,
        201–2
    Marie Sen 202
    The Crystal Messenger 201–2, 326
Hoan, Pham Huy 168, 170
Hoan, Tran Quoc 40
Hoi An Port, Chan family chapel
        235
Hollywood, action heroes 346–7
Holocaust 237
Holy See 271, 273
Honda Dream II motorbikes 15,
        230, 331–3
Honecker, Erich 159
Hong Kong 7, 231, 286, 343
    boat people 58, 149, 307, 316
    economy 136, 303
    martial arts movies 346–7
    Political and Economic Risk
        Consultancy 133

Hong Kong – *contd*
  Vietnamese Communist Party 83
Hong, Nguyen Viet 331–2
Houston, Texas 322–3
  Vietnamese 317
Hu, Feng 180
Huan, Nguyen An 204–5
Hue 3, 211, 271
  Archbishop of 266–7
  Buddhist church 281
  court 291
  mausoleums 45
  Museum 32
  Tien Mu Pagoda 281
Human Rights Watch 119
Hung kings 36–7, 73, 208
Hung, Tran Anh 12, 173, 346–7
Hungarian Uprising 106
Hunyh, Father 268–9
Huong, Duong Thu 183–9, 191,
  198–200
  Beyond Illusions 186
  Love Story Told Before Dawn
    185–6
  Paradise of the Blind 186–7
Huu, Nguyen Quang 270
Huu, To 69–70, 179–81
Huynh, Vu Dinh 39–40, 110

Independence League 179
India 69
  Buddhism 307
IndoChina 11, 13, 21
  French colonialism 9–10, 210,
    212, 243, 264
  governors-general 43
  Hanoi declared capital 211
  Japanese forces (1940) 49
  landscapes 26
  movies 12
  see also Dalat; Hanoi
Indochine 12–13
Indonesia 290, 303
  investors 133
  rural poverty 62
  stock market 7
Information, and Culture, Ministry

  of 161
Institutes of
  Cinematography 346–8
  Criminology 339
  Economic Management 143
  International Cultures 182–3
  Marxism-Leninism 107, 111
  Military Nutrition and Clothing
    67
  Nutrition 66
  Philosophy 292
  Sociology 143
Interior Ministry 84, 122, 172–3,
  175, 187, 225
international
  architects 41, 43, 213–14, 217,
    234–5
  capitalists 144
  Communist movement 107
  companies 345
  economic development 293
  law 299
  media tycoons 349
  pop culture 343
  publishing companies 171
  rice prices 60
  socialist solidarity 87
Internet 167–8
Iraq 163
Irish, Catholicism 266

Japan 48, 50, 140, 156, 343–4
  Doremon comic books 343
  Imperial Court 263
  Indochine, forces in (1940) 49
  Keidanren 134
  market 344
  Portuguese missionaries 263
  Shinto temples 212
  South China Sea 299
Jiang Zemin, Chinese president
  297–9
John Paul II, Pope 270–3

Karnow, Stanley 22
Kass, Patricia 326–7
Ke Cho, Red River 205

Keidanren, Japan 134
Khai, Pham Van 93, 100
Khe Sanh 22
Khmer Rouge 284, 297
Khruschev, Nikita 103, 106
Khue, Le Minh 220–1
   'Scenes from an Alley' 222
Kiet, General Ly Thuong 283
Kiet, Prime Minister Vo Van 74, 79,
   87–94, 99–100, 117, 124, 132,
   138, 141, 143, 147–8, 150, 166,
   224–5, 247, 274, 297
   wife and children 88
Kim Il-Sung, mourning for 98
Kinh, Hoang Dao 232
Kissinger, Henry 86, 108, 296
Kokko, Ari 144–5
Korea 293
Kraft Foods 79
Kremlinology 81
Kuomintang 179
Ky, Petrus 210–11

La Courneuve, Paris 119–20
La Vang basilica 267–8
Labour, Ministry of (Molisa) 149
Lai, Nguyen Xuan 275
Lai, Tuong 143
Lam Dong 278
Lan, Bang Ba 47–8
Lan, Nguyen Ngoc 165, 176
Lang Son 283, 285
Lang, Tam, 'I Pulled a Rickshaw'
   74–5
Lanh, Nguyen Thi 29–30
Lao Dong newspaper 168, 170,
   251
Lao Dong Party 107
Laos 234, 289
Le Corbusier 217, 220
Le Hiep 234–5
Le, Hung 319–21
Le May, General Curtis 184
Leclerc, General Jacques Philippe
   50
Lee (Korean) 293
Lee Kuan Yew 293

   Singaporean leader 289
Lenin, Vladimir 85, 137
   statues 97, 353
Leningrad Scientific Research
   Centre for Town Planning and
   Construction 219–20
Leninism 2
Lennon, John
   'Give Peace a Chance' 330
   'Hey Jude' 333
L'Europeo 23
LG Group 147–8
L'Humanité newspaper 120
Li Tana, 'Peasants on the Move'
   233
Li Peng 297
Lien, Nguyen Van 258–9
Lien, Ta Ngoc 196
Lieu, Prince 73
Linh, Nguyen Van 94, 114, 116,
   155–7, 178–9, 184, 189, 199,
   297–9, 334, 353
Linh, Thuy 254
Linh, Viet 51–2
literature 189
Little House on the Prairie 343
Liu Shaoqi, President 295, 298–9
Loc, Nguyen Quang 291–2
Loc, Phung Gia, 'The Night of that
   Day, What a Night!' 157–9, 169
Lockhart, Greg 1 9 6
Logan, William 220
Loi, emperor Le 230
Long, Emperor Gia 43, 198, 211
Long, Ha Phi 172–3
Long Tho Pagoda, Dalat 276–8
Los Angeles Times 24, 123, 318
Lu, Dat 316–17
Luong, Tran Duc 93, 100
Luu, Khoi T. 318–19, 321
Luu, Truong Quang 314–15, 321
Luyen, Nguyen Truc 43
Ly Dynasty 208, 293
Ly, Emperor 209
Ly, Khanh 329–30
Ly, Nguyen Van 271
Ly (Vietnamese) 293

Macau 129, 286
McCain, Senator John 142
McCarthy, Mary 24–5
McNamara Line 32
McNamara, Robert 44
Maginot Line 32
Mahayana Buddhism 261
Mai, Le 164, 200, 281, 296
Mai, Nguyen Thi 343
Malaysia 7, 290, 303
    South China Sea 299, 301
    Viet Kieu 310
Malraux, André, *The Royal Way* 347
Man, Tran Cong 161
Mang, Emperor Minh 264
Manh, Nguyen Dang 179
Manh, Nong Duc 39
Mao, Vu 340–1
Mao Zedong 67, 84, 107, 124, 179,
        189, 265, 295–6
    guerrilla warfare 284
    Little Red Books 296
    'On Contradiction' 294
    'On Practice' 294
    Revolution 294
    Youth 326–7
Maoism 38, 85, 88–91, 103–4, 107–8,
        113, 181, 265
    class war 122
    guerrillas 297
Marian festival 267
Market-Leninism 2, 87, 150–51,
        155, 292–3, 353
Marr, David 118, 337–8
Marx, Karl 38, 155
Marxism 25, 65, 83, 87, 96–7, 104,
        107, 125–6, 153, 169, 260, 295,
        353–4
    class system 292
    doctrines 150–2
    history 179
    legacies 242
    Mandarins 25
    pageantry 80
    scientific nature 292
    states 85, 182
    war machine 12

Marxist-Leninism 3, 83, 85, 154, 293
    eternal rule 86
    faith 107
    governments 289
    Institute of 107, 111
Mekong Delta 12, 48–9, 243–4, 302
    flood-relief mission 280
    region 59, 88
    rice 60, 284
Melbourne 319, 321
    Vietnamese community 321
Mencius (disciple of Confucius)
        292
migration from countryside to
        cities 232–3
Military Nutrition and Clothing,
        Institute of 67
Minh, Dang Nhat 348
Minh, Duong Van 324
Mischief Reef 301
Miss Saigon 28
Missionaries of Charity 275
Molisa (Ministry of Labour) 149
Montagnards 8
Moscow
    Beijing rivalries 107, 113–14
    Cinematography Institute 348
    Pushkin Institute 193
    radio line to 155
MTV 328
Muoi, Huu 348
Muoi, Premier Do 81–3, 94–6, 100,
        112–13, 138, 150, 159–60,
        271–2, 297
    Party Congress (1996) 314
Murdoch, Rupert 349
My, Nguyen Thi 139–40
My, Phung Van 111

'Nam' 11, 13–16, 21, 24–6
    museums 32
    World Wide Web 13
Nam Dinh Textile Company 145–6
National
    Administration for Tourism 141–2
    AIDS Committee 251
    anthem 182

Assembly 24, 90–1, 121
    members 132
    sessions 81, 124
    South Vietnamese doctor 325
    Vietnam News Agency 163
Book Award 16
Institute of Nutrition, Hanoi 66
Liberation Front 346–7
Library 211
United Front for the Liberation
    of Vietnam 323
Neo-Confucianism 126
New York
    Committee to Protect
        Journalists 324
    Vietnamese community 317
New York Times
    Magazine 22
    'Saigon: The Sequel' 14
New Yorker 25
Ngan, Nguyen Ngoc, 'The Two
    Ducks' 53
Nghe An province 163, 295
Nghi, Huynh Van 273
Nghi Tam lakeside area 209
Nghia, Le Minh 301
Ngoc, Huu 35
Ngoc, Le Hong 104–5
Ngoc, Nguyen 179, 196
NGOs 249, 255
    Oxfam report 228
Nguoi Hanoi (the *Hanoian*) 159
Nguoi Lao Dong (the *Worker*) 169,
    234
Nguoi Viet, Los Angeles newspaper
    324
Nguyen Dang Giai, Pagoda, Hanoi
    210
Nguyen Du School 193
Nguyen Dynasty 43, 74, 198, 264,
    292
Nguyen, Hoang Ngoc 141
Nguyen, Jimmii 335
Nguyen, Nguyen Van 258
Nguyen, Theodore 322–3
Nha Trang 134, 160, 272
    Bishop of 266

Nhan Dan newspaper 85, 90, 119,
    122, 153–4, 161–2, 164–5,
    172–3, 175, 228, 233, 280
Nhan Van (Humanism) 181
    Giai Pham movement 179, 182–3
Nhu, doctor Ly 71
Nhu, Madam, South Vietnam 329
Nien, Nguyen Dy 315
Ninh, Bao 30–1, 190–4, 198–9
    The Sorrow of War 20–1, 190–3
    'Wild Wind' 191
Ninh Hiep village 18, 71–2
Ninh, Lu Trong 334
Nixon, President Richard 296
Nobel Peace Prize 86, 108
Noi Bai Airport, Hanoi 220, 272
North, Oliver 13
North Vietnam 25, 32, 50, 59, 267
    Vietminh control 265
Nung minority 40
Nuoc mam (fish sauce) 63–5

Oanh, Nguyen Xuan 141
Ong, Hai Thuong Lan 66
open societies 68–9
Orange County, California,
    Vietnamese 122–3, 317–18, 335
Oshin television series 343

Packer, Kerry 349
Pao, Judge 138, 350
Papal Bull (1493) 299
Paracel Islands 299
Paris 124, 213, 220
    La Courneuve 119–20
    Palais Garnier 232
    peace talks 108
    Tin, Colonel Bui 119–20
    Vietnamese ambassador 124
Pasteur Institute 64
Paterniti, Michael 14–15
peaceful evolution 90, 153
People's
    Army 23, 84, 88–91, 339–40
    Court of Investigation 118, 129
    Inspectorate 133
    Republic (1949) 288

Peregrine Capital Vietnam 316
Petersen, Douglas 'Pete' 142
Phai, Bui Xuan 230
Phan, Nguyen Ha 90–2
Phat Diem 266, 268–9, 271
Phieu, General Le Kha 7, 91, 93, 100
Philippines 10, 239, 281, 299, 301, 303
Phong, Nguyen Dam 323
Phu Nu (Woman) magazine 171
Phu Quoc Island 63–5, 258
Phu Yen village 157
Phuc, Nguyen Vinh 232
Phuoc, Pham Huy 129–32, 152
Phuong, Cao Ngoc 53–4
Phuong, Do 82, 163
Planning and Investment, Ministry of 175
Pol Pot 297
Politburo 40, 80, 87, 89, 92, 95, 110, 112, 139, 150
   cleansing 296
   Ho Chi Minh monument 41
   meetings 90
   members 135, 162
   speeches 154
   Standing Board 80–1, 84
Political and Economic Risk Consultancy, Hong Kong 133
Portugal
   missionaries 263
   world oceans 299
post-1986 literature 53
Poulo Condore Island 116
Presidential Palace 33, 42–3, 215, 320
Press Law (1989) 159–61
Prochnau, William, *Once Upon a Distant War* 19–20
Prospect magazine 353
Protestants 259, 262, 289
Public Security Bureaux 171
Pulitzer Prize 16, 20
Pushkin Institute, Moscow 193

Quan Doi Nhan Dan (the *People's Army*) 153–4, 161–2, 166, 191

Quan, Lady Thanh, 'Remembering the Past in the City . . .' 204
Quan, Phung, 'What My Mother Once Told Me' 176
Quan Su Pagoda, Hanoi 281
Quan, Tran Hong 341
Quang Binh province 184
Quang Ninh province 288, 305
Quang, Phan 165
Quang, Tran Huy, *Van Nghe* 38–9
Quang Tri 32–3, 267
   battle of 67
Quang, Vu 273
quoc ngu 36
Quoc Tu Giam 3
Quyen, Luu Quang 2–3

Radio France Internationale (RFI) 165–6
Radio Free Asia (RFA) 166
Rather, Dan 22
Reagan-era, Communist hostility 323
Red Army 83
Red Book 76
Red Guards, demonstrations 296
Red River 209
   basin 49, 72
   delta 35, 48–9, 265, 288
   dyke 224
   Ke Cho 205
   villages 34
Religious Affairs Commission 37, 270, 273–4
Renan, Ernest 26
Research Institute of Military Nutrition and Clothing 67
The Resistance Tradition 116
Returnee Assistance Programme (RAP) 149
Revolution (1945) 1, 48, 91, 103, 105, 179, 182, 186, 243
   documents 97
   propaganda 96
Reydellet, Bertrand 263–4
river deltas 62, *see also* Mekong Delta; Red River delta

Roh Tae-Woo, South Korean
    president 174
Roman Catholics 262–3, 265, 267,
    270, 275
  church 88, 259, 270, 273–5, 279,
    281–2
  missionaries 263
  nations, HIV 239
  pilgrimages 266–7
  Vietnam South 266
Rome, church activities 274

Safer, Morley 22
Saigon 14–15, 42, 211, 237, 263, 305
  Buddhist monks 204
  Communists take over (1975)
    305
  Ecole Française d'Extrême-Orient
    212
  fall of 112–13, 192, 316, 330
  Ho Chi Minh museum 43–5
  Institute of Cinematography
    346–7
  Presidential Palace 33, 42–3, 215,
    320
  restaurants 129–30
  River 309
  student movement 141
  Ton San Nhat Airport 190, 192,
    309, 314
  Viet Cong 279
  youth 329
  see also Ho Chi Minh city
Saigon Giai Phong newspaper 268,
  287
Saigon Tiep Thi (Saigon Marketing)
  164, 174
Saigon Times Weekly 312–13
'The Saigonese' 166–7
Sam, Lai Van 349
San Diego, survey of Vietnamese
  refugees 311
San Jose, California
  Vietnamese 317
    organisation 167, 323
Sarraut, Governor-General Albert
  212

The Scent of Green Papaya 12, 21
Scholars Uprising (1874) 264
Schwarzkopf, General Norman 22
Sen, Amartya 68–9
  Seventeenth Parallel 32
Sheehan, Neil 19, 22, 25
Singapore 136, 175, 290, 292, 303,
  333
  Lee Kuan Yew 289
Sino-Soviet split (1960) 113–14, 296
Son, Huynh Phu 339
Son La province 197
  prison 108–9
Son, Pham Ngoc 330
Son, Trinh Cong 329–30
Song Huong (Perfume River) journal
  197
Sontag, Susan 8, 13, 24–5
South China Sea 289, 298–302, 310
South Korea 7, 174, 290, 292–3
South Vietnam 26, 32–4, 107, 115,
  185, 324, 329
  Buddhist Church 279
  Catholics 266
  government 141, 242
    surrender (1975) 75, 86, 119,
      122–3, 162, 305
  leaders 115
  police 92, 117
  prisons 140–1
  religious groups 263
  revolutionaries 116
  subjugation 112–13
  Viet Cong 115
Southeast Asia 62, 137, 234, 288,
  291, 300
  camps 149, 316
  Confucianism 290
  Japan market 344
  overseas Chinese 304
Soviet Bloc, former nations 255–6
Soviet Union 151–2
  advice 113
  aid 58, 97
  archives 108
  cars 156
  cinema 346

Soviet Union – *contd*
  collapse 2, 141
  Communism, collapse 353
  control 284
  diplomats 114
  Ho Chi Minh mausoleum 42,
    45
  Ho Chi Minh, President 38
  last structure designed 43
  Marxism 96
  military advisors 108
  novels 328
  political training 106
  swing against 108
  weapons 296
Spain
  Catholicism 266
  world oceans 299
Spratly Islands 299–301
Stalin, Joseph 101, 106, 124, 146,
    163
  Youth 326–7
Stallone, Sylvester 183
Stasi techniques 251
Steele, Danielle 13
Stone, Oliver 13
Sweden 192

Tai, Tran Tuan 303
Taiwan 133, 265, 290, 303, 333, 343
  South China Sea 299, 301
Tamexco 131, 152
Tan, Tran Trong 80–2
Tank 843; 33
Taoism 235, 260, 292
Tap Chi Cong San journal 200, 340
Tap Chi Quoc Phong Toan An journal
    260–1
Taylor, Keith 195, 291–3
Temple of Literature, Hanoi 2–3,
    291
Teresa, Mother 275
Tet new year holidays 4–5, 56, 73–4,
    131, 159–60, 206, 248, 257
Tet Offensive (1968) 23, 85, 117
Thach, Nguyen Co 86, 156, 297–8,
    306

Thai Binh province 135, 275, 282
  riots (1997) 227–8, 275–6
Thai Nguyen steel works 287
Thailand 7, 62, 76, 88, 290, 303
  architects 234
  college students 341
  economy 140
  Gulf of 63
  HIV 239
  injecting drug users 239
  investors 133
  pirates 310, 344
Thang Long, City of the Ascending
    Dragon 208, *see also* Hanoi
Thang, Vo Thi 141–2
Thanh, Ngo Ba 24
Thanh, Nguyen Trung 109–13
Thanh Nien 169, 244, 277
Thanh, The 171
Thao, Phung, *Café Alone* 336
Therevada Buddhism 261
Thi Huong Examination Hall,
    Hanoi 211
Thien, Nguyen Chi, *My Rice
    Portion* 47
Thiep, Nguyen Huy 100, 189,
    194–9, 293–4
  'A Sharp Sword' 195
  'Chastity' 195
  'Fired Gold' 43, 195, 197–9
  Song Huong (*Perfume River*)
    journal 197
  'The General Retires' 194–5
  Vang Lua (Fired Gold) 43, 195,
    197–9
Tho, Huu 85
Tho, Le Duc 86, 104, 108–9
Thong, Huynh Sang 204
Thu, Nguyen (film maker) 27
Thu, Professor Nguyen Tai 292
Thuan, Bishop François-Xavier
    Nguyen Van 272–3
Thuy, Nguyen Xuan 339
Thuy, Tran Van 348
Thuy, Xuan 108
Tiananmen Square massacre 216,
    297

Tien Phong 158

Tien, Tuong Nang, 'Communism and Guigozcanism' 54

Tiep, Hoang Nhu 41

Tin, Colonel Bui 119–25, 128, 162–3
 BBC interviews 165
 Following Ho Chi Minh 124, 161–2

Tinh, Emperor Canh 267

Tinh, Tran Tam 266

Tinh, Tue 66
 The Miraculous Effects of the Southern Pharmacopoeia 65–6

Tinh, Vuong 121

To, Emperor Ly Tai 208

Ton Dao, church 268–9

Ton, King Le Thanh 229

Ton San Nhat Airport, Saigon 190, 192, 309, 314

Tonkin, North Vietnam 50

Total (French oil firm) 147

Toubon, Jacques 184

Tran dynasty emperor 65

Trang An 229

Tri, Emperor Thieu 264

Trinh dynasty 263

Truc, Nguyen Trung 316

Truong Son Cemetery, Quang Tri 33

Tu, Nguyen Dinh 82

Tuan, Nguyen 71

Tung, Dao Duy 91, 112–3, 167

Tung, Nguyen Song 36

Tung, Paul Cardinal Pham Dinh 270

Tuoi Tre Cuoi 172–4

Tuoi Tre newspaper 164, 169, 336, 340

Tuong, Nguyen Manh 109

Ukraine 150–52

UNAIDS agency 239

UNHCR 307

United Buddhist Church of Vietnam (UBCV) 279–81

United Nations
 Children's Fund (UNICEF) report (1997) 61
 human rights 112
 report on quotas (1996) 59

United States 11, 153, 164, 167
 anti-war activists 24–5
 armed forces 26, 44, 90
 Asians, crime 318
 authors and books 1, 185
 bombing raids 88, 117, 184, 219, 259
 capitalism 3
 conflicts with 21
 cultural integration 319
 drugs 318
 embargo 2, 8, 79, 344
 ethnic humour 319
 expatriates 14
 extremist groups 323
 famine 51
 film locations 346–7
 human rights 127
 imperialism 13, 296
 Information Service 166
 investors 31–2
 Ivy League 318
 movies 1, 16
 multi-national 322
 nuclear attack 265
 political groups 323
 prisoners of war 142, 229
 prostitution 318
 relations with 272
 scholarship 122
 Seventh Fleet 319
 South Vietnam intervention 24
 threat from 89
 trade fair, Hanoi 79
 troops missing in action 86
 university libraries 13
 veterans 15, 32
 victories over 24
 Viet Kieu 122–3, 311, 316–19, 321–4, 329–30, 335
 violence 318
 War Crimes Museum (later War Remnants Museum) 31, 323

VAC system of food production 69

Van Mieu Institute 291

Van Nghe magazine 157–9, 179, 184, 196

'A Prophecy Fulfilled' 38–9

Vatican 265, 271–73, 281

Veterans' Association 116

Vichy French regime 49–50

Vien, Nguyen Khac 200–1, 242–3

Vien, Nguyen Tach 71

Viet Cong 26, 29, 92, 118–19, 141
  Cambodia base 30
  guerrillas 346–7
  networks 85
  Saigon 279
  songs about 330
  South Vietnam 115
  veterans 115

Viet Hoa 302, 304–7
  Bank 303

Viet Kieu (overseas Vietnamese) 6, 122–3, 127, 184, 309–25
  communities 310–11, 314–15, 321, 323, 329–30, 335
  entertainers 335–6
  festivals 317

Viet Minh 49–50

Vietminh 232, 265, 294–6
  Independence League 179

Vietnam
  abortions 253
  abuses 102, 137, 159, 168
  advertising revenues 171
  agriculture 59, 64
  aid donors 137–8, 144, 150
  anti-Communists 123
  aphrodisiacs 78
  architects and architecture 43, 214, 234,
  artists 179, 182
  associations 354
  banking system 354
  banned imports 286–7
  bia om (hugging bar) 82–3
  bicycles 286
  bike racing 331–2
  boat people 58, 149, 307
  broadcasts 120, 124, 165, 185, 314–15

buildings 235

bureaucracy 129–52

ca phe cut chon (coffee beans) 75–6

cats 78

cemeteries 33–4

children, nutrition 61–2

Chinese 288, 303–4, 306, 308

church festivals 268

citizenship 313

civil society 241–2, 352

co-operatives 58

coal industry 288, 305–6

collectivisation 57–8, 61–2, 88

communal canteens 67

consumer-oriented society 79

consumers 344–6, 350

contraceptives 253

crime 105, 246, 334, 339

Criminal Code 105

culture 3, 16, 33, 35, 198, 292, 324, 345
  activities and services 247
  associations 182
  identity 65
  and political campaigns 108
  purges (1950s) 113

Cultural Revolution 296, *see also* Revolution (1945)

currency reform 58

cymbals and litanies 177–203

dead 45

death sentences 138

Democratic Republic 214

demographics 98–9

dictatorship 87

diet 61

dissidents 104, 119, 124–6, 128, 165

dogs and snakes 76–7

dragons 208, 235

drug addiction 289, 354

drug users 238–9, 241–3, 246–7, 252–4, 318, 332, 339
  needle exchange programmes 239, 250, 255
  see also social evils

dual citizenship 313
economy 2, 69, 151, 155, 297, 341, 354
   changes 55–6, 141
   crime 134
   growth 114, 133, 352
   independence and security 287
   recovery 71
   reforms 72, 89, 104, 205, 268, *see also Doi Moi*
education 99, 316, 340–1, 354
electricity 288
excommunication 101–28
exiles 123
families 125
famine (1945) 47–62
farmers 59, 69, 88
feast 63–79
feudalism 35, 43, 294
film industry 22, 27, 346–7
films 338
first dynasty 337–8
food 49, 52, 54–5, 63, 65–6, 68–72, 75–9
   state controls 58
   vegetables 68
   see also famine
football hooliganism 332
foreign investment 7, 144, 156, 350
forestry 62
freedom and dissent 352
freedom of
   movement 265, 274
   speech and assembly 6, 103, 137
friends 6
gambling 345
gay men 238
golf course 9
government 88–91, 97, 124, 127, 146, 171
   post-colonial 221
grain 48
history 11–12, 44, 51, 124, 204–36, 258, 294, 337–8, 352

official versions 177
holiest site 266–7
houses and businesses confiscated 313
human rights 137, 153, 170, 260, 280–1, 314–15
   activists 106
   organisations 127
   and responsibilities 137
hunger 79, *see also* famine
identity 198
image abroad 121
incomes 49, 70, 344
industrialisation and modernisation 87
inflation (1995) 60
information 155, 176
   sources 6, 109, 185
institutions 153
intellectuals 107–9, 127, 181, 196, 198, 260, 336
investments 315
investors 133–4, 137–8, 144, 147
jailed writers 117–19
job market 342
journalism 14, 22, 157, 159–64, 168–71, 174, 177, 226, 278, 280
jungles 68, 147
labour, movement 115, 168, 241
land 205
   reforms 57, 103, 109, 113, 181, 186, 265–6, 295
landscape 27
language, romanised writing 36
law 105, 118, 134, 136, 139
reform 136–7
lawyers 139
leaders 25, 112–3, 159
libel laws 170
licenses 137, 170
machine age 44
market
   economies 139
   reforms 155
martial arts movies 342
mausoleums 43, 45

Vietnam – *contd*
Ho Chi Minh, President 40–3, 45, 84
media 161, 163–4, 167–8, 170, 175–6, 328, 342
medical plants and spices 71
medicine 66, 71
military 67–8, 153, 242
motor-bikes 331–3, 336
museums 31–4, 43–5, 97, 166, 323
music 327–8, 330
national
dish 55
identity 352
mythology 229
poem 178, 244
nationalism 87, 293, 334
nationalist ideas 69
neo-liberal economists 138
networks and associations 85, 254
new appetites 74
new economic zones 125, 242, 269, 305–6
newspapers 159–60, 165, 172–4, 176, 178, 229, 275, 339 *see also* Nguoi Lao Dong; Nguoi Viet; Nhan Dan; Saigon Giai Phong; Tuoi Tre
nutrition 59, 61–2, 66, 68, 354
officials 143, 146, 158
corruption 133, 159, 244, 354
memorials 34
openness 4–5
organisations 115, 167
patriotism 106
peace generation 334
performers world tours 327
personality cults 126
petty injustices 5
'pillars of state' 90–1
pioneers (1990's) 11, 15
police, newspaper 172–3, 202, 250
politics 82, 90–1, 94, 121, 124, 181
culture 6, 25
leaders 140–1, 198

scientists 94
popular culture 327, 342–3, 346, 350–1
population 1
porcelain 286
pornography 247, 345
post-war generation 337
poverty 55, 168, 354
press 153–4, 159, 176, 339
freedom 159–60
taboo subjects 163
priests 265, 268–71, 274
prisoners, mistreatment 104
prisons 316
camps 125
literature 117–19
projects 147
prostitution 168, 238, 241–5, 247, 252–4, 318, 345, 354
re-education camps 53–4, 103, 125, 269, 272–3, 316
rectification classes 182
reforms 35, 145, 352, 355
religions faith 257–82, 352
freedom 6, 262, 272
groups 114, 123
persecution 104
rituals 35, 259
restaurants 75, 77–8, 129–30
reunification (1975) 103, 107, 113, 295–6
revitalisation (1990s) 55
revolutionaries 115
rice 55–62, 72, 284
cakes 69–70, 73
ruling class 94
sainthoods, Hanoi 270
saints' days 35
savings rate 333
saying 63
secret police 109
security 118, 153, 171, 342
smuggled cars 286, 289
snake restaurants 77
social
affairs, ministry of 149
changes 79, 107

control policies 251
evils 237–56
issues 254
order 334
problems 248, 255
scientist survey (1990) 57
socialism 2, 87–9, 125–126, 144
failings (1980s) 352
socialist culture ministries 298
society 77, 171, 354–5
state
censorship 177, 348
companies 143–45, 354
controls 58–60, 252
steel and cement markets 146
students 296, 341
tabloids 173
technocrats 140
telecommunications 168
television 138, 224, 253, 350
channels 176
foreign investment 350
news 101–2
series 32, 253–4
textiles 49, 286
'Three Nos' campaign 345
tiger hunting 10
tourism 13, 26–9, 31–2, 278
traditions 36, 72, 276
transport links 288
troops 1
underground papers 166–7
university professors 341
venison biltong 75–6
villages 217–19, 222, 242, 264, 297
violence 318
vocational training centres 149
warriors 190
weapons 286
wild plants, edible 68
women 172–4, 286, 289, 319, 322
Union 30, 249
writers 177–203, 254
young people 326–51
students survey (1992) 338
survey (1992), juvenile crime
334, 339

youth 6, 332
organisations 169, 249
conference (1988) 339–40
Vietnam Investment Review 175, 307
Vietnam News 36
Vietnam News Agency (VNA) 81,
163
Vietnam State Bank 131
Vietnam War 1, 26–7, 44–6, 49, 288
mourning and remembrance
34
shortages 69
theme parks 33
veterans 34, 119, 155
Vietnamese
Architects' Association 41, 43
Organisation to Exterminate
Communists and Restore
the Nation 324
overseas 127, 184, *see also* Viet
Kieu
Vietnamese-Algerian film, *The Dust
of Life* 346–7
Vietnamese-Americans 315–8
Vietnamese-Soviet Cultural Palace,
Hanoi 221, 335
village festivals 35, 263
Vincennes, Paris, architects and
planners congress 213
Vinh Phu, temple 37
Voice of America (VOA) 165
Voice of Vietnam 165
VTV 348–50
Vung Tau 322
Vuong, Hung 337–8

War Remnants Museum
Danang 31
Ho Chi Minh City 166, 323
Webb, James 347
Western
delicacies 78
multinationals 293
performers 343
politicians 94
popular culture 350
tabloids 176

Westminster, Orange County,
    Vietnamese 317
White Book 296
White Horse Temple, Hanoi 209
*The Wind Blows through Light and
    Dark* (television series), 253–4
Womack, Brantly 286, 288
World
    Bank 312, 333
    Communist community 293
    Cup quarter-final 98
    Economic Forum 134
    Health Organisation 66
    news agencies 163
    oceans 299
    open economies 136

Wide Web 13, 167
Wright, Gwendolyn 210, 212–14
Writers' Association 157, 192

Xuan Loc Diocese 282
Xuan, Nong Thi 40

Yugoslavia, Serb leaders 306
Yunnan province 288

Zen
    Buddhism 276
    variants 261
Zhou, Enlai 296
Zinoman, Peter 199